READING ADRIENNE RICH

UNDER DISCUSSION
David Lehman, General Editor
Donald Hall, Founding Editor

Volumes in the Under Discussion series collect reviews and essays about
individual poets. The series is concerned with contemporary American
and English poets about whom the consensus has not yet been formed
and the final vote has not been taken. Titles in the series include:

Reading Adrienne Rich

Reviews and Re-Visions, 1951–81

Edited by Jane Roberta Cooper

Ann Arbor

THE UNIVERSITY OF MICHIGAN PRESS

2002   2001   2000   1999   7   6   5   4

Library of Congress Cataloging in Publication Data
Main entry under title:

Reading Adrienne Rich.

   Bibliography: p.
   1. Rich, Adrienne Cecile—Criticism and interpretation
—Addresses, essays, lectures. 2. Feminism—Addresses,
essays, lectures. I. Cooper, Jane Roberta, 1959–
PS3535.I233Z87   1984   811'.54   83-23377
ISBN 0-472-09350-9
ISBN 0-472-06350-2 (pbk.)

Preface

I wanted this collection to be both comprehensive and representative. The result is, of necessity, a two-sided book. The essays that comprise the bulk of the book speak eloquently for themselves; they interpret Adrienne Rich's work on the terms she has chosen in the last decade. The poetry reviews are included primarily for their historical value; they document the reception of Rich's poetry by the critics, and the changing consciousness of her readers since the fifties. Within the reviews section there is a decisive split: the pieces written before *Diving into the Wreck* betray the blind spots of masculine literary culture—the consistent, sometimes subtle erasure of women's themes in readings of Rich's early poems. As she wrote more incisively about women's lives, the selective perception of some of her early admirers gave way to overt antifeminism. Those who had tokenized the "poet's poet" of the fifties and sixties dismissed Rich when she began to tap the source of her strength in "the common world of women."[1] The reviews I have selected of her volumes since *Diving into the Wreck* exemplify the explosive power of women coming into our own. Taken together, the two parts of the reviews section provide a context which reveals differences between feminist and patriarchal understandings of poetry, criticism, and gender.

Rich's own recent prose is another source of feminist readings of her poetry. Her essays synthesize her ideas about language, feminist theory, and women writers, as she reflects on her earlier poems and selves. Thus the materials on her essays are particularly appropriate in this collection about her poetry. The reviews and studies in the final section range from Gloria Bowles's bold response to Rich's recent writings about "compulsory heterosexuality" and black women's fiction, to Alexander Theroux's willful misreading of *Of Woman Born*. The latter I have included as an extended footnote, a complement to Kathleen Barry's piece on censorship. Like the reviews she criticizes in greater detail, Theroux's "attack is, first, a signal . . . that through feminist analysis we are challenging patriarchy at its core." It is reprinted here because I am ever mindful of the power of the world view it represents.

> . . . No art, no writing, exists that is not ultimately political. . . . Language and images have the capacity to bolster privilege and oppression, or to tear away at their foundations.[2]

The women whose essays are at the heart of the collection share this belief. They neither subscribe to the fallacies nor tolerate the omissions of androcentric culture. Rich's poetry demands a scrupulous "re-vision" of history with a woman's eye to what can be salvaged. The writers interpret her work from an historical perspective that links our lives with those of our foremothers; they share Rich's determination to recover "the memory, context, continuity"[3] of female experience. I cannot introduce all of the essays here, but I do want to give readers some sense of the range of the first section of the book.

In "The Angels Chiding," Claire Keyes takes a retrospective look at Rich's nascent feminism in *Snapshots of a Daughter-in-Law*. Using Rich's journal entries from the fifties and sixties, she studies her early disaffection with the institution of motherhood, and the peculiarly feminine conflicts between love and anger, creation and relation. Keyes attributes Rich's "fairly consistent lack of female identification" to the limitations of her historical milieu, and marvels at the woman who dared, in 1960, even to *hear* the voices that told her to "smash the mould straight off" ("Snapshots of a Daughter-in-Law").

In her essay on the "Twenty-One Love Poems," Adrian Oktenberg reflects on the everyday meanings of "disloyalty," lesbian love, and life outside the law. The subject of the "Love Poems" is not simply the inner event shared by the lovers but the politics of their resistance in the patriarchal world. The passion and clarity of the lovers is "the embryonic beginning of a woman-centered civilization."

Gertrude Hughes's "Imagining the Existence of Something Uncreated" surveys Rich's affinities with and divergences from the Emersonian tradition. Hughes studies Rich's and Emerson's ideas about history and power, negative capability and otherness, with particular attention to the commonality among women which Emerson could not imagine. For women, "transcendence" means living through and beyond the patriarchal assumptions that restrict us. In Hughes's view, Rich partly shares and partly counters Emersonian ideals; but she always "radically revises the origins and history—the sources and direction—of the very consciousness Emerson called for."

Susan Stanford Friedman's essay is a study of the influence of H.D. in *The Dream of a Common Language*. A poetic foremother whose work is only now becoming available, Hilda Doolittle's bequest to Rich has been underestimated. Most critics have been content to study the influence of Frost, Auden, and Stevens; a few, including Rich herself, have explored the influence of Dickinson, Plath, and Sexton; but Friedman's essay amplifies Rich's own effort to trace her work back through a women's tradition. It reveals the striking similarities in Rich's and H.D.'s language and imagery, their shared concern with male violence, and the genesis of their love for women.

Poetry has always been Adrienne Rich's way of getting at the disparity between the "world as it is" and "as it might be" ("The Spirit of Place"). For more than thirty years she has written from the edge of an order she did not create, about the possibilities of one which would be more in keeping with her desire. That desire has undergone "changes elemental and minute" ("Phantasia for Elvira Shatayev") since she was a Yale Younger Poet, and sometimes her past—especially her poetry before *Snapshots of a Daughter-in-Law*—does not seem to belong to her. Yet there are continuities even in Rich's changes; her "fierce attention" ("Like This Together") to change itself has long enabled her to "use what we have / to invent what we need" ("Leaflets"). In repossessing women's common experience, Rich makes us available to ourselves and one another. She gives to women a vision of the future that honors our past and invites our continuing assertion of women's prerogatives.

This collection is dedicated to those who have taught and learned with me about "the common world of women." I want to thank the people whose critical support, reassurance, and persistent questioning have helped me to expand my sense of the possible—and to integrate it into my living.

I am grateful for the perspective, clarity, and commitment of my professors and advisers at Wesleyan University. Joan Hedrick and Richard Ohmann encouraged me to do considerable "re-vision"—of literature, history, education, and daily life. Gertrude Hughes pushed me to ask the questions I needed to ask. If it weren't for her, I still might not know that poetry matters. I am grateful for financial assistance from the Olin Fellowship, Department of English, Wesleyan University, which covered the costs of a summer's research.

I thank Pat Camden for her impeccable typing and for kindness and irreverence which lifted my spirits.

Linda Howe's expert copyediting and sensitive suggestions for the bibliography made a difference in both the process and the product.

Shirley MacDaniel helped me chart a good course long ago when she asked me what I wanted to learn and challenged me to take my work seriously. Beverly Hinton listened attentively, matched and heightened my enthusiasm in the early stages of the book, and shared a "cable of blue fire" ("Phantasia for Elvira Shatayev") which I continue to cherish. Leslie Landau provided much of the lifeblood of this book; with indelible affection, she reminded me repeatedly that not finishing it was not an option. Susan Freinkel, Deborah Ehrenthal, Maria Rodriguez, and Joan Massey provided large amounts of warmth, support, criticism, distraction, food, beer, and advice—all at the right times. David Engstrom has been an exemplary friend and tenacious optimist throughout. Steve Kelley's affection and intelligence have helped me in countless ways. My parents, Sandra and David Cooper, have cared for me with wisdom and patience.

It has been a privilege to work with the women who contributed to this collection. I want to express my gratitude to them and to my editor, Donald Hall, for their enormous patience.

NOTES

1. Adrienne Rich, "Conditions for Work: The Common World of Women," in *On Lies, Secrets and Silence* (New York: Norton, 1979), p. 203.

viii

2. Adrienne Rich, "Notes For a Magazine," *Sinister Wisdom* 17 (1981):4.

3. Adrienne Rich, Foreword to *The Coming Out Stories,* ed. Susan J. Wolfe and Julia Penelope Stanley (Watertown, Mass.: Persephone Press, 1980), p. xii.

Contents

xii

PART ONE *Contemporary Essays on Rich's Poetry*

JUDITH McDANIEL

"Reconstituting the World"
The Poetry and Vision of Adrienne Rich

A life I didn't choose
chose me . . .

—1961

Only she who says
she did not choose, is the loser in the end.

—1976

The will to change dramatically distinguishes the career of Adrienne Rich from many contemporary artists. Accepting at first the roles assigned by society, Rich moved from dutiful daughter/apprentice to mother/creator, excelling—poetically, at least—within the boundaries of her sex, generation and class. At midlife she began to break out of those boundaries: "Locked in the closet at 4 years old I beat the wall with my body / that act is in me still."[1] Writing poems that were no longer nice, in forms that reflected her mind's straining for new visions, the poet began to challenge, and in recent years her work has reflected her life changes—from daughter-in-law to radical lesbian feminist.[2] The process of this growth is recorded for us in her poetry.

While apparently accepting the traditional female roles in early life, nonetheless feelings of strain and stifled emotion characterize Adrienne Rich's first two volumes.[3] The opening poem in *A Change of World,* "Storm Warnings," sets the tone of both books:

The glass has been falling all the afternoon,
And knowing better than the instrument

Reconstituting the World was first published as a monograph (Argyle, N.Y.: Spinsters, Ink, 1978). Reprinted by permission from Spinsters, Ink and the author.

> What winds are walking overhead, what zone
> Of gray unrest is moving across the land,
> I leave the book upon a pillowed chair
> And walk from window to closed window, watching
> Boughs strain against the sky

The controlled iambic rhythm, broken appropriately in the first, fourth, and sixth lines by an anapest as the wind strains against the glass, contains the threat of violent weather, just as the imagined room protects the poet. The form of the poem is a device, used exactly as the drawn curtains and the hurricane lanterns, as a "defense against the season; / These are the things that we have learned to do / Who live in troubled regions." Another scene of restrained violence follows with "Aunt Jennifer's Tigers" who pace harmlessly across the embroidered tapestry, while her own energy is submerged; she lies "ringed with ordeals she was mastered by." Rich herself was unaware of the tensions her poems illustrate: later she was to write, "In those years formalism was part of the strategy—like asbestos gloves, it allowed me to handle materials I couldn't pick up barehanded."[4] To fill the role of poet, to win the approval of those whom she imitated, Rich had nearly crafted herself out of feeling. Like many of the women she described, these early poems seem nearly suffocated by self-control.

Rich's poetic adaptation was not unique. Barbara Bellow Watson, in an essay on women and power, reminds us that

> women, like other groups with minority status, adopt various forms of accommodation to protect themselves. The most essential form of accommodation for the weak is to conceal what power they do have and to avoid anything that looks like threat or competition.[5]

Just as these early poems seldom focused specifically on the woman described, concealing her in metaphors of tapestry, uncharted seas and skies,[6] so too Rich's first expressed aesthetic accommodated the power of a masculine school of critical thought. "At a Bach Concert" affirms that "form is the ultimate gift that love can offer" and admonishes, "A too-compassionate art is half an art. / Only such proud restraining purity / Restores the else-betrayed, too-human heart." The self-conscious use here of the rhymed form, the frequent hyphens, enclose the meaning in an archaic restraint. The exact meaning of these words must then be carefully extracted. Form, not the more amorphous "craft," is the preferred value of this early Rich aesthetic. Only through controlled, restraining forms can the emotion be communicated safely. The danger is twofold. Two great a compassion is sentiment, not art; and the artist may reveal more of herself than is safe for her, or than her critical audience would wish to read. Rich's essential transformation as an artist was a movement away from this aesthetic toward an art that allowed a far more personal expression, allowed her to take risks as a poet and a compassionate woman.

Snapshots of a Daughter-in-Law,[7] published eight years after Rich's second volume, marks a significant change in style and attitude. The title of the volume is personal; it also emphasizes an awareness of her role within the forms of marriage. She is no longer the young woman who could change her world arbitrarily, nor the poet whose craft is compared to that of the diamond cutter.

> The poem was jotted in fragments during children's naps, brief hours in a library, or at 3 A.M. after rising with a wakeful child. I despaired of doing any continuous work at this time. Yet I began to feel that my fragments and scraps had a common consciousness and a common theme, one which I would have been very unwilling to put on paper at an earlier time because I had been taught that poetry should be "universal," which meant, of course, nonfemale.[8]

Here, the poet is a mother/wife/daughter-in-law whose life is given over to others, and that circumstance significantly affects her subject and, increasingly, the form of her poem. At times, the numbering of the sections within the title poem seems the only controlling factor, argument and syntax giving the reader little direction.

In "Snapshots of a Daughter-in-Law" Rich shows us a young woman who is beginning to realize that her identity is not that of the women she has been given as models: "Nervy, glowering, your daughter / wipes the teaspoons, grows another way." Like Joan of Arc, this protagonist hears voices; but hers bid her not to sacrifice herself: "*Have no patience. / . . . Be insatiable. / . . . Save yourself; others you cannot save.*" These are not the voices of angels, but of monsters, the inevitable accompaniment of growing self-awareness and self-involvement for women. And these monsters do not come from another sphere; they are from within: "A thinking woman sleeps with monsters. / The beak that grips her, she becomes."

No specific political connections enlighten the protagonist of this poem. Rich celebrates those several predecessors who remained strong and produced their writing, such as Mary Wollstonecraft and Emily Dickinson, but the future is vague and awkwardly expressed:

> Well,
> she's long about her coming, who must be
> more merciless to herself than history.
> Her mind full to the wind, I see her plunge
> breasted and glancing through the currents,
> taking the light upon her
> at least as beautiful as any boy
> or helicopter,
> poised, still coming,
> her fine blades making the air wince
>
> but her cargo
> no promise then:
> delivered
> palpable
> ours.

The image of the helicopter represents both power and deliverance and its blades are weaponlike. But the ludicrous shape, the emphasis on a technological rather than a natural event, make this leap of the imagination a farfetched one. What we wish to believe is the wistful voice at the poem's end: a promise of selfhood that is "delivered," "palpable" and "ours." The theme of the poem is the role of a woman poet; the problem, in 1960, was one of inadequate models for that mode of female achievement.

While the political perspective of *Snapshots of a Daughter-in-Law* is nebulous, Rich does attempt in this volume to discuss, if not resolve, the problem she must have seen in applying her previously stated aesthetic to this new style of writing. "The Roofwalker" compares the poet to a construction worker balanced precariously on a rafter, "exposed, larger than life, / and due to break my neck." The female poet has labored "with infinite exertion" and succeeded in laying "a roof I can't live under." Her exertions were thwarted because "A life I didn't choose / chose me"—the life this volume depicts of mother, wife and daughter[9]—and thwarted because "even / my tools are the wrong ones / for what I have to do." Rich is not specific, may not be sure herself whether those wrong tools are the problem of gender identification—a woman writing in a man's voice and poetic form—or simply the problem of a formal style which made writing difficult with infants to care for. But both are connected to the use of a language which the poet is finding increasingly awkward. The phenomena Rich wishes to describe—a new female identity, the nuances of a male/female relationship—make impossible demands on a limited and sexist vocabulary. This combination, the wrong tools and the need to build, leave the poet exposed and vulnerable. Taking changes in her writing, the poet sees herself "naked, ignorant, / a naked man fleeing / across the roofs." With only a small difference, however, with a little less existential courage or curiosity, she could reduce these impulses to mere fantasies, daydreams, instead of her own reality. She could

> be sitting in the lamplight
> against the cream wallpaper
> reading—not with indifference—
> about a naked man
> fleeing across the roofs.

The debate between the possibility of actively engaging in change, or passively watching others take those risks, is the keynote of this volume. In "Prospective Immigrants Please Note" Rich presents the challenge directly:

> Either you will
> go through this door
> or you will not go through.
>
> If you go through
> there is always the risk
> of remembering your name.

Rich tries to present both options fairly: "If you do not go through / it is possible / to live worthily." But she will not let the reader escape the reality that to refuse growth and change inevitably means that "much will blind you, / much will evade you, / at what cost who knows?" The matter-of-fact tone of these short terse lines suggests forcibly that Rich herself has gone through the door.

This choice necessarily separates Adrienne Rich from many of her female antecedents—from Christina Rossetti and Emily Dickinson,[10] certainly. A condition of their art required them to choose isolation, to close the door rather than pass through it. Her decision to encounter the self in the world allies her—emotionally and poetically—with several of her contemporaries. "The Roofwalker," for example, is dedicated to Denise Levertov and seems to be a response to Levertov's "From the Roof" in which a woman bringing in the wash on her Manhattan rooftop becomes the transformer and the transformed, watching and taking part in the sensuous, teeming life beneath her. And Rich experiences in this volume a problem of voice similar to that which plagued Levertov. In the fifties and sixties it was difficult for a woman to escape the fact that poet was a masculine noun. In Levertov's prose piece, "The Poet in the World," in a grotesque and awkward allegory, the female poet gives birth to a male child who becomes the poet-he, who then goes into the world to experience it. Similarly, in "Snapshots of a Daughter-in-Law" the standard of beauty and achievement is still male. The woman of the future, Rich tells us, will be "at least as beautiful as any boy."

Snapshots of a Daughter-in-Law was a book ignored by the critics, written off, Rich says, as "being too bitter and personal." In her next book she retreated from those earlier insights: ". . . something in me was saying, 'If my material, my subject matter as a woman is going to be denied me, then there is only *one* other subject for me and that is death.' That's why *Necessities of Life*[11] is a book about death."[12] And it is why *Leaflets*[13] is permeated with anger, diffused nervous tension and unfocused hostility. *Leaflets* opens with "Orion," the you addressed in the poem is the poet herself, "the active principle, the energetic imagination."[14] This aspect of her personality, that energy and self-involvement out of which the poetry is written, is on the defensive and will fight for its life:

> Breathe deep! No hurt, no pardon
> out here in the cold with you
> you with your back to the wall.

That image of defiant extremity recurs and becomes more specific: "Did you think I was talking about my life? / I was trying to drive a tradition up against the wall." And finally, "I can't live at the hems of that tradition— / will I last to try the beginning of the next?" The tradition that is forcing her to the wall, forcing her to live and write on its outskirts, is patriarchy, and this is specifically recognized in Rich's restatement of the theme of Auden's "Musée des Beaux Arts." Auden insisted that "about suffering they were never wrong, / The Old Masters: how well they understood / Its human position." Rich sees that the scenes haven't changed, "We stand in the porch, / two archaic figures: a woman and a man." But her perspective on suffering is unique: "The old masters, the old sources, / haven't a clue what we're about." She is not declaring, as one critic suggested with irritation, that "human experience in general is so radically disparate that even the old masters could fail to intimate our problems, provide us with a clue."[15] She *is* insisting that the old masters, the patriarchy, have cut themselves off from female experience; as her own sense of herself as a woman who has been forced to the edges of male culture becomes more conscious, she realizes how little that culture represents her own needs and desires.

Like the four-year-old flinging herself against the closet door, the images in *Leaflets* strike out against that cultural entombment. Blood, fire and war converge in the repeated identification of the poet with the red fox:

> The fox, panting, fire-eyed,
> gone to earth in my chest.
> How beautiful we are,
> she* and I, with our auburn
> pelts, our trails of blood,
> our miracle escapes,
> our whiplash panic flogging us on
> to new miracles!

In "5:30 A.M." Rich is sure that she and the fox will die, the hunters, "inanely single-minded / will have our skins at last." In "Abnegation" the woman poet and the vixen share a common birthright: ". . . no archives, / no heirlooms, no future / except death."

"No future / except death" is a distinct recognition by Adrienne Rich of the aesthetics expressed by the "confessional poets."[16] But Rich's identification with the confessional poets is not complete. In "On Edges" words appear which indicate that Sylvia Plath is the source of this reverie/nightmare: "dressing-gowns," "monster," "lampshade." Still, Rich is a translator who, taking a "torn letter," cannot "fit these ripped-up flakes together." She recognizes and agrees that "the blades on that machine / could cut you to ribbons." The blades are not the dangerous helicopter blades from "Snapshots of a Daughter-in-Law," but the relentless keys of the poet's typewriter. And the "delicate hooks, scythe-curved intentions / you and I handle," are, in this poem of Rich's, words—in a literal sense, commas, the expression of a hesitation or silence. The last two poems of Sylvia Plath's life were "Edge" and "Words." "Words" are the axe's edge for Plath; "words dry and riderless" take on a life of

---

*In the original version of the poem, this pronoun is "he." Rich explains why she has changed some pronouns in her preface to *Poems: Selected and New, 1950–1974* (New York: Norton, 1975), p. xv.

their own, endangering the poet's life. Rich is willing to acknowledge this danger, to become the renegade:

> . . . I'd rather
> taste blood, yours or mine, flowing
> from a sudden slash, than cut all day
> with blunt scissors on dotted lines
> like the teacher told.

Rich echoes Plath's "the blood jet is poetry." But that which differentiates her from the confessional poets is her insistence that poetry/words/language have a "function" that "is humane." Adrienne Rich will encounter the danger, but her belief in a direction for the future will allow her to survive that encounter.

In *Leaflets,* then, Rich connects the problem of survival to the problem of communication: a primary theme of her mature poetry. *"Tell me what you are going through—,"* the man asks in "Leaflets," "but the attention flickers" and he cannot hear her response, cannot hear her plead, *"Know that I exist!"* The words she tries to write in the "Ghazals" are "vapor-trails of a plane that has vanished" and she implores the reader, "When you read these lines, think of me / and of what I have not written here." In the last "Ghazal," dedicated to her husband, she wishes for some magic incantation to protect them from the suffering they will have to endure, and she asks him, speaking "as a woman to a man / . . . How did we get caught up fighting this forest fire, / we, who were only looking for a still place in the woods?"

Within a year, Rich wrote a poem that begins to analyze politically that question: "how did we get caught?" "Tear Gas"[17] announces:

> The will to change begins in the body not in the mind
> My politics is in my body, accruing and expanding with every
>   act of resistance and each of my failures.

The subjective physical self is now seen as the focus for profound political change. Economically, a woman's body has always been a political object, controlled by a man, a master, a religion or a government. This new war will not be over until the woman can assert control over her own destiny, physical and cultural. To achieve both, she needs

> . . . a language to hear myself with
> to see myself in
> a language like pigment released on the board
> blood-black, sexual green, reds
> veined with contradictions
> bursting under pressure from the tube
> staining the old grain of the wood

The tensions here are palpable and explosive and the language seems inadequate. Rich protests, "but this is not what I mean / these images are not what I mean." It will be years before women find the images they need for this expression; but Rich now knows the direction of the search. She is moving "toward a place where we can no longer be together" as men and women; she is moving toward "another kind of action."

To effect this journey to a new place, a new action, Rich must first create a new language, a new way to express women's experience. The task is enormous, but not impossible; for she means to shape this new language, not through new words, but through new perceptions, so that we may first see ourselves in the new place. The old language causes pain, suffering, and isolation because it does not acknowledge or portray the human situation in a truthful way. One corrective, insists Rich, when "we are confronted with the naked and unabashed failure of patriarchal politics and patriarchal civilization," is to make an accurate record of human feelings by rewriting the stories and myths that purport to represent our deepest reality. And she is determined that "the sexual myths underlying the human condition can and shall be recognized and changed."[18] *The Will to Change*[19] and *Diving into the Wreck*[20] represent a sophisticated and passionate attempt to give us a new vision of ourselves. These volumes recognize that myths and legends have had a complex interrelationship with the development of civilization and the concommitant development of the consciousness of the self. Rich returns again and again to images of humankind's prehistoric and preconscious state and then carefully leads us toward a new and altered perception. The process is one of rebirth and conscious recreation.

The Will to Change opens with a poem that moves us carefully back into a state where "the last absolutes were torn to pieces." The image of "November 1968" is an incinerator of autumn leaves, the smoke from which beings "to float free / . . . the unleafed branches won't hold you / nor the radar aerials." The smoky essence of the leaves, drifting into the air and disappearing, becomes a metaphor for the human return to a preconscious state in which the self and the environment are one, before the individual begins to differentiate itself from the group or its surroundings. As the poet watches this process—individual leaves merging into smoke—she wonders:

> How you broke open, what sheathed you
> until this moment
> I know nothing about it
> my ignorance of you amazes me

"Study of History" charts the vagaries of human development when it is not consciously controlled. The poem describes a river at night. Lights on the shore opposite the viewer are occasionally blotted out by the "unseen hulls" of passing barges. The viewer cannot see the barges, only knows that the lights go out and then reappear. Cause and effect cannot be determined. Here, the river is formed, irrevocably and inexplicably, it would seem. And the poet, "lying in the dark, to think of you," reminds herself that this place is not the origin of the river and that

> . . . we have never entirely
> known what was done to you upstream
> what powers trepanned
> which of your channels diverted

Like any human personality, those early processes and boundaries that form the present are only visible as an occasional light winking on and off.

Rich's most straightforward attempt to present a corrective to "what was done to you upstream" is "Planetarium," in which she attempts to rewrite some of the myths and legends which have misrepresented women's potential. It is a poem, she says, "in which at last the woman in the poem and the woman writing the poem become the same person. . . . It was written after a visit to a real planetarium, where I read an account of the work of Caroline Herschel, the astronomer, who worked with her brother William, but whose name remained obscure, as his did not."[21] What Caroline Herschel saw changed our earthly vision of the sky—"What we see, we see / and seeing is changing"—and the poet sees Caroline Herschel and gives the reader a new way of seeing a female reality. Rich knows that all of our lives we have been "bombarded" by the old myths about women, women "doing penance for impetuousness." Those messages reach all of us, always:

> I have been standing all my life in the
> direct path of a battery of signals
> the most accurately transmitted most
> untranslateable language in the universe

But in this poem, the poet, like the astronomer, becomes an active agent of change. No longer the passive receptacle of others' descriptions of her,

> . . . I am an instrument in the shape
> of a woman trying to translate pulsations
> into images   for the relief of the body
> and the reconstruction of the mind.

Her theme is the will to change; the very conscious reappraisal of Caroline Herschel suggests one direction for this change: "Writing as Re-Vision."[22]

"The Burning of Paper Instead of Children" attempts a much more difficult process of change. It is a poem about language, and once again we sense a real ambivalence here toward the power of the written word, which Rich both denies and affirms. The headnote of the poem quotes Daniel Berrigan, on trial in

Baltimore for burning draft records: "I was in danger of verbalizing my moral impulses out of existence." And the poem itself is a verbalization of the poet's own moral impulses about her sense of her function and purpose in a violent society.

The first section of the poem asserts that the symbolic act (burning a book) is less important to the poet than the burning of a child, or Joan of Arc. Yet she learns of Joan's martyrdom in a book, *The Trial of Jeanne d'Arc,* and is so mesmerized by the telling of the story that "they take the book away / because I dream of her too often." This irony—the paradox of the power of words versus the power of action—runs through the poem. The poet reads the knowledge which allows an identification with Joan of Arc, and she concludes part one of the poem with the realization, "I *know* it hurts to burn" (emphasis mine).

"To imagine a time of silence" is the attempt of the second section, and the poet proposes communication through touch. Physical love allows a "relief / from this tongue   this slab of limestone / or reinforced concrete." Verbalization is a gravestone, as the Indians discovered who, in the poet's imagination, communicated "in signals of smoke" until "knowledge of the oppressor" gave them language. The ambivalence of the poem is never more profoundly realized than in the terse conclusion of this section: "this is the oppressor's language / yet I need it to talk to you."

The poem does not conclude in the fifth and final section, it ignites. The languages of Frederick Douglass and Jeanne d'Arc were "pure" because their languages and their actions coincided; their languages were their actions: thus, "a language is a map of our failures" and our successes. This is the knowledge that will incite human change. With the realization that "I cannot touch you now," that earlier hope of a personal, physical communication is negated:

I am in danger. You are in danger. The burning of a book arouses no sensation in me. I know it hurts to burn. There are flames of napalm in Catonsville, Maryland. I know it hurts to burn. The typewriter is overheated, my mouth is burning, I cannot touch you and this is the oppressor's language.

"My politics," Rich had written earlier, "is in my body." When we realize how inextricably related are all of our modes of expression, the lives we live become integrated into new political potential. She shows its complexity to us:

> Trying to tell the doctor where it hurts
> like the Algerian
> who has walked from his village, burning
>
> his whole body a cloud of pain
> and there are no words for this
>
> except himself

In this single image Rich unites the words, the pain, the body, and the politic. A vivid example of her poetic imagination, the precise visualization of an abstraction is a technique she has perfected as a mature poet, and will continue to use.

Each of the poems in *The Will to Change* is a further commentary on this political reality, from the myth of Orpheus as it is rewritten by Eurydice to the more specific directions in "Shooting Script." The penultimate section of the poem returns to the image of the river from "Study of History." Now the poet is not a silent observer on the shore of the river; she is on the river, although "once it would not have occurred to / me to put out in a boat, not on a night like this." Now, she is encountering life, having chosen to go through the door of life changes, and part of this choice includes pledging "myself to try any / instrument that came my way. Never to refuse one from conviction / of incompetence." Learning new ways is not easy and again we are reminded that the old life gave women the "wrong tools" for the task: "I had no / special training and my own training was against me." Still, she is out on the moving river. "I watched the lights on the shore I had left for a long time; each / one, it seemed to me, was a light I might have lit, in the old days." It is a process she describes as pulling "yourself up by your own roots."

In the poems that followed *The Will to Change,* Rich continued to focus on these three problems: changing the language, rewriting the myths, and returning to the sources from which our conscious actions originate. The poems about language are characterized by anger and frustration. The first poem in *Diving into the Wreck* is titled "Trying to Talk with a Man" and the experience is compared to testing bombs. "The Phenomenology of Anger" finds words and images to describe a rage so profound it could lead to "Madness. Suicide. Murder. / Is there no way out but these?" When she dreams of meeting her enemy, she imagines acetylene

> raking his body down to the thread
> of existence
> burning away his lie
> leaving him in a new
> world; a changed
> man

This anger, Rich says, is not female hysteria. It has real sources in the daily existence of women:

> Today, much poetry by women—and prose for that matter—is charged with anger. I think we need to go through that anger, and we will betray our own reality if we try, as Virginia Woolf was trying, for an objectivity, a detachment. . . .
> Both the victimization and the anger experienced by women are real, and have real sources, everywhere in the environment, built into society. . . .[23]

In other prose writing, Rich began at this time (1972) to articulate more specifically a political perspective that elaborated the insights of her poems. She understands patriarchy as "any kind of group organization in which males hold dominant power and determine what part females shall and shall not play. . . .[24] Not only is this artificial restraint a source of anger to women, Rich finds that

> men—in so far as they are embodiments of the patriarchal idea—have become dangerous to children and other living things, themselves included; and that we can no longer afford

to keep the female principle—the mother in all women and the woman in many men—straitened within the tight little postindustrial family, or within any male-induced notion of where the female principle is valid and where it is not.[25]

In those poems in which she is trying to rewrite some of the old myths and stories, Rich is very consciously trying to combat this tendency of the patriarchy. She will not let Orpheus's failure of direction limit her, "a woman in the prime of life." She wants women to "explore the condition of connectedness as a woman. Which is something absolutely new, unique historically, and which is finally so much more life-enhancing"[26] than exploring the condition of women's alienation. In "Translations" the narrator has become aware that women need not compete and become enemies over a man's affections. They are ignorant that "this way of grief / is shared, unnecessary / and political." It is political because of the unequal power held by the man. Again, in "From a Survivor" Rich's narrator addresses a man with whom she had made "the ordinary pact / of men & women in those days." She has a new vision of that pact, no longer accepts the myth that he can define or control her. His body "is no longer / the body of a god / or anything with power over my life." Her new life is "a succession of brief, amazing movements / each one making possible the next."

"Diving into the Wreck" is Rich's most complex use of an image of rebirth. This time her tools are carefully chosen: she has "read the book of myths, / and loaded the camera, / and checked the edge of the knife-blade." It is necessary to know the old stories before embarking on a journey to change them. This journey is to record the sources of our origin, hence the camera. The knife is less obvious, until one remembers Rich's frequent earlier warnings—that the journey is dangerous. As the narrator descends, the water turns from blue to green to black. There is the effect of "blacking out," becoming unconscious, while still remaining in control. As she begins to move in this new element, the swimmer learns that "the sea is not a question of power." It is, rather, the all encompassing "deep element" in which she must learn "to turn my body without force." She has come "to explore the wreck . . . / to see the damage that was done / and the treasures that prevail." The wreck is a layered image: it is the life of one woman, the source of successes and failures; it is the history of all women submerged in a patriarchal culture; it is that source of myths about male and female sexuality which shape our lives and roles today. Whichever, the swimmer came for "the wreck and not the story of the wreck / the thing itself and not the myth." She explores the wreck and records for us her experiences of the cargo, "the half-destroyed instruments . . . the water-eaten log / the fouled compass." But no questions are answered here for those who have not found their own way to this place; we are given no explanation for why the wreck occurred. Nor is there any account of the swimmer's return, the use to which she puts this new information. It is as if Rich still found herself in the dilemma at the end of "Snapshots of a Daughter-in-Law" when it seemed impossible to record an image of the "new woman." Indeed, she said in 1974, two years after "Diving into the Wreck,"

I absolutely cannot imagine what it would be like to be a woman in a nonpatriarchal society. At moments I have this little glimmer of it. When I'm in a group of women, where I have a sense of real energy flowing and of power in the best sense—not power of domination, but just access to sources—I have some sense of what that could be like. But it's very rare that I can imagine even that.[27]

"From an Old House in America," published in 1975, irrevocably makes Adrienne Rich's connection with the lives of other women. Thinking of Emily Brontë in her life-long isolation, she writes: "I place my hand on the hand of the dead, invisible palmprint / on the doorframe." In the poem she reaches out "to comprehend a miracle beyond / raising the dead: the undead to watch / back on the road of birth." The road, for American women, has been grotesquely difficult; and in a series of breathtaking vignettes Rich does indeed look back on the road to watch her own birth. Slaves, witches, pioneers, women chained together, hung together, or dying alone, whatever the history of individual lives has been, each was a victim of a power that took her life out of her own control. Finally, for the poet, after the repression, murder, exploitation characterizing these women's lives, she finds:

A dream of tenderness

wrestles with all I know of history
I cannot now lie down

with a man who fears my power
or reaches for me as for death

or with a lover who imagines
we are not in danger

The implications of this declaration are clear: the dream of tenderness is in loving other women. The mind leaps back to the earlier assertion in "The Phenomenology of Anger":

"The only real love I have ever felt
was for children and other women.
Everything else was lust, pity,
self-hatred, pity, lust."
This is a woman's confession.

In her two most recent books Adrienne Rich explores the potential for women's power. Her prose work, *Of Woman Born: Motherhood as Experience and Institution,* shows that potential interfaced against the dark power of the patriarchy. She writes of women's quest "for models or blueprints of female power which shall be neither replications of male power nor carbon copies of the male stereotype of the powerful, controlling destructive woman."[28] She asks vindication for the belief "that patriarchy is in some ways a degeneration, that women exerting power would use it differently from men: nonpossessively, nonviolently, nondestructively."[29] *The Dream of a Common Language*[30] opens with a poem entitled "Power." The complexities of this power are inherent in the story of Marie Curie, who discovered the vital properties of uranium, and who died from radiation poisoning, "denying / her wounds   came   from the same source as her power." Marie Curie did not know—literally—how to handle power. Once again Rich's poetic image—the woman holding in her "suppurating" fingers the test tube of uranium, source of energy and death—unites the abstract and political difficulties of power.

"Phantasia for Elvira Shatayev" further explores the danger of accepting and using power. In this poem the women's climbing team dies in an attempt on a mountain, dies, in the words of the team leader, while seeing in the struggle "*my own forces so taken up and shared / and given back*" by each of the women on the team. Nothing is lost. They lose their lives. But each of us must die and these women "*know now we have always been in danger / down in our separateness . . . but till now / we had not touched our strength.*" They will choose to survive only to live a life of their own choosing: "*We will not live / to settle for less.*" But they will not die, living in Adrienne Rich's poem as the poet assumes the voice of Shatayev, taking up her vision and sharing it, giving back to the women who died a new kind of life. The climb and the poem are a communal endeavor.

Language, poetry, contains a power of its own. And the poet has a responsibility to that power, to the power of consciousness, self-awareness and growth. "Origins and History of Consciousness" is a poem about Adrienne Rich's lifelong commitment to poetry. We enter the space in which she creates, share her process of analyzing and testing each idea that enters a poem. Writing poetry has always been a life-serious undertaking for this woman:

> No one lives in this room
> without confronting the whiteness of the wall
> behind the poems, planks of books,
> photographs of dead heroines.
> Without contemplating last and late
> the true nature of poetry. The drive
> to connect. The dream of a common language.

The necessities of a larger world call the poet (and reader) out of the drama of the intensely personal—" the drive / to connect"— to an integration of the personal and the larger political realities. It is this necessity, finally, that has brought Rich's poetic voice beyond that range explored by the confessional poets. "Even in her most personal lyrics," critics have recognized, she "stretches all human activities on the frame of social and political consciousness."[31] Her poetry

> does not solely rely upon an . . . emotional relationship to the poet and the poetic vision. Adrienne Rich's poetry maintains its autonomy, states its case, evolves its arguments, and at all times relates the personal to the objective, temporal, timeless, to the universal. Adrienne Rich never avoids either interior or exterior examination, never takes a stand that is not consciously chosen and firmly reinforced. Her poetry engages its subject; no conclusion is gained without a test.[32]

Within the later poems, this testing occurs more and more frequently in the use of dialogue, quotations (as in the journal segments from "Phantasia for Elvira Shatayev" or the letter fragments in "Paula Becker to Clara Westhoff") and the accrual of emotion and meaning in the repeated use of a particular image.

A silent beast, for example, stalks through *The Dream of a Common Language,* but the image is not new for Rich. The very early poem, "Aunt Jennifer's Tigers," the gorillas of "The Observer," Rich's identification with the hunted fox in *The Will to Change,* have all prepared for our encounter with Rich's image of incipient power, our sleeping "dumb beast, head on her paws, in the corner." In "Splittings" the beast is the pain of self-separation inflicted by the expectations of a patriarchal culture. And, "what kind of beast would turn its life into words?" asks "Love Poem VII," drawing on the expectation and fear of the power of self-revelation. The caged beast (or the empty cage) surfaces in image after image, as in "Natural History" or in "Mother-Right," when the mother and child run from the father/oppressor, "the woman   eyes sharpened in the light / heart stumbling   making for the open."

The beast becomes manifest in "The Lioness." Like women, she knows more than she has experienced. The poet addresses her:

> In country like this, I say, the problem is always
> one of straying too far, not of staying
> within bounds. There are caves,
> high rocks, you don't explore. Yet you know
> they exist. Her proud, vulnerable head
> sniffs toward them. It is her country, she
> knows they exist.

The poet stands watching the lioness and although she sees much from that perspective, sees that the power of the beast is "half-abnegated" and that "three square yards / encompass where she goes," there is no overt recognition that the lioness is caged. Standing on the outside, looking perhaps between the bars, the poet naturally sees only the lioness. It is a partial vision: not true. The poet must learn more than sympathy; she must be able to enter the lioness's frame of reference, and this she does:

> I look into her eyes
> as one who loves can look,
> entering the space behind her eyeballs,
> leaving myself outside.
> So, at last, through her pupils,
> I see what she is seeing . . .

From inside, the cage, of course, is visible. The lioness knows what lies in the distance—freedom, "the volcano veiled in rainbow"—and she sees what is immediately before her, that which was not strikingly visible from the outside:

> a pen that measures three yards square.
> Lashed bars.
> The cage.
> The penance.

The poet now sees and understands those elements that create the oppression of one who is like and unlike her.

"Hunger," dedicated to Audre Lorde, is the poem in this volume that deals most specifically with these elements of oppression. Adrienne Rich sees the desolation, the wasteland that encompasses a large part of the female experience. Once again, she sees at first from her own limitations, seeing "in my Western skin, / my Western vision," a landscape that is alien:

> huts strung across a drought-stretched land
> not mine, dried breasts, mine and not mine, a mother
> watching my children shrink with hunger.

The transition here is subtle, but encompassing. The land is *not hers,* the breasts are *"mine* and *not mine,"* but they are *"my* children" (emphasis mine). The involvement is complete and necessary. Because Rich says, if they can convince us that "our pain belongs in some order," that, for example, some of us will suffer a little, and some of us will suffer more because we are more powerless, or black or lesbian, and that's just the way it is, then "they *cán* rule the world." We are separated from one another and powerless as long as suffering can be "quantified," as long as the question can be asked:

> Is death by famine worse than death by suicide,
> than a life of famine and suicide, if a black lesbian dies,
> if a white prostitute dies, if a woman genius
> starves herself to feed others,
> self-hatred battening on her body?

Adrienne Rich also knows that no analysis of the problem of hunger by a white middle-class American can be separated from one's own sense of class guilt, of passivity—even when that passivity stems from the knowledge that circumstances are so complex that one person of good will can do little or nothing to effect change. "I stand convicted by all my convictions—" Rich confesses, "you, too." We will not, she says, accept the responsibility of our vision:

> We shrink from touching
> our power, we shrink away, we starve ourselves
> and each other, we're scared shitless

of what it could be to take and use our love,
hose it on a city, on a world,
to wield and guide its spray, destroying
poisons, parasites, rats, viruses—
like the terrible mothers we long and dread to be.

But our failure, the failure of women and mothers and lesbians and all of those whose very existence depends on maintaining a precarious balance, is a failure of nerve: "even our intimacies are rigged with terror," and we confess this, as our "guilt at least is open." Our powers are expended on the struggle to survive and "to hand a kind of life on to our children / to change reality for our lovers."

Other failures are more damning:

The decision is feed the world
is the real decision. No revolution
has chosen it. For that choice requires
that women shall be free.

The words are deceptively simple; there are no images. The tone is matter-of-fact, straightforward. There are three simple statements and the connections which lead to their conclusion have everything to say about a feminist apprehension of power, the failures and necessities of power relationships.

The center of *The Dream of a Common Language* is a group of lesbian love poems, originally published as a separate booklet[33] and reanthologized here. It is an appropriate choice for continuing the theme of power, for in these poems Rich shows us a glimpse of the power generated by love, specifically the love of women for women:

You've kissed my hair
to wake me. *I dreamed you were a poem,*
I say, *a poem I wanted to show someone . . .*
and I laugh and fall dreaming again
of the desire to show you to everyone I love,
to move openly together
in the pull of gravity, which is not simple,
which carries the feathered grass a long way down
the upbreathing air.

There is a special recognition in "your small hands, precisely equal to my own," the recognition that "in these hands / I could trust the world. . . ." The strength in these poems is the discovery of the self in another, the range of knowing and identification that seems most possible in same-sex love: the encounter of another's pain, for example, leaves the poet knowing "I was talking to my own soul." Out of that sharing grows the ability to choose solitude "without loneliness," to define one's own sphere of action and growth:

> I choose to be a figure in that light,
> half-blotted by darkness, something moving
> across that space, the color of stone
> greeting the moon, yet more than stone:
> a woman. I choose to walk here. And to draw this circle.

The choice, here and in most of Adrienne Rich's poetry, is of a process, a way of becoming, rather than a narrowly defined end.

That emphasis on process can also be found in her frequent images of women creating beautiful quilts out of small pieces of fabric and experience that many women have made, saved and cherished, "piecing our lore in quilted galaxies," as she says in "Sibling Mysteries." In "Natural Resources" she gathers up "these things by women saved,"

> these ribboned letters, snapshots
>
> faithfully glued for years
> onto the scrapbook page
>
> these scraps, turned into patchwork

and the effort is the poet's attempt to give women back the past that has been lost to us, a past of "humble things" without which we have "no memory / no faithfulness, no purpose for the future / no honor to the past." She tells us it is against this knowledge of other women that we must now analyze and test our perceptions and visions for the future.

Adrienne Rich was once accused of "the will to be contemporary," an unhappy influence on her poetry, as she was "neither a radical innovator nor the voice of an age."[34] She is, in fact, both. No poet's voice has spoken as hers has in this period of profound social change in the relations between women and men, among women themselves. In the nearly three decades in which Adrienne Rich has been writing poetry, the quality of her vision and of her poems has been unique. We find again in these poems

> . . . no mere will to mastery,
> only care for the many-lived, unending
> forms in which she finds herself.

Her voice and her work are distinguished by a commitment to "the fibers of actual life" and to change, a commitment that is unmatched in her poetic generation.

> I have to cast my lot with those
> who age after age, perversely,
>
> with no extraordinary power,
> reconstitute the world.

NOTES

1. Adrienne Rich, "Tear Gas," in *Poems: Selected and New 1950–1974* (New York: Norton, 1975), p. 140.

2. By publishing two poems in the anthology *Amazon Poetry*, Rich has included herself in the prefatory note which announces that all of these poems "were written by women who define themselves as lesbians. And who have chosen, by publishing their poetry here, to affirm publicly that identity." *Amazon Poetry*, ed. Joan Larkin and Elly Bulkin (New York: Out & Out Books, 1975), p. 9.

3. *A Change of World* (New Haven: Yale University Press, 1951) and *The Diamond Cutters* (New York: Harper & Brothers, 1955).

4. "When We Dead Awaken: Writing as Re-Vision," *College English* (October 1972): 22.

5. Barbara Bellow Watson, "On Power and the Literary Text," *Signs* 1 (Autumn 1975): 113.

6. E.g., "Aunt Jennifer's Tigers," "Mathilde in Normandy," "Unsounded," and "For the Conjunction of Two Planets" in *A Change of World*.

7. *Snapshots of a Daughter-in-Law* (New York: Harper & Row, 1963).

8. "When We Dead Awaken," p. 24.

9. "My husband spoke eagerly of the children we would have; my parents-in-law awaited the birth of their grandchild. I had no idea of what *I* wanted, what *I* could or could not choose." Adrienne Rich, *Of Woman Born: Motherhood as Experience and Institution* (New York: Norton, 1976; pb. ed. New York: Bantam, 1977) p. 5.

10. "I read the older women poets with their peculiar keenness and ambivalence: Sappho, Christina Rossetti, Emily Dickinson . . . I know that my style was formed first by male poets: by the men I was reading as an undergraduate—Frost, Dylan Thomas, Donne, Auden, Mac-Niece, Stevens, Yeats." In "When We Dead Awaken," p. 21.

11. *Necessities of Life* (New York: Norton, 1966).

12. "Adrienne Rich and Robin Morgan Talk About Poetry and Women's Culture," in *The New Woman's Survival Sourcebook,* ed. Susan Rennie and Kirsten Grimstad (New York: Knopf, 1975), p. 107.

13. *Leaflets* (New York: Norton, 1969).

14. "When We Dead Awaken," p. 24.

15. Robert Boyers, "On Adrienne Rich: Intelligence and Will," *Salmagundi* 22–23 (Spring–Summer 1973): 140.

16. For example, Sylvia Plath, Anne Sexton, John Berryman, Robert Lowell.

17. First published in *Poems: Selected and New 1950–1974* (1975), p. 139.

18. Preface to *Poems: Selected and New 1950–1974,* pp. xv–xvi.

19. *The Will to Change* (New York: Norton, 1971).

20. *Diving into the Wreck* (New York: Norton, 1973).

21. "When We Dead Awaken," p. 25.

22. The subtitle of the essay, "When We Dead Awaken: Writing as Re-Vision."

23. "When We Dead Awaken," p. 25.

24. "The Antifeminist Woman," in *On Lies, Secrets and Silence* (New York: Norton, 1979), p. 78.

25. "The Antifeminist Woman," pp. 83–84.

26. "Adrienne Rich and Robin Morgan Talk About Poetry," p. 106.

27. "Three Conversations," in *Adrienne Rich's Poetry,* ed. Barbara Charlesworth Gelpi and Albert Gelpi (New York: Norton, 1975), p. 119.

28. "The Kingdom of the Fathers," *Partisan Review* 43 (Spring 1975): 25. This section appeared in a prepublication excerpt of *Of Woman Born,* but was not included in final publication.

29. *Of Woman Born,* p. 57.

30. *The Dream of a Common Language* (New York: Norton, 1978).

31. Willard Spiegelman, "Voice of the Survivor: The Poetry of Adrienne Rich," *Southwest Review* 60 (Autumn 1975): 386.

32. Mary Titus, "Adrienne Rich's Poetic Process" (Senior thesis, Skidmore College, 1978), p. 66.

33. *Twenty-One Love Poems* (Emeryville, California: Effie's Press, 1976).

34. Boyers, p. 144.

CLAIRE KEYES

"The Angels Chiding"
Snapshots of a Daughter-in-Law

> When . . . one reads of a woman possessed by the devil, or of a
> wise woman selling herbs, or even a remarkable man who had a
> remarkable mother, then I think we are on the track of a lost
> novelist, a suppressed poet, or some Emily Brontë who dashed her
> brains out on the moor, crazed with the terror her gift had put her
> to.
>
> —Virginia Woolf, A Room of One's Own

Snapshots of a Daughter-in-Law[1] reveals Adrienne Rich's obsession with demons. They may also be angels. The poems are ambivalent about this. In essence, these demons take over a woman caught between expressing her creative energies and remaining in her traditional role as a woman. No compromise seems possible. In her third volume of poetry, Adrienne Rich cannot imagine a coming-together of the woman and the poet with any sort of harmony, for the contemplated shift to womanly creativity violates the taboos of sexual identity. Within this conflict lies the necessity for a female aesthetic, the development of which will challenge assumptions about artistic creativity, masculinity and femininity. Two decades beyond these poems, Rich comments that "for centuries women have felt their active, creative impulses as a kind of demonic possession. But no less have men identified and punished such impulses as demonic. . . ."[2] The struggle going on in Adrienne Rich's poems constitutes a threat to male supremacy, to the concept of woman as Other, and to our sense of what it means to be "human." No wonder, then, that Rich's personae fear reprisal and regard the forces tormenting them as demonic.

"The Angels Chiding" is part of Claire Keyes's Ph.D. dissertation, "The Aesthetics of Power: A Stylistic Approach to the Poetry of Adrienne Rich" (University of Massachusetts, 1980). Reprinted by permission of the author.

The demons may be recognized in two ways. Both ways stem from clues given in the title poem. In its second section, Rich names the demons ironically as angels. Certainly not the carriers of good tidings, these angels harass the daughter-in-law with various maxims that have a Blakean ring; that is, they turn selfishness into a value: *"Have no patience." "Be insatiable." "Save yourself; others you cannot save."* Immediately following the maxim passage, Rich writes, "A thinking woman sleeps with monsters. / The beak that grips her, she becomes." Clearly we are to read "the angels chiding" the woman in section two as monsters. I go further and call them demons because *chiding* in this context recalls an earlier poem, "Living in Sin," in which a woman was "jeered by the minor *demons*" (my emphasis). The nature of the angels/demons depends on the verbs *chide* and *jeer,* both of which involve the sense of rebuke. Chide carries the meaning "to goad" or "to impel." Jeer means "to taunt." In both of these verbs, there is a quality of pressure or insistence, and the hint of a strong force able to perform the chiding. Thus the term *demon* is simply more useful than angel because it conveys more of the sense which involves Rich. Demon derives from the Greek *daimon:* a divine power, fate or god; in other words, some force capable of overwhelming a person—not necessarily to evil. Demons destroy, but in the act of destruction, the creation of a new self occurs. Thus the process involved in the recognition of Rich's demons requires noticing 1) an overwhelming hostile force and 2) a conflict that could result in the reshaping of the psyche along the lines of the self-attention the demon demands.

Selfishness in these poems always carries with it the suggestion of artistic creativity. Because the artist is a woman, Rich's struggle with the demons commands special interest. In her 1972 essay, "When We Dead Awaken: Writing as Re-Vision," Rich addresses this conflict directly:

Now, to be maternally with small children all day in the old way, to be with a man in the old way of marriage, requires a holding-back, a putting-aside of . . . imaginative activity, and demands instead a kind of conservatism. I want to make it clear that I am *not* saying that in order to write well, or think well, it is necessary to become unavailable to others, or to become a devouring ego. This has been the myth of the masculine artist and thinker; and I do not accept it. But to be a female human being trying to fulfill traditional female functions in a traditional way *is* in direct conflict with the subversive function of the imagination. The word traditional is important here. There must be ways, and we will be finding out more and more about them, in which the energy of creation and the energy of relation can be united.[3]

Because her need to do so is greater than man's, the woman artist is more likely to discover ways to unite "the energy of creation and the energy of relation." Such a discovery would constitute a basic element in a *female* tradition. Lacking such a tradition at the time *Snapshots* was written, Adrienne Rich is torn because her demons of selfishness seem to negate her womanhood as they push her toward being an artist. Because the life of an artist demands a quality of selfishness women have abjured, many settle for a pretty pleasing which Rich condemns: "When to her lute Corinna sings / neither words nor music are her own." Adrienne Rich's poetry moves towards shaping a Corinna who creates her own words and music. Such a woman exercises her creative power with no concern for being labeled "harpy, shrew and whore."

In her essay "The Kingdom of the Fathers," Rich cites Anne Hutchinson as "merely one example" of a woman who was punished because she exercised her powers. In "Snapshots of a Daughter-in-Law" she brings in all women whose "crime" was

> only to cast too bold a shadow
> or smash the mould straight off.

> For that, solitary confinement,
> tear gas, attrition shelling.
> Few applicants for that honor.

Rich herself boldly takes on the poetic subject of being a woman, a "daughter-in-law." By using the phrase "in-law," Rich stresses women's status in the patriarchal structure, criticizing the oppression of women and the suppression *by women* of their own powers. Because the poet fears reprisal, she writes other poems in which she maintains an identification with men, either in adopting a male persona, taking on male attitudes or imitating male poets, primarily Yeats. In other poems, she returns to the themes of "Daughter-in-Law," but her strategy remains oblique. She is possessed by another demon—the specter of male approval. What she risks in her title poem, she takes back. Thus she vacillates between expressing her female energy and maintaining the status quo. The demon that haunts Rich's poetic consciousness is the expression of womanhood as a special power. She is not even sure what that uniqueness *is*, but she experiences it as a repressed force, deviant and threatening because it is not male. This demon does battle with the specter of male approval. The result is a stand-off. Rich's ambivalence toward power is a key to the tensions in this volume. In earlier poems, she exhibited a more hidden ambivalence in which the dormant energies of the female personae were gently restrained. In *Snapshots,* the energies are very much awake. Rich's ambivalence is closer to the surface and, therefore, the poems are angrier.

A woman possessed by demons is taken over by an evil spirit, something "unclean" that torments her. Demons can be a divine power, fate or god. Thus the issue comes down to a woman's knowledge of a power within herself, a force by which she can transcend her subjectivity, a power, that is, which would make her fully human. Yet in the universe of Rich's third volume of poems, the demons are not finally regarded as a positive force. Rich focuses her attention on how crazy one becomes when demons take over. In part, the demon conundrum validates Phyllis Chesler's thesis in *Women and Madness* that "women are labeled as crazy to prevent them from having access to their own powers."[4] We might add that women themselves, at times, participate in the labeling. A woman who does not attend her demons could, of course, have "the old consolations" (Ghost of a Chance"). In addition to remaining within the feminine tradition, this means, for Adrienne Rich, a series of poems in which she assumes a male persona or identifies with a male experience *to the exclusion of the female.* In reading these poems, we can observe a pattern similar to the one Rich notes in the works of poets Sylvia Plath and Diane Wakoski:

> It strikes me that in the work of both Man appears as, if not a dream, a fascination and a terror; and that the source of the fascination and the terror is, simply, Man's power—to dominate, tyrannize, choose, or reject the woman. The charisma of Man seems to come purely from his power over her and his control of the world by force, not from anything fertile or life-giving in him. And, in the work of both these poets, it is finally the woman's sense of *herself*—embattled, possessed—that gives the poetry its dynamic charge, its rhythms of struggle, need, will, and female energy.[5]

We will not find a "Daddy" in *Snapshots,* or a tatooed motorcyclist. We do find a fascination with maleness and a male-identification much tamer than anything in Plath or Wakoski, but more insidious because Rich seems unaware of it. For example, Rich dedicates the last poem in the volume, "The Roofwalker," to Denise Levertov, but writes the following:

> A life I didn't choose
> chose me: even
> my tools are the wrong ones
> for what I have to do.
> I'm naked, ignorant,
> a naked man fleeing
> across the roofs
> who could with a shade of difference
> be sitting in the lamplight
> against the cream wallpaper
> reading—not with indifference—
> about a naked man
> fleeing across the roofs.

What kept Adrienne Rich from writing "a naked woman"? Would that have been too sexual? If so, to whom? Or doesn't it seem something perverse: a fear of not being universal, that is, not male. According to Rich's own dating, this poem was written in 1961, one year after she completed her title poem. Thus her vacillation, her ambivalence towards *womanly* power, dominates the emotional climate of the volume, creating the displacement of "The Roofwalker" and similar avoidances in other poems.

Only in her title poem does she reveal a sense of herself as "embattled, possessed." In "Daughter-in-Law" Rich's poetry carries the "dynamic charge" she notes in Plath and Wakoski. In it, Rich doesn't hide behind a male mask, although she still maintains her distance by referring to the woman hearing demonic voices as "she" not "I." On the whole, *Snapshots* fails as a volume of poetry because Rich backs away from the "rhythms of struggle, need, will, and female energy" she marks in other contemporary women poets. *As a woman,* she relinquishes the struggle to claim the power of the poet for herself. Her failure has aesthetic consequences because the poems pull at one another and their credibility is strained. If the poet is not sure about her function as a poet, then her poems appear weak and tentative. Such poems cannot be major poems because they are afraid of the truths contained in the voices of the demons. Such voices are taboo: "*Have no patience.*" "*Be insatiable.*" They violate the feminine tradition.

The demons that occupy Adrienne Rich press against such feminine "values" as passivity, submission and masochism. In some of the poems she clearly wants to overthrow those traits, but she confuses the issue by seeing other women as the enemy instead of developing a sense of identification with them. In "A Woman Mourned by Daughters," the tension operates between the old tradition embodied in the mother and the rumblings of the daughters which haven't crystalized yet into any "new" tradition. The title is ironic; the daughters resent the mother as an oppressive and overwhelming force. Dead, she remains formidable:

> You are swollen till you strain
> this house and the whole sky.
> . . . .
> What is it, if not you,
> that settles on us now

like satin you pulled down
over our bridal heads?
. . . .
And all this universe
dares us to lay a finger
anywhere, save exactly
as you would wish it done.

The antagonism Rich postulates in this poem between the mother and her daughters exemplifies the fairly consistent lack of female identification in the volume. It surfaces in the title poem as well, though I'll deal later with that poem in its own right. At issue here is the fact that Rich's poetic consciousness places the odium on the mother rather than regarding the older woman as similarly victimized. Fleetingly, she recognizes in the poem the light, ephemeral quality of the woman before she became wife and mother:

And yet you were a leaf,
a straw blown on the bed,
you had long since become
crips as a dead insect.

Once lively and natural as "a leaf, / a straw," the woman turned "crisp" with rigidity. These lines call to mind the portrayal of similar women in *The Diamond Cutters,* women who were "sharp of tongue and quick,"[6] women who lost their vibrancy to the compromises of marriage. There, Rich sympathized; here, she denigrates. Her hostility can be regarded as displaced anger. She can't strike out at the entrenched social institution of marriage nor at men. Then everything would crumble, both sexual relationships and the careful schooling she's giving herself in the major male poets. Other women are an easier, more culturally-sanctioned target.

Woman-hating is part of a cultural pattern which treats a mother-in-law, for example, as either a joke or a virago. Contempt for women is nothing new. Behind the daughter-in-law in Rich's volume there is a mother-in-law called to task. Rich's denigration of women is part of the overall pattern of the volume, a pattern which indicates that the poetic consciousness of Adrienne Rich is still located on the side of a masculine tradition in literature. Because she writes within that tradition, she delays the discovery of the female aesthetic so crucial to her development as a poet. In a volume which contains the forceful, woman-identified title poem, Rich's holding onto her male personae, male attitudes and blatant male identification weakens her credibility as a poet and brings about such poems as "The Loser," "The Knight," and "Antinoüs: The Diaries"—poems in which she adopts either a male voice or a male persona. When regarded as studies for Rich's title poem, these take upon a poignant relevance.

"The Knight" and "The Loser" appear side by side and come before the title poem; "Antinoüs" comes afterward. Each takes up a strand of the title poem's argument: "Well, / she's long about her coming, who must be / more merciless to herself than history." Each poem masks this theme in various guises. In "The Knight," for example, the speaker identifies with a male hero described in paradoxical terms: outwardly he appears strong and forceful; inwardly he trembles. His impoverished inner self makes a mockery of his brave and public mask. The "lump of bitter jelly" that is "his eye" betrays

> rags and tatters
> that cling to the flesh beneath
> and wear his nerves to ribbons
> under the radiant casque.

Since the Yeats influence upon Rich's subject matter, diction and imagery is obvious in other poems ("At Majority," "The Loser"), his "Sailing to Byzantium" comes to mind as a possible parallel, particularly his second stanza:

> An aged man is but a paltry thing,
> A tattered coat upon a stick, unless
> Soul clap its hands and sing, and louder sing
> For every tatter in its mortal dress.

The word "tatter" is the most overt link; the concept of the flesh as weak or puny, the deeper connection. But where Yeats's poem moves towards the immortality of the soul, Rich's focuses upon the freeing of the weak, inner man and the effect of the liberation. In her last stanza we recognize her desire for freedom countered by her fear of its repercussions:

> Who will unhorse this rider
> and free him from between
> the walls of iron, the emblems
> crushing his chest with their weight?
> Will they defeat him gently,
> or leave him hurled on the green,
> his rags and wounds still hidden
> under the great breastplate?

In the case of the knight, freedom from the armor which constrains him means defeat or death. The only question is whether his enemy is gentle or violent. If it is the latter, his secret vulnerability will remain hidden. The significant feature of this poem is that Rich imagines the exposure of male weakness as positive ("free him from between / the walls of iron") and yet deadly ("hurled on the green"). "Few applicants for that honor." If the manifestation of female strength is taboo, signs of male weakness are imagined by Rich as similarly punishable. Either way, she is caught in a firm set of beliefs about sex roles.

"The Loser" echoes Yeats's poems of longing for the beautiful Maud Gonne, in particular his "The Folly of Being Comforted," but more so "No Second Troy" with its lines:

> What could have made her peaceful with a mind
> That nobleness made simple as a fire,
> With beauty like a tightened bow, a kind
> That is not natural in an age like this,
> Being high and solitary and most stern?

Yeats regards the woman he loves as another Helen; Rich appropriates the yearning of his male speaker, but abandons the myth. The gloss on her poem reads, "A man thinks of the woman he once loved: first, after her wedding, and then nearly a decade later." In the second part, when the speaker regards the older woman taking in her wash, Rich plunges her Yeatsian beauty into an antiheroic, domestic scene:

> I see you strip the squeaking line,
> your body weighed against the load,
> and all my groans can do no good.
>
> Because you still are beautiful,
> though squared and stiffened by the pull
> of what nine windy years have done.
> You have three daughters, lost a son.
> I see all your intelligence
> flung into that unwearied stance.

In the last lines of the poem, the speaker returns to the woman's intelligence, describing her house as "lit by the friction of your mind." So far, the Yeats parallel holds, in particular the way in which the minds of both women are associated with fire. The difference, of course, lies in the domestication of Rich's housewife, whose fires, unlike Maud Gonne's, are banked. Like the armor the knight wears in the preceding poem, the woman's exterior has been "squared and stiffened." Furthermore, her husband has "chafed [her] beauty into use." *Chafe* means "to annoy" or "to vex"; it's similar to chide. Unfortunately, no angels chide this woman. The regret in the poem lies in the speaker's loss of the beautiful woman to another man; the real loss has been the woman's creative fire. She attended one demon—that of male approval—but neglected the other.

Read out of context in *Snapshots,* "The Loser" appears as a positive statement about the beautiful endurance of the ordinary woman. And, of course, the poem *says* this. What it doesn't say about the loss of the woman's creative fire draws more attention because it seems a secret even to the poet. Rich has various strategies for keeping her secrets from herself. In "Antinoüs: The Diaries," she again chooses a male speaker. A dramatic monologue, the poem recounts the diary-thoughts of "a beautiful youth, favorite boy of Emperor Hadrian, who drowned in the Nile, perhaps a suicide, in A.D. 130." Rich's note to this poem, added in 1973, continues, "I let the young man speak for me,"[7] a gloss she could not have written in 1959. "Antinoüs" is a devastating commentary upon a life lived by compromising the self. Rich withholds any mention of suicide; to mention it would go beyond the scope of her speaker. Instead she gives us, by means of his voice, the reasons for the suicide. Another suicide not mentioned by the poem, but endorsed by the choice of speaker, is the stifling of a creative woman. "Antinoüs" is about captivity; as in other poems, fire imagery plays an important role.

Why Antinoüs? He is a kept boy, a beautiful youth, a favorite; in sum, an appropriate mask for a woman in a traditional role. In the evenings, he says, he "need[s] to be out, / walking fast, fighting the fire / that must die, light that sets my teeth on edge with joy." Once again, Rich names fire as something that must be repressed.

In the second stanza, Antinoüs finds himself inside where "fires snap" and he hears "poetry of furs and manners. / Why do I shiver then?" The fire imagery in this stanza makes possible a distinction between the fire of the creative imagination and those fires that surround the "poetry of furs and manners." Rich's goal is to define the true sources of her poetry, but all conventions go against her. Worse, she has absorbed these conventions, like Antinoüs in the last stanza:

> The old, needless story. For if I'm here
> it is by choice and when at last
> I smell my own rising nausea, feel the air
> tighten around my stomach like a surgical bandage,
> I can't pretend surprise. What is it I so miscarry?
> If what I spew on the tiles at last,
> helpless, disgraced, alone,
> is in part what I've swallowed from glasses, eyes,
> motions of hands, opening and closing mouths,
> isn't it also dead gobbets of myself,
> abortive, murdered, or never willed?

In these lines, Rich depicts a boy who has "miscarried" himself. In her title poem, she more overtly describes her true concern—

the aborted selves of women. Hence, part 8 of "Snapshots of a Daughter-in-Law" *in toto:*

> "You all die at fifteen," said Diderot,
> and turn part legend, part convention.
> Still, eyes inaccurately dream
> behind closed windows blankening with steam.
> Deliciously, all that we might have been,
> all that we were—fire, tears,
> wit, taste, martyred ambition—
> stirs like the memory of refused adultery
> the drained and flagging bosom of our middle years.

Fire heads the list of "all that we [women] might have been, / all that we were." It is not curious that Rich's imagination finds fire an appropriate metaphor for the power women have killed in themselves. For purposes of clarification we can turn to the myth which tells how Prometheus stole the fire from Zeus and gave it to man, thereby initiating all that we know as civilization. Denis Donoghue defines the nature of that fire in a passage which describes well the imagery in Adrienne Rich's poetry and the kind of power that involves her:

> We have found the stolen fire identified with reason and knowledge, but it is probably better to identify it with the symbolic imagination; we have not grown so accustomed to the creative power of the imagination as to think it common, in the nature of the human case, like knowledge or reason. We think imagination a wonderful power, unpredictable and diverse, and we are satisfied to call it divine and to ascribe to it an early association with the transgression. A Promethean says of it that it is the most precious part of man, perhaps the only precious part, the only respect in which man's claim to superior character is tenable.[8]

Donoghue defines imaginative power as "unpredictable and diverse." Along with calling it "divine," he marks its "early association with transgression." These qualities, which make it "the most precious part of man," coincide with the meanings that surround *daimon* and help us understand the Promethean nature of Adrienne Rich's fire imagery. In addition, a reading of "Snapshots of a Daughter-in-Law" provides the awareness that it is not man alone who can possess the "wonderful power" of the imagination and thereby claim a "superior character." Rich's subject is woman.

In her essay "When We Dead Awaken" she comments upon this time in her life:

> In the late fifties I was able to write, for the first time, directly about experiencing myself as a woman. The poem was jotted in fragments during children's naps, brief hours in a library, or at 3 A.M. after rising with a wakeful child. I despaired of doing any continuous work at this time. Yet I began to feel that my fragments and scraps had a common consciousness and a common theme, one which I would have been very unwilling to put on paper at an earlier time because I had been taught that poetry should be "universal," which meant, of course, nonfemale. Until then I had tried very much *not* to identify myself as a female poet. Over two years I wrote a ten-part poem called "Snapshots of a Daughter-in-Law," in a longer, looser mode than I'd ever trusted myself with before. It was an extraordinary relief to write that poem. It strikes me now as too literary, too dependent on allusion; I hadn't found the courage yet to do without authorities, or even to use the pronoun "I"—the woman in the poem is always "she."[9]

The "common theme" which connects all the sections of the poem is a woman's relationship to creative power: how she wants yet fears it; how she regards her desire for power as demonic and angelic at the same time; how using her power means going against *all* patriarchal traditions. All these strands move toward a definition of power not as force or control but as the ability to transform. In this last respect, words and images surrounding fire continue to play an important role. Section 1 of the poem sets up the antagonism between the older woman, "once a belle in Shreveport," whose "mind now moulder[s] like wedding-cake" and her daughter who "wipes the teaspoons, grows another way." The way she grows is the subject of section 2: she hears voices. Unlike Joan of Arc, she is not driven to service for

God, King and country—but to herself. She experiences such a call as madness:

> Banging the coffee-pot into the sink
> she hears the angels chiding, and looks out
> past the raked gardens to the sloppy sky.
> Only a week since They said: *Have no patience.*
>
> The next time it was: *Be insatiable.*
> Then: *Save yourself; others you cannot save.*
> Sometimes she's let the tapstream scald her arm,
> a match burn to her thumbnail,
>
> or held her hand above the kettle's snout
> right in the wooly steam. They are probably angels,
> since nothing hurts her any more, except
> each morning's grit blowing into her eyes.

The voices distract the woman; as a result, she burns herself. The three acts of burning are deliberate. She fights fire (the call to creativity) with fire (the tapstream, the match, the steam) in order to deaden her longing. To a certain point, she succeeds "except [for] each morning's grit blowing into her eyes." That grit—the sand in her eyes that causes pain and tearing—is Rich's metaphor for what follows. Section after section unravels the troubled history of women.

Barbara and Albert Gelpi refer to Adrienne Rich as "pioneer, witness, prophet."[10] In the midsection of "Snapshots" she is witness—to woman's history, to her half-beginnings, to her rankling discontent:

> Knowing themselves too well in one another:
> their gifts no pure fruition, but a thorn,
> the prick filed sharp against a hint of scorn . . .
> Reading while waiting
> for the iron to heat,
> writing, *My Life had stood—a Loaded Gun—**
> in that Amherst pantry while the jellies boil and scum.

---

*Compare the first edition of *Snapshots of a Daughter-in-Law* (New York:

When she refers to Dickinson's poem but does not name Emily Dickinson, Rich pulls together two strands in her handling of power; she dovetails the aspects associated with fire or burning ("waiting for the iron to heat") with the sense of women's repressed energy, possibly phallic, certainly associated with masculinity and destructiveness ("a Loaded Gun").[11] We have come a long way from Rich's "An Unsaid Word" with its woman who "stands . . . still" even though "she . . . has power." While "Snapshots" expresses Rich's ideas about women and power more overtly, there is a holding back, a reservation inherent in her reluctance to bring in personal concerns. Nonetheless, these concerns surface in the attention she gives the subject of women's art: "When to her lute Corinna sings / neither words nor music are her own." Once again, women's unsaid word claims Rich's attention. She possesses, however, what Corinna does not. Adrienne Rich *knows* more than Corinna and she points the direction for other women with the questions of part 6:

> Pinned down
> by love, for you the only natural action,
> are you edged more keen
> to prise the secrets of the vault? has Nature shown
> her household books to you, daughter-in-law,
> that her sons never saw?

Woman's limitation ("pinned down / by love") could become her strength if we were to regard both the love which is woman's "natural action" and her "keen" edge as instruments by which she can gain access to Nature's "household books." That is, because woman *is* closer to Nature ("pinned down") and has ordinarily been regarded by man as *representing* Nature, her "natural action" enables her to discover what is necessary for the ordinary maintenance and furtherance of life. In "Snapshots," therefore, Rich's voice emerges in its visionary power. Seeing and understanding the nature of woman's experience she creates

---

Harper & Row, 1963) where this line reads: "*This is the gnat that mangles men. . . .*"

a vision of possible fulfillment: "the secrets of the vault," Nature's "household books." In 1977, she will urge women "to help the earth deliver." In the power of her imagination, she is Promethean. She would steal the fire and give it to women.[12]

Sections 7 to 9 of the poem recognize the obstacles to such a path as she has chosen, primarily the full weight of male disapproval. Mary Wollstonecraft was labelled "harpy, shrew and whore." Stasis is the alternative to male disapproval and Rich's diction in section 9, particularly her terms of address, show her contempt for those women who refuse change. She calls them "darling" and "ladies": "Sigh no more, ladies. / Time is male / and in his cups drinks to the fair." Those who are not fair, whose crime is "to cast too bold a shadow," are rewarded with "solitary confinement, / tear gas, attrition shelling. / Few applicants for that honor." Adrienne Rich is one of those applicants, for she is pioneer as well as witness and prophet. How she avoids the destruction she foresees is the map charted by her subsequent volumes. In the present poems, the act of writing down her own demons exorcises them.

As pioneer, Rich experiences herself as ahead of other women. By means of poetry, she has freed herself of the demons that taunted her. She looks back at other women who are still caught, doesn't particularly sympathize with them, and emerges as somewhat contemptuous. For example, "Readings of History," a 1960 poem, dwells in part 2 upon Luigi Pirandello and how he appropriated his mad wife's ravings for his writing. Rich reconstructs the confrontation between the artist and his wife, successfully splitting off the "mad" woman from the creative artist. Her speaker's sympathies lie with Pirandello:

> The present holds you like a raving wife,
> clever as the mad are clever,
> digging up your secret truths
> from her disabled genius.
> She knows what you hope
> and dare not hope:
> remembers
> what you're sick
> of forgetting.

What are you now
but what you know together, you and she?

She will not let you think.
It is important
to make connections. Everything
happens very fast in the minds
of the insane. Even you
aren't up to that, yet.
Go out, walk,
think of selves long past.

Despite her attention to Pirandello, Rich expresses the value of the wife's ravings: she is clever, aware of secret truths, and knows the importance of making connections. In sum, she sounds like a poet, but without the poet's facility with words. Pirandello's wife cannot shape her "ravings" into the considered art of her husband.

Why is she—Madame Pirandello, Adrienne Rich, other women—"so long about her coming"? The remaining poems in *Snapshots* settle into depression over this topic or avoid it while Rich returns to imagining what it's like to be a man ("The Roofwalker"). In one poem, "The Afterwake," Rich presents domesticity itself as the obstacle. The speaker is a woman, perhaps a young mother concerned over a sick child. Returning to a favorite situation of *The Diamond Cutters*, Rich allows us to enter the mind of a woman awake in the middle of the night. Other recurrent themes emerge:

Nursing your nerves
to rest, I've roused my own; well,
now for a few bad hours!
Sleep sees you behind closed doors.
Alone, I slump in his front parlor.
You're safe inside. Good. But I'm
like a midwife who at dawn
has all in order: bloodstains
washed up, teapot on the stove,
and starts her five miles home

walking, the birthyell still
exploding in her head.

Yes, I'm with her now: here's
the streaked, livid road
edged with shut houses
breathing night out and in.
Legs tight with fatigue,
we move under morning's coal-blue star,
colossal as this load
of unexpired purpose, which drains
slowly, till scissors of cockcrow snip the air.

We recognize the demons, imaged here in the roused nerves, "the birthyell still / exploding in her head"; the sense of something overwhelming, the "colossal . . . load / of unexpired purpose"; the hint of new birth contained in the figure of the midwife herself; and the woman's traditional role battling with her own need to create. Certainly, the woman in the poem is capable of making connections: she becomes, in effect, the midwife. The poem, however, is aborted. It goes no further than describing the situation of great womanly fatigue, the special struggles of a woman trying to fulfill a traditional role and attend her demons.

As midwife or poet, Rich acknowledges and names her demons, but she cannot embrace the fullness of their creative potential. Few clues in her cultural or historical background direct her to new, woman-centered uses of her demons. When *Snapshots* was written, she was still deeply influenced by male poets.

She imitates the great moderns—Yeats, Frost and Stevens among them—and she identifies with the poetic tradition created by them and their predecessors. She does not locate herself in the context of a tradition developed by other women. This is, perhaps, an American problem. In England, women novelists, at least, could look back upon the great novelists of the nineteenth century: Austen, the Brontës, George Eliot. In Canada, as well, women writers have been difficult to ignore.[13] In the United States, even as recently as the early sixties—the time of *Snapshots*—the literary establishment recognized no strong women poets besides Emily Dickinson. A woman writer needs a sense of a woman's active role in the shaping of a literary heritage. As long as poetry is regarded as what men write, a woman writing poetry must deny a crucial part of herself: her female identity. We can locate such a denial in the powerful prophetic conclusion of "Snapshots of a Daughter-in-Law," where Rich longs for the full expression of a female consciousness, yet manages to sabotage it at the same time.

Another one of the fragments with a "common consciousness and a common theme," part 10 of the title poem is a close paraphrase of a passage in Simone de Beauvoir's *The Second Sex*.[14] Rich shares de Beauvoir's grasp of the secondary status of women and a similar desire to change that status. Thus she concludes her poem in a vision of woman emerging from the darkness of her past:

> Well,

> she's long about her coming, who must be
> more merciless to herself than history.
> Her mind full to the wind, I see her plunge
> breasted and glancing through the currents,
> taking the light upon her
> at least as beautiful as any boy
> or helicopter,
> poised, still coming,
> her fine blades making the air wince

> but her cargo
> no promise then:
> delivered
> palpable
> ours.

Simone de Beauvoir writes, "She is a helicopter and she is a bird"; Rich emphasizes "beautiful as any *boy* / or helicopter." Once again, why couldn't she write "beautiful as any girl"? Granted, she would lose the alliterative pattern of "breasted," "beautiful" and "boy," but deeper reasons than music govern Rich's word choice.

48

"Beautiful as any boy" sums up the whole complex of Rich's poetic consciousness in this volume. Yes, the "she" is beautiful as she comes into her own power; and yes, Rich continues to regard that coming in male imagery, "as a boy." Thus she is torn between two demons: the demon of woman's creative flowering and the demon of masculine approval. With the latter, she can still be applauded as a writer of universal themes. With the former, she ventures into unexplored territory—like Emily Dickinson in the preceding century, but public: a pioneer, witness and prophet. Adrienne Rich's ultimate goal is the shaping of a strong women's tradition in American literature. To this end, she herself must develop a female aesthetic.

Thus *Snapshots of a Daughter-in-Law* demonstrates that Adrienne Rich cannot reconcile *what* she is (a poet) with *who* she is (a woman). She won't be able to effect this reconciliation until she finds new terms for power, and ultimately a new language capable of embracing female energy and creativity. Furthermore, she must recognize that the problem is not simply hers but inherent in a patriarchal culture which denies full status to women. In the process of developing a female aesthetic, her next book, *Necessities of Life,* [15] initiates her movement toward a redefinition of power. In these poems she regards the power-to-control as basically destructive. She rejects such power and moves toward the kind of transforming power which will become the basis of her female aesthetic.

NOTES

1. *Snapshots of a Daughter-in-Law: Poems 1954–1962* (New York: Harper & Brothers, 1963; New York: Norton, 1967).

2. Adrienne Rich, *Of Woman Born: Motherhood as Experience and Institution* (New York: Norton, 1976; pb. ed. New York: Bantam, 1977), p. 54.

3. Adrienne Rich, "When We Dead Awaken: Writing as Re-Vision," in *On Lies, Secrets and Silence: Selected Prose, 1966–1978* (New York: Norton, 1979), p. 43.

4. Adrienne Rich, "Three Conversations," in *Adrienne Rich's Poetry,* ed. Barbara Charlesworth Gelpi and Albert Gelpi (New York: Norton, 1975), p. 114; Phyllis Chesler, *Women and Madness* (New York: Doubleday, 1972).

5. "When We Dead Awaken," in *On Lies, Secrets and Silence,* p. 36.

6. "Autumn Equinox," in *The Diamond Cutters* (New York: Harper & Brothers, 1955), p. 63.

7. *Adrienne Rich's Poetry,* p. 16.

8. Denis Donoghue, *Thieves of Fire* (New York: Oxford, 1974), p. 61.

9. "When We Dead Awaken," in *On Lies, Secrets and Silence,* pp. 44–45.

10. *Adrienne Rich's Poetry,* p. xi.

11. Rich deals with the subject of Emily Dickinson in "Vesuvius at Home: The Power of Emily Dickinson" (1975), in *On Lies, Secrets and Silence,* pp. 157–83.

12. Toward the end of the volume, Rich takes Prometheus as her subject in a poem called "Always the Same." The line, "to help the earth deliver," is from "Natural Resources," in *The Dream of a common Language* (New York: Norton, 1978), p. 67.

13. See Karla Hammond's "An Interview with Margaret Atwood," *American Poetry Review,* September/October 1979, pp. 27–29. Atwood characterizes the conflict between woman and poet as "part of the American tradition. I can see why an American woman would say 'the poet is a man, and "poetry" is what men write', because I'm familiar with those university courses: Romantic writers, all men. Then they'd include Emily Dickinson. Even now American universities habitually ignore women writers in favor of men. It isn't that Canadian men are nicer or less sexist. They would have done that in Canada, too, if they could have. But they couldn't because the tradition was already fairly heavily populated by women."

14. Glossed in *Adrienne Rich's Poetry,* p. 16n; Simone de Beauvoir, *The Second Sex,* trans. H. M. Parshley (New York: Knopf, 1953), p. 729.

15. *Necessities of Life: Poems 1962–1965* (New York: Norton, 1966).

MARIANNE WHELCHEL

Mining the "Earth-Deposits"

Women's History in Adrienne Rich's Poetry

"Living   in the earth-deposits   of our history"[1] is the first line of "Power," a poem that explores the famous Marie Curie's history, and that opens Adrienne Rich's *The Dream of a Common Language*. The volume's last poem, similarly concerned with history, concludes with lines praising the "ordinary" woman who also makes history,

> pulling the tenets of a life together
> with no mere will to mastery,
> only care for the many-lived, unending
> forms in which she finds herself,
> becoming now the sherd of broken glass
> slicing light in a corner, dangerous
> to flesh, now the plentiful, soft leaf
> that wrapped round the throbbing finger, soothes the wound;
> and now the stone foundation, rockshelf further
> forming underneath everything that grows.
>
> (P. 77)

The earth metaphor persists, but the two poems indicate an overall shift in Rich's exploration of women's history from poems focusing on the individual, named woman to those focusing on unnamed, "ordinary" women or groups of women.

Marianne Whelchel read this paper at the University of Pittsburgh "Conference on Women in the Arts" in March 1980. She presented an expanded explication of Rich's "Phantasia for Elvira Shatayev" at the Great Lakes College Association Women's Studies Conference in November 1980; it is reprinted in *Toward a Feminist Transformation of the Academy: II, Proceedings of the Sixth Annual GLCA Women's Studies Conference,* published by the Great Lakes College Association, 1982. Reprinted by permission of the author.

Since her 1951 first volume, *A Change of World,* and throughout the fifties and sixties she has given us images of individual women—Emily Dickinson, Russian poet Natalya Gorbanevskaya, astronomer Caroline Herschel—strong women who have achieved, but often in isolation and at the cost of misinterpretation and actual physical threat. In some cases Rich has gratefully identified with these women, finding them the sisters and models who have lifted her from her estrangement as a woman and a poet, and she has celebrated their achievements against great odds. Throughout the late sixties and the seventies she has continued to create individual portraits, but she has tended increasingly to write about the unnamed women who have collectively made history: those of prepatriarchal times, those who settled the American West, those who have simply carried out the ordinary, day-to-day activities necessary to sustain life. And she is now eager to identify with these nameless women "who age after age, perversely, / with no extraordinary power, / reconstitute the world."[2]

Using women's history in her poetry, Rich participates in the movement among feminists—historians, sociologists, anthropologists—to reclaim, preserve, and evaluate women's lives. She explores how this history has affected her own experience and women's experience collectively. And certain poems, because of a particular woman's history, enable her to make feminist critiques of patriarchal institutions such as war and marriage, and to redefine important concepts such as power and love. Increasingly, her poems about women's history are overtly political, even revolutionary. Rich believes in the necessity of a feminist revolution and she wants her poetry to contribute to that revolution.

Rich's first poem dealing with women's history, the 1951 "Mathilde in Normandy," based on the legend that William the Conqueror's Queen Mathilde and her court ladies wove the Bayeau Tapestry, prefigures many of Rich's later concerns. She presents both the individual figure, Mathilde, and her unnamed court ladies; she deals with women's art—here a particularly female art, weaving; and she undertakes a critique of war. Although the historical accuracy of the legend has been challenged, assumptions about the women's experience and achievement as tapestry weavers have not. The legend would have it that the

Bayeau Tapestry was woven as a pleasant pastime by ladies whose lords had deserted them for the world's real business, war. Rich challenges this view of the women's enviable ease:

> Say what you will, anxiety there too
> Played havoc with the skein, and the knots came
> When fingers' occupation and mind's attention
> Grew too divergent, at the keen remembrance
> Of wooden ships putting out from a long beach,
> And the grey ocean dimming to a void,
> And the sick strained farewells, too sharp for speech.[3]

Rich challenges, too, the notion that women's work is ultimately less significant, less lasting than men's by focusing on the irony that the tapestry itself "should prove / More than the personal episode, more than all / The little lives sketched on the teeming loom" (p. 53). The shuttle's work outlasts the sword's. Further, the poem embodies a subtle critique of war in this statement about the importance of women's work, in the sympathetic exploration of the women's feeling, and in the depiction of tapestry images which put down male bravado: "the outlandish attitudes of death / In the stitched soldiery"; "the *little* lives sketched" (emphasis mine).

Several of Rich's poems about individual women deal with writers; others present women of note who are not writers, but whose experience Rich nevertheless relates to her own as a poet. Important among such poems from the sixties are those about Emily Dickinson, Natalya Gorbanevskaya and Caroline Herschel.

"I Am in Danger—Sir—" gives a feminist reinterpretation of Emily Dickinson's much misunderstood "withdrawal" from the world. The poem begins

> "Half-cracked" to Higginson, living,
> afterward famous in garbled versions,
> your hoard of dazzling scraps a battlefield,
> now your old snood
>
> mothballed at Harvard
> and you in your variorum monument

equivocal to the end—
who are you?[4]

As she does in many of her poems using women's history, Rich confronts the difficulties in establishing the actual facts. So much has gone unrecorded, been misrecorded or misinterpreted by men such as Thomas Wentworth Higginson, Dickinson's literary mentor. Nevertheless, Rich starts with the known facts—she sees Dickinson caring for house and garden but always with a mind to her poetry—and moves from there to conjecture that Dickinson, so distressed by the "spoiled language" around her, withdrew to preserve her own integrity:

> and in your half-cracked way you chose
> silence for entertainment,
> chose to have it out at last
> on your own premises.

(P. 33)

The careful wording of these lines stresses the active nature of Dickinson's withdrawal. Though her poetry has become a "battlefield" for male critics and biographers (as the poem's opening suggests), Rich insists that Dickinson herself was not driven back, not vanquished like a defeated general; she chose her retreat not out of weakness but out of a conscious decision "to have it out at last" on *her* terms.[5]

Perhaps Rich's personal experience around the time she wrote this poem (1964) gave her the insight and sympathy for this reading of Dickinson's experience. Though at that time she wrote no poems about it, she later said much about the difficulties of writing poetry while filling the traditional female roles as wife and mother. These difficulties may have given her the insight to see Dickinson's radical, atypical behavior not as evidence of weakness or aberration, but as a necessary and reasonable choice. To see it in this light is to give it an essentially feminist interpretation, something no critic had yet done.

"For a Russian Poet," for Natalya Gorbanevskaya, is the first of Rich's poems about real women in which she openly relates her own experience to that of the woman in the poem. It is from *Leaflets: Poems 1965–1968,* a collection that reveals Rich's struggle to move beyond the sense of powerlessness she feels before the immense social and political problems of the sixties to a consistent activism. Written partly in 1967 and partly in 1968, the poem combines the two impulses and is pivotal in Rich's development.

Section 1 establishes Gorbanevskaya's importance to Rich; she recalls how Gorbanevskaya's poetry has long given her a sense of Russian life and how they have shared similar visions and political concerns. The second section describes their mutual despair at contemporary social and political breakdown: "but this year we both / sit after dark with the radio / unable to read, unable to write."[6]

The poem's third section, based on Gorbanevskaya's account of her participation in a nonviolent protest action against the Soviet invasion of Czechoslovakia, contrasts sharply with the first two. Rich imagines herself with the poet and her little boy demonstrating in Red Square: "At noon we sit down quietly on the parapet / and unfurl our banners" (p. 29). Though Gorbanevskaya was later arrested, Rich thinks with satisfaction that they have succeeded in making "a great jagged torn place / in the silence of complicity" (p. 29). The poem ends on a strong note as Rich identifies herself with the Russian poet's protest. Here Rich preserves this woman's history, celebrates her action, and presents her as a model for political activism.

If Rich identifies as poet-activist with Natalya Gorbanevskaya, she identifies as poet-seer with astronomer Caroline Herschel. The 1968 poem "Planetarium" was inspired by an actual visit to a planetarium where Rich first learned that there had been women astronomers and heard particularly about Caroline Herschel, little-known sister and colleague of the famous William.[7] The first half of the poem vividly establishes Herschel's extraordinary achievement in the male world of astronomy:

a woman   'in the snow
among the Clocks and instruments
or measuring the ground with poles'

in her 98 years to discover
8 comets[8]

Hence the poem functions to reclaim women's history. And by emphasizing the fact of Herschel's femaleness and thus her kinship with Rich and her female audience, the poem presents Herschel as a model for female achievement:

> she whom the moon ruled
> like us
> levitating into the night sky
> riding the polished lenses

(P. 13)

The above lines, which play on the centuries-old witch image of the eccentric or unusual woman, along with lines describing the heavens Herschel surveys as filled with "Galaxies of women, there / doing penance for impetuousness" (p. 13) recall the persecution throughout history of women who have defied social expectations. In a sense, they warn the audience. Nevertheless, Rich moves in the poem's second half to full identification with Caroline Herschel. Using images from astronomy appropriate to both Herschel's career and to her own as a poet, she affirms her role as receiver and transmitter of truths that can transform.

> I am bombarded yet   I stand
>
> I have been standing all my life in the
> direct path of a battery of signals
> the most accurately transmitted most
> untranslateable language in the universe
> . . . .
> I am an instrument in the shape
> of a woman trying to translate pulsations
> into images   for the relief of the body
> and the reconstruction of the mind.

(P. 14)

Rich begins to articulate a revolutionary concept of poetry's function. By equating her vision with Herschel's, she suggests that as Herschel's vision changed the body of knowledge in astronomy, her own poet's vision can effect change in consciousness. Significantly, in this poem Rich for the first time identifies her aggressive, creative spirit with a woman. In the Emily Dickinson poem she called Dickinson "masculine / in singlemindedness" (p. 33) and in "Orion" (1965) she found inspiration in looking at a constellation representing a male mythic figure. Here, identifying her spirit with Caroline Herschel's, Rich records the "reconstruction" of her own mind.[9]

In a 1977 interview Rich commented, "It's not as interesting to me to explore the condition of alienation as a woman as it is to explore the condition of connectedness as a woman."[10] Although she continues in the seventies to write poems about individual women achievers, she often shows these women in relationships with other women who help make possible their achievement. Two such poems are "Paula Becker to Clara Westhoff" and "Phantasia for Elvira Shatayev." Both poems present women supporting each other in ways they are not supported in traditional heterosexual relationships. Exploring their history, Rich shows the potential for transformation of women's lives through connections made among women. Both poems are examples of what I define as revolutionary poetry. I would suggest that revolutionary poetry, as opposed to merely consciously political poetry, moves beyond exploration, criticism and analysis to posit alternatives to currently existing social structures and personal relationships. The revolutionary poet desires and assumes community with the audience and, in fact, attempts through rhetorical strategies as well as content to forge that community.[11]

The poem "Paula Becker to Clara Westhoff," based on the relationship between the too-little-known painter Modersohn-Becker and her even lesser-known sculptor friend, begins with an epigraph that identifies them, gives the dates of their lives, and explains that before their marriages—Becker's to painter Otto Modersohn and Westhoff's to poet Rainer Maria Rilke—the two women had lived and worked together in Paris and Berlin. Here Rich self-consciously reclaims women's history.[12] The poem itself is cast as a letter written by Becker after her marriage in which she tells her friend about her pregnancy, her wish not to have a child at that time, and her fears of what the child's birth may mean to her work as an artist. Casting the poem as a letter enables Rich to use Paula Becker as a mouthpiece for some of her central themes: the particular difficulties of the female artist and the way patriarchally defined marriage and motherhood allot love and nurturance to women, power and creativity to men.

Recreating Becker's thought, Rich presents her marriage as a concession to social convention which allowed continued intimacy with a man but not with a woman. Rich suggests that Becker would clearly have preferred to continue to live and work with Westhoff. Now married, she understands how marriage and children threaten the woman artist's work but not the man's. If there are children, the assumption is that the wife alone will care for them:

> this child will be mine
> not his, the failures, if I fail
> will be all mine. [13]

Not only does the wife nurture the children, but she nurtures her husband as well. In reference to Clara's marriage, Paula points out how a male artist profits through marriage while a female artist is exploited:

> Rainer, of course, *knows* more than Otto knows,
> he believes in women. But he feeds on us,
> like all of them. His whole life, his art
> is protected by women. Which of us could say that?
> Which of us, Clara, hasn't had to take that leap
> out beyond our being women
> to save our work? or is it to save ourselves?

(P. 43)

She admits to Clara her own need for the support that women traditionally provide for others, and suggests that in a continued relationship between them they might have provided it for each other:

> Sometimes I feel
> it is myself that kicks inside me,
> myself I must give suck to, love . . .

I wish we could have done this for each other
all our lives, but we can't . . .[14]

(P. 44)

Their mutually supportive relationship stands as a positive alternative to traditional marriage. Elsewhere Rich has written that she does not accept the male myth that to achieve, the artist must "become unavailable to others, or . . . become a devouring ego." She believes "there must be ways . . . in which the energy of creation and the energy of relation can be united."[15] As the poem presents the relationship between Becker and Westhoff, these two energies are no longer split apart but are both embodied in each woman.

In "Phantasia for Elvira Shatayev" Rich presents an even more fully realized vision of women in a cooperative, sustaining relationship that allows, even requires, the unity of love and power. Elvira Shatayev was the leader of an eight-woman mountain-climbing team, "all of whom died in a storm on Lenin Peak, August 1974."[16] Despite the team's failure to actually reach their goal, and despite their consequent deaths, Rich celebrates their attempt as representative of the achievement possible for women in community.

The poem is a straightforward monologue spoken from beyond death by Shatayev who recalls the team's experience and interprets its meaning. Though the poem is named for her, she clearly stands as representative of the group: "If in this sleep I speak / it's with a voice no longer personal / (I want to say *with voices*)" (p. 4, italics in original). Before speaking of their climb together, Shatayev recalls briefly her own and her companion's slowly evolving commitment to each other:

> For months   for years   each one of us
> had felt her own *yes*   growing in her
> slowly forming   as she stood at windows   waited

(P. 4)

No simple matter, their commitment required radical changes "elemental and minute" that enabled them to deliberately "choos[e] ourselves   each other   and this life." Using her own experience, Shatayev contrasts "this life" with marriage.

Recalling a climb with her husband "... when I trailed you in the Caucasus" (p. 4), she asserts that this life allows achievement not possible in traditional relationships with men. "Now I am further / ahead   than either of us dreamed   anyone would be" (p. 4). Rich's use of "anyone" makes clear that the usual division of love and power in marriage hurts and limits men as well as women.

The women are "further ahead" because in their commitment to each other they have experienced a new kind of love:

> *I have never loved*
> *like this   I have never seen*
> *my own forces so taken up and shared*
> *and given back*
> *After the long training   the early sieges*
> *we are moving almost effortlessly in our love*
>
> (Pp. 5–6; italics in original)

Unlike the self-sacrificing "love" traditionally expected of women as wives and mothers, this love is united with power. The self-affirmation and achievement that each woman experiences can take place only in community. Here Rich is not interested in the mere self-affirmation of the individual woman achiever—the token woman. She underlines this point by imagining Shatayev's diary:

> In the diary as the wind   began to tear
> at the tents over us   I wrote:
> *We know now we have always been in danger*
> *down in our separateness*
> *and now up here together but till now*
> *we had not touched our strength*
>
> (P. 6; italics in original)

The women's experience becomes a model for the community of women Rich increasingly calls for in her poetry—women acting together, supporting each other, accomplishing together. Their venture is transformed into myth as they "stream / into the unfinished   the unbegun / the possible" (p. 5). These lines not only eulogize the team but they also challenge the audience to finish what the women of the poem have begun and even to conceive "the possible" on a yet grander scale. Other lines work similarly:

> choosing ourselves   each other   and this life
> whose every breath   and grasp   and further foothold
> is somewhere   still enacted   and continuing
>
> (P. 5)

The poem is revolutionary in both content and form, for it not only posits alternatives but often through rhetorical strategies challenges the audience to adopt them. Rich invites the audience to go even further in conceiving revolutionary alternatives than she or the women have yet done.

Although, as we have seen, Rich continues in the late sixties and seventies to write about named historical women, in her latest work she has turned more and more to exploring the lives of "ordinary" women past and present. In 1974 Rich rejected the National Book Award as an individual for *Diving into the Wreck*. Instead, she and the other nominees, Audre Lorde and Alice Walker, accepted it

> in the name of all women whose voices have gone and still go unheard in a patriarchal world, and in the name of those who, like us, have been tolerated as token women in this culture, often at great cost and in great pain. . . . We dedicate this occasion to the struggle for self-determination of all women, of every color, identification or derived class. . . .[17]

This commitment to the collective welfare of women informs Rich's recent poetry which attempts to recover the experiences of those women "whose voices have gone and still go unheard. . . ."

A cluster of poems from *Diving into the Wreck*—including "Incipience," "After Twenty Years," Waking in the Dark"—presents images of a slowly evolving women's community struggling to create new female roles outside those assigned by patriarchy, images of women

who kept their secrets from each other
walked the floors of their lives in separate rooms
and flow into history now as the woman of their time[18]

These images depict a grass-roots movement of women striving for self-determination. Poems in *The Dream of a Common Language,* particularly "Natural Resources" and "Transcendental Etude," include vivid images of the ordinary women whose daily work has in the past and continues today to keep life going. Rich's profound respect for these women is obvious. Two major poems since *Diving,* "From an Old House in America" and "Sibling Mysteries," deal specifically and extensively with women of American history and women of prepatriarchal times.

"From an Old House in America" (1974) is set in the Vermont farmhouse where Rich spends her summers. Composed of sixteen parts (essentially mediations), the poem moves back and forth between the present moment in the old house and evocations of the poet's personal past, the past of other women who lived in the house, and the history of American women. The poet recalls this history to understand how it has conditioned her own experience and that of all American women. She wants to perceive her difficulties with her husband in a larger context and she needs to know how history has shaped female-male relationships. As she recounts the history, we see the origins of the destructive division of power along sex lines, divisions that have constricted the lives of most women. Mothering both men and children, most women are—as she tells us again and again in her poetry—as yet unborn to themselves. Lines from the poem inform us that a miracle "beyond / raising the dead" would be to watch "the undead" "back on the road of birth."[19] It is to effect this birth that she explores the American past.

Reconstructing this history is, of course, difficult because records are scarce or nonexistent. Early in the poem Rich addresses this issue as she ponders the lives of the women who lived in the farmhouse before her: "Other lives were lived here: / mostly un-articulate" (p. 235). The use of "un-articulate" focuses on failure to articulate rather than on the inability to do so. Here as elsewhere, Rich modifies language to make it disclose her feminist perceptions. Nevertheless, her female predecessors have left their mark: "yet someone left her creamy signature / in the trail of rusticated / narcissus . . ." (p. 235). Rich imaginatively reconstructs and reinterprets female history out of the traces that do remain—the flower gardens, diaries, journals and details mentioned by male historians and misinterpreted or seen as insignificant.

In the poem's central section she recalls those women who came to America, usually against their wills, to populate the "new country."

> Foot-slogging through the Bering Strait
> jumping from the *Arbella* to my death
>
> chained to the corpse beside me
> I feel my pains begin
>
> I am washed up on this continent
> shipped here to be fruitful
>
> my body a hollow ship
> bearing sons to the wilderness
>
> sons who ride away
> on horseback, daughters
>
> whose juices drain like mine
> into the *arroyo* of stillbirths, massacres
>
> Hanged as witches, sold as breeding-wenches
> my sisters leave me
>
> (Pp. 238–39)

The painful vignettes illustrate that from the first, American women have been defined by their sexuality and valued primarily as breeders of men who carry out the business of ever-raping and expanding the American frontier. The frontier experience, central to American history and consciousness and often romanticized, has meant—as Rich reconstructs it—the draining of female energies and the separation of women from each other.

This separation she views as integral to women's self-devaluation.

> I have lived in isolation
> from other women, so much
>
> in the mining camps, the first cities
> the Great Plains winters
>
> Most of the time, in my sex, I was alone
>
> (P. 239)

She also finds in this history the origins of the harmful dissociation of powers along sexual lines. This has been destructive not only to women and men, but it has also led to war and to ecological disaster.

> It was made over-simple all along
>
> the separation of powers
> the allotment of sufferings
>
> her spine cracking in labor
> his plow driving across the Indian graves
>
> her hand unconscious on the cradle, her mind
> with the wild geese
>
> his mother-hatred driving him
> into exile from the earth
>
> (P. 240)

As Rich sees misogyny interrelated with this separation of the sexes, she also attributes women's self-hatred to it. If women are defined primarily as mother-nurturers, their experiences as mothers must determine their self-esteem. In a passage based on diary quotations and public records taken from *Wisconsin Death Trip*,[20] Rich dramatically gives painful capsule histories of women's desperate responses to failure in their mother roles. One woman views her seven-year inability to conceive a child as punishment from God: "my punishment is my crime / what I have failed to do, is me . . ." (p. 241). Another woman, "her children dead of diptheria, . . . / set herself on fire with kerosene" (p. 241).

The recollection of our history as American women is so painful for Rich that she must fight her desire to escape this past and dissociate herself from the pain of her sisters either by retreat into romantic love or by acceptance of privileged status as token successful woman. Her need to understand her experience and to help her sisters "back on the road of birth" is so great, however, that she ultimately rejects these temptations and asks her audience to do the same:

> Isolation, the dream
> of the frontier woman
>
> leveling her rifle along
> the homestead fence
>
> still snares our pride
>
> (P. 245)

She calls this dream suicidal and asserts her connection with other women in the poem's final line: "Any woman's death diminishes me" (p. 245).

Using the first person pronoun, Rich continually identifies with the women whose history she recalls. In so doing she underscores the point that her seemingly simple affirmation "I am an American woman" (p. 238) is really a profound recognition of how her present has been shaped by the past she explores. Further, her identification with women across the boundaries of class, race and time, and her final line, "Any woman's death diminishes me," make a pledge of solidarity with her American sisters to end the isolation so central to the American female experience and to work to transform the social order. And through her use of the first person plural pronoun, Rich draws her audience into the community she envisions in the poem: "we have done our time / as faceless torsos licked by fire / we are in the open, on our way" (p. 242).

Rich believes the women's community she longs for and affirms is possible only if women achieve a positive acceptance of their primary relationship with their mothers.[21] She believes the mother-daughter relationship is constantly undercut in patriarchy where, traditionally, the daughter's affection and allegiance are expected to shift very early from the mother to the father in preparation for the daughter's eventual marriage. Rich views the patriarchal separation of mother and daughter as integral to the separation of women from one another, to the directing of their primary allegiance to men, and to their consequent underrating of themselves and relationships with other women. Thus, the mother-daughter relationship must be worked through both for the sake of the particular relationship itself and for the sake of community and strength among women.

"Sibling Mysteries" is essentially a working out in poetry of this analysis of the mother-daughter relationship. In the poem Rich gives glimpses of ordinary women during prepatriarchal history, a time when she imagines women were strong and experienced positive bonds with each other. She juxtaposes images of strength and connectedness with images of separation under patriarchy and with recollections—some taken from her diary—of her estrangement from both her mother and her sister. In the poem's present time she effects a reconciliation with her sister. The poem suggests that this reconciliation is made possible partly through an understanding of how women's original strength and rapport with each other were broken down during patriarchal history. This knowledge enables Rich and her sister to recognize and affirm their early bonds with their mother and finally with each other.

Rich dedicates the poem to her sister whom she addresses in the opening section, which is filled with positive images of women from prepatriarchal history—women attuned to nature and their creative powers as mothers and makers of tools and cultural artifacts. She requests of her sister:

> Remind me how we walked
> trying the planetary rock
> for foothold
> . . . .

> smelling the rains before they came
> feeling the fullness of the moon
> before moonrise
> . . . .
> Remind me how the stream
> wetted the clay between our palms
> . . . .
> how we traced our signs by torchlight
> in the deep chambers of the caves[22]

The images reclaim female history and reassure Rich and her audience that women are potentially strong.

In the poem's second section Rich asks her sister to recall their original relationship with their mother:

> Remind me how we loved our mother's body
> our mouths drawing the first
> thin sweetness from her nipples
> . . . .
> how she floated great and tender in our dark
> or stood guard over us
> against our willing

(P. 48)

She needs to be reminded of this early close relationship because, according to the rest of the section, it was quickly made taboo as the daughters were required to accept their mother's primary allegiance to their father:

> and how we thought she loved
> the strange male body first
> that took, that took, whose taking seemed a law
>
> and how she sent us weeping
> into that law

(P. 48)

Sections 3 and 4 place their personal estrangement from their mother in the context of women's history in various cultures under patriarchy. Rich suggests through vivid images and direct statements how this estrangement occurs, how it is built into patriarchal law and ceremonies. The sections emphasize male domination and devaluation of women. She asks her sister to remind her "how beneath / the strange male bodies / we sank in terror or in resignation / and how we taught them tenderness— / . . . how we ate and drank / their leavings, how we served them / in silence, how we told / among ourselves our secrets" (p. 49). Other images recall women burned at the stake, "the pregnant set to drift, / too many mouths for feeding" (p. 50).

Mingled with these images of oppression are images suggesting that women's intuitive knowledge and potential power, if brought into the open and communalized, could be subversive. In the poem's final lines Rich celebrates her current unity with both her mother and her sister:

> The daughters never were
> true brides of the father
>
> the daughters were to begin with
> brides of the mother
>
> then brides of each other
> under a different law
>
> Let me hold and tell you

This unity is partially a result of the demystification of patriarchal history and its laws. We have seen that women's experience in patriarchal history is not the "nature of things." Hence, through the recollection and understanding of myth, history, and personal experience, Rich finds the way back to unity with her mother and her sister. Essentially, the poem asserts anew the mother-daughter reunion celebrated in the ancient rites, the Eleusinian mysteries.[23] The title "Sibling Mysteries" implies a comparable reunion of sisters.

The poem has ritual, ceremonial qualities. Rich rehearses the history of women's oppression and separation from each other against an evocation of a mythic time when we were strong. The use of "we" in relating women's prepatriarchal history works rhetorically to reclaim early women's power and unity for Rich and her audience. The repetition of requests—"remind me," "hold me"—and of clauses similarly introduced—"how we walked," "how we dwelt," "how she sent"—lends an incantatory, ceremonial quality to the poem. Very personal, the poem is also public, for Rich views her experiences with her mother and sister in a mythical and historical context that includes all women. Thus, the female audience she seems to assume is brought into the experience of the poem, into the celebration of this new mystery. Both "Sibling Mysteries" and "From an Old House in America" may be called revolutionary poetry in that Rich attempts to involve the audience and thereby effect changes in consciousness and action.

Rich "min[es] the earth-deposits of our history" to bring to light women whose lives have been forgotten, undervalued, misinterpreted. She celebrates individual women and offers them to us for inspiration and models. As she restores and validates the experience of unnamed women who have collectively made our history, she looks closely at their lives to understand how they shape our own. She finds there the sources of our oppression, but she finds there, as well, alternatives to oppression. She invites us to use these alternatives so that we may reshape our futures and, thus, reconstitute our world.

NOTES

1. Adrienne Rich, "Power," in *The Dream of a Common Language: Poems 1974–1977* (New York: Norton, 1978), p. 3. Subsequent references to this poem will appear parenthetically in the text.

2. "Natural Resources," in *The Dream of a Common Language*, p. 67.

3. Adrienne Rich, "Mathilde in Normandy," in *A Change of World* (New Haven: Yale University Press, 1951), p. 52. Subsequent references to this poem will appear parenthetically in the text.

4. Adrienne Rich, *Necessities of Life: Poems 1962–1965* (New York: Norton, 1966), p. 33. Subsequent references to this poem will appear parenthetically in the text.

5. In her essential 1975 essay, "Vesuvius at Home: The Power of Emily Dickinson," Rich, with the advantage of much fuller research

into the details of Dickinson's biography, elaborates this feminist analysis of Dickinson's choice. The essay is collected in *On Lies, Secrets and Silence: Selected Prose 1966–1978* (New York: Norton, 1979).

6. Adrienne Rich, *Leaflets: Poems 1965–1968* (New York: Norton, 1969), p. 28. Subsequent references to this poem will appear parenthetically in the text.

7. Rich gave this commentary about the poem's genesis at a University of Connecticut poetry reading, April 9, 1975.

8. Adrienne Rich, *The Will to Change: Poems 1968–1970* (New York: Norton, 1971), p. 13. Subsequent references to this poem will appear parenthetically in the text.

9. Rich herself has called "Planetarium" a "companion poem to 'Orion'" in that the two poems document the shift in identification of her poet-self from a male to a female figure. "When We Dead Awaken: Writing as Re-Vision," in *On Lies, Secrets and Silence*, p. 47.

10. Blanche M. Boyd, "Interview: Adrienne Rich," *Christopher Street* 1 (January 1977): 14.

11. My thoughts on revolutionary poetry have been influenced by a number of sources, among them the article "Tom Eliot Meets the Hulk at Little Big Horn: The Political Economy of Poetry," by Marge Piercy and Dick Lourie, in *Literature in Revolution,* ed. George Abbott White and Charles Newman (Chicago: Northwestern University Press, 1972).

12. When I first heard Rich read the poem in March 1976, she encouraged the audience to see Becker's art, scheduled to be exhibited in 1977. For the poet to read the poem and so comment is to participate in restoring women's culture.

13. *The Dream of a Common Language,* p. 42.

14. In her poetry since *Diving into the Wreck* Rich frequently uses birth imagery in relationship to women's needs to give birth to themselves. For instance, women "in love" in the traditional sense are seen as "unborn" to themselves and in need of playing "midwife" to their own consciousness ("When We Dead Awaken," in *Diving into the Wreck*).

15. "When We Dead Awaken," in *On Lies, Secrets and Silence*, p. 43.

16. *The Dream of a Common Language,* p. 4. Subsequent references to this poem will appear parenthetically in the text.

17. Adrienne Rich, as quoted in *Adrienne Rich's Poetry,* ed. Barbara Charlesworth Gelpi and Albert Gelpi (New York: Norton, 1975), p. 204.

18. "After Twenty Years," in *Diving into the Wreck*, p. 13.

19. Adrienne Rich, *Poems: Selected and New 1950–1974* (New York: Norton, 1975), p. 238. Subsequent references to this poem will appear parenthetically in the text.

20. The Gelpis identify this source (see *Adrienne Rich's Poetry*, p. 82).

21. My summary of Rich's position is taken from her essay "Motherhood and Daughterhood," in *Of Woman Born: Motherhood as Experience and Institution* (New York: Norton, 1976).

22. *The Dream of a Common Language*, p. 47. Subsequent references to this poem will appear parenthetically in the text.

23. Rich discusses the Eleusinian mysteries in *Of Woman Born*, pp. 237–40.

ADRIAN OKTENBERG

"Disloyal to Civilization"
The *Twenty-One Love Poems* of Adrienne Rich

"A man's world. But finished."

From the beginning, in poetry as well as prose, Adrienne Rich has taken up the questions posed of patriarchy by Virginia Woolf in *Three Guineas:*

> . . . Let us never cease from thinking,—what is this "civiliza-
> tion" in which we find ourselves? What are these ceremonies
> and why should we take part in them? What are these profes-
> sions and why should we make money out of them? Where in
> short is it leading us, the procession of the sons of educated
> men?[1]

From the "respect [for her] elders" (W. H. Auden)[2] and "beauti-
ful lies" (Rosellen Brown)[3] in her early work, through the trou-
bled evasions, erasures, zigzag roofwalks later on, to the con-
frontation "with the naked and unabashed failure of patriarchal
politics and patriarchal civilization"[4] which is the chief necessity
of her mature work, Rich has returned to these questions over
and again. In the "Twenty-One Love Poems,"[5] Rich confronts
"this 'civilization' in which we find ourselves" for perhaps the
most concentrated and sustained moment in her poetry, and
pronounces herself, more explicitly than ever, disloyal to it.

It is not my purpose to describe the personal, political, or
poetical development which led Rich to arrive at these poems,
although that development as it is revealed in her work is fas-
cinating and the "Twenty-One Love Poems" are a culminating
point in it. The chronicle of tremors and quakes which her work

---

Previously unpublished, 1981.

has undergone up to this point, while essential to an understanding of her poetry, will be left to others. I wish to focus instead on what will undoubtedly remain one of the peaks of that development, to offer a reading of the "Twenty-One Love Poems" which, while not ignoring the climb, surveys in some detail the view from the height.

"Every peak is a crater," Rich writes (in poem XI of the series), indicating the dialectical nature of her enterprise. For throughout the "Twenty-One Love Poems" she is concerned with not one but two civilizations; the constant play of her mind is between (and beyond) them. The first is "this still unexcavated hole / called civilization, this act of translation, this half-world" (V) in which we are forced to live; it is the patriarchal peak, the sum or the summit of what men have created. Its apex is the city, the center of industry, commerce, law, culture. It is appropriate, and necessary, that the poems begin there.

> Wherever in this city, screens flicker
> with pornography, with science-fiction vampires,
> victimized hirelings bending to the lash,
> we also have to walk. . . .

> (I)

The speaker's disloyalty to this "civilization" is immediately apparent, for the culture of the sons of educated men displays at its apex its most meaningful artifacts: the imagery of violence, human distortion, gynephobia, horror. Woolf's question was, "Where . . . is it leading us . . . ?" Sweet Honey in the Rock sang, "B'lieve I'll run on . . . see what the end's gonna be."[6] But they, and Rich, and anyone else who cared to see, saw that the end would be death and destruction. That to avoid disaster, the procession of the sons of educated men must be diverted or halted. That disloyalty to civilization is not a crime (see XIII), but the essence of pragmatism. That disloyalty has become urgent necessity.

But patriarchal civilization is only the starting point, the thesis, for the argument. Rich is equally concerned to grasp and place beside it, as opposition and reproach, another conception of civilization—one that is woman-centered, woman-identified, woman-created. ("To bring forward" or "raise" or "emerge" are perhaps more appropriate verbs for this process, for a civilization which is of use to women is conceived of in the "Twenty-One Love Poems" as having been buried beneath or behind that constructed by men—see V.) While the violence of patriarchal civilization is palpably before us (concrete, assaultive, unavoidable), the struggle to imagine a woman-centered way in the world is of a different character.[7] Because we live, and have lived for centuries, under patriarchy, it must remain in large part the task of the moral imagination; because it is an act of imagination, it is fraught with mistakes, lapses, fears, confusions, setbacks, loops. It sometimes takes on the quality of shadowboxing; our powers of imagination can be weak, dim, or clouded; but the pain of error, fault, or missed connections is intense nevertheless. "No one has imagined us," the poet writes (I). She means that no man, no work of literature, no part of patriarchal culture has taken into account the possibility of two women together, loving each other, and of this as the embryonic beginning of a new, woman-centered civilization. She means that there are no guides or models for this task, so that "whatever we do together is pure invention" (XIII).

The poet also means that the "we" of the "Poems" (two women, lovers; by extension, other women together: "an army of lovers cannot fail") must undertake this essential work of the imagination as individual human beings in the world. In writing, "No one has imagined us," Rich suggests that the lovers of the "Poems" are not only fictive creations, but also, simultaneously, real human beings. The decisions they make have consequences in the actual world, the world of pain and struggle, life and death. Whatever is imagined by them must be created daily, under pressure of events. "A life I didn't choose / chose me . . . ," Rich wrote in an earlier poem,[8] and now she would no longer wish to turn away, but would embrace, the choice. She sees that "we need to grasp our lives inseparable / from those rancid dreams, that blur of metal, those disgraces" (I).

Necessity requires that the work of the imagination be conducted under conditions by which most women have always worked—without leisure, without space or privacy, without retreating from the immediately pressing and mundane demands of life.[9] Women must grasp their lives whole, and extract beauty ("the red begonia," "the long-legged young girls" of poem I) from conditions of ugliness—because other conditions are not available to be chosen. In opposition to patriarchal civilization, Rich attempts to imagine a woman-identified one; the latter remains as yet dim, fragmentary, rough. The "Twenty-One Love Poems" are also a partial documentary record, as if tape-recorded (XVII), of two people engaged in this effort, of their gains and losses, taken at a certain point in the struggle and in their lives.

Rich's procedure is by a method necessarily oxymoronic, paradoxical, contradictory, shocking. Her lovers exist in a patriarchal context, within which they represent, and attempt to create, a way of living profoundly at odds with it. Rich lives among the artifacts and debris of "modern" civilization, yet she knows it is dead ("the unabashed failure . . ."). Its values are dead both in the sense that they no longer hold meaning for us (e.g., patriotism: "*I think that men love wars,*" from IV), and that they lead to extinction (the polluted rivers and massacres of VII). The structures and institutions with which she must deal are patriarchal (cities in I, war in IV, culture in V, heterosexism in XIV), yet her true allegiance, and deeper identification, are to modes of thinking and relating which do not subscribe and are fundamentally opposed to patriarchal rules.

The underground life of the lovers in the "Poems" is constantly alluded to, and comes from the deeply buried parts of the "primitive" psyche, which continually assert themselves:

> . . . my own animal thoughts:
> that creatures must find each other for bodily comfort,
> that voices of the psyche drive through the flesh
> further than the dense brain could have foretold. . . .
>
> (X)

The speaker's thoughts are "animal" (X), she tells her dreams (II), identifies with "beasts" and "wolverines" (VII), with animals' instinct for physical contact and comfort (X), with planets, dream-ghosts (XII), outlaws and hallucinated transformations

(XIII). The lovers feel "animal passion" (I), their lovemaking is described in terms of forest ferns and caves ("THE FLOATING POEM, UNNUMBERED"), the impression they leave is of "some ghost" (XVII), they speak to each other in a dream (XIX), one communicates with the other as "to my own soul" (XX).[10] The *sotto voce* stream, or the subtext, of the "Poems" is the secret life of women—those who are openly disloyal to patriarchal forms are secretly loyal to antipatriarchal ones.

To express paradoxical thoughts, the poet requires a language of paradox. The imagery of the "Poems" is also substantially oxymoronic, and this contributes to the shock of the reader's response. Visionary poetry from Sor Juana Inés de la Cruz to Judy Grahn is oxymoronic in just this way:

> No one has imagined us. We want to live like trees,
> sycamores blazing through the sulfuric air,
> dappled with scars, still exuberantly budding,
> our animal passion rooted in the city.
>
> (I)

> to move openly together
> in the pull of gravity, which is not simple,
> which carries the feathered grass a long way down
>   the upbreathing air.
>
> (II)

> I touch you knowing we weren't born tomorrow,
> and somehow, each of us will help the other live,
> and somewhere, each of us must help the other die.
>
> (III)

> my body still both light and heavy with you
>
> (IV)

> such hands might carry out an unavoidable violence
> with such restraint, with such a grasp
> of the range and limits of violence
> that violence ever after would be obsolete.
>
> (VI)

Every peak is a crater.

(XI)

the innocence and wisdom of the place my tongue
      has found there—
         (THE FLOATING POEM, UNNUMBERED)

Across a city from you, I'm with you,
. . . .
your generous, delicate mouth
where grief and laughter sleep together.

(XVI)

two people together is a work
heroic in its ordinariness,
the slow-picked, halting traverse of a pitch
where the fiercest attention becomes routine. . . .

(XIX)

. . . nor any place but the mind
casting back to where her solitude,
shared, could be chosen without loneliness,
not easily nor without pains to stake out
the circle, the heavy shadows, the great light.
I choose to be a figure in that light,
half-blotted by darkness. . . .

(XXI)

Two women who are lovers in heterosexist society live with
contradictions embedded in their most intimate thoughts and
feelings. What they experience as beautiful, and as absolutely
natural, the rest of society views as ugly and perverted. Those
who exist in biologically female bodies in a world where only
male ones are considered "human" must daily deny the most
basic facts about their experience. Feminists who recognize
emotional, communal, or political bonds with women as prima-
ry, or who assert the centrality of "women's" issues to society as
a whole, or who seek to project woman-identified values where
masculinist ones hold hegemony, are under no illusions about

the ubiquity of patriarchal power. Those who are disloyal to civilization have no reason to obey, or even to recognize, its rules ("we're out in a country that has no language / no laws . . ." from XIII). Living in such a world *is* a paradoxical project for them; they float, unnumbered, in a world of anchored numbers. Why should not their laughter also contain grief, why could not their solitude be shared? And why should not gravity reverse itself, and pull grass up with the "up-breathing air"?

The adoption of antipatriarchal attitudes requires the most clarified vision, the most searching re-vision of received wisdom; nothing in it can be taken for granted. The struggle for clarity is one of the themes of the "Twenty-One Love Poems," as it is of Rich's work in general. This is a poet of celebrated intelligence, "a woman sworn to lucidity,"[11] for whom nothing is simple, to whom nothing is given. She believes in intelligence, which for her carries an active value, as others believe in the redemptive value of grace. In an earlier poem, she wrote:

> Only our fierce attention
> gets hyacinths out of those
> hard cerebral lumps,
> unwraps the wet buds down
> the whole length of a stem.[12]

In the "Twenty-One Love Poems," she wrote:

> If I could let you know—
> two women together is a work
> nothing in civilization has made simple,
> two people together is a work
> heroic in its ordinariness,
> the slow-picked, halting traverse of a pitch
> where the fiercest attention becomes routine
> —look at the faces of those who have chosen it.
>
> (XIX)

In the decade between the writing of those two poems, the "fiercest attention" of the focused mind, which seems an effort of supreme will (in the heterosexual context?) in the earlier poem, becomes routine (among women?). Its transformative power has not dissipated over time but has, if anything, increased. The "faces of those who have chosen it" ("it" being "two women together") are beatified not only by love, but also by the intense intellectual work in which they are involved.

But the struggle for clarity cannot be the work solely of the mind, as love cannot be the expression solely of the body. One critic has noted that the intensity of Rich's recent work comes in part from the fact that "mind and passion test and confirm each other,"[13] as they must in any good poetry. But for Rich the test is more rigorous than for most, and the confirmation is by no means assured beforehand. Her quest for intellectual clarity, the naming and placing of it in the larger cultural, historical, or planetary (XII) context, remains "hard," "cerebral," lumped, incomplete, unless passionate linkage can be made—and made to hold. For years, readers have shared her attempt to forge this link (one reason her work holds such fascination), and it is also why there is such relief and joy when she writes, in III: "And you, you move toward me with the same tempo." The lovers *meet,* minds and passions equally joined, as they have not met before in Rich's poetry.[14]

The fully engaged, intellectual and passionate meeting of *these* lovers is unique in the poetry that I know, and I am not speaking of the fact that the lovers are women (though that fact, acknowledged and celebrated, is still so rare in literature that its importance is not to be minimized). The meeting of lovers in the "Twenty-One Love Poems" is unique because it is on terms which are consciously antipatriarchal; lovers who are disloyal to patriarchal civilization strive to free themselves from its attitudes even in their intimate relations, even in themselves. This is a profoundly liberating process, and it is charted in the "Poems". This is what make the "Twenty-One Love Poems" new, not the fact that the lovers are women. Women have always loved each other, in literature as in life, but they have usually accepted, and done so within, patriarchal forms.

Nothing is given to these lovers—outlaws of patriarchy— neither language nor laws (XIII): "whatever we do together is pure invention." Much of the action of the "Poems" describes the process of trial and error by which the lovers must explore their love. Conventional love, as patriarchy would have them experience it, is useless ("the maps they gave us were out of date / by years . . ." from XIII). They use the only maps available, their own minds and passions. Much "courtly" or "romantic" baggage is jettisoned as so much dead weight.[15] One such item is the notion of lover as subject, beloved as object, and merger as unattainable ideal—one of the characteristic dichotomies of patriarchal thinking. Here are "two lovers of one gender, / . . . two women of one generation" (XII); their lives are seen as merging in a single poem (see II), and "it could be written with new meaning" (XII). The lovers are not human beings divided eternally by rigid categories of difference, but individuals linked by circumstance and choice (XVII).

Indeed, the familiar structure of romantic tragedy is explicitly rejected. Not fate but accident brings the lovers together:

> No one's fated or doomed to love anyone.
> The accidents happen, we're not heroines,
> they happen in our lives like car crashes,
> books that change us, neighborhoods
> we move into and come to love.
>
> (XVII)

No fatal or foredoomed flaw, but mortal choice and responsibility, determines the course of their love:

> If I cling to circumstances I could feel
> not responsible. Only she who says
> she did not choose, is the loser in the end.
>
> (XV)

The traditional "choices" for women, self-destruction, suicide, martyrdom, are recognized for the deathtraps they are:

> Well, that's finished. The woman who cherished
> her suffering is dead. I am her descendant.
> I love the scar-tissue she handed on to me,

but I want to go on from here with you
fighting the temptation to make a career of pain.[16]

(VIII)

The climax provides no spectacle of disaster,

> *Tristan und Isolde* is scarcely the story,
> women at least should know the difference
> between love and death. No poison cup,
> no penance. . . .

(XVII)

only the drone of an anticlimactic, analytical voice:

> . . . Merely a notion that the tape-recorder
> should have caught some ghost of us: that tape-recorder
> not merely played but should have listened to us,
> and could instruct those after us:
> this we were, this is how we tried to love,
> and these are the forces they had ranged against us,
> and these are the forces we had ranged within us,
> within us and against us, against us and within us.

(XVII)

For that kind of drama is out of date; its conventions do not, cannot, illuminate the images of these women.

A drama or literary structure that does is still largely unmapped, still in the process of discovery. Like the nineteenth-century feminists who compiled *A History of Woman's Suffrage* while the vote was in the process of being won, we know we must work it out while we are also living it ("—and yet, writing words like these, I'm also living," from VII). The language, the laws, the "charted systems" (XIII) of patriarchy must be transmuted, like the violence of poem VI, into a structure at once recognizable, yet fully expressive of and responsive to, our female passions and minds.

The form of the "Twenty-One Love Poems" also forces a transmutation of more traditional forms for love poems. Many have commented on how Rich's mature work has opened up, her lineation becoming less regular, her syntax more fluid, and so on,[17] and I do not propose to repeat that discussion. But there are two aspects of form in the "Twenty-One Love Poems" on which I feel I can comment.

The first is that, while they *look* like other, perhaps more familiar, love poems, they are in fact dissimilar. It is true that they are a sequence of short, free-verse lyrics; the speaker in the poems is a lover who addresses a beloved; the tone of the poems is intense, passionate, aching, intimate; the poems follow the course of a romantic relation over a relatively short time; the sequence comprises a testament to the beloved, a justification of the lover, and a fictive record of the relationship. In such respects the "Twenty-One Love Poems" do not differ substantially from the sonnets of Shakespeare, Matthew Arnold's "Marguerite" poems, the "Sonnets from the Portuguese," or the love poetry of Emily Dickinson, to all of which they owe a great deal. The "Twenty-One Love Poems" succeed so well in making the leap from the particular to the universal, they are so sensual, swift, and immediate in their impact, that it is possible to read them as if the tantalizing fragments of Sappho had been taken up by a poet of equal stature, and completed at last.

But it would be a mistake to read them that way for the reasons I have outlined. Rich has never been a particularly personal, certainly not a confessional, poet, and it is important to recognize that the "Twenty-One Love Poems" are not an anomaly in her work. They do not represent a private interlude in the work of a poet whose great theme has always been social relations; they are in no sense a departure or retreat from that theme. In fact, they deepen and extend it. While the poems may appear to be the private utterances of the lover to the beloved, while readers may appear to be privileged to eavesdrop on this most intimate relation, we are nevertheless expected to notice and remember the fact that these are only appearances. The "Poems" are political to their roots, and to ignore or minimize this aspect of the matter is to distort them.

Second, the "Twenty-One Love Poems" are constructed in such a way as to open up the whole of Rich's work; they are highly self-referential.[18] More than most contemporary poets,

Rich has fashioned a body of work rather than an accumulation of poems; the "Twenty-One Love Poems" demand to be read in the context of that work, both poetry and prose. Almost every line reflects on or reverberates off of something Rich has written elsewhere, creating a montage of images and associations. This poet who has been so influenced by film has observed that "the continuity and unity flow from the associations and images playing back and forth. . . ."[19] I have already noted, for example, the "fierce attention" which recurs in poems written years apart; when it resurfaces, the phrase enriches both contexts in which it appears. There are many such examples of recurring words, phrases, images, or ideas which are renewed or expanded each time they appear. The phrase "artists dying in childbirth" (in V) recalls Rich's great poem, "Paula Becker to Clara Westhoff";[20] "neighborhoods / we move into and come to love" (XVII) recaptures the last line of an earlier poem, "Shooting Script";[21] the reference to midwives' hands, eschewing forceps in the delivery of a child (VI), finds an explanation in *Of Woman Born;*[22] "Every peak is a crater. This is the law of volcanoes . . ." (XI) most directly recalls Rich's essay on Emily Dickinson, "Vesuvius at Home";[23] "the Eleusinian cave" (VI) brings to mind Rich's description of the Eleusinian mysteries in *Of Woman Born;*[24] "the slow-picked, halting traverse of a pitch" (XIX) reminds us of "The Roofwalker," who is "due to break my neck,"[25] and so on.

By inserting external references into the fictive world of the poems, Rich seems to be deliberately blurring the formal distinctions between fictive and natural discourse.[26] Many contemporary writers adopt this procedure; Rich is not alone, or particularly innovative, in this respect. By making reference to extraneous matters, literary or otherwise, the writer's intention is not to set up a bar to comprehension but rather to expand its field. If the reader has encountered nothing else by Rich, the "Twenty-One Love Poems" are of course perfectly comprehensible and moving. But if the reader can also connect the references in these poems to Rich's previous work, then her experience of the "Twenty-One Love Poems" gains in depth and range.

references do not slacken or degenerate into a private guessing game or code. Only Rich and her friends can identify "Kenneth" in V; the common reader must wonder whether Burke or Koch or Pitchford is involved. By now we know enough of Rich to assume that if Kenneth's full identity would add further dimension to the poem, we would have it, and leave it at that. Contrast Rich with the numerous references to friends in the work of O'Hara, Ginsberg, or Ashbery, and note the difference. Rich's references do not result in an enclosed system or zero-sum game, nor in damage to the poems.

The one extraneous reference we lack is the identity of her lover. I doubt that it matters. Rich has never conspicuously named her husband or sons either, nor is it necessary for her to do so in the important poems in which they figure. Colette: "One is always writing for someone."[27] Whether that someone appears in the work itself, in the flesh as it were and by name, is another question.

The "Poems" remain, then, consummate *fictive* acts; but the fact that Rich blurs the distinction between fictive and natural utterance heightens their intimacy. An impression is thereby achieved of speed, immediacy, and emotional compression. It is as if Rich has so much to say, and her need to say it is so urgent, that she resorts to a kind of emotional speedwriting or shorthand—an abbreviation of associations caused by the pressure of emotion. The "Poems," like Sappho's, become almost transparent and accessible. The result is that the reader is practically vaulted into the "Poems"; the effect is breathtaking.

None of this, however, can explain or do justice to the most striking effect created by the "Twenty-One Love Poems"—they are remarkably appealing. People's reaction to them is visceral, and I have reason to doubt that this response is limited to those readers—lesbian, or feminist, or female—who might be predisposed to favor this particular writer or these particular poems. It would be a sociological, rather than a poetical, enterprise to attempt to "identify" the "factors" which contribute to the appeal of the "Poems," and a futile one. But we can at least speculate on why these particular love poems are so affecting.

I have already suggested some likely reasons, but the most obvious one is that Rich has touched a nerve. We have all understood with Woolf that "the procession of the sons of educated men" is leading us to death and destruction; the evidence for that is everywhere inescapable. In the "Twenty-One Love Poems," Rich has succeeded, heavily against the odds, in putting us in touch with a powerful counterforce. By rejecting the patriarchal dichotomy between mind and passion, and suggesting instead their unification, she has begun to articulate an idea that it is difficult for most of us even to imagine. The project of the "Poems"—ultimately to unite the Greek concepts of *eros* and *agape,* or in the Gandhian formulation, *satyagraha* and *ahimsa*—is to suggest the regenerative power of knowledge united with love.[28]

The "Twenty-One Love Poems" are *feminist* in that they are woman-identified; they acknowledge, define and explore one set of the possibilities of love between women; they recognize the connection, the primary bond, between women as a source of integrity and strength.[29] They are also *radically* feminist in that they constitute a critique, a re-vision, of patriarchal notions of love. "Civilization" has shaped our consciousness of love, and therefore our experience of it, into gynephobic, patriarchal forms; Rich has chosen to "smash the mold straight off."[30] In struggling both to imagine and to live a way of loving which breaks that mold, in transmuting that struggle into art through the medium of poetry, Rich has provided us with a wealth of clues and insights. That the struggle ended in failure—at least in terms of the longevity of the love relationship described in the poems—is also instructive and of use to us. The struggle against patriarchy is an essential one; the "Twenty-One Love Poems" are a new labyris—and a banner of continuing beauty—for all those engaged in it.

NOTES

The title is taken from Lillian Smith via Adrienne Rich: "Freud said once that woman is not well acculturated; she is, he stressed, retarded as a civilized person. I think what he mistook for her lack of civilization is woman's lack of *loyalty* to civilization. . . ." Lillian Smith, "Auto-biography as a Dialogue between King and Corpse," in *The Winner Names the Age: A Collection of Writings by Lillian Smith,* ed. Michelle

Cliff (New York: Norton, 1978), p. 191. Cited by Adrienne Rich in "Disloyal to Civilization: Feminism, Racism, Gynephobia," in her *On Lies, Secrets and Silence: Selected Prose 1966–1978* (New York: Norton, 1979), p. 275.

I wish to thank Judith Weissman, Jane Roberta Cooper, Robin Becker and Leslie Lawrence for their helpful comments on earlier versions of this essay, and the directors of the Helene Wurlitzer Foundation of Taos, New Mexico, for an extended residency during which it was written. This paper, along with all my work, is dedicated to Barbara Herrnstein Smith—poet, critic, photographer, exemplary friend.

1. Virginia Woolf, *Three Guineas* (New York: Harcourt, Brace, 1966), pp. 62–63; first published 1938.

2. "[Rich's poems] . . . are neatly and modestly dressed, speak quietly but do not mumble, respect their elders but are not cowed by them, and do not tell fibs: that, for a first volume, is a good deal." W. H. Auden, Foreword to *A Change of World*. Reprinted in this collection, pp. 209–11.

3. "Rich's poems fall into two major categories, it's necessary but not sufficient to say that: the beautiful lies, whole and conventional, of the early period; everything that's followed her recognition that there is nothing apolitical, neither statement nor act. . . ." Rosellen Brown, "The Notes for the Poem Are the Only Poem," *Parnassus* 4 (Fall/Winter 1975): 50.

4. Adrienne Rich, Foreword to her *Poems: Selected and New 1950–1974* (New York: Norton, 1975), p. xv.

5. The "Twenty-One Love Poems" are in Rich, *The Dream of a Common Language, Poems 1974–1977* (New York: Norton, 1978), pp. 25–36. First published as a separate volume by Effie's Press, Emeryville, Calif. in 1976.

6. Bernice Reagan, "B'lieve I'll Run On . . . See What the End's Gonna Be." The song is the title cut of an album by the same name, by the group Sweet Honey in the Rock (Redwood 3500).

7. "[T]he sea is another story / the sea is not a question of power," from "Diving into the Wreck," in Rich, *Poems: Selected and New,* p. 196.

8. From "The Roofwalker," in Rich, *Poems: Selected and New,* p. 63.

9. See "Conditions for Work: The Common World of Women," in Rich, *On Lies, Secrets and Silence: Selected Prose 1966–1978* (New York: Norton, 1979), p. 203.

10. Nor is it an accident that the sequence concludes, in XXI, with the image of a woman walking alone at Stonehenge. The labyris, "the sacred double ax of Crete, symbol of the goddess and of matriarchal

rule," appears carved on the stones there. See Elizabeth Gould Davis, *The First Sex* (New York: Putnam, 1971), p. 80.

11. From "I Dream I'm the Death of Orpheus," in Rich, *Poems: Selected and New,* p. 152.

12. From "Like This Together," in Rich, *Poems: Selected and New,* p. 77.

13. Albert Gelpi, "Adrienne Rich: The Poetics of Change," in *Adrienne Rich's Poetry,* ed. Barbara Charlesworth Gelpi and Albert Gelpi (New York: Norton), p. 141.

14. And more successfully later. ". . . two women, eye to eye / meauring each other's spirit, each other's / limitless desire, / a whole new poetry beginning here." From "Transcendental Etude," in Rich, *The Dream of a Common Language,* p. 76. Any work published by Rich after this volume is beyond the scope of this essay.

15. But some, forgotten or unexamined, remains. I have said that the poems are an act of the moral imagination in which confusions, setbacks, and loops are inevitable. One such point of confusion appears in II, in which the speaker desires to show the lover "the poem of my life." A few lines later, it becomes clear that the speaker's life *is* her beloved. "*I dreamed you were a poem,* / I say, *a poem I wanted to show someone. . . .*" The attitude here revealed is a paradigm for the way women are supposed to address the (male) lover in romantic patriarchal literature, on the order of "you are my love, my life, my all." As such, it is a throwback to a way of thinking which the "Poems" as a group reject.

16. The prosaic language of these lines is another lapse—or leak—involving here the poet's effort to translate politics into poetry. "LEAK: There are leaks comparable to water leaks in the consciousness of every person. . . ." Monique Wittig and Sande Zeig, *Lesbian Peoples: Materials for a Dictionary* (London: Virago, 1980), p. 96.

17. See, e.g., Albert Gelpi, "Adrienne Rich: The Poetics of Change," in *Adrienne Rich's Poetry,* ed. Gelpi and Gelpi, pp. 142–45; Suzanne Juhasz, *Naked and Fiery Forms, Modern American Poetry by Women: A New Tradition* (New York: Harper Colophon, 1976), pp. 186–200; Helen Vendler, *Part of Nature, Part of Us: Modern American Poets* (Cambridge: Harvard University Press, 1980), p. 251.

18. The "Poems" include references to literature by others as well. The "Victorian poet" of XVIII is Matthew Arnold, whose poem, "To Marguerite, in Returning a Volume of the Letters of Ortis," concludes as follows:

> Who order'd, that their longing's fire
> Should be, as soon as kindled, cool'd?
> Who renders vain their deep desire?—

A God, a God their severance rul'd;
And bade betwixt their shores to be
The unplumb'd, salt, estranging sea.

From *The Poems of Matthew Arnold, 1849–1867* (London: Oxford University Press, 1922), p. 135. Philoctetes "hurting with an infected foot" in VIII is from the play of the same name by Sophocles, in *The Complete Greek Drama,* vol. 1, ed. Whitney J. Oates and Eugene O'Neill, Jr. (New York: Random House, 1938), p. 555. The legend of Tristan and Iseult appears in many places in literature (Beroul, Malory, Tennyson, E. A. Robinson), but Rich's reference in XVII no doubt refers to the music-drama by Richard Wagner, in which the lovers drink from a poisoned wedding cup. She has earlier referred to "Götterdämmerung" (in XIII), the last part of Wagner's tetralogy, "Der Ring des Nibelungen." "Der Rosenkavalier" (XIII) is the opera by Strauss. In V, Swift is seen "loathing the woman's flesh while praising her mind. . . ." Swift praised the minds of the two most important women in his life, to whom he played tutor and mentor: Esther Johnson, of the *Journal to Stella,* and Esther Vanhomrigh, of the long poem *Cadenus and Vanessa.* As for his "loathing the woman's flesh," evidence is abundant in his writing, a single line sufficing: "Celia, Celia, Celia shits." "Goethe's dread of the Mothers" (V) appears in *Faust,* part 2, act 1, scene 5:

Mephistopheles:	Unwilling, I reveal a loftier mystery.—
	In solitude are throned the Goddesses,
	No space around them, Place and Time still less;
	Only to speak of them embarrasses.
	They are THE MOTHERS!
Faust (terrified):	Mothers!
Mephistopheles:	Hast thou dread?
Faust:	The Mother! Mothers!—a strange word is said.

Goethe, *Faust,* trans. Bayard Taylor (Boston: Houghton Mifflin, 1882), pp. 65–66. Eckermann, Goethe's friend, stated that the Mothers are the "creating and sustaining principle, from which everything proceeds that has life and form on the surface of the Earth." See Notes, pp. 352–53. I am unable to locate the reference to Claudel (V), whose vilification of Gide is anyway inherent in the situation. Claudel: devout Catholic and conservative. Gide: anticlerical and radical homosexual. St. Pierre and Miquelon (XIV) are islands in the Atlantic just off the southern coast of Newfoundland. Finally, intuition based on similar experience tells me that the Xerox in the mail (IV) may have come from

Amnesty International, the organization that aids prisoners of conscience around the world.

19. Quoted by Albert Gelpi in *Adrienne Rich's Poetry,* p. 144.

20. In Rich, *The Dream of a Common Language,* p. 42.

21. In Rich, *Poems: Selected and New,* p. 182. The line is: "To pull yourself up by your own roots; to eat the last meal in / your old neighborhood."

22. Adrienne Rich, *Of Woman Born: Motherhood as Experience and Institution* (New York: Norton, 1976), pp. 142–51.

23. See "Vesuvius at Home: The Power of Emily Dickinson," in Rich, *On Lies, Secrets and Silence,* p. 157. Volcanoes appear often in Rich's poems. See, e.g., "Re-forming the Crystal," in Rich, *Poems: Selected and New,* p. 227–28.

24. See Rich, *Of Woman Born,* pp. 237–40.

25. See Rich, *Poems: Selected and New,* p. 63.

26. My understanding of such distinctions is derived from Barbara Herrnstein Smith, *On the Margins of Discourse: The Relation of Literature to Language* (Chicago: University of Chicago Press, 1978), esp. pp. 14–40. Natural discourse is essentially historical in character, and is the utterance of a temporal voice which, once having existed, passes from the scene. Conversations, letters, biographies are instances of natural discourse. Fictive discourse is ahistorical; it is the stuff of which poems and novels are made. Because it is ahistorical, we can reenter and reexperience it at will. One of Smith's arguments is that the two modes operate by virtue of characteristics suitable to themselves, and that we confuse them at our peril. When Rich writes, in XVIII, ". . . I am Adrienne alone. And growing colder," the statement is fictive because it is made in a poem. The speaker of it is therefore a fictive "Adrienne." It is *not* the statement of Adrienne Rich, a woman who lives in western Massachusetts, who writes poems, who is feeling cold—because such an understanding of it is appropriate only to natural discourse. My argument here is that Rich does not confuse, but deliberately *merges,* elements of fictive and natural discourse, in order to enlarge her readers' consciousness of the poems. It is a method used by many contemporary poets, whether or not they have been instructed by Smith.

27. *Letters from Colette,* ed. Robert Phelps (New York: Farrar, Straus and Giroux, 1980), p. 146.

28. My argument here, perhaps, is somewhat confused by the patriarchal connotations of the words used. The essential component of *eros* is usually identified as physical passion, whereas *agape* represents a more disinterested, sometimes termed "Christian," version of love based on the Golden Rule. *Satyagraha* is inadequately translated as "passive resistance," and *ahimsa,* as "nonviolence." The original meanings,

"truth/firmness" for the former, and "the negative of/injury" for the latter, are better, both being more active and less weak. For a useful discussion of the matter, see Joan V. Bondurant, *Conquest of Violence: The Gandhian Philosophy of Conflict,* rev. ed. (Berkeley: University of California Press, 1965), esp. pp. 15–35. Put simply, my claim here is that by breaking down the patriarchal dichotomy between mind and passion, the "Poems" offer a glimpse of what experience would be like if both were free. I have in mind nothing in the least mystical—only visionary.

29. See Adrienne Rich, "Compulsory Heterosexuality and Lesbian Existence," *Signs* 5 (Summer 1980):631–60.

30. The phrase is from "Snapshots of a Daughter-in-Law," in Rich, *Poems: Selected and New,* p. 50.

JOANNE FEIT DIEHL

"Cartographies of Silence"
Rich's *Common Language* and the Woman Poet

> Every age has its characteristic faults, its typical temptation to
> overemphasize some virtue at the expense of others, and the
> typical danger for poets in our age is, perhaps, the desire to be
> "original." . . .
>   Radical changes and significant novelty in artistic style can
> only occur when there has been a radical change in human
> sensibility to require them. . . . (W. H. Auden, Foreword to
> *A Change of World*)[1]

The "radical change in human sensibility" W. H. Auden finds
essential to poetic originality is at once documented and created
in Adrienne Rich's *The Dream of a Common Language*.[2] Here Rich
describes the dream of finding a language with the capacity to
free itself from its own history, the power to escape the length-
ening shadows of the patriarchal tradition of poetry in the West.
That such a vision carries with it a risk—the danger of silencing
the poetic or linguistic imagination—is neither surprising nor
new. For the woman poet's need to find or reinvent a language
in which she can seize the power and prerogatives of the origi-
nating voice has been the central challenge for all strong nine-
teenth- and twentieth-century women poets. In the wake of the
Romantics' self-conscious identification of the male poet as
quester and poetry as the language of desire, women who wish
to write repeatedly strive for ways to appropriate language, to
claim it for female experience. If the title of Rich's volume ac-
knowledges the visionary character of such an enterprise, it also
names its audience, for what she wishes to discover is a language

First published in *Feminist Studies* 6 (Fall 1980). Reprinted by permission of
Feminist Studies and the author.

that, while freeing itself from the exclusionary dominance of patriarchy, establishes a new, antithetical commonality of readers, a language spoken by and for other women. Rich's title contains an allusion to Virginia Woolf's sense of commonality as she described it in her introductory essay to *The Common Reader*. Here Woolf quotes from Dr. Johnson's "Life of Gray": " 'I rejoice to concur with the common reader; for by the common sense of readers, uncorrupted by literary prejudices, after all the refinements of subtilty and the dogmatism of learning, must be finally decided all claim to poetical honours.' "[3] Rich makes clear that she shares with Woolf the desire to speak not to an exclusive, educated, and advanced audience, but to those who share the concerns, desires, and burdens that define them as being excluded from the tradition of patriarchy, the lineage of male readers and writers who have dominated literature in the West. Rich aims, moreover, to reach beyond the "exceptional" women who have developed an awareness of their situation, and who have the means to articulate their burden, to reach beyond this educated class of consciousness to those deprived of such opportunities. It is from her sense of audience and the politics that determines such a choice that the literary method of her poems develops. The desire to convert ordinariness into a new mythos leads Rich to explore the conversational aspects of a language close to speech, in which secrets are laid open and wishes, too long silent, find their voice.

How can woman, that perpetual "other" of male consciousness, the object of his desire, create either the linguistic and/or social conditions that establish *her* not as the mediator of inspiration, the maculate whore-mother-muse of tradition, but as the predominant, shaping consciousness; the inventor of relationships that inform art? Although Rich's major nineteenth-century predecessors, Elizabeth Barrett Browning, Christina Rossetti, and Emily Dickinson, did find ways of breaking through the male dominance of language to discover new possibilities for the word, the difficulty of their search for imaginative priority does not, of course, fade with time. There can be no "final solution" for a woman who faces the accumulative force of a tradition that has its origins in the Homeric voice and which echoes with renewed strength in our post-Miltonic assumptions about the nature of language and the patriarchal perceptions of image-making itself.[4] It is just this need to find a way of piercing the web of traditional discourse to open and extend her dialogue with the predominant culture that Rich explores in *The Dream of a Common Language*. Her search for a shared mythology becomes a means of reclaiming a common experience for women that takes her into history, on an archaeological dig for lost possibilities of metaphor. In a recent essay on Denise Levertov, Rich, and Muriel Rukeyser, Rachel Blau DuPlessis remarks on this remythologizing process in Rich's poem, "Diving into the Wreck":

> In this poem of journey and transformation Rich is tapping the energies and plots of myth, while re-envisioning the content. While there is a hero, a quest, and a buried treasure, the hero is a woman; the quest is a critique of old myths; the treasure is knowledge: the whole buried knowledge of the personal and cultural foundering of the relations between the sexes, and a self-knowledge that can be won only through the act of criticism.[5]

The opening poem in *The Dream of a Common Language* describes a similar revising of myth—again the hero is a woman and the treasure is not simply scientific knowledge, but knowledge of self as the poet describes an attempt to reach into the earth for the sources, the origins of woman's distinctive power.[6] Rich first combs through the "earth-deposits" of "our" (female) experience of history to discover the amber bottle with its bogus palliative which will not ease the pain "for living on this earth   in the winters of this climate." The second gesture of the poem is toward a text and model: the story of Marie Curie, a woman who seeks a "cure," denying that the "element she had purified" causes her fatal illness. Her refusal to confront the crippling force of her success and to recognize the deadly implications of original discovery enables Curie to continue her work at the cost of her life. Denying the reality of the flesh, "the cracked and suppurating skin   of her finger-ends," she presses on to death:

> She died   a famous woman   denying
> her wounds

```
         denying
         her wounds       came       from the same source as her power
```

Here, in the poem's closing lines, Rich uses physical space and the absence of punctuation (an extension of Dickinson's use of dashes) to loosen the deliberate syntactic connections between words and thus introduce ambiguities that disrupt normative forms. The separation between words determines through the movement of the reader's eye—the movement past the "wounds" where it had rested the first time—the emphasis on the activity of denial and its necessary violation. The second "denying" carries the reader past the initial negativity of a woman's denying self-destruction by extending the phrase "denying / her wounds" into "denying / her wounds   came   from the same source as her power." Denial is an essential precondition for the woman inventor's continuing to succeed; what she is denying, of course, is the inevitable destruction of self in her work, as well as the knowledge that her power and her wounds share a common source. Like Curie, this book's later poems inform us, the woman poet must recognize a similar repression of her knowledge that what she is doing involves a deliberate rejection of the borrowed power of the tradition, the necessity of incurring the self-inflicted wounds which mark the birth of an individuated poetic voice.

Why should the process of image making, using language for one's own ends, be, in Rich's words, "mined with risks" for women?[7] And how are these pressures different from those confronting men? The poems respond directly to these issues and suggest that women are not only secondary in status, but are also latecomers to a patriarchal world of images. In a culture where words are formed and assigned their dominant associations by men, women, in order to speak at all, must either subvert their own speech by using the patriarchal tongue or else seek for themselves experiences available only to women—what it means to be a daughter, the emotions of a lesbian relationship, the process of childbirth—experiences which would then serve to free the woman poet through her choice of subject from the history of patriarchal associations. Thus, Rich insists upon the authority of, as well as the necessity for, solely female experience. Other women poets, of course (Sylvia Plath, Anne Sexton, and their contemporaries), have written of this need and described it. Each in her own way asserts that the power of language depends upon the originative capacity of the woman poet, her ability to create a linguistic context freed from the prescriptive tradition of male-dominated images. Rich's "Phantasia for Elvira Shatayev," for example, attempts to replace the received image of the male adventurer, the rugged masculinity of the climber, with the woman hero. In this poem, which speaks through the voice of the leader of a women's climbing team whose members died in a storm on Lenin Peak, Rich provides a narrative that supports the need to climb to a fresh place, to discover a ground where emotions stifled for years can be expressed. Describing an experience customarily associated with men and showing instead the physical courage of women is an alternative way to demonstrate how female consciousness can transgress and repossess male territory. The newness of the possibility for free expression depends upon an isolation complete and uncompromised, a quest that demands the sacrifice of life itself to reach it. In the courageous spirit of Dickinson's "If your nerve deny you, Go above your nerve," the climbers adjust to a cold matched only by the blood's will to turn still colder. In a dream, Elvira Shatayev voices her intent—to speak not as an individual, but with a language shared by this team of women climbers, a voice that achieves authority through the heroic and fatal struggle to the summit. But what these women learn transcends (thus calling into question) the power of language itself. Leaving behind the separation that exists between women on the earth below, the climbers discover that

> What we were to learn   was simply   what we had
> up here   as out of all words   that *yes*   gathered
> its forces   fused itself   and only just in time
> to meet a *No* of no degrees
> the black hole   sucking the world in

Only through a rejection of tainted or "grounded" language, in this will to confront physical challenge, can the "yes" be fulfilled. Although the voice we hear is triumphant in its achieved independence, the voice is of a woman dead. Yet even after death, Shatayev guards against her husband's powers of appropriation as he pursues the team to discover their fate. If, in the past, his wife has trailed him through the Caucasus, she escapes this secondariness in death:

> Now I am further
> ahead   than either of us dreamed   anyone would be

Her "self" merges with the land:

> I have become
> the white snow packed like asphalt by the wind

And death completes the commonality of the climbers:

> the women I love   lightly flung   against the mountain
> that blue sky
> our frozen eyes unribboned   through the storm
> we could have stitched that blueness   together   like a quilt

After her husband finds the bodies and tells his story, Shatayev insists that the women's experience does not end; their death engenders a physical metamorphosis into the world's being which continues the internal transformation of their climb. But this union of mind and spirit, this sharing of love, grows only as the women leave the world; in the diary, which must be "torn" from the dead climber's fingers (as if, even in death, she were still insisting that the words belonged to her alone), Shatayev had written:

> *What does love mean*
> *what does it mean   "to survive"*
> *A cable of blue fire ropes our bodies*
> *burning together in the snow   We will not live*
> *to settle for less   We have dreamed of this*
> *all of our lives*

The burning, ice-blue cable of connections holds the climbers, enforcing as it symbolizes the symbiotic relationship among the women and between life and death as well. These women who "will not live to settle for less" lose their lives in the attempt to reach new possibilities for living. Here Rich asserts the belief (echoed throughout these poems) that what women seek, this new ground, is a space where love and language find meanings that transgress the rules of society and supersede the tradition of a male-dominated discourse. Like Marie Curie in "Power," achievement depends upon the sacrifice of one's life. In the face of such a sacrifice, Rich keeps asking, can we achieve this requisite freedom and survive?

If the climate in which women live proves stultifying, if our language has become too tainted to trust, can we find a world more congenial to an imagination that seeks a reawakening of the powers of language and a field for its own intelligence? What determines the success or failure of this enterprise for Rich is whether she can stake out a territory freed from traditional identities and associations; she cannot forget the history of poetry because it is not hers. As outsider, Rich seeks a way to reappropriate language, to find a means of forcing language to free itself from its patriarchal origins. Yet Rich embarks on this search not in innocence, but aware that she must necessarily banish, repress, or "consign to oblivion" the possibility that language may resist if not finally defeat her attempts to establish an alternative language capable of reaching beyond male experience into the exclusive relationships between women. Although love between women becomes a way of discovering fresh ground, of defining a world that will and can only be described by women, the play of desire and the formal character of language cannot, of course, simply be destroyed. Nevertheless, asserting the priority of experience, Rich turns to address the woman who seeks to map a territory for such a language and faces the problem of conceiving a poetics based on transgression, a violation of societal expectation. The desire to make things whole, to love "for once with all [her] intelligence,"[8] becomes a / move to cast out the relation of male self and female/male other, to reassert mother-daughter intimacy, and thus validate the emotional self-sufficiency of women. Placing woman-woman relationships at the center of poetic attention may establish the experiential basis for figurative discourse no longer dependent upon the traditional patterns of heterosexual romance.

Rich's poetics of transgression become a source of "truth" in her "Twenty-One Love Poems." In the center of the book, she enacts the poetic theories she asserted in the volume's beginning and the assertions she will return to at its close. Here Rich attempts to make a poetry that refuses to succumb to the lies she must utter while living within the confines of a heterosexual culture. These poems demonstrate the difficulties of fusing a poetics out of politics, for they raise a question fundamental to Rich's project: If women have been stifled by being kept in a heterosexual society they reject, can a rejection of that society's mores itself free the poet, and thus restore to her the capacity of originative language? On this subject, Rich elsewhere remarks that "heterosexuality as an institution has also drowned in silence the erotic feelings between women. I myself lived half a lifetime in the lie of that denial. That silence makes us all, to some degree, into liars."[9]

To express, openly and without hesitation, her feelings as they develop in a lesbian relationship becomes a way of escaping the "silence and lies" which heretofore governed "women's love for women." Out of this assertion of truthfulness, Rich discovers, in her own terms, new possibilities for "truth": "When a woman tells the truth she is creating the possibility for more truth around her."[10] The relation of a lesbian ontology to the poetic praxis is not, however, so direct as Rich would have us believe. Merely to eliminate an overt stigma, to reject the veil of obfuscation, will not of itself produce good poetry no matter how liberating a gesture for the poet's psyche. What this lesbian relationship, as a ground of experience, does offer the woman poet, is the possibility of escaping the anxieties of male-dominated poetic influence. Ideally, Rich can thus draw on both female and male precursors while maintaining the authority that comes from a description of life that at once taps the more generally recognized emotions associated with eros, while simultaneously centering the poetry in a relationship that excludes the male consciousness—hence, the male poet.[11] Helpful though sexual truth-telling may be, however, it does not resolve the more difficult problem these poems so starkly articulate: the difficulty of reinventing names for experience, of placing the female Self at the center of this mimetic process. In her essay,

"When We Dead Awaken: Writing as Re-Vision," Rich discusses the relationship between woman's survival in this world and man's authority as the one who names what we experience:

> And this drive to self-knowledge, for women, is more than a search for identity: it is part of our refusal of the self-destructiveness of male-dominated society. A radical critique of literature, feminist in its impulse, would take the work first of all as a clue to how we live, how we have been living, how we have been led to imagine ourselves, how our language has trapped as well as liberated us, how the very act of naming has been till now a male prerogative, and how we can begin to see and name—and therefore live—afresh. [12]

The politics of experience becomes in *The Dream of a Common Language* a question of style; for the poems either assert in a strong rhetorical voice or enact in a more muted conversational manner, the distinction between gender-based differences in language. As Rich herself states, "Poetry is, among other things, a criticism of language."[13] More specifically in the "Twenty-One Love Poems," Rich proceeds to make a myth out of the dailiness of her experience; because, as she asserts, "No one has imagined us." The female poet, like Adam in the Garden, can name rather than rename the world around her. This transference foremost allows the woman to be both subject and object of consciousness, the agent of desire and its aim. The poems' language, their attempts to bear witness to the individual, private quality of an intimate relationship, moves between tones of understatement and forthright assertions of the difficulties sustaining such a poetry in the face of a tradition of silence, in the face of "centuries of books unwritten piled behind these shelves" (V). What these poems seek to accomplish is to combine a self-consciousness associated with starting an alternative poetic ground based on a lesbian relationship, a world without men, and an attempt to convert a specific intimacy into a paradigm that maps the possibilities of such a relationship for a radically alternative poetics. Rich confronts the inherent problem of combining these aims as she questions the mythopoetic enterprise itself—the conversion of private experience into an alternative program: "What kind of beast would turn its life into words? / What atonement is this all about?" (VII). But Rich sees this attempt also as a kind of evasion from the even more disruptive goal of centering the female self and making that self the origin for naming all that stands outside it:

And how have I used rivers, how have I used wars
to escape writing of the worst thing of all—
not the crimes of others, not even our own death,
but the failure to want our freedom passionately enough
so that blighted elms, sick rivers, massacres would seem
mere emblems of that desecration of ourselves?

(VII)

The question of renaming the world is at the heart of these poems because Rich perceives the necessity of escaping the boundaries of convention to make a new world "by women outside the law" (XIII). These poems also mirror the conviction that only by choosing one's own life freely and by making one's choice into a language can women begin to redefine poetry, appropriating for themselves the power of naming. The "Love Poems" close with Rich's assertion of the autonomy she seeks and the corollary mythos she creates through them:

I choose to be a figure in that light,
half-blotted by darkness, something moving
across that space, the color of stone
greeting the moon, yet more than stone:
a woman. I choose to walk here. And to draw this circle.

(XXI)

Echoing Aurora Leigh's decision, "I choose to walk at all risks," Rich shares her choice; the tradition reaffirmed continues.[14]

Yet such exclusionary tactics as Rich employs in the "Twenty-One Love Poems" do not necessarily release the poet from her own linguistic anxieties; the word can never free itself of its accrued meanings as emotion here strives to do. If the woman poet discards traditional images, where will she discover her First Idea? Power inheres in the word; it cannot rid itself of centuries of connotation. Knowing this, Rich turns away from the outspoken word, the power of the voice, to advocate a language that borders on silence. Thus the gesture of isolation, the exclusionary act itself, may, Rich speculates, provide an untainted source of female power. Consequently, the poems in this volume address, in various ways, the need to minimalize language, to divest the word of its accretions of power by replacing it with actions identified as preserving and sustaining a woman's integrity. Rich most powerfully resolves the difficulties of her apparently contradictory poetic aspirations in two of these poems: "Paula Becker to Clara Westhoff" and "A Woman Dead in Her Forties," for both poems achieve the balance between intimacy and assertion toward which Rich strives throughout this volume. In both poems, the speaker's words are shadowed by death; in the earlier poem, Becker writes to Westhoff, and her words gain for us a sorrowful resonance as her mingled hopes for her work combine with her sense of bewildered regret to prophecy unwittingly her death in childbirth and her last words, "What a pity." Again, as in the "Twenty-One Love Poems," we are readers who overhear—only this time, the imaginative reconstruction of the letter Becker writes adds a further distance; thus, Rich is able through this double distancing and through her voice of intimacy at once to use her words in a conversational, muted way and to make her language attain its dramatic character, for the letter itself is not a private document, but becomes through our reading of it a public performance. This same sense of violated yet shared intimacy controls "A Woman Dead in Her Forties," only here the survivor speaks of all she could never say while her friend was still alive. Again the death endows her words with renewed pathos; and the difficulty of speech, the price for honoring the taboo of silence, is measured by the irrevocable silence of death itself. Once more, we overhear words meant for another, and this act of overhearing enables the poem successfully to mediate between a conversational language (an intimate voice) and the power to transform this language into performance, into the language of poetry.

Yet such poems, although they do balance, can only provisionally resolve the underlying linguistic questions to which Rich returns throughout her work. If the poet cannot trust even the words she writes, her voice must be relegated to silence; but, if silence will not suffice, the problem remains: how to control the distrust of the very language the woman poet must invoke? The claims to be made for silence—its capacity for interrupting the repetition-compulsion of the activity of naming, the danger either of echoing or antithetically mimicking the patriarchal voice—achieve an eloquent expression of their own:

> Silence can be a plan
> rigorously executed
>
> the blueprint to a life
>
> It is a presence
> it has a history   a form
>
> Do not confuse it
> with any kind of absence[15]

But this power of silence potentially casts a shadow, for the very refusal to speak may not be a simple desire to escape the strictures of conventional discourse, but may, in the absence of any interpretative gesture, signify the negative act of willful withholding. The tension between these possibilities cannot be resolved within silence, but must seek its resolution in the margins of discourse. By margins, I mean the outermost edges where Rich can best mediate between the desire for speech and her need to respect the communicative forces of silence: the margins of discourse become for Rich the thoughts that precede or follow conversations, momentary impressions, the internalized voice that she returns to throughout the volume.

In "Cartographies of Silence," a mapping of the possibilities and dangers of the word, the poet expresses her longing for a language that would itself be a "pure" imaging forth; she desires an impossible linguistic form that would transcend discourse through its own originating presence, leaving the burden of meaning to silence:

> The silence that strips bare:
> In Dreyer's *Passion of Joan*

Falconetti's face, hair shorn, a great geography
mutely surveyed by the camera

If there were a poetry where this could happen
not as blank spaces or as words

stretched like a skin over meanings
but as silence falls at the end

of a night through which two people
have talked till dawn[16]

In this linguistic utopia, poetry would win freedom from voic-
ing either by the signifying power of physical presence (the
camera's moving in silently to survey Falconetti's face), or by
the mutual plenum of meaning created by a night of intimate
conversation. In both instances, a temporary resolution is
achieved. The ultimate irresolution of the character of silence,
however, does not allow Rich to evade the more precise de-
mands of speech. In her earlier poems—one thinks particularly
of "Shooting Script"—Rich had attempted to employ cinematic
techniques—splicing, close-ups, fade-outs, to writing; but in her
most recent work, she insists upon the distinctions between the
two media.[17] Despite her occasional envy of "the pure annun-
ciations to the eye," what Rich, as a matter of fact, keeps choos-
ing "are these words, these whispers, conversations / from
which time after time the truth breaks moist and green." These
words, which close the poem "Cartographies of Silence," com-
plete the allusions in its last movement that equate the act of
renaming the world, of remaking the land, with the power of
speech: the capacity for renewal and for rebirth. Like those cele-
brants of the Eleusinian rites, the woman poet should celebrate
her choice; "these words, these whispers, conversations," that
will bring, as did the goddess the hierophants worshipped, a
return of Spring to the world.[18] The woman poet becomes, as in
the myth of Demeter and Korê, through her very presence, the
regenerative power of life. Consequently, although Rich is
drawn to silence, her poems refuse to relinquish the life-giving
possibilities of an eloquence based upon the vocative powers of
the word, the truth-telling capacities of the woman poet who

defies convention to redefine the nature of performative language itself.

The central paradox of this volume resides in the poems' assertion of this move toward a new mode of writing, toward a gentle poetics antithetical to the aggression of the patriarchal tradition of Western poetry, while at the same time claiming the bold, heroic nature of this enterprise. Consequently, Rich shifts from the intimate voice of inner conversations to the rhetorical formulation of the need for an alternative form of power. Although the reader may initially be puzzled by this disjunction as she moves from poem to poem, the two modes are interdependent; for the apparently heterogeneous voices cohere around a common purpose—to strive toward overcoming the delimiting properties of language itself. The "radical change in sensibility" Rich at once explores and articulates depends in part upon the appropriation of a Whitmanian expansiveness for women; she is here to experience, as *only a woman can,* "the rainbow laboring to extend herself / where neither men nor cattle understand."[19] She envisions woman as explorer—a miner, whose headlamp, as we by now might expect, casts a ray like the weight of death. Despite the lethal dangers which the woman poet's light reveals, she alone can enter her sacred ground. We hear Rich invoking the Whitman of "The Sleepers," with all his confidence in the prepotent self, as she describes woman's solitary voyage:

> The cage drops into the dark,
> the routine of life goes on:
>
> a woman turns a doorknob, but so slowly
> so quietly, that no one wakes
>
> and it is she alone who gazes
> into the dark of bedrooms, ascertains
>
> how they sleep, who needs her touch
> what window blows the ice of February
>
> into the room and who must be protected:
> It is only she who sees; who was trained to see.

She wanders all night in her vision, and her freedom draws upon the power Whitman had claimed for himself. Note how close Whitman himself comes to her assertion of universal consciousness, as he appropriates the metaphor of birth to inform his return to the world of night, dreams, and death:

I will duly pass the day O my mother and duly return to you;
Not you will yield forth the dawn again more surely than you will
    yield forth me again,
Not the womb yields the babe in its time more surely than I shall be
    yielded from you in my time.[20]

This is the voice of the divinating American poet: Emerson, the father; Whitman, the son—members of the descendant tradition of a powerful patriarchy that claims for itself the possibility of an awful knowledge, a universal transparency that enables men to see and know the dreams of their mothers and daughters. Women face such a company, each of whom asserts that he is "the man-who-would-dare-to-know-us." In response, Rich creates experiences which exclude men; she envisions a world of women, a kind of love in which men play no part.

From this renewed ground of being, what kind of poetry? In lieu of aggressive consciousness, the powerful men of imagination, what possibility? Or, to ask these questions in another way, can language survive if we divest it of its appropriative power over the world of things? This is the heart of the problem, and, like other originating tensions, its power lies in its capacity to resist solutions. In the final passages of "Natural Resources," the poem that earlier made Whitmanian claims for the female imagination, Rich turns to gentleness, a conserving stoicism, as ways of combating aggression without diminishing the capacity for verbalization. "These scraps, turned into patchwork / . . . a universe of humble things"—what options do these offer?[21] Woman must, Rich asserts, strive against the assaults of both life and language; she must seek to save, but the burden is in the labor, the bringing forth. Returning to the rainbow which *labors* to extend itself, the natural work only a woman can understand, Rich closes this poem with her counterclaim against the male tradition:

The women who first knew themselves
miners, are dead. The rainbow flies

like a flying buttress from the walls
of cloud, the silver-and-green vein

awaits the battering of the pick
the dark lode weeps for light

My heart is moved by all I cannot save:
so much has been destroyed

I have to cast my lot with those
who age after age, perversely,

with no extraordinary power,
reconstitute the world.

But can such stoic gentleness, or biological capacity, create an
individuating language? Or is the very act of finding words and
sending them out of oneself, an activity that must imply vio-
lation, a gesture of trespass against the world? Here Rich faces
her most severe challenge: at once to speak of the place without
violating its presence and find a common language that repudi-
ates the mode of aggression in favor of a discourse of
conservancy:

if I could know
in what language to address
the spirits that claim a place
beneath these low and simple ceilings,
tenants that neither speak nor stir
yet dwell in mute insistence
till I can feel utterly ghosted in this house.[22]

The poet searches for a spider thread that will lead her back to
the origins of discovery, the answers that will inform her histor-
ical moment.[23] Seeking a "directive" that will lead her home,
Rich turns to housewifely duties—"brushing the thread of the

spider aside," a thread she earlier hoped might lead her to the source of lucid understanding, which now she must sever rather than spin in order, paradoxically, to re-form the thread of poetic continuity. Merely to preserve appearances is not to save them.

Yet if the gentle occupations of the housewife of language will not suffice, what alternatives remain for the woman poet? Rich explicitly rejects the American Romantics' belief in the poem as performative act:

> And we're not performers, like Liszt, competing
> against the world for speed and brilliance
> (the 79-year-old pianist said, when I asked her
> *What makes a virtuoso?—Competitiveness.*)
> The longer I live the more I mistrust
> theatricality, the false glamour cast
> by performance, the more I know its poverty beside
> the truths we are salvaging from
> the splitting-open of our lives.[24]

To deny a language of competition, to reject the performance, "cut the wires, / find ourselves in free-fall," is to experience a risk akin to that of living in a world where self-other relations are dissolved, where no comfort of precedence exists, where the tradition casts the word into a void:

> No one who survives to speak
> new language, has avoided this:
> the cutting-away of an old force that held her
> rooted to an old ground[25]

What that new poetry will depend upon are the origins of the poet's vision; and in the final lines of this volume's final poem, "Transcendental Etude," Rich shows us her vision through an extended simile:

> Vision begins to happen in such a life
> as if a woman quietly walked away
> from the argument and jargon in a room
> and sitting down in the kitchen, began turning in her lap

> bits of yarn, calico and velvet scraps,
> laying them out absently on the scrubbed boards
> in the lamplight, with small rainbow-colored shells
> sent in cotton-wool from somewhere far away,
> and skeins of milkweed from the nearest meadow—
> original domestic silk, the finest findings—[26]

This would be a poetry of what is close, precious through personal association, and drawn from the domestic landscape. Such a poetry would pull "the tenets of a life together / with no mere will to mastery, / only care for the many-lived, unending / forms in which she finds herself." The woman, in a return to a kind of "negative capability" that results in imagistic poetry would find herself

> becoming now the sherd of broken glass
> slicing light in a corner, dangerous
> to flesh, now the plentiful, soft leaf
> that wrapped round the throbbing finger, soothes the wound;
> and now the stone foundation, rockshelf further
> forming underneath everything that grows.[27]

It is she who protects by becoming, who re-creates by combining into the form of art the foundations of life, a life not of argument or jargon (a life of intellectual displacement); but a life so close to its sources, so open to one's experiences, that it provides the foundations for a new home and a new world. The woman becomes this foundation as she creates her language out of what she knows, the acceptance of the common, the life-sustaining forces that allow her to grow and to write.

NOTES

1. Reprinted in this collection, pp. 209–11. In her essay, "When We Dead Awaken," Rich remarks on the predicament of patriarchal poetry in this "historical epoch": "To the eye of a feminist, the work of Western male poets now writing reveals a deep, fatalistic pessimism as to the possibilities of change, whether societal or personal, along with a

familiar and threadbare use of women (and nature) as redemptive on the one hand, threatening on the other. . . ." See "When We Dead Awaken: Writing as Re-Vision," in *On Lies, Secrets and Silence: Selected Prose, 1966–1978* (New York: Norton, 1979), p. 49.

2. *The Dream of a Common Language: Poems 1974–1977* (New York: Norton, 1978). Unless otherwise indicated, all quotations in the essay are from this volume.

3. Virginia Woolf, *The Common Reader: First Series* (New York: Harcourt, Brace & World, 1953), p. 1.

4. For a brilliant discussion of women readers' and writers' responses to Milton, specifically to *Paradise Lost,* see Sandra M. Gilbert, "Patriarchal Poetry and Women Readers: Reflections on Milton's Bogey," *PMLA* 93 (May 1978): 368–82.

5. Rachel Blau DuPlessis, "The Critique of Consciousness and Myth in Levertov, Rich, and Rukeyser," in *Shakespeare's Sisters: Feminist Essays on Women Poets,* ed. Sandra Gilbert and Susan Gubar (Bloomington and London: Indiana University Press, 1979), p. 295. Originally published in *Feminist Studies* 3 (Fall 1975).

6. The poem is entitled "Power." For another treatment of Marie Curie's story within the context of an extended poetic discussion of women and creativity, see William Carlos Williams's *Paterson, Book Four,* section 2.

7. The phrase "mined with risks" appears in Rich's essay "Vesuvius at Home: The Power of Emily Dickinson," in *On Lies, Secrets and Silence,* p. 166.

8. "Splittings," p. 11.

9. Rich, "Women and Honor: Some Notes on Lying," in *On Lies, Secrets and Silence,* p. 190.

10. Rich, "Women and Honor," p. 191.

11. Consider, for instance, the echoes of Robert Lowell's *Notebook: 1967–68* in Rich's "Twenty-One Love Poems" (in *The Dream of a Common Language,* pp. 25–36). I would suggest that here Rich draws freely upon Lowell's tone, his form, the recounting of the dailiness of his life, because she claims for herself an alternative centrality in the poetic tradition.

12. *On Lies, Secrets and Silence,* p. 35.

13. "Power and Danger: Works of a Common Woman," in *On Lies, Secrets and Silence,* p. 248.

14. See Elizabeth Barrett Browning, *Aurora Leigh,* book 2, in *The Poetical Works of Elizabeth Barrett Browning* (Boston: Houghton Mifflin, 1974) p. 106.

15. "Cartographies of Silence," p. 17.

16. "Cartographies of Silence," p. 18.

17. See "Shooting Script," sections 1, 8, 13, and 14 in *Poems: Selected and New 1950–1974* (New York: Norton, 1975), pp. 173–82.

18. "Cartographies of Silence," p. 20.

19. "Natural Resources," p. 60. The following two quotations are also from this poem.

20. Although in her discussion of literary influences ("When We Dead Awaken," in *On Lies, Secrets and Silence,* p. 39) Rich does not mention Whitman, he clearly has had an impact on her work. Rich's "The Corpse-Plant," in *Necessities of Life* (New York: Norton, 1966), quotes Whitman in its headnote: *"How can an obedient man, or a sick man, dare to write poems?"* Both the tenor and the scope of her recent work remind one of the Whitmanian assertion of an expansive intimacy. The passage cited here is the closing verse paragraph of the 1855 version of "The Sleepers."

21. "Natural Resources," p. 66.

22. "Toward the Solstice," p. 69.

23. Robert Frost's "Directive," with its language of domesticity and spiritual search for origins, may be the poem Rich is addressing, if only indirectly, in "Toward the Solstice." To assess just how far Rich has come from her first volume of poems, one need only compare her self-conscious echoing of Frost and others in the earlier work and her dialectical appropriation of the voices of past poets, both male and female, in her most recent work. For analyses of this progress in Rich's poetry, see Albert Gelpi, "Adrienne Rich: The Poetics of Change," and Wendy Martin, "From Patriarchy to the Female Principle: A Chronological Reading of Adrienne Rich's Poems," in *Adrienne Rich's Poetry,* ed. Barbara Charlesworth Gelpi and Albert Gelpi (New York: Norton, 1975), pp. 130–48 and 175–89.

24. "Transcendental Etude," p. 74.

25. "Transcendental Etude," p. 75.

26. "Transcendental Etude," p. 76.

27. "Transcendental Etude," p. 77.

JANE VANDERBOSCH

Beginning Again

> *I found god in myself*
> *and I loved her*
> *loved her fiercely*
> —Ntozake Shange, *for colored girls who have considered suicide*
> *when the rainbow is enuf: a choreopoem*

During Adrienne Rich's thirty-year journey to educate herself through her art, both she and her work have gone through many changes. While these changes began slowly enough, they have accelerated in the last decade. This acceleration is due primarily to the influence of the women's movement in her life and on her work. For Rich, in becoming a feminist, has used it to catapult herself into a whole new way of perceiving reality. In one of many testaments, she outlined how it has influenced her life and work:

> . . . the women's movement connected for me with the con-
> flicts and concerns I'd been feeling when I wrote *Snapshots of a*
> *Daughter-in-Law,* as well as with the intense rapid politiciza-
> tion of the 1960s New Left. It opened up possibilities, freed
> me from taboos and silences, as nothing had ever done; with-
> out a feminist movement I don't see how I could have gone
> on growing as a writer.[1]

Feminism affected two interrelated areas of Rich's work: it freed her from the "taboos and silences" that had limited her perception, and it "opened up [new] possibilities" for seeing and interpreting her experience. By expanding the limits of her per-

This essay is part of Jane Vanderbosch's Ph.D. dissertation, "The Education of Adrienne Rich: From Re-Vision to Revelation" (University of Iowa, 1980). Reprinted by permission of the author.

ception, feminism broadened the boundaries of her vision as well.

Defining herself now according to her experiences as a woman, Rich also defines reality according to a feminist aesthetic. Her first explicit attempt to do this occurs in *Diving into the Wreck*. While the majority of poems in the collection are taken up with describing what it is like to survive as a female in the wasteland of the male, there are two poems, "The Stranger" and the title poem, which, when taken together, constitute a "revision" of Rich's sense of herself.

Rich identifies herself in these poems as a being who combines male and female characteristics. In "Diving," for example, she names herself both "the mermaid whose dark hair / streams black" and "the merman in his armored body."[2] And when she adds, "I am she: I am he," Rich goes beyond the indirection of metaphor to name herself an androgyne; she defines herself as one of those "possibilities" that feminism "opened up."

If, in "Diving," Rich sets herself in feminist opposition to stereotypes of masculine and feminine, in "The Stranger," she addresses the very efficacy of sex-linked language:

> if they ask me my identity
> what can I say but
> I am the androgyne
> I am the living mind you fail to describe
> in your dead language
> the lost noun, the verb surviving
> only in the infinitive
> the letters of my name are written under the lids
> of the newborn child[3]

The irony of this declaration is impressive and exact. By defining herself a "lost noun" from a living language, she implies that English, not Greek, is a "dead language." By so carefully distinguishing between the parts of speech, she questions the power of names (as nouns) to describe identity and she defines herself in terms of action by referring to herself as a verb.

While the androgyne is certainly the most unusual image in *Diving,* there are a number of problems connected with it. The "lost noun" is a being which combines sex-linked characteristics. Rich has described the male in her most extreme poems as her "enemy," a "prince of air and darkness," a killer, and a marital tyrant.[4] She has defined her relationship to the male as adversarial, angry, and bitter.

The female part of the androgyne, on the other hand, is as vaguely outlined as the male is sharply defined. The female is an unknown quantity, a nebulous factor in the whole, which is defined more by potential than by actuality. This results in an ideal composed of equal parts of what the poet says she doesn't know and what she says she hates.

The problems connected with the androgyne are clarified, though not resolved, by looking at it as a being serving two symbolic functions. That is, it signifies Rich's final attempt to integrate the male and the female into a holistic vision of the human and it represents her first attempt to define what it means to be female. Seen from this second angle, the androgyne symbolizes the poet's belief that women are androgynous because they have had to learn the male in order to survive in the patriarchal world and to retain the female in order to exist as women.

Once Rich's sense of herself as a female became more secure, the androgyne became expendable. This suggestion is not at odds with Rich's own perspective on the subject, though it does imply more than the poet explains. In an interview published three years after *Diving,* she "re-vised" her own estimate of the image by first describing it as "seductive . . . as a liberal solution" and then by maintaining that:

It's essentially the notion that the male will somehow incorporate into himself female attributes—tenderness, gentleness, ability to cry, to feel, to express, not to be rigid. But what does it mean for women? The "androgyny people" have not faced what it would mean in and for society for women to feel themselves and be seen as full human beings. [Thus] I don't think of androgyny as progress anymore, I think it's a useless term. . . .[5]

A useless term because it does not help women be or feel themselves, androgyny is now defined and discarded according to a stricter feminist standard: "But what does it mean for women?"

While some critics, notably Robert Boyers, would contend that this standard is itself a "rigid" ethic that narrows rather than expands the poet's vision, Rich seems to regard it as simply more precise.[6]

Rich's regard, in turn, seems to stem from her decision to define the human in terms of the female, not the female in terms of the human. In this critical shift, the once-favored androgyne, now a remnant of "patriarchal definitions," is not allowed a quiet passing. In a poem from *The Dream of a Common Language*, Rich declares:

> There are words I cannot choose again:
> *humanism   androgyny*
>
> Such words have no shame in them, no diffidence
> before the raging stoic grandmothers:
>
> their glint is too shallow, like a dye
> that does not permeate
>
> the fibers of actual life
> as we live it, now[7]

Rich's coup de grâce may be inelegant but it does accomplish its purpose. In disposing of the androgyne, Rich puts her readers on notice. Henceforth, her journey into the female will be the only journey; the "we," which will be more directed, will have no detours into "humanism" or "androgyny."

Journeying to the female center allows Rich to define what it means to be a woman from the inside, without resorting to definitions that are outside her experience or her context. This she does with what Margaret Atwood, in reviewing *Dream*, termed "authority." Atwood, in that review, went to the heart of the matter when she paraphrased the poet's quest:

> These poems are by an older poet, and possibilities, especially possibilities for heroism, have contracted in the face of the actual. Miss Rich is now asking: How, given the world and its history—which in her eyes must be seen as a history of

oppression for all women and many men—how, given vio-
lent and shoddy America, can anyone live and affirm?[8]

Atwood's question is important because it cuts through the
complexity of the collection to repeat one of its basic themes,
and rhetorical because she is aware of the answer. In an earlier
review of the poet's work Atwood had recognized, given Rich's
view of the world, that

the task of the woman, the She, the powerless, is to concen-
trate not on fitting into the landscape [of contemporary cul-
ture] but on redeeming herself, creating a new landscape,
getting herself born.[9]

The task of the poet, like "the task of the woman," is to affirm
herself rather than deny a "violent and shoddy America."
    This is precisely the task that Rich undertakes in *The Dream of
a Common Language*. It is not altogether different from what she
was trying to do in *Diving* except for the fact that Rich now
writes to, for, and about women. To go back for a moment: in
Diving, Rich wrote about women surviving in the landscape of
the male. She described their efforts to affirm the female in
themselves in the face of what she termed "the tragedy of
sex."[10] She also recreated a "lost noun" to speak of her own
dream for reconciling opposites. *Dream* does as much; it, too,
tells of the survival of women "in a world masculinity
made / unfit for women or men."[11] In addition, though, it
speaks of a new landscape that is metaphorically within the body
of women and offers a woman-identified definition of the
female.
    Dream, then, is a radical extension of *Diving*. No longer di-
recting either her energies or her attention to describing the male
environment in which the female must try to "live and affirm,"
Rich is now intent on getting the She in all women born. By
imagining an exclusively female landscape, she can explore her
understanding of who the She is by examining Her from the
inside. In other words, as *Diving* was the poet's internalization of
the male, *Dream* is her projection of the female. This shift of
perspective, subtle though it is, makes a world of difference.

Directing her full attention to the ideally female and the women who attempt to make this ideal a reality, Rich is able to imagine a collective and archetypal world.

Three things stand out in this world: the landscape itself, Rich's insistence that female interrelationships are the dominant feature of the landscape, and her definition of the virgin as the self-actualizing woman. The features are facets of the same phenomena; the parts—a woman's sense of herself, her relationships with other women, and her environment—add up to a female vision of wholeness.

The relation of the landscape to the She is the easiest feature to examine. The way Rich describes it, the landscape seems to resemble the Great Steppes of Russia: it is ancient, vast, and relatively unexplored. Rich reminds her readers that:

> we're out in a country that has no language
> no laws, we're chasing the raven and the wren
> through gorges unexplored since dawn
> whatever we do together is pure invention[12]

The women exploring this landscape have, like the country itself, no precedents, "no language / no laws." Bereft of the familiar, they are forced to rely on themselves and one another to discover the She in this landscape of the mind. Since the female is a place of imagination where "pure invention" is the keynote, the explorers' mission, as implied in the poem, is to bring this state of mind into a state of being.

The place that Rich is describing is the region of the archetypal female. It is also, on a more ordinary level, any place where women come together to discover who they are as women. Borrowing the title of a utopian novel by Charlotte Perkins Gilman, this "country" could be called "Herland." This name conveys the dual level of Rich's metaphor: "Herland" is at once the place "out there" that women collectively explore and the interior region of the self that each woman must locate and define.

A chosen place, it is for Rich also a holy place because it is the center of female mystery and belief. In this country,

Every peak is a crater. This is the law of volcanoes,
making them eternally and visibly female.
No height without depth, without a burning core,
though our straw soles shred on the hardened lava.
I want to travel with you to every sacred mountain
smoking within like the sybil stooped over her tripod,
I want to reach for your hand as we scale the path,
to feel your arteries glowing in my clasp,
never failing to note the small, jewel-like flower
unfamiliar to us, nameless till we rename her,
that clings to the slowly altering rock—
that detail outside ourselves that brings us to ourselves,
was here before us, knew we would come, and sees beyond us.

(P. 30)

This poem, XI of the "Twenty-One Love Poems," presents the
female landscape in miniature. The She is both the "volcano"
and the women who "scale the path." The "jewel-like flower"
that grows on the side of the mountain has a physical corollary
in the clitoris. Again, the female is not one thing any more than
it is one place. It is everywhere, any place that women perceive
to be "eternally and visibly female." Existing on the land and in
the body, it is both Nature and Woman.

What is interesting about this particular lyric is not only how
Rich parallels the natural and the womanly (the flower and the
clitoris, the burning core and the glowing arteries), but also her
belief that women have the power to name their environment as
well as themselves. When Rich and her friend define the "jewel-
like flower," the poet pointedly reminds the reader that the
flower was "nameless till we re-name[d] her." "Renaming" is
analogous to "re-vision" here; the flower—like an "old text"—
is seen "with fresh eyes" and given a fresh name.[13] Like the
sybils of ancient Greece, these women prophesy a mysterious
vision that is not of this world. In the case of these modern
sybils, the vision is an exclusively female one which they (rather
than the male priests of the Greek sanctuaries) interpret by the
act of naming.

In presenting this portrait of the female, Rich also offers a vision of the work that is before all women: reclaiming and renaming the "eternally and visibly female" without the benefit of laws or language. For Rich, women must do this not only to reassert their power to name but also to reestablish the bonds between themselves and nature that have been broken by patriarchal interpretations of the feminine.

That these bonds have been broken is clear to the poet. She writes of the rupture in "The Lioness." Here, equating animal with woman, Rich imagines how the split may be healed. The poem opens with the woman, absorbing the naturalness of the animal, saying simply:

> The scent of her beauty draws me to her place.
> . . . .
> The lioness pauses
> in her back-and-forth pacing of three yards square
> and looks at me. Her eyes
> are truthful. They mirror rivers,
> seacoasts, volcanoes, the warmth
> of moon-bathed promontories.
> Under her haunches' golden hide
> flows an innate, half-abnegated power.
> Her walk
> is bounded. Three square yards
> encompass where she goes.[14]

The lioness is, even in a caged "place," a mirror of the natural. Her animal energy flows toward the observer who is drawn by the "scent of her beauty." Watching the lioness watch her, the woman is unconsciously aware of her own animal power. She argues with herself about making too much of this scent:

> *In country like this,* I say, *the problem is always*
> *one of straying too far, not of staying*
> *within bounds. There are caves,*
> *high rocks, you don't explore. Yet you know*
> *they exist.* Her proud, vulnerable head
> sniffs toward them. It is her country, she
> knows they exist.

(P. 21)

Debating with herself, the speaker presents the rhymed alternatives: "straying too far" or "staying / within bounds." She is, Odysseus-like, "of two minds"; because of her loyalties, she is caught between one "country" and another. Rationalizing that knowledge and feelings about unseen places are sufficient, she is brought short by the lioness' sensate awareness. The natural is this animal's "country" and "she knows" in a way that the woman takes on faith that the "caves, / high rocks . . . exist." The animal does not need to meditate on the limits of existence: she has not forgotten where she came from.

Shifting from interior monologue back to narrative, the poem concludes:

> I come towards her in the starlight.
> I look into her eyes
> as one who loves can look,
> entering the space behind her eyeballs,
> leaving myself outside.
> So, at last, through her pupils,
> I see what she is seeing:
> between her and the river's flood,
> the volcano veiled in rainbow,
> a pen that measures three yards square.
> Lashed bars.
> The cage.
> The penance.
>
> (Pp. 21–22)

Breaking out of her solipsism by leaving herself "outside" and then empathizing "as only one who loves" can, the woman comes to identify with the animal. In that act of empathy, she also sees that her life has been circumscribed by her intense desire for privacy, for a personal space ("three yards square") as the lioness is circumscribed by the "lashed bars." The woman comes to see and share the "penance" that she and the animal have had to make.

The message of "The Lioness" is not the penance, however. It is the cage, the context of the female in a miniature "three yards square." It is the spatial dynamic that allows the woman first to observe and then to share the physical imprisonment of the animal. Together, they share the unnaturalness of the "cage." In realizing that the lioness' situation and her own are identical, the speaker sees that she, too, is "a stranger to this place." She and the animal are both in exile; both are removed from their natural habitat and are forced to spend their days remembering or imagining the freedom of that other "country." Developing an affinity with the animal, the woman discovers that the lioness' world is not very different from her own. And while empathy is what enables the speaker to see beyond the "lashed bars," it is not enough for Rich. She wants more than occasional acts of revelation or involvement; she envisions connection among all women.

In "Origins and History of Consciousness," she speaks of the limits of empathy, the limits of one woman loving another, one "warm animal" dreaming of "another animal."[15] While it is clear that Rich affirms the relationship, it is equally clear that she regards it as insufficient. Of love and physical intimacy between women, she says:

> It isn't simple
> to wake from sleep into the neighborhood
> of one neither strange nor familiar
> whom we have chosen to trust. Trusting, untrusting,
> we lowered ourselves into this, let ourselves
> downward hand over hand as on a rope that quivered
> over the unsearched. . . . We did this. Conceived
> of each other, conceived each other in a darkness
> which I remember as drenched in light.
>
> (P. 9)

Even before the reader can marvel at this exploration of intimacy, Rich has already changed direction. Shifting emphasis by the use of a single line placed near the right margin of the page, a transition line that connects the stanzas while it separates their tones, she immediately brings the poem to conclusion by declaring:

I want to call this, life.

But I can't call it life until we start to move
beyond this secret circle of fire
where our bodies are giant shadows flung on a wall
where the night becomes our inner darkness, and sleeps
like a dumb beast, head on her paws, in the corner.

(P. 9)

For Rich, sexually intimate relationships between women do not suffice. Beyond "this secret circle of fire," a fire that hides as much as it reveals, Rich imagines another world. She imagines a light and free space beyond the fire where women can be more than "dumb beasts" sleeping their lives away "in the corner."

While the conclusion recalls Yeats's "The Second Coming" ("And what rough beast, its hour come round at last, / Slouches toward Bethlehem to be born?"[16]), it is equally reminiscent of the poet's own "Diving into the Wreck." Here, two women, instead of the single explorer in "Diving," climb down "hand over hand" to discover their sexuality amid the "wreckage" of a male-defined culture. They, too, learn that they must go beyond the physical or material; they must uncover what has been lost or hidden from them. While Rich does applaud their exploration, she exhorts the lovers to climb out of themselves and share what they have learned with the larger "body" of women. She wants all women to explore the female in themselves in the light, not merely to conceive of one another in darkness.

Implicit in "Origins" is a recognition that the life of the beast in the cage is actually a life lived in exile. The necessity of escaping the exile is echoed in "Cartographies of Silence." In this poem Rich speaks of another kind of relationship between two women that can also result in a glimpse of the She. Explaining the possibilities of her aesthetic relationship with her readers, she wonders

If at the will of the poet the poem
could turn into a thing

121

a granite flank laid bare, a lifted head
alight with dew

If it could simply look you in the face
with naked eyeballs, not letting you turn

till you, and I who long to make this thing,
were finally clarified together in its stare[17]

In this fragment from "Cartographies," it is as if Rich has taken parts of the relationships she described in "Origins" and "The Lioness" and combined them into a third, one that transects the sexual and the empathetic.

Rich realizes through her narrator that the animal is "the thing itself and not the myth." She considers the words between herself and her readers to be an aesthetic relationship that combines the sexual passion of the one and the emotional empathy of the other. This aesthetic relationship is the basis for the poet's "dream of a common language" ("Origins," p. 7). It is a relationship in which the woman who writes and the woman who reads are connected both by the "thing" (i.e., the female) and by "the story of the thing." Doubly connected and "finally clarified" by their instinctive connection to the female and their symbiotic connection to each other as writer and reader, women reading women alter the boundaries of traditional aesthetics. (An analogue to the dynamic that Rich describes is the Christian concept of a triune Godhead: the bond of love between the Father and the Son is a unique and coexisting entity, the Holy Spirit. Rich seems to be saying that the bond between the woman writer and the woman reader creates a third entity, that "thing" that "is nameless till we rename her.")

Rich also implies that as women strengthen relationships (the sensual, the empathetic, and the aesthetic) among themselves, they somehow do enter into this female "country." This culture is a preexisting entity that only needs to be exercised in order to be found. In trying to locate this "thing," the poet "re-vises" yet another relationship. She takes the bond between herself and her blood sister in "Sibling Mysteries"[18] and demonstrates how to transform a seemingly ordinary relationship into an aesthetic one. As this transformation is essential to Rich's "re-vision," some care will be taken to examine how it functions in the poem.

"Sibling Mysteries" is a fairly long poem broken into six roughly chronological sections. Rich opens it in the imperative voice. The first section is a string of demands (much like any sister might make of another) that reach all the way back into prehistory. "Remind me how we walked," she charges,

> feeling the fullness of the moon
> before moonrise
>
> unbalanced by the life
> moving in us, then lightened
> yet weighted still
>
> by children on our backs
> at our hips, as we made fire
> scooped clay   lifted water
>
> Remind me how the stream
> wetted the clay between our palms
> and how the flame
>
> licked it to mineral colors
> how we traced our signs by torchlight
> in the deep chambers of the caves
> . . . .
> I know by heart, and still
> I need to have you tell me,
> hold me, remind me
>
> (Pp. 47–48)

Rich is not only personal here, she is also panoramic. She asks that her sister verbally and physically help her to remember herself as part of a women's tradition that stretches back to the primordial. She asks the sister to help her recall the deeds of their foremothers: as bearers of life, as thieves of fire, as makers of utensils and art. Ascribing to mothers the roles of civilizers and life givers, the poet claims the bond of matrilineal descent. Carol Muske, in examining Rich's claim, concludes that her "refusal to assume . . . the 'approved past' in poetry" and history is more than an act of feminist rebellion.[19] Instead, it is a positive and alternative method of integrating the past into the present. Says Muske:

> . . . the matrilineal heritage does not seem to proceed hierarchically, "down to us," as in patriarchy, but horizontally, *across* the ages. Virginia Woolf [also] tried closing in on this idea once during some random theorizing in her diary: "Yet I am now and then haunted by some semi-mythic very profound life of a woman, which shall be told on one occasion; and time shall be utterly obliterated; future shall somehow blossom out of the past."[20]

Muske's perception that Rich, like Woolf, is trying "to close in" on the idea of integrating women's lives "*across* the ages," does make sense. Rich aims at an awareness of the simultaneity of women's existence; she reaches back into the past to claim a particularly female heritage in order to "re-vise" the present and envision a more feminized future.

The second section of "Mysteries," still written in unrhymed triplets (and mirroring, perhaps, the triune relationship of the mother to her daughters), compares all female relationships "*across* the ages." The reminder here is not only of a collective past but of a simultaneous present, the experience of being "of woman born."[21]

> Remind me how we loved our mother's body
> our mouths drawing the first
> thin sweetness from her nipples
>
> our faces dreaming hour on hour
> in the salt smell of her lap   Remind me
> how her touch melted childgrief
>
> how she floated great and tender in our dark
> or stood guard over us
> against our willing

(P. 48)

For Rich loving "our mother's body" combines a desire for pleasure and a need for security. The mother's milk, for example, that "first thin sweetness," bonds the daughter to her even after the umbilical cord has been cut; it also mitigates the child's sense of difference between herself as "the Me" and the mother as "the Not-Me." The sensuousness of this dyad, this first connection of the she-child to the woman-mother, is evoked by the sucking, touching, "dreaming hour on hour / in the salt smell of her lap." It is a precedent in a Proustian way: the first memory of these sensations will connect all future sensations of this sort back to the first experience of them, back to the woman with whom they were first shared.

Rich is hinting at other types of connection here, connections that are more subtle than the simply physical ones. For one thing, she is maintaining that the mother's body is a metaphor for life. Her lap, like the amniotic sac (or an ocean teeming with life), is salty; the milk from her nipples is sweet. The tether between the mother who feeds and the daughter who is fed goes beyond that moment of birth to include successive moments of being.

The connection of physical life with the life of the mind is the most subtle of all the connections made in this poem. As the baby dreams "hour on hour," her role in relation to her mother is reversed by the first stirrings of thought. No longer suspended in the mother's womb, the daughter now enfolds the mother in her mind ("she floated great and tender in our dark"). The child's consciousness of the mother as a separate but similar being dramatically culminates in her "birthing" the mother into an existence apart from her own.

The mother-daughter relationship as drama is the theme of the remainder of this section and the rest of the poem. The mother's relationship to the father provides, from the daughter's point of view, the essential conflict. Rich recalls her own memories of that painful moment when her mother's love was diverted by the "law," that moment when

> we thought she loved
> the strange male body first
> that took, that took, whose taking seemed a law

and how she sent us weeping
into that law

(P. 48)

This "law" is, as Rich uses the term, an institutionalized mimicry of the experiential bond between the mother and daughter. The father's "taking," as if he were a child, is an act of imitation of the mother-child bond. The legitimation of this mimicry is, then, an intrinsic irony of the "law." That the daughters, sharers in the mother's body, are "sent weeping into the law" is the culmination of the irony: the daughters will grow into women who will henceforth only give to husbands who will only take.

The irony culminates in "the tragedy of sex." The daughter is taught by the mother to forget her connection with the female in herself and her mother and to forge bonds now only with men. This transformation of intimacy from a sensual connection to a sexual bond is the "law." And in learning to live within the law, the daughter is trained not only to forget but also to deny that a female connection existed at all. Asking her sister to confirm this, Rich insists:

> I know, I remember, but
> hold me, remind me
> of how her woman's flesh was made taboo to us

(P. 49)

In reversing Freud's Oedipal theory, Rich distinguishes between the known and the learned. The daughter "knows" the mother's body as she knows her own. Yet, says the poet, she is trained to deny that knowledge; she learns to teach men lessons about what she is supposed to have forgotten.

The daughter, like her mother before her, is to teach men tenderness. She is to transform her first memory of it into a sexual and civilizing learning experience for them. Rich recalls the lessons she taught men as sensuously as she recalled the lessons she was taught by her mother; she remembers

> . . . how we taught them tenderness—
>
> the holding-back, the play,

> the floating of a finger
> the secrets of the nipple

(P. 49)

Speaking not of sexual technique but of the half-forgotten memories of sensuous intimacy, Rich's variations on certain words—"tender," "floated," and "nipples"—words that she had used earlier to evoke the relationship to the mother, underscore the abuse of knowledge. Women are taught to deny the source of their knowledge with men and to refuse the benefits of their knowledge to each other. Based on the premise that a woman becomes an adult by somehow developing amnesia about her childhood, this abuse of knowledge is one of the "mysteries" that Rich reveals in the poem, her ironic "re-vision" of a woman's coming of age.

This coming of age involves for Rich the "splitting" of the female self. As a woman must be silent about the real source of her "secrets," she is unable to acknowledge that part of herself which is the repository of such knowledge. Rich speaks of the ensuing schizophrenia when she admits

> how we dwelt in two worlds
> the daughters and the mothers
> in the kingdom of the sons

(P. 49)

This split from the female self, this dwelling in "two worlds" with two different "laws" and two sets of meaning, is for the poet the price all women pay for their survival in a male-dominated world ("the kingdom of the sons"). It comes from trading "secrets" for survival in a world that Rich likens to a "feast / where the fathers sucked the bones" (p. 50). Rich's ire at this arrangement, what she terms elsewhere "the separation of powers / the allotment of sufferings," is reinforced by her savage description of "the fathers."[22] They are "sucking bones"—presumably women's bones—in their vicarious and voracious efforts to subsume the female into themselves. Their behavior is in sharp contrast to the daughters who earlier had sucked not bones, but the "thin sweetness from her nipples."

Having sketched the difficulties a woman faces in discovering the She in herself in the first three sections of the poem, Rich outlines what must be done in the last three. She describes the attempt to connect with the female as analogous to her own attempt to reconnect with her blood sister. This attempt is painful because it is an admission that even though she and her sister share in the "sibling mysteries" with the mother, they "are not really friends, and [only] act the part of sisters" (p. 50).

Having named the current relationship between them as a theatrical one, one where both women "act" their parts in the sexual tragedy, Rich chooses to remind her sister of their original connection. No longer needing to be reminded herself, she now speaks with a new force and urgency. She evokes first the memory of the night they began to break down the barriers that divided them, the night their father lay dying. This memory is special to Rich because it is the night the sisters "burned [their] childhood," that period of their lives when they had been governed by the "law." Accepting as minor the differences that their separate life experiences have wrought ("our hair has fallen long / or short at different times"), Rich implores her sister to be mindful of the more essential experiences that they have in common: they were born of the same woman, "driven down the same dark canal" (p. 51).

Rich's drive to connect herself and her sister does not end with memory of an archetypal experience. She plunges into the present in the last two sections of the poem. Enclosed again in a female connection (as she was once enclosed in the womb, then in the lap), Rich defines herself, her sister and, indeed, all women by both their past and their present when she declares

> we are translations into different dialects
>
> of a text still being written
> in the original

(P. 51)

The simultaneity of female experience now is seen in terms of the language of "the original." That the text is "still being written" is proof of the ongoing nature of the process, a process that Atwood had described earlier as "getting . . . born." In this process, Rich's memory of the past and the activities of the present merge into the realization of possibilities, fuse into a "dream of a common language." As language and memory fuse, the forgotten becomes legitimated and the "law" becomes unnecessary.

As the female is realized in the relationship of the sisters, the poet allows a sense of triumph to mingle with her former urgency. Finished with asking for or demanding answers of her sister, Rich concludes by stating what she herself has learned through the course of the poem:

> The daughters never were
> true brides of the father
>
> the daughters were to begin with
> brides of the mother
>
> then brides of each other
> under a different law
>
> Let me hold and tell you

(P. 52)

Having broken through the laws and language of the fathers to a more fundamental if "different law" of the mothers, Rich concludes by recording the secrets of this matrilineal code. It is, she notes, a code of primary bonding between women, a law that designates them first "brides of the mother / then brides of each other." Essentially a law of instinctive connection between daughters, it is based upon a sensual bond with "the great and tender" mother of all women.

As ongoing as "re-vision," this bonding is also as critical to understanding Rich's feminist vision. It is a personal prototype of sisterhood. Including as it does the empathetic, the passionate and the aesthetic, this bonding connects each woman with her sisters through the recognition of the She in every female relationship. For Rich, female bonding is not an abstract phrase; it is one of those possibilities which feminism opened up to her and to all women.

Sisterly relationships between women—as friends, lovers, siblings, and daughters of the She—are the dominant feature of Rich's female "country." She provides a composite portrait of the woman who would be a sister. Through a number of poems about individual women, she describes the characteristics that a sisterly woman seems to possess: an independence from "patriarchal interpretations of femininity" and a self-defined integrity. These two characteristics, present in greater or lesser degrees in nearly all the poems about specific women, are also the chief attributes of the virgin. Rich herself is aware of this, for in *Of Woman Born*, published two years before *Dream*, she noted that

> the Moon Mothers, according to [Esther] Harding, were virgins, in the great primal sense of the word—not the undeflorated girl, but the woman who belongs to herself, or, in the Eskimo phrase, "She-who-will-not-have-a-husband." She has many lovers, and many sons, . . . [but is] still associated primarily with what Harding terms "Woman's Mysteries."[23]

Rich's concept of the virgin, a "woman who belongs to herself," is a classical rather than a contemporary one; it stresses a woman's independence as "unwed" rather than her ignorance as "chaste." It is the virgin's behavior, not her role, which defines her. So, too, in Rich's use of the behavior (she does not use either the term "virgin" or "virginal" in the collection), it is possible to detect a formative definition of the sisterly woman.

The poet's most careful delineation of the virginal occurs in her persona poems. Rich's use of persona in *Dream* is a departure from the traditional form. Her speakers are neither fictive nor nameless; they are real people with whom the poet identifies. In "Paula Becker to Clara Westhoff" and "Phantasia for Elvira Shatayev," for example, Rich uses poetry itself as an act of reconstruction and relationship between women.

In identifying with these women, Rich invites her readers into the sisterhood. Like the observer in "The Lioness," Rich leaves herself outside and "enters the space" of these other women's lives. Writing as if she were Becker or Shatayev, not the poet observer, Rich connects with what is virginal in them, in herself, and in the aesthetic relationship between them. Elvira Shatayev, the subject of the major persona poem of the collection, is the "leader of a women's climbing team, all of whom died in a storm on Lenin Peak, August, 1974."[24] "Phantasia," written as though it were the climber's journal, focuses on the Russian woman's convenant with the female in herself, in the other climbers, and in the mountain.

Rich opens the poem with the women's deaths, as if to get this fact out of the way quickly. While she is more intent on describing how Shatayev lived rather than how she died, the climber's death is described in an oddly comforting way. It is comforting in the same way Dickinson's "Because I could not stop for Death" is; both poems stress the ordinariness of death as an experience. Dickinson does so by imagining it as a social call and Rich by imagining it as a change in weather:

> The cold felt cold until our blood
> grew colder   then the wind
> died down and we slept

(P. 4)

Opening the poem as she does, Rich evokes—through repetition and slant rhyme—the feeling that death is but the comparative version ("cold . . . colder") of a common physical sensation. The ordinariness of death, then, becomes the context from which to measure life. Speaking to herself, Shatayev discloses what her death has taught her about life:

> If in this sleep I speak
> it's with a voice no longer personal
> (I want to say *with voices*)
> When the wind tore   our breath from us at last
> we had no need of words
> For months   for years   each one of us
> had felt her own *yes*   growing in her
> . . . .
>
> What we were to learn   was simply   what we had
> up here   as out of all words   that *yes*   gathered
> its forces   fused itself   and only just in time

                    to meet a *No* of no degrees
                    the black hole   sucking the world in

(P. 4)

What is crucial to this stanza is Shatayev's discovery that her "voice [is] no longer personal," that she speaks "*with voices*" that extend beyond the ego. Her discovery is nearly identical to the speaker's in "Meditations for a Savage Child." In that earlier poem, Rich advised, "Go back so far there is another language / . . . [that] is no longer personal."[25] As the stanza unfolds, the realization that "voice" can be substituted for "word" or language becomes another more subtle discovery; one that reinforces Rich's belief here, as in "Sibling Mysteries," that women's "voices" do speak "*across* the ages." Rich's suggestion is quite simple: the oral is more fundamental than the literary. It is the primal whisper behind all speech, the human sound that most approximates the wind.

These voices seem to be saying that the "*yes*" which confronts the "*No* of no degrees" is the essence of female power and one of life's natural "forces." As Shatayev learns before her death, the female—when "gathered" and "fused"—can and does "meet" and integrate the fact of death, that "black hole   sucking the world in." She comes to learn that the power of the female is every woman's legacy ("was simply what we had") and that when shared with other women becomes the primary fact of any woman's life.

Having revealed her thoughts to the reader, Shatayev now speaks to her husband of the lessons she learned on the mountain. Of pitting oneself against Nature, she notes that in this, her last climb, she and the other women of the team ("the women I love") did not attack, assault or conquer the mountain; they simply became part of it. She notes as well that her husband, who climbs toward her ostensibly to bury her "against advisement," must recognize the motives behind his own behavior:

                    You come (I know this)   with your love   your loss
                    strapped to your body . . .
                    . . . .
                    to give us burial in the snow   and in your mind
                    While my body lies out here

> flashing like a prism   into your eyes
> how could you sleep   You climbed here for yourself
> we climbed for ourselves
>
> (P. 5)

Dying to Shatayev is to become part of life's possibilities ("the unfinished" and "the unbegun"). In this sense, the women's existence may cease but their part in the "story" of existence does not "end." It continues not only in the husband's memory and the legends of Lenin Peak but also in the reality of the still-living mountain,

> this mountain   which has taken   the imprint of our minds
> through changes elemental and minute
> as those we underwent
> to bring each other here
> choosing ourselves   each other   and this life
>
> (P. 5)

Through "changes elemental and minute," the mountain provides a choice. It enables them, in becoming part of the "unbegun," to "choose" the female in all its forms; to identify with one another in life and, in death, to merge with "the armature of rock beneath these snows" (p. 5).

Shatayev finishes her journal by explaining the consequence of those choices. The final stanzas vivdly describe the approach of death (in the singular) and the power of the living (in the plural):

> In the diary I wrote: *Now we are ready*
> *and each of us knows it*   *I have never loved*
> *like this*   *I have never seen*
> *my own forces so taken up and shared*
> *and given back*
> *After the long training*   *the early sieges*
> *we are moving almost effortlessly in our love*
>
> In the diary as the wind   began to tear
> at the tents over us   I wrote:
> *We know now we have always been in danger*

> down in our separateness
> and now up here together   but till now
> we had not touched our strength
>
> In the diary torn from my fingers I had written:
> *What does love mean*
> *what does it mean   "to survive"*
> *A cable of blue fire ropes our bodies*
> *burning together in the snow   We will not live*
> *to settle for less   We have dreamed of this*
> *all of our lives*
>
> (Pp. 5–6)

As the wind begins to tear Shatayev from life, she speaks again of the natural "forces" implied in the team's love for its members. Having "taken up" their "separateness" like an offering, the women share in their collective gift to each other: the love that flows among them. The strength of this love, which tethers them to each other in death as in life like an ice-crusted "cable of blue fire," is the dream that will not allow them "to settle for less."

That Shatayev and her team perish is sobering. But the poem is itself as incautious as the climbers' dreams or the team's burial by Shatayev's husband. "Against advisement," the poem maintains that the dreaming is as important as the dream, that the process of extending the "I" is as crucial as the "we" that results.

Rich does not lament these women; nor does she exalt them. She simply appreciates that they did what they dreamed, what they wanted. And while Rich does not describe them as heroes any more than she defines them as virgins, she does allude to the heroism of women who attempt to be integrated and independent. In "Natural Resources" she says:

> My heart is moved by all I cannot save:
> so much has been destroyed
>
> I have to cast my lot with those
> who age after age, perversely,

                    with no extraordinary power,
                    reconstitute the world.

                                            (P. 67)

Those who "reconstitute the world" are the women who strug-
gle to get the female "born." These heroes are, in the most
radical sense, lovers. They, like Shatayev or the narrator of
"Twenty-One Love Poems," are women who have consciously
chosen to love the female in themselves and others. While a
number of Rich's women lovers who willingly "cast their lot"
with other women are lesbians, it is, as Olga Broumas points
out,

> not the physical which defines this love as lesbian, but the
> absolute and primary attention directed at the other. Sister-
> hood—that is, primary and bonding love from women—is,
> like motherhood, a capacity, not a destiny.[26]

Rich's heroes and explorers, then, are ordinary women who
choose to love women as they love the female. For Rich, as for
Broumas, their sisterhood is "a capacity" which they choose to
realize heroically in the midst of a woman-hating culture.

Born of woman and directing an "absolute and primary at-
tention" to the women they love as daughters, sisters and
friends, the narrators and personae of *The Dream of a Common
Language* explore and define the geography of the female. They
extend their boundaries to include all women in their definition
of the female. Exploring it as a "country" that is both outside
and inside themselves, they reconstitute the world by destroying
the dichotomies that have kept them separate and afraid, sleep-
ing, "like a dumb beast, head on her paws, in the corner."

In one sense, the poem that most typifies Rich's dream of a
female language is "Splittings." It names the dichotomies that
the woman who would love women must confront. And the
love that it encourages is the epitome of the virginally female
that pervades all the poems.

> My body opens over San Francisco like the day-
>   light raining day   each pore crying the change of light

I am not with her   I have been waking off and on
all night to that pain   not simply absence but
the presence of the past   destructive
to living here and now . . .[27]

Juxtaposing images—the daylight "rains" and the skin "cries"—
in a tight, enjambed and internal rhyming, the poet names the
forces that are ranged against women lovers. These forces—
unless suffering and "myths of separation"—are forces within
the self that deny female love even as it is offered.

Rich realizes that she has two "lovers," her absent friend and
her present pain. By admitting that she can choose to love or not
to love (i.e., to suffer), she faces up to her own attraction to
pain, an attraction as powerful and more stereotypical than her
love. She further confronts the fact that she must internalize pain
in order for it to exert power over her. She admits that if she
were to "refuse" pain, it

                              would have to stand
off from me and listen   its dark breath still on me
but the mind could begin to speak to pain
and pain would have to answer:

                                   We are older now
we have met before   these are my hands before your eyes
my figure blotting out   all that is not mine
I am the pain of division   creator of divisions
it is I who blot your lover from you
and not the time-zones nor the miles
It is not separation calls me forth   but I
who am separation   And remember
I have no existence   apart from you

                                        (P. 10)

Encountering pain by anthropomorphizing it, Rich admits that
since pain has no existence apart from her, she is pain. Distanc-
ing herself from pain (as physically as she is distanced from her
lover), she begins to view her choices less romantically. She sees
that pain is like a cancer which she allows to grow and "blot
out" the healthier parts of her feelings. Her insight enables her to

reject pain, accept love, and refuse to assume—as many poets in the past have—that they are interchangeable.

Demythologizing her love, Rich accepts finally that feeling is not identical with feeling pain; she chooses "still to feel" but

> . . . not to suffer uselessly
> to detect primordial pain as it stalks toward me
> flashing its bleak torch in my eyes   blotting out
> her particular being   the details of her love
> I will not be divided   from her or from myself
> by myths of separation
>
> (P. 11)

Choosing "not to suffer uselessly" is also for Rich to choose life over anti-life (that which she describes as "destructive / to living here and now"). Opting to both live and affirm the present, the real, and the female, she dismisses (as false) those feelings that emanate from fear of responsibility or "myths of separation." She refuses to manufacture doubts that would blind her to who she is and what she knows. Refusing as well to be detoured by what she should feel, the poet moves through the man-made glyph of despair to enter into that free and female place where she is most fully alive and most fully herself.

Rich concludes "Splittings" by reviewing in a somewhat more political fashion the choices that she has made. As she reviews them, she reconstitutes her personal world:

> The world tells me I am its creature
> I am raked by eyes   brushed by hands
> I want to crawl into her for refuge   lay my head
> in the space   between her breast and shoulder
> abnegating power for love
> as women have done   or hiding
> from power in her love   like a man
> I refuse these givens   the splitting
> between love and action   I am choosing
> not to suffer uselessly   and not to use her
> I choose to love   this time   for once
> with all my intelligence
>
> (P. 11)

Choosing to integrate heart and mind, body and soul in the ordinary act of being alive, Adrienne Rich provides (though she herself would not say so) another example of that particularly female heroism detailed in "Phantasia for Elvira Shatayev." Her love for a woman, "heroic in its ordinariness," is her affirmation of life in the face of all that would destroy or distort it.

Rich's choice, finally, "to love   this time   for once / with all my intelligence," is her personal testament to the female and her commitment to women made manifest. By her act of faith in the female, Adrienne Rich in *The Dream of a Common Language* brings "re-vision" to the point of revelation.

NOTES

1. Elly Bulkin, "An Interview with Adrienne Rich," *Conditions: One* 1 (April 1977): 51.

2. Adrienne Rich, "Diving into the Wreck," in *Diving into the Wreck: Poems 1971–1972* (New York: Norton, 1973), p. 24.

3. Rich, "The Stranger," in *Diving*, p. 19. Rich here is influenced by the work of her friend, Mary Daly. In *Beyond God the Father* (Boston: Beacon, 1973), Daly speaks of women's "conscious, communal participation in God the Verb."

4. See "The Phenomenology of Anger," "A Primary Ground," "Waking in the Dark," and "Rape" in *Diving*.

5. Bulkin, pp. 61–62.

6. Robert Boyers, "On Adrienne Rich: Intelligence and Will," *Salmagundi* 22–23 (Spring–Summer 1973): 132–48.

7. "Natural Resources," in *The Dream of a Common Language: Poems 1974–1977* (New York: Norton, 1978), p. 66.

8. Margaret Atwood, "Unfinished Women," *New York Times Book Review*, June 11, 1978, pp. 7, 42.

9. Margaret Atwood, review of *Diving into the Wreck*, *New York Times Book Review*, December 30, 1973, pp. 1–2. Reprinted in this collection, pp. 238–41.

10. "When We Dead Awaken," *Diving*, p. 8.

11. "Merced," *Diving*, p. 36.

12. Poem XIII of "Twenty-One Love Poems," in *Dream*, p. 31. Further references to the "Love Poems" will be cited parenthetically in the text.

13. Rich, "When We Dead Awaken: Writing as Re-Vision," in *On*

Lies, Secrets and Silence: Selected Prose, 1966–1978 (New York: Norton, 1979), p. 35.

14. "The Lioness," in *Dream*, pp. 21–22. Further references to this poem will be cited parenthetically in the text.

15. "Origins and History of Consciousness," in *Dream*, p. 8. Further references to this poem will be cited parenthetically in the text.

16. William Butler Yeats, "The Second Coming," in *Modern Verse in English: 1900–1950*, ed. Daniel Cecil and Allen Tabe (New York: Macmillan, 1958), p. 117.

17. "Cartographies of Silence," in *Dream*, p. 19.

18. "Sibling Mysteries," in *Dream*, pp. 47–52. Further references will appear parenthetically in the text.

19. Carol Muske, "Backward into the Future," *Parnassus* 7 (Fall/Winter 1979): 81.

20. Muske, p. 81.

21. A reference to Rich's semi-autobiographical prose work, *Of Woman Born: Motherhood as Experience and Institution* (New York: Norton, 1976).

22. Rich, "From an Old House in America," in *Poems: Selected and New, 1950–1974*, p. 240.

23. *Of Woman Born* (New York: Norton, 1976; pb. ed. Bantam, 1977), p. 96.

24. Rich, "Phantasia for Elvira Shatayev," in *Dream*, p. 4. Further references to this poem will be cited parenthetically in the text.

25. Rich, "Meditations for a Savage Child," in *Diving*, p. 58.

26. Olga Broumas, Review of *The Dream of a Common Language*, *Chrysalis*, no. 6 (1978): 111. Reprinted in this collection, pp. 274–86.

27. Rich, "Splittings," in *Dream*, p. 10. Subsequent references to this poem will appear parenthetically in the text.

GERTRUDE REIF HUGHES

"Imagining the Existence of Something Uncreated"

Elements of Emerson in Adrienne Rich's *Dream of a Common Language*

A *New Yorker* drawing of a few years ago shows two well-heeled women earnestly assessing their lives over lunch at a restaurant. "I got what I wanted," confides one to the other, "but it wasn't what I expected." Ralph Waldo Emerson could have said the same about American poetry. In his 1844 essay, "The Poet," he rhapsodized about the powers and mission of the poet, saying that the poet is "a liberating god" who, as "the Namer or Language-maker," could tap "that *dream*-power" (the italics are Emerson's) which all persons possess, but only poets know how to use. Emerson complained that America had not yet produced a native version of the poet he envisioned.

> I look in vain for the poet whom I describe. We do not with sufficient plainness or sufficient profoundness address ourselves to life, nor dare we chaunt our own times and social circumstances. . . . We have yet had no genius in America, with tyrannous eye, which knew the value of our incomparable materials. . . .[1]

Soon enough Emerson had one version of his poet in the Whitman of the 1855 edition of *Leaves of Grass*. Though he fully acknowledged Whitman's genius in the famous letter of praise and salutation he sent the younger poet after reading *Leaves,*

This essay is a chapter of Hughes's book-in-progress about the visionary feminism of five women poets, *Genius and Gender,* which is forthcoming from Wesleyan University Press. Reprinted by permission of the author.

Emerson was understandably abashed at the form in which his literary prayers were answered. The same might have been true if he could have read Dickinson. On the one hand, he would have been more comfortable than she herself was with her rebellions against Calvinism, and he might well have recognized his own Orphism in her wild originality. On the other hand, her formidable insistence on exploring the pains and risks of the extreme states of soul she called "circumference" (borrowing her term from his own essay, "Circles") would almost surely have seemed morbid and perverse to his more serene love of expansiveness.[2] But in any case he himself could have written the letter in which Emily Dickinson urged her sister-in-law and next-door-neighbor, Susan Gilbert Dickinson, "Cherish Power—dear—Remember that stands in the Bible between the kingdom and the Glory because it is wilder than either of them. Emily."[3] By "wild" Emerson always meant radically free, and both the wildness of power and the power of wildness were Emerson's great themes from his earliest celebrations of self-reliance in *Nature* (1836) and *Essays, First Series* (1841) to his most mature praise of "the Beautiful Necessity" in *The Conduct of Life* (1860).

For Adrienne Rich, too, ideas of power constitute the subject of all her researches into the energies of women's lives. How these energies have been denied, diverted, or ignored, how they have nevertheless survived and have sustained, and how they must be maintained and can be tapped—these are the themes of her poetry, her prose, and, it seems, her living. Fundamentally, Rich means the same thing by power as Emerson does: "not power of domination, but . . . access to sources," as she says in one of her "Three Conversations" with Albert and Barbara Charlesworth Gelpi.[4] But Rich's poetry and prose provide an access to sources that Emerson was certainly not anticipating when he complained that no American poet had as yet used the "incomparable materials" and spoken to the "social circumstances" that America offered. Rich studies social circumstances and materials that it is extremely unlikely Emerson had in mind. Over and over in essays and poems, her research into women's lives reveals unacknowledged sisterhood (for instance *Jane Eyre* in the hands of male-dominated criticism);[5] unacknowledged service ("The phrase 'wages for housework,'" she writes in an essay, "has the power to shock today that the phrase 'free love' possessed a century ago");[6] unacknowledged isolation (like the loneliness to which patriarchal notions of family life have consigned mothers and pregnant women);[7] unacknowledged accomplishments of women; and, always, the unacknowledged costs of those female achievements that *have* been officially recognized.

Emerson could not possibly have anticipated, and he might well not have approved or even recognized, that Rich's work is part of the effort which his own work called for. Nevertheless her writings both fulfill and exceed his requirements for a historically pertinent poetry of power and empowerment. Hearing her work in his context emphasizes how profoundly she affirms female potentialities, but this intertextual approach has at least two possible dangers. On the one hand, stressing that Rich's poetry exceeds Emerson's vision could have the effect of using Rich as a kind of exemplar to reproach Emerson with. Her work would then become a literary joke at his expense, and ultimately both poets would be cheapened. Alternatively, an intertextual reading can show that Rich's "fierce attention" to women's lives (Emerson's more patriarchal diction would call it her "tyrannous eye") repeatedly makes her affirm our scandalously neglected and drastically underused power. That approach would use Emerson's work to legitimate Rich's. It would ruinously depoliticize her by overlooking that she celebrates specifically female powers and identifies specifically patriarchal obstructions. In what follows I will try to survey Rich's affinities with Emerson and her divergences from him, not to use them against each other but to show that Rich defies Emerson without denying his vision. She retains its enabling power without perpetuating, let alone condoning, its blind spots.

Rich's poem "Incipience," which is about the creative force of latency and also about the way it should be handled, is a revealing text for a survey of how her vision relates to Emerson's. Opening oneself to power in the sense of unrealized potential is their shared theme, and in this poem Rich is at her most Emersonian when she recognizes the potency of what she calls, following Emerson, the "uncreated." But in cautioning how much care and collaboration and deliberation this potency requires of its users, Rich adds considerations that Emerson leaves out of account. In the poem's opening lines, for instance, Rich wonderfully describes a preternatural sensitivity to the latent power in a given environment, but she also specifies that this heightened awareness is occurring at a time when it is impossible to act upon it.

> 1. To live, to lie awake
> under scarred plaster
> while ice is forming over the earth
> at an hour when nothing can be done
> to further any decision
>
> to know the composing of the thread
> inside the spider's body
> first atoms of the web
> visible tomorrow
>
> to feel the fiery future
> of every matchstick in the kitchen[8]

Rich asks you to imagine a time when you could experience such a sensitivity to latent power that the still unspun spider's web and the fiery future of every matchstick in the kitchen would feel real to you. But would those latent powers be available to you? No. For their presence is making itself felt at "an hour when nothing can be done / to further any decision."

It is not pessimism but experience that speaks here. Clearly and ecstatically as she feels what Emily Dickinson called "possibility" ("a fairer house than prose"), Rich just as completely recognizes that the fiery future latent in those kitchen matches guarantees nothing, not even explosion, let alone warmth. Consequently, in the next lines a certain diminishment has occurred. The matchsticks' fiery future seems to have become the smouldering anger that Rich keeps seeing on the faces of women, while the intricate promise of the web inside the spider's body seems to have dwindled to the striations of air inside an ice cube, which Rich is helplessly counting and recounting. Notice how the lines combine frustration and celebration:

> Nothing can be done
> but by inches. I write out my life
> hour by hour, word by word
> gazing into the anger of old women on the bus
> numbering the striations
> of air inside the ice cube
> imagining the existence
> of something uncreated
> this poem
> our lives

(P. 192)

Is Rich defeated by the discrepancy between the vast energies available and the tiny opportunities for using them, or is she evoking the depth and fullness of that "something uncreated" on which she can draw as she works to imagine its very existence, which is also the existence of "this poem / our lives"?

The second part of "Incipience" tells what it is like to imagine the existence of something uncreated: it is harder but more companionable than just lying in bed at 4:00 A.M. feeling uncannily akin to the latencies around one. It is a shared waking dream that makes a mockery of mere wish-fulfillments. In this part of the poem, Rich and a friend—"we"—"sit up smoking and talking of how to live" while "a man is asleep in the next room," dreaming that a female is dissecting his brain. In his dream he struggles to solve what seems to him an inconsistency: how a neurosurgeon fit to operate on *him* can be a woman. Resourcefully, his unconscious comes up with the acceptable solution: Marie Curie; that's who must be operating on him. The female neurosurgeon of the man's dream must be acceptable to him or else he will, of course, awaken; and Marie Curie—exceptional woman, patriarchal idea of a female scientist, one whose achievement cost her her life—this token woman of science fills the bill handily.

Meanwhile, in the other room, Rich and her friend are indeed dissecting the man's brain, though in ways he cannot dream of and still remain asleep. They are identifying his dreams as the standard wish-fulfillments of a male whose right to dominate is endangered. His dreams, they understand, are not motivating visions but lulling fantasies that function to prevent him from awakening rudely to his own misconceptions and to the threat these two women pose. Most importantly, the two women know that they are "outside the frame of his dream." True, they are not free of its implications—far from it. The steep landscape of scarred volcanic rock over which they are stumbling in the poem's closing lines demonstrates that. But unlike the idealized, isolated female figure of the man's dreams, these women who are stumbling are also "hand in hand . . . and guiding each other."

To conceive the existence of something uncreated entails a vision that is both satiric and ecstatic, and it requires action that is both laborious and communal. Satire, ecstacy, community, and work—these are Rich's attitudes and subjects in *The Dream of a Common Language* as she imagines both the existence of something uncreated and the effort to realize it in poems and lives.

Emerson insisted that behind everything created stood "immortal, necessary, *uncreated,* natures, that is, . . . Ideas."[9] The uncreated is a causal force, and Emerson constantly urged his audiences to open themselves to it. The openness he advocated is demanding in two senses; it requires a willingness to risk constant vulnerability to new tasks and the vitality to maintain constant dissatisfaction with what has already been achieved, "for that which is made instructs how to make a better." This requirement of a constant receptivity to what may be new affects Emerson's view of history, and it contrasts revealingly with Rich's.

In his 1841 essay on the subject he articulated his famous conviction that "there is properly no history only biography."[10] He meant, of course, that no individual needs to be cowed by the past achievements of others, for greatness is available to all persons at all times if they too will but tap the energies of the over-soul or universal mind. "Of the works of this mind," says

Emerson, "history is the record" and it challenges each new generation to surpass it.[11] For Emerson, history is a *fable convenu* which must be divested of its insidious implications that newcomers are latecomers.

Rich would agree that history is shaped by individuals, but her attitude toward the obverse—that individuals are shaped by history—introduces a critical complication that Emerson overlooked. For Rich, too, history is a *fable convenu* but of a more sinister kind. Perniciously, patriarchal writers and interpreters of "the" record have conspired to make women think of ourselves as powerless, as liars, as petty competitors incapable of cooperation, as dependents, as resources to be used rather than as users of resources. Rich and Emerson both fear history; Emerson that his readers will be intimidated by it, Rich that hers will ignore it or deny it. For both, history is an encumbrance, but while Emerson wanted to dispose of the record altogether, Rich wants to expose the disgraceful evidence it contains.

While patriarchal history chronicles victories and victors, feminist history registers a record of resistance, and thus it may be called a history of enemies. This is not to say that feminist history doesn't celebrate women's power. Emphatically it does, particularly in the hands of Adrienne Rich. But it also serves to expose oppression and oppressors—a mission that Emerson failed to consider when he mused on the lessons history offers. Increasingly in her career of writing and reading, and teaching her audiences to think with her "how we can use what we have / to invent what we need,"[12] she has undertaken to tell the stories of women's oppression and women's resistance. She has unearthed evidence of resources depleted by all kinds of abuse, including non-use. She has uncovered also a record of heroic resilience. Because it is a history of survivors, the record that Rich retrieves for her readers inspires a more tragic recognition of powers than the history of inexhaustible capacity that Emerson celebrates. It awakens consciousness of our passion for survival, yes, but also of the counterforces against which that passion somehow prevailed and must continue to prevail.

To enable women to identify and resist these counterforces, Rich is committed to working like the backhoe in "Power," the poem that opens *The Dream of a Common Language*.[13]

> Living   in the earth-deposits   of our history
>
> Today a backhoe divulged   out of a crumbling flank of earth
> one bottle   amber   perfect   a hundred-year-old
> cure for fever   or melancholy   a tonic
> for living on this earth   in the winters of this climate

The amber bottle that the backhoe turns up has sobering, even sinister, implications. When the poem continues, it becomes clear that it is a souvenir of the disease it was used to cure as much as it is a momento of healing. For Rich goes on to muse how Marie Curie—that patriarchally endorsed Uncommon Woman of Science—could be killed by the destructive power of her own discovery because she could not acknowledge that "her wounds   came   from the same source as her power."

Far from indicting Curie for this fatality, Rich mourns her and indicts her killer, the seductive, destructive forces of patriarchal competitiveness. In this first poem of *The Dream of a Common Language* and in the final one, "Transcendental Etude," Rich presents the lure of prima donna performance as a virulent enemy to achieving the dream of any commonality at all. From "Transcendental Etude":

> . . . We aren't virtuosi
> . . . .
> And we're not performers . . .
> . . . .
> The longer I live the more I mistrust
> theatricality, the false glamour cast
> by performance, the more I know its poverty beside
> the truths we are salvaging from
> the splitting-open of our lives.
>
> (P. 74)

If power is access to sources, then disablement is isolation of all kinds, from the singular brilliance of Marie Curie to the numbed withdrawal of the caged beast in "The Lioness" or the enforced muteness of the woman in "The Poet" who is "dumb / with loneliness." The first three poems in *The Dream of a Common Language* achieve a complex and subtle synthesis of the forces and counterforces involved in refusing isolation and trying to embrace commonality. The first, 'Power," dramatizes the story of Curie's success so as to identify how seductive and destructive a concept singular achievement can be. The second, "Phantasia for Elvira Shatayev," dramatizes the transcendent energies available to those who conceive their effort otherwise.

Rich designed an intricate presentation for this "Phantasia," dedicated, as her headnote explains, to the "leader of a women's climbing team, all of whom died in a storm on Lenin's Peak, August 1974." Building on Shatayev's diaries, Rich has Shatayev tell the story of her team's venture from the vantage point of death (a vantage point Emily Dickinson frequently chose). But Rich's imagination of her ecstatic utterances gives them a specific audience *in* time as well as a transcendental point of origin *beyond* time. Rich's Shatayev is specifically addressing her surviving husband as he climbs toward the scene of her death to pay homage to her effort which, he supposes, has been defeated because it ended in her death. The husband is mistaken. With tact and respect, Shatayev thanks him for his sentiment, but she candidly and definitively rejects the critical misconception that engendered it: "You climbed here for yourself / we climbed for ourselves." His grief is sincere, her tone suggests; she admires and appreciates his courage in making the dangerous climb "against advisement / to give us burial"; but his comprehension of the team's deeds and his own accomplishment is grievously limited. Misconstruing their story as having ended—ended sadly—he presumes to bury what is in fact alive, and she tells him so in most Emersonian terms:

> When you have buried us   told your story
> ours does not end   we stream
> into the unfinished   the unbegun
> the possible

This uncreated that Shatayev's husband presumes to bury cannot be killed. But though it is endless, it is not sourceless, and Rich very characteristically has Shatayev measure its superhuman vitality by remembering the

        . . . changes elemental and minute
        . . . we underwent
    to bring each other here
    choosing ourselves   each other   and this life
    whose every breath   and grasp   and further foothold
    is somewhere   still enacted   and continuing

The strength that Rich and Shatayev celebrate is no unaccounta-
ble visitation; it is not some sourceless fortune or grace. It has a
history of technique and apprenticeship ("the long train-
ing   the early sieges"), and of psychological preparation
("For months for years   each one of us / had felt her own
yes   growing in her / slowly forming   as she stood at win-
dows   waited / for   trains   mended   her
rucksack   combed her hair"). At the same time, this struggle,
this power that is the opposite of Curie's, does have ecstatic,
mysterious intensity. If one feels its intensity to be other-
worldly, one should, the poem implies, ask, "other than *whose*
world?"

By choosing a minor key for her affirmation on behalf of
Shatayev, Rich gives it a dignity and serenity that would be
missing if she had chosen differently. Imagine the poem ad-
dressed by Shatayev to a daughter, or to a group of women she
had left behind, or to her dead teammates and you can see how
Rich has taken care to avoid whimsy and self-congratulation.
Her "Phantasia" is an elegy for the physical death of the climb-
ing team but more for the killing misconceptions with which
patriarchal love and loyalty would mourn them. Rich identifies
and mourns what really kills—the husband's well-intentioned
but misconceived love; and she praises what really lives and
enlivens—the threatened and overwhelmed but still continuing
sisterwork of Shatayev and her teammates.[14] Austerely, Rich
blends celebration and indictment in an affirmation that refuses,
as does Emerson's, to accept limiting conceptions of power.

The power that interests Rich and Emerson cannot be limited
or dominated because it does not seek to limit or dominate. For
both of them, power is access to sources; but while Emerson
simply affirms the source as an inexhaustible energy and concen-
trates on the risks and glories of access, Rich closely examines

the sources in her ongoing effort to explore accesses to them. Ultimately for Rich, women are one another's sources of power. Access to other sources results in the deadly strength of a Curie instead of the vitalizing strength of a Shatayev.

These first two poems in *The Dream of a Common Language* complement one another. Isolated power fatally seduces Marie Curie in the first; lovingly shared power triumphs over death— though not over patriarchal misunderstanding—in the second. Then, in "Origins and History of Consciousness," the poem where her title phrase, "the dream of a common language," actually occurs, Rich adds a sobering third vision of the ways isolation can corrupt power: Two women arduously achieve mutual love but must still renounce it as a withdrawal from life because it leaves unchanged the life of the world around them.

Section 1 describes the setting—the poet's study. The history of consciousness in this room haunts anyone who would write poetry here. "No one lives in this room / without confronting the whiteness of the wall / behind the poems"—the blank pages still to be filled, the audiences still to be reached. Sleeping in this room is no easier than writing here. "No one sleeps in this room without / the dream of a common language." Sleep, in section 1, seems to be both dreaded and desired and, by implication, so is the dream it entails. The poet opposes her lonely sleep in this room to the enviable yet pitiable sleep of heterosexual lovers:

> Thinking of lovers, their blind faith, their
> experienced crucifixions,
> my envy is not simple. . . .

She has dreamed that her solitary sleep would be murderously cold only to find that "the water / is mild." Surprisingly, her watery sleep supports her as if she were a "warm amphibious animal" and keeps her safe from "the hunter, the trapper / the wardens of the mind." Asleep, the "warm animal dreams on / of another animal" and it is not clear—at least to me—whether that other animal is a predator or an expected mate, a threat to peace or a desire that cannot be lulled. In either case, the lonely sleep achieved in this setting, like the lonely efforts to write poems here, is marked by an inescapable dream, the dream of a common language.

The next two sections describe waking—first in this room and then, in section 3, "into the neighborhood." Whereas the imagined sleep of the first section was a solitary release from pursuit and entrapment, a real sleep of lovers has taken place as section 2 opens. Since Rich dramatizes their union as a triumphant if fearsome alternative to the heterosexual union that she so painfully rejected in section 1, she implies that these are lesbian lovers. They have found and chosen each other after arduous, wasteful years of enforced separation, and their union is described as a triumph of mutuality. Yet, once awakened and recalled to their environment, the lovers experience it with pain and a sense of entrapment. "[A] scream / of someone beaten up far down in the street" reminds each to "listen to her own inward scream" which, as survivor of "this city, / this century, this life," each bears ineradicably within her.

Their ardent, endangered love makes their awakening "not simple," and Rich develops its complexity in section 3.

> It's simple to wake from sleep with a stranger,
> dress, go out, drink coffee,
> enter a life again. It isn't simple
> to wake from sleep into the neighborhood
> of one neither strange nor familiar
> whom we have chosen to trust. . . .

From these lines, which open section 3, it seems at first that the difficulty or complexity Rich is acknowledging concerns the risks of partnership that the two lovers experience as a couple, for she describes their loving as an adventure of shared danger and mutual accomplishment:

> . . . Trusting, untrusting,
> we lowered ourselves into this, let ourselves
> downward hand over hand as on a rope that quivered
> over the unsearched. . . .

The expedition has been a success and it is summarized as a conception:

> . . . We did this. Conceived
> of each other, conceived each other in a darkness
> which I remember as drenched in light.

The poem might have ended here or with the half line that follows: "I want to call this, life." If it had, it would have celebrated a revolutionary union—two lovers who are "neither strange nor familiar" because these categories do not apply.[15] But the poem's coda accomplishes a more stringent re-vision of the origins and history of consciousness, and it should be read very closely. Here are the closing lines:

> I want to call this, life.
>
> But I can't call it life until we start to move
> beyond this secret circle of fire
> where our bodies are giant shadows flung on a wall
> where the night becomes our inner darkness, and sleeps
> like a dumb beast, head on her paws, in the corner.

Notice how the demanding, haunting room of the poem's opening passages reasserts itself once again here at the end. The square room will not accommodate "the secret circle of fire" the lovers have made there; its walls mock their bodies into grotesque shadows. Moreover, the room does accommodate yet another sleeper—the "dumb beast, head on her paws, in the corner." Still waiting to be awakened to the dream of a common language, the beast is a mute reproach to the lovers. The two women's ecstatic conception of each other proves to be a secret circle that excludes the beast in the corner, and the poem ends by acknowledging that their union has not met her needs. This third poem in *The Dream of a Common Language*, then, suggests that the dream is to be more than a mere wish-fulfillment, the kind that keeps the dreamer suspended in sleep; it is to be a waking dream, a vision that can engage and direct action.

There is something deeply Emersonian about Rich's severe

renunciation of her lovers' union. Like Emerson, she will not rest in accomplishment no matter how arduous has been the effort or how astonishing and worthy the outcome. In fact, Rich's image of a "secret circle of fire" may be read as an allusion to Emerson's famous insistence, "Around every circle another can be drawn."[16] Rich seeks to "unsettle all things,"[17] especially complacency. But whereas concentric circles provide an apt image for the ceaseless expansiveness he wants to urge upon his audiences, her conception of ongoing initiative includes a complexity that his centrifugal sweep misses. All Emerson's new circles expand from a single, if paradoxical, center—"the infinitude of the private man." But the center of the secret circle Rich's lovers have drawn is a damaging secret (or lie, or silence)—namely, that women are forbidden to love women.

One of Rich's great gifts to her readers—perhaps her most valuable one—has been her discovery that women's love for women is the source of energy to which our access has been most cripplingly blocked and her effort to reclaim that access for us. To do this she has had to develop a consciousness that is as radically unintimidated by custom and as radically willing to reject societal constructs and "historical" precedent as Emerson could possibly wish. Even in her lesbian/feminism, then, Rich does not so much diverge from Emerson's goals as exceed them. Her work of helping women to open ourselves to our love for one another is in the tradition of demanding openness that he inaugurated, while at the same time it radically revises the origins and history—the sources and direction—of the very consciousness he called for.

Written from 1972 to 1974, "Origins and History of Consciousness" completes the opening triad of *The Dream of a Common Language* by introducing what Rich will later call the "radical complexity" from which the meanings of women loving women can eventually expand.[18] During the period 1972–1976 her work on *Of Woman Born: Motherhood as Experience and Institution* was revealing to her how extensively patriarchal deracination and debasement of motherhood and daughterhood incapacitates women by denying us each other's love and intimacy. Among many other works in *The Dream of a Common Language,* the

"Twenty-One Love Poems" (1974–1976) attempt to inaugurate reform of this atrocity. As a poet, Rich would agree with Emerson's dictum about political revolution: "Every reform was once a private opinion and when it shall be a private opinion again, it will solve the problem of the age."[19] That is, she would agree that poetry can function as an agent of reform only insofar as it explores the poet's private experience of corruption. Patriarchal denials of Mother-Right become for her "the problem of the age" (a long age, at that); and because Rich means that women loving women should be a radiating center of reform, she made her "Twenty-One Love Poems" the core of *The Dream of a Common Language*.

True to Emerson's understanding that reform begins with and results in private conviction, these poems are never merely private, for all their intimacy and ardor. They are political poems in the sense Rich herself articulates in this passage from her essay on the work of Judy Grahn.

> No true political poetry can be written with propaganda as an aim, to persuade others "out there" of some atrocity or injustice. . . . *As poetry,* it can come only from the poet's need to identify her relationship to atrocities and injustice, the sources of her pain, fear, and anger, the meaning of her resistance.[20]

In these "Twenty-One Love Poems," Rich identifies her relationship to the atrocities and injustices that originate from the complex fact that she puts with such eloquent simplicity in poem I: "No one has imagined us." All kinds of disabling self-conceptions issue from that enormity. By not officially existing, women who love women—whether as mothers and daughters, as sisters, as lesbians, or as colleagues and friends—have to struggle even to believe in the existence of their own love, let alone to live that love. "[F]ighting the temptation to make a career of pain" (VIII), women who love women must identify the injuries but refuse to be the injured party.

Many other poems in *The Dream of a Common Language* expose the fundamental atrocity whereby women have been denied access to each other by being denied access to our mothers. "Sibling Mysteries" (1976), "Hunger" (1974–1975), and "Mother-Right" (1977) are three important examples. In these, as in the "Twenty-One Love Poems," Rich adapts to feminist uses Emerson's insight that reform is never truly public until it is generally private. Radically, she reconceives and reapplies this cherished Emersonian principle, taking his insight even more seriously than he himself could.

From beginning to end *The Dream of a Common Language* recalls Emersonian visions and rhapsodies, because it affirms energies that are potentially limitless (or at least are still to be imagined). At the same time, these poems confirm the misnaming, misuse, and misunderstanding that beset women's energies, impeding women's access to them. Having begun the volume with three poems in which she rechannels those Emersonian ideas of power that are especially congenial to her, Rich ends it with a poem she calls "Transcendental Etude," as though to invite comparison with the Emersonian tradition.

To be sure, the poem appears in the final section, which she has called "Not Somewhere Else but Here"—in overt defiance of any universalized, mystifying "beyond." But disclaiming mystery is very much a part of the transcendentalist tradition anyway. "The word Miracle, as pronounced by Christian Churches," warned Emerson, "gives a false impression; it is Monster. It is not one with the blowing clover and the falling rain."[21] He enjoined transcendental visionaries to focus on the commonplace here and now, not on what Emily Dickinson was soon to scorn as "the further heaven."[22] With Yankee shrewdness Emerson and Dickinson themselves suspected the dangers of romantic wonder; they were aware that awe, however sincere, can trivialize rather than vitalize because it makes strange what ought to be familiar.

Still, as a feminist, Rich is conscious that women experience this danger particularly, and thus her defiance of visionary mystifications radically refocuses the traditional wariness. Too often women have been regarded as "somewhere else" by men who saw themselves as "here." Otherness has been a particular threat to women because women have for so long been made to play "NOT ME" to men's "ME" (to borrow the terms Emerson uses for distinguishing crea*tive* selfhood from merely crea*ted* nature). For Rich as for Whitman the most important use of imaginative vision is to overcome otherness, and not just by making the strange familiar but by intuitive identifications that refuse this dichotomy altogether.

"Transcendental Etude" doesn't immediately hit its stride. There is something awkward and affected about the opening idyll. If Rich's car startles the deer, how can she hear well enough over the engine to know that "one / gave a hoarse intake of breath" before springing away into the maples? Meanwhile, Rich's *poetic* ear seems to fail, letting her write such clumsy lines as,

> Three months from today they'll be fair game
> for the hit-and-run hunters, glorying
> in a weekend's destructive power.

But toward the end of the second verse paragraph, she achieves her authentic sound, with its lyrical accuracy ("musing heifers," a farmland "slanting its planes"), its exhilarated urgency, and its audacious, effective repetitions ("life" used three times in six lines):

> I've sat on a stone fence above a great, soft, sloping field
> of musing heifers, a farmstead
> slanting its planes calmly in the calm light,
> a dead elm raising bleached arms
> above a green so dense with life,
> minute, momentary life—slugs, moles, pheasants, gnats,
> spiders, moths, hummingbirds, groundhogs, butterflies—
> a lifetime is too narrow
> to understand it all, beginning with the huge
> rockshelves that underlie all that life.

(P. 73)

With this Whitman-like passage she strikes the keynote of her "Transcendental Etude." In its many intricately related passages she will be trying to "understand it all." She will be studying life; nothing less. In her attempt to achieve a transcendent vision while still staying "not somewhere else but here," she will be practicing the appropriate technique—that is what études are for.

The most celebrated moment of transcendence in American letters is the epiphany Emerson describes in *Nature* when he becomes a transparent eyeball:

Standing on the bare ground,—my head bathed by the blithe air and uplifted into infinite space,—all mean egotism vanishes. I become a transparent eyeball; I am nothing; I see all; the currents of the Universal Being circulate through me; I am part or parcel of God. The name of the nearest friend sounds then foreign and accidental: to be brothers, to be acquaintances, master or servant, is then a trifle and a disturbance.[23]

When Emerson transcends his ego boundaries and becomes a transparent eyeball, he is nothing, he sees all, and the currents of life flow through him. When Rich transcends her ego boundaries, the negative capability she achieves has a different quality.[24] Rather than becoming *nothing,* as Emerson did, Rich experimentally becomes *anything.* By her intuitive identifications she flows into life as well as letting life flow through her.

Such intuitive identification occurs in the climactic movement of "Transcendental Etude," the poem's closing rhapsody, where Rich significantly adapts the transcendental stance that she has provisionally adopted throughout the poem, starting with its very title. The closing rhapsody begins with this declaration: "Vision begins to happen in such a life"—that is, a life in which a woman can start to know herself, free of patriarchal definitions of womanhood or selfhood. Rich then develops the actual rhapsody as an extended simile. When "vision begins to happen" it is as if a woman quietly withdraws into the peace of her own kitchen and there reflectively fingers various objects, freely composing them *and herself* into various experimental forms (pp. 76–77). Rich catalogues a miscellany of simple things—scraps of yarn and velvet, a fragile seashell, a cat whisker, a petunia petal, a finch's feather, and other oddments. These the woman combines "absently" in a female version of loafing and inviting one's soul. If the mood recalls Whitman, Rich's emphasis on vision as a creative activity enhanced or impeded by the claims that ordinary things make recalls Emerson's return to his image of visionary transparency at the end of *Nature*.

When vision fails, says Emerson, it is because "the axis of vision is not coincident with the axis, of things, and so they appear not transparent but opaque."[25] Matter obstructs spirit unless imaginative or visionary seeing restores the lost transparency of things and makes them once again revelations. For Emerson, things are monumental; they darken the light that they should be memorializing, and to transcend their materiality you must position your own eye so that it realigns things with their source of significance.

The metaphor of obstructed light will not serve Rich. Though she too wants to unify a disabling division, the split she deplores is a division between two kinds of work, not the split between revelatory vision and blank or meaningless vision that pains Emerson. When the woman at the end of "Transcendental Etude" composes and recomposes her assortment of oddments, she is not transcending their monumental meaninglessness by endowing them with significance. They are too trivial to obstruct much light anyway and sufficiently suggestive so that endowing them with significance can hardly be the point of her activity. Transcending these emblematic tokens requires "no mere will to mastery," Rich explicitly insists, but "care for the many-lived, unending / forms in which she finds herself. . . ."[26] To appreciate how this care constitutes a transcendence, you have first to appreciate the ordinary care it transcends. In "Natural Resources" Rich has provided her readers the necessary opportunity.

In sections 11 and 12 of the poem, she looks at a collection of trivia and does not see the transcendent care that her visionary woman is freed to experiment with. Instead, she sees an enormity, "the enormity of the simplest things" (p. 65). The unacknowledged, unpaid, unrelieved female care that Rich sees congealed in these things is an outrage. It is November, a day or two after Thanksgiving. "Women simmer carcasses / of clean-picked turkeys" while they set stained table linen to soak and put away until the next festivity the cutglass dishes they have already washed. In enumerating these seasonal things—which now grace holiday tables and will someday be undervalued relics spread on barn tables for a rummage sale—Rich evokes the female labor they represent.

As she goes on to catalogue the things to be found at a barn sale—letters, snapshots, scraps of material, clean white rags—she emphasizes the work congealed in each item. The letters have been carefully tied into packets with ribbon, the snapshots "faithfully glued for years / onto the scrapbook page." The scraps have been saved for making patchwork or doll clothes, the clean rags "for stanching blood" (pp. 65–66). Like "the child's height penciled on the cellar door," each of these "things" is actually an eloquent phase in a very particular process, the specific work women have performed: cleaning up what others have made dirty, salvaging what others have used up, stanching, remaking, storing for the future. "These things by women saved / are all we have of them" (p. 65). They are the honorable remains of lives and labors that have been systematically dishonored.

In "Natural Resources" Rich does not specifically connect this dishonored labor with imaginative labor, but in her essay, "When We Dead Awaken: Writing as Re-Vision" (1971), she does. There, in a passage that anticipates her rhapsodic extended simile at the end of "Transcendental Etude," she speaks from personal experience of "the discontinuity of female life with its attention to small chores, errands, work that others constantly undo, small children's constant needs," and she tries to "analyze the real nature of the conflict" between this work and imaginative work, like that of writing poems:

> . . . a certain freedom of the mind is needed—freedom to press on, to enter the currents of your thought like a glider pilot, knowing that your motion . . . will not be suddenly snatched away. . . . You have to be free to play around with the notion that day might be night, love might be hate; nothing can be too sacred for the imagination to turn into its opposite or to call experimentally by another name.[27]

Here, just as she will do seven years later in "Transcendental Etude," she emphatically rejects the patriarchal solution to this conflict between daily chores, which demand "a kind of conservatism," and imaginative work, which has a "subversive function."

> I want to make it clear that I am *not* saying that in order to write well, or think well, it is necessary to become unavailable to others, or to become a devouring ego. This has been the myth of the masculine artist and thinker; and I do not accept it.

Instead of splitting "the energy of creation and the energy of relation" she wants to find ways to transcend that splitting, and this transcendence is the vision that "begins to happen" in the life of the woman in "Transcendental Etude." Significantly, all the objects that the woman is reflectively fingering are remains, but most of these items cannot be restored for daily use. Rather, they await and receive a reassembly that the woman can make without regard to the immediate need of others. At the same time, Rich defies any observer to say that what her freely associating woman may be making has anything to do with patriarchal "culture." "Such a composition has nothing to do with eternity, / the striving for greatness, brilliance," Rich insists. Nor does it have anything to do with conventional notions of "domesticity." Combining the energies of relation with the energies of creation, this devoted, experimental composing transcends them both. It is an experiment in becoming the "unending / forms in which she finds herself." In the poem's marvelous final lines, the woman proceeds to become, imaginatively,

> . . . now the sherd of broken glass
> slicing light in a corner, dangerous
> to flesh, now the plentiful, soft leaf
> that wrapped round the throbbing finger, soothes the wound;

and now, in a climactic return to that underlying rockshelf of the poem's opening rhapsody,

> . . . the stone foundation, rockshelf further
> forming underneath everything that grows.

In many ways Rich's rhapsody is as transcendent a vision as any transparency Emerson could desire. But instead of transcending by heroically realigning the axes of a universe that is sadly out of kilter, Rich's woman is not fixing or conquering anything. She is neither abdicating nor indulging her own abilities to patch, to store, and to salvage. Freeing these capacities from male-dominated conceptions of what they are good for, she is using them to imagine the existence of something uncreated—herself as a free giver and partaker of life.

NOTES

1. Ralph Waldo Emerson, "The Poet," in vol. 3 of *The Complete Works of Ralph Waldo Emerson,* ed. Edward W. Emerson, Centenary Edition (Boston: Houghton Mifflin, 1903), pp. 30 and 32. See also 21, 40, 37. All subsequent references to Emerson are to volumes in this edition, which is abbreviated as *W.*

2. For Dickinson's ambivalence about her own unorthodoxy, see Albert Gelpi, *The Tenth Muse* (Cambridge: Harvard University Press, 1975), pp. 229–36. For Emerson's Orphism and its relation to Whitman and Dickinson, see Harold Bloom, *Figures of Capable Imagination* (New York: Seabury Press, 1976), chapters 3, 4, and 5. For Dickinson's use of "circumference," see Gelpi, pp. 270–78 and also Gelpi, *Emily Dickinson: The Mind of the Poet* (Cambridge: Harvard University Press, 1965), chapter 5.

3. *Letters of Emily Dickinson,* ed. Thomas H. Johnson and Theodora Ward (Cambridge: Harvard University Press, 1958), vol. 2, p. 631, letter #583.

4. *Adrienne Rich's Poetry,* ed. Barbara Charlesworth Gelpi and Albert Gelpi (New York: Norton, 1975), p. 119.

5. Adrienne Rich, "Jane Eyre: The Temptations of a Motherless Woman," in *On Lies, Secrets and Silence: Selected Prose 1966–1978* (New York: Norton, 1979), pp. 89–106.

6. Rich, "Conditions for Work: The Common World of Women," in *On Lies, Secrets, and Silence,* p. 206.

7. Rich, "The Antifeminist Woman," in *On Lies, Secrets and Silence,* p. 84.

8. Rich, *Poems: Selected and New 1950–1974* (New York: Norton, 1975), p. 191.

9. Emerson, *Nature, W,* I, 56; my emphasis.

10. Emerson, "History," *W,* II, 9.

11. Emerson, "History," *W,* II, 3.

12. Rich, "Leaflets," in *Poems: Selected and New* p. 120.

13. Rich, *The Dream of a Common Language: Poems 1974–1977* (New York: Norton, 1978). Hereafter, page numbers will be given in parentheses in the text for citations from the longer poems when the location is not readily evident from the text itself.

14. Judith McDaniel, *Reconstituting the World: The Poetry and Vision of Adrienne Rich* (Argyle, New York: Spinsters, Ink, 1978), p. 18, makes a cognate point about "Phantasia." See also her explication of "Power." "Reconstituting the World" is reprinted in this collection, pp. 3–29.

15. From a conversation with Jane Roberta Cooper, Spring 1980.

16. Emerson, "Circles," *W,* II, 301.

17. Emerson, "Circles," *W,* II, p. 318.

18. Rich, "The Meaning of Our Love from Women Is What We Have Constantly to Expand," in *On Lies, Secrets and Silence,* p. 227.

19. Emerson, "History," *W,* II, 5.

20. Rich, "Power and Danger: Works of a Common Woman," in *On Lies, Secrets, and Silence,* p. 251; Rich's emphasis. Note that Rich is speaking here specifically, though not exclusively, about love poetry.

21. Emerson, "Divinity School Address," *W,* I, 129.

22. *The Poems of Emily Dickinson,* ed. Thomas H. Johnson. 3 vols. (Cambridge: The Belknap Press, Harvard University Press, 1955): #569.

23. Emerson, *Nature, W,* I, 10.

24. For Rich on ego boundaries and negative capability, see "Three Conversations" in *Adrienne Rich's Poetry,* ed. Gelpi and Gelpi, pp. 114–15.

25. Emerson, *Nature, W,* I, 73.

26. Joanne Feit Diehl, " 'Cartographies of Silence': Rich's *Common Language* and the Woman Poet," *Feminist Studies* 6, (Fall 1980): 541–43, astutely compares Rich to Whitman and makes related points about caring and noncompetition. The essay is reprinted in this collection, pp. 91–110.

27. Rich, *On Lies, Secrets and Silence,* p. 43. The subsequent quotations in this paragraph all come from the same page.

WENDY MARTIN

A Nurturing Ethos in the Poetry of Adrienne Rich

Adrienne Rich has observed that

> Feminism means finally that we renounce our obedience to
> the fathers and recognize that the world they have described is
> not the whole world. Masculine ideologies are the creation of
> masculine subjectivity; they are neither objective, nor value-
> free, nor inclusively "human." Feminism implies that we rec-
> ognize fully the inadequacy for us, the distortion, of male-
> created ideologies, and that we proceed to think, and act, out
> of that recognition.[1]

If masculine ideologies are inadequate, a more comprehensive
perspective must be defined which includes the experience of
women and other disenfranchised people: this has been the mis-
sion of Adrienne Rich.

Feminism, for Rich, is a commitment to a nurturing ethos
and to a comprehensive vision of life which honors all people. In
contrast to patriarchal religions such as early American Puritan-
ism, which viewed human beings as corrupt and blamed wom-
en for the fall of man, feminism is centered in the belief that
males and females of all ages and races are entitled to equal rights
and resources; that no elite group of privileged men has been
ordained to dominate the rest of society. Unlike religious (and
romantic) traditions which are based on the opposition of God
and the Devil, virtue and vice, saints and sinners, spirit and
flesh, feminism insists on the significance of daily experience.
Criticizing American culture with its Puritan origins, which

praises the feats of extraordinary men at the expense of the ordinary labor of the general population, Rich urges women to honor the truths of their own lives—the capacity for bringing forth and sustaining life—and to extend this perspective to the entire cosmos.

In an effort to understand what female experience has actually been, Adrienne Rich has documented her own evolution from traditional dependency through anger and rebellion against patriarchal values, to a commitment to the female principle—an active, nurturing ethos.[2] Rich's poetry from *A Change of World* (1951), *The Diamond Cutters* (1955), *Snapshots of a Daughter-in-Law* (1963), to *Leaflets* (1969) and *The Will to Change* (1971) explores the complex relationships of twentieth-century men and women. They record the willfulness of the dominant male as well as the cultivated docility of the subservient female, and document Rich's own struggle to overcome the inertia and emotional paralysis which result from years of conditioned passivity.

In *Diving into the Wreck* (1973), Rich no longer looks for a man to protect her, as she begins to act on her own behalf. While her previous work explores the complexity of a modern marriage with hurt, anger, and resentment churning beneath the surface, this and subsequent volumes—*Poems: Selected and New* (1975), *The Dream of a Common Language* (1978), and *A Wild Patience Has Taken Me This Far* (1981)—contend with the complex task of balancing the desire for psychological autonomy with the need for commitment and for community.

In the conclusion to her prose study, *Of Woman Born: Motherhood as Experience and Institution* (1976), Rich urges her readers to

> . . . imagine a world in which every woman is the presiding genius of her own body. In such a world women will truly create new life, bringing forth not only children (if and as we choose) but the visions, and the thinking, necessary to sustain, console, and alter human existence—a new relationship to the universe. Sexuality, politics, intelligence, power, motherhood, work, community, intimacy will develop new meanings; thinking itself will be transformed.[3]

Here Rich elaborates a theme which has been central to her recent poetry—the necessity for women to free themselves from the cultural constructs which mediate their experience in order to determine for themselves the meaning of their lives. The key to this transformation of consciousness is a "passionate attention to *all* female experience."[4]

In *The Dream of a Common Language* and *A Wild Patience Has Taken Me This Far,* Adrienne Rich stresses the importance of a reverence toward life in its many forms, human and natural. "Transcendental Etude" (1977), one of her most sustained lyric poems to date, honors the fertility of the earth and the complexity of nature. This poem is a meditation on the web of interrelated life:

> I've sat on a stone fence above a great, soft, sloping field
> of musing heifers, a farmstead
> slanting its planes calmly in the calm light,
> a dead elm raising bleached arms
> above a green so dense with life,
> minute, momentary life—slugs, moles, pheasants, gnats,
> spiders, moths, hummingbirds, groundhogs, butterflies—
> a lifetime is too narrow
> to understand it all, beginning with the huge
> rockshelves that underlie all that life.[5]

This is a long poem which is not broken into sections; the lyrical language flows without pause or interruption as Rich finds her full poetic voice: "a whole new poetry beginning here / Vision begins to happen in such a life." The perspective in this poem is not fragmented or partial. Instead of focusing on flowers, trees, or meadows, Rich takes in the entire landscape and does not sacrifice the whole to the part; she understands that the countryside before her involves an intricate system of relationships in a strong yet sensitive balance. Comparable to Anne Bradstreet's "Contemplations" in its profound appreciation of nature's plenitude, this poem, unlike the Puritan Bradstreet's, does not attribute the splendor of the landscape to God. Here there is no progress from earth to heaven but rather an acceptance of earth for its own sake. The hierarchical or stratified universe of Anne Bradstreet's poetry is replaced by a detailed appreciation of diverse interdependence.

The title of the poem is double-edged because Rich wants to

be grounded in life, not released from it. Transcendence, in this instance, does not lead to a rising above ordinary experience but the dissolution of artificial categories that prevent us from seeing and appreciating life in its extraordinary variety; moreover, transcendence also means the possibility of living in harmony with nature, a commitment to growth not destruction:

> pulling the tenets of a life together
> with no mere will to mastery,
> only care for the many-lived, unending
> forms in which she finds herself.[6]

In contrast such poems as "Culture and Anarchy" (1978), which takes its title from Matthew Arnold's essay published in London in 1869, provide a feminist alternative to the Puritan imperative to tame and control nature in the name of God's elect. A tribute to generativity, and to the life cycle which includes death as well as birth and growth, this poem sustains the lyrical celebration of nature begun in "Transcendental Etude":

> Leafshade stirring on lichened bark
> Daylilies
> run wild, "escaped" the botanists call it
> from dooryard to meadow to roadside
>
> Life-tingle of angled light
> late summer
> sharpening toward fall, each year more sharply
>
> This headlong, loved, escaping life[7]

The insistent rise and fall of the lines, the dropped word or phrase set below the primary line, create a sense of the inevitable movement towards death.

In contrast to the acceptance of the life cycle in this poem, the following passage from Samuel Sewall's description of the landscape of seventeenth-century New England, *Plum Island,* voices the conviction that the purpose of human life on earth is to prepare for an afterlife, to transcend corporeal existence to become "Saints in Light":

> As long as any Cattel shall be fed with the Grass growing in the Medows, which do humbly bow down themselves before Turkie-Hill; As long as any Sheep shall walk upon Old Town Hills, and shall from thence pleasantly look down upon the River Parker, and the fruitfull Marishes lying beneath; As long as any free and harmless Doves shall find a White Oak . . . to perch, or feed, or build a careless Nest upon . . . So long shall Christians be born there; and being first made meet, shall from thence be Translated, to be made partakers of the Inheritance of the Saints in Light.[8]

Although Sewall clearly appreciates nature, his desire to be "translated" to Heaven bifurcates his experience in such a way that his life and the life around him are not inextricably intertwined; instead, nature is merely a harbinger of his heavenly destination.

The understanding and acceptance of the profound connection between nature and human life in Rich's poetry permits a vision which overcomes the habitual separation of mind and body, self and other:

> *I am the lover and the loved,*
> *home and wanderer, she who splits*
> *firewood and she who knocks, a stranger*
> *in the storm . . .*[9]

Because she can accept diversity in nature, the poet is able to accept the complexity of her emotions and experience. Refusing to dichotomize her emotions, Rich achieves psychic wholeness, not through repression, but by confronting the widest possible range of her feelings. "Integrity" (1978) describes this consciousness:

> Anger and tenderness: my selves.
> And now I can believe they breathe in me

as angels, not polarities.
Anger and tenderness: the spider's genius
to spin and weave in the same action
from her own body, anywhere—
even from a broken web.[10]

Rich's poetry documents a determination to accept and live
through pain, jealousy, anxiety, fear, even the threat of psychic
disintegration rather than repudiate large areas of experience.
Through her phenomenological approach, Rich has explored
such difficult subjects as anger and female sexuality—orgasm,
menstruation, pregnancy, childbirth—and she has done so
"with no mere will to mastery" but with a respect for the full
range of her emotions, however difficult.

In her effort to recall the experience of women whose lives
were not recorded by historians and to restore significance to the
daily lives of countless women, Rich uses the resonant word
"remember"—to reconstitute as well as to recollect female expe-
rience past and present. "Culture and Anarchy" (1978) uses ex-
cerpts from the diaries, letters, and speeches of Susan B. An-
thony, Ida Husted Harper, Jane Addams, Elizabeth Cady
Stanton, and Elizabeth Barrett Browning, to flesh out the por-
traits of these women whose struggles for the equality of wom-
en have been so often overlooked.

An energy I cannot even yet
take for granted: picking up a book
of the nineteenth century, reading there the name
of the woman whose book you found
in the old town Athenaeum
beginning to stitch together
Elizabeth Ellet
Elizabeth Barrett
Elizabeth Blackwell
Frances Kemble
Ida B. Wells-Barnett
Susan B. Anthony[11]

This commitment to excavate the female past is extended to
include all women, past and present, whose lives are not re-

corded by official historians or acknowledged by authorities to be important. "Frame" (1980) narrates the experience of a young black woman who is arrested, jailed, and beaten in Boston in 1979 for waiting for a bus during a snowstorm in the lobby of a newly constructed building. It is written from the perspective of a woman who was not physically present but who bears witness to the event nevertheless:

> What I am telling you
> is told by a white woman who they will say
> was never there. I say I am there.[12]

Similarly, Rich writes poems in memory of Paula Modersohn-Becker, Clara Westhoff, Marie Curie, Elvira Shatayev, Ethel Rosenberg and Simone Weil as well as for her grandmothers, her sister, her mother, her lovers in an effort to preserve the meaning of their lives. And in the eight part poem "Turning the Wheel" (1981), she turns her attention to the lives of the Hopi and Navaho women of the Southwest:

> I try to imagine a desert-shamaness
> bringing water to fields of squash, maize and cotton
> but where the desert herself is half-eroded
> half-flooded by a million jets of spray
> to conjure a rich white man's paradise
> the shamaness could well have withdrawn her ghost.[13]

Bearing witness to the lost lives of women past and present in a world that has been misused by patriarchal exploitation has been one of the major themes of Adrienne Rich's recent poetry; for her the liberated woman is one who is able to embrace life as process, an unfolding which requires continuous effort and a willingness to confront the quotidian truths:

> Freedom. It isn't once, to walk out
> under the Milky Way, feeling the rivers
> of light, the fields of dark—
> freedom is daily, prose-bound, routine
> remembering. Putting together, inch by inch
> the starry worlds. From all the lost collections.[14]

In contrast to the epiphanal moments of Sewall's narrative, in which nature is seen as God's handiwork, Rich's poem reminds us that the Earth is a dwelling place which sustains all forms of life day by day. In her work, a nurturing ethos replaces the imperative to dominate or transcend ordinary experience.

NOTES

1. Adrienne Rich, Foreword to *Working It Out,* ed. Sara Ruddick and Pamela Daniels (New York: Pantheon, 1977), p. xvii.

2. I have discussed this evolution in detail in the following studies: "A Chronological Reading of Adrienne Rich's Poetry," in the *Norton Critical Edition of Adrienne Rich's Poetry* ed. Barbara Charlesworth Gelpi and Albert Gelpi (New York: Norton, 1975), pp. 175–89; *The Poetry of Adrienne Rich, American Writers* monograph series, ed. Leonard Unger (New York: Charles Scribner's Sons, 1979); "'To Study Our Lives'— The Poetry of Adrienne Rich," *Ploughshares* 5 (1980): 172–77; "Adrienne Rich—The Evolution of a Poet," in *American Writers Today,* ed. Richard Kostelanetz (Washington, D.C.: International Communication Agency, 1982). See also the chapters on Adrienne Rich in Wendy Martin, *An American Triptych: Anne Bradstreet, Emily Dickinson, Adrienne Rich* (Chapel Hill: University of North Carolina Press, 1984).

3. Rich, *Of Woman Born: Motherhood as Experience and Institution* (New York: Norton, 1976; pb. ed. New York: Bantam, 1977), p. 292.

4. Rich, *On Lies, Secrets and Silence: Selected Prose 1966–1978* (New York: Norton, 1979), p. 133.

5. Rich, *The Dream of a Common Language: Poems 1974–1977* (New York: Norton, 1978), p. 73.

6. "Transcendental Etude," in *The Dream of a Common Language,* p. 77.

7. "Culture and Anarchy," in *A Wild Patience Has Taken Me This Far: Poems 1978–1981* (New York: Norton, 1981), p. 10.

8. Samuel Sewall *Plum Island,* quoted in Perry Miller, *The New England Mind: From Colony to Province* (Cambridge: Harvard University Press, 1953), p. 190.

9. "Transcendental Etude," in *The Dream of a Common Language,* p. 76.

10. "Integrity," in *A Wild Patience,* p. 9.

11. "Culture and Anarchy," in *A Wild Patience,* p. 11.

12. "Frame," in *A Wild Patience,* p. 48.

13. "Turning the Wheel," part 3, "Hohokam," in *A Wild Patience,* p. 54.

14. "For Memory," in *A Wild Patience,* p. 22.

SUSAN STANFORD FRIEDMAN

Adrienne Rich and H.D.:

An Intertextual Study

Adrienne Rich's *The Dream of a Common Language* opens its
search for women's life-giving power by invoking the stern
determination of the poet H.D., who wrote in the third volume
of her war *Trilogy:*

I go where I love and where I am loved,
into the snow;

I go to the things I love
with no thought of duty or pity.[1]

Published during World War II, H.D.'s epic presents the mod-
ern poet's search in the midst of war for a regenerative Love
symbolized by the changing forms of the Goddess. Rich's epi-
gram from the *Trilogy* is an appropriate beginning for her own
volume, in which her quest for the common language of women
names the love between women as the life force countering the
death-trip of patriarchy. Virginia Woolf wrote that "a woman
writing thinks back through her mothers."[2] H.D., who died in
1961 just as Rich's second volume of poems appeared, is just
such a literary foremother. She hovers as a rich presence nour-
ishing the evolution of the younger woman's poetic vision to-
ward the woman-identified, gynocentric feminism of *The
Dream of a Common Language.* This essay will explore not only

A shorter version of this essay was read at the Conference on Women Writing
Poetry in America at Stanford University (1982), and it appeared in *Signs* 9
(Winter 1983). For their insightful and supportive criticism, the author would
like to thank Gertrude Hughes, Rachel Blau DuPlessis, Marilyn Arthur, and Jane
Roberta Cooper. Reprinted by permission of the author and *Signs.*

the nature of that influence, but also the mutual illuminations evident in their lives and texts.

H.D.'s influence on Rich begins within the larger context of Rich's own brilliance as a critic and the place she has created for herself within the family of women, particularly women writers. By no means an exclusive influence, H.D.'s presence in Rich's thought results from her feminist commitment to unearth the "natural resources" in women's common lives, in the women's culture which has survived in spite of the patriarchy, whether lived out in women's intangible experiences or named in women's art.[3] In her classic essay on awakening consciousness, "When We Dead Awaken: Writing as Re-Vision," Rich identified "re-vision" as an active form of "seeing with fresh eyes," literally a revision which selects, shapes, and relates knowledge to ultimately feminist contexts. As an act of passionate intellect essential for women's survival, re-vision deconstructs patriarchy and uncovers "how the very act of naming has been till now a male prerogative, and how we can begin to see and name—and therefore live—afresh."[4] Rich's search through women's literary tradition for how women have seen and named their lives has fed her own poetic survival and growth.

Rich's stance toward women writers is distinctly compassionate and noncompetitive. It embodies a feminist theory of reading in which the underlying receptivity inevitable in any literary influence overlaps with her desire to build a tangible women's culture. One writer's receptivity to the ideas of another depends upon a preexisting common bond, a conscious or subconscious identification of lives and ideas that allows the process of influence to proceed. Through her conscious search for a family of women who write as women, about women, Rich has intensified this process of bonding in order to transcend the divisions to which she believes the patriarchy determines women. In contrast to Carolyn Kizer's satiric anger in "Pro Femina," Rich's criticism never condemns or destroys, but rather decodes the woman's life and work to reveal what is illuminating and useful for herself and by extension, other women.[5] This approach reverses the family constellation Harold Bloom has identified for male writers whereby the "sons" regard previous writers as literary "fathers" with all the rivalry and ambivalence of a young boy in the throes of the Oedipus complex.[6] The family model of influence is a powerful paradigm for Rich's reading, but what she has described as the potential of mother-daughter relationships characterizes her approach to her literary mothers and sisters:

> We are, none of us, "either" mothers or daughters; to our amazement, confusion, and greater complexity, we are both. Women, mothers or not, who feel committed to other women, are increasingly giving each other a quality of caring filled with the diffuse kinds of identification that exist between actual mothers and daughters. . . .
>
> To accept and integrate and strengthen both the mother and the daughter in ourselves is no easy matter, because patriarchal attitudes have encouraged us to split, to polarize, these images, and to project all unwanted guilt, anger, shame, power, freedom, onto the "other" woman. But any radical vision of sisterhood demands that we reintegrate them.[7]

Rich does not project onto other women writers her own emotions or desires, but attempts instead to regard these women as mothers and sisters trapped in patriarchy, damaged inevitably in some way by that experience, and struggling to devise some mechanism of speech.

The nurturant attitude pervading Rich's reading and writing about women artists involved her in a selective process whereby she highlighted certain aspects of women's lives and work and placed their hesitations and contradictions within the context of patriarchally imposed difficulties. Different women writers came through this process to represent a variety of strategies by which women have confronted, subverted, transformed, or been silenced by patriarchy. The result of this feminist approach to reading has been essays of critical brilliance which have not only opened up new perspectives on various women writers, but also identified the very issues undergoing exploration in her own poetic development. Her early essay on Anne Bradstreet (1966), for example, discusses the movement in Bradstreet's poetic development from ordinary "public" poems to extraordinary poems "written in response to the simple events in a woman's life"; in her own poetry of the sixties, Rich was herself gradually changing from a poet who had erased all traces of gender to one who explored the dailiness of a woman's life, who was beginning to see the links between the personal and the political.[8] Rich's compassionate argument with Woolf on anger and women's writing in "When We Dead Awaken" (1971) paralleled the first substantial explosions of her own rage in "The Phenomenology of Anger" (1972) and the other poems of anger in *Diving into the Wreck*.[9] Like Woolf, the evolution of the vision embodied in Rich's own art is mirrored in her critical essays on other writers. Consequently, examination of Rich's ideas about women writers helps to pinpoint the precise area of influence on her own poetic development.

The powerful presence of H.D. in *The Dream of a Common Language* and the brilliant reading which stands behind it are a case in point. A quick glance through Rich's essays would suggest that H.D. has been relatively unimportant to her. Her occasional and scattered references to H.D. contrast with her extended discussions of Bradstreet, Dickinson or Woolf, and do not seem to explain the central position she has given H.D. among all her literary foremothers by opening her major poetic statement of her lesbian–feminist vision with lines from the *Trilogy*.[10] However, a closer look at what Rich has written about H.D., combined with the ideas and questions she has brought with her to her reading of H.D.'s works, demonstrate that Rich has closely connected this poet with her own lesbian feminism. Rich has seen in H.D. a comprehensive critique of the violence at the core of patriarchy, a quest for the personal and mythic maternal principle to counter the patriarchy, and the exploration of rich bonds between women as friends and lovers to feed their emotional, intellectual, and erotic lives. These ideas, which Rich found in H.D., go to the very heart of her evolving feminist theory after the publication of *Diving into the Wreck* (1973) and constitute the recurring themes of *The Dream of a Common Language*.[11] Her interaction with H.D. is consequently a touchstone that reveals the larger process of change in Rich's theoretical and poetic formulations of feminism.

In "The Antifeminist Woman" (1972), by her own account

the seed for *Of Woman Born* (1976), Rich identified patriarchy as an institution that is not only unjust to women, but also dangerous to all living things:

> I am a feminist because I feel endangered, psychically and physically, by this society, and because I believe that the women's movement is saying that we have come to an edge of history when men—insofar as they are embodiments of the patriarchal idea—have become dangerous to children and other living things, themselves included; and that we can no longer afford to keep the female principle enclosed within the confines of the tight little postindustrial family. . . .[12]

In kinship with the New Left intelligensia of the sixties, Rich had already demonstrated in her poetry her alienation from the atmosphere of the Cold War, the threat of the atomic bomb, racist violence, and the Vietnam War. But by the early seventies, Rich firmly connected the public culture of violence with the politics of the personal and the system of patriarchy—as a poem like "Trying to Talk with a Man" (1971), set near a bombing test sight, vividly demonstrates.[13] In both her prose and poetry, Rich determined to counter the violent core of patriarchy through a feminist re-vision of the "female principle"—the qualities of Eros centered in birth, life, and love, which the patriarchal ethos has displaced onto women and thereby made a real current in women's culture.[14]

Motherhood, as both institution and experience, is at the symbolic center of this "female principle" as Rich identified it in "The Antifeminist Woman" and later developed it in *Of Woman Born*. Understanding why feminist theory had to begin by "exploring whatever else woman is and might be besides a body with uterus and breasts," Rich nonetheless stated: ". . . I believe that a radical reinterpretation of the concept of motherhood is required which would tell us, among many other things, more about the physical capacity for gestation and nourishment of infants and how it relates to psychological gestation and nurture as an intellectual and creative force" (*LSS*, p. 77). Rich called for the use of woman's procreative potential as the symbolic paradigm of the life force which must counter the "death-spiral" of patriarchy. This led Rich into a revisionist mythmaking with traditions of matriarchy, mother-right, and the great goddesses of a possibly prepatriarchal era. Throughout her research into ancient history and prehistory, Rich sought to fuse the shards of "*gynocentric* . . . periods of human culture which have shared certain kinds of woman-centered beliefs and woman-centered social organization."[15]

Rich's analysis of patriarchal violence and the symbolic "primacy" of the mother is encoded in H.D.'s epic works more fundamentally than in the work of any other poetic foremother. Rich has described her discovery of H.D.'s book-length epics of war as her recovery of "the passion for survival"—"the great theme of women's poetry":

> In my college years we studied the "great" long poems of modernism. . . . But we did not read, and courses in modern poetry still do not teach, H.D.'s epic poem, "Trilogy," in which she confronted war, nationalist insanity, the ruin of the great cities, not mourning the collapse of Western civilization but turning back for her inspiration to prehistory, to a gynocentric tradition. H.D. insisted that the poet-as-woman should stop pouring her energies into a ground left sterile by the power-mongers and death-cultists: *Let us leave / the place-of-a-skull / to them that have made it. . . .* For women, the "breakdown" of Western "civilization" between the wars and after the holocaust has never seemed as ultimate and consequential as it has for men. . . . What the male poets were mourning and despairing over had never *been* ours, and, as H.D. saw, what we have yet to create does not depend on their institutions; would in fact rather be free of them. She saw that for her as a woman poet, "the walls do not fall"— there are living sources for her that transcend the death-spiral of patriarchy. (*LSS*, pp. 256–57)

Rich's reading of H.D., shaped by the concerns she had already voiced in "The Antifeminist Woman," is an accurate one. The exploration of violence and the vision of Love embodied in the avatars of female divinity form the motivating purpose and symbolic centers of both H.D.'s modernist epics of war, *Trilogy* and *Helen in Egypt*. H.D. lived through two world wars in London, experiences she did not shun but regarded as shattering forces in both the personal and public domains of history. Sharing the despair and consequent search for new meanings with friends like Pound, Williams, and Eliot, H.D. brought her perspective as a woman to her quest to understand the patterns ordering a world governed by destruction. In stark contrast to these male mythmakers, H.D. identified the violence epitomized by war as the central force of disintegration. She self-consciously adapted Sigmund Freud's theory of Eros and Thanatos as the primal instincts of the unconscious to create her apocalyptic mythos of death and resurrection, Love and War, L'Amour and La Mort as the underlying forces of history.[16]

Freud did not associate Eros with women and Thanatos with men. Nor did H.D. when she wrote the *Trilogy* shortly after the Battle of Britain. But consistent with Rich's reading of the *Trilogy*, H.D. did suggest that the world had lost touch with the female forms of divinity and that the search for life amidst death was inextricably connected with recovery of the Goddess—or, in Rich's terms, the "female principle."

H.D.'s re-vision of culture and resurrection of the Goddess takes a number of forms throughout *Trilogy*.[17] But the central vision of the epic is the Goddess' appearance in the poet's dream, which is always for H.D. the oracle of the unconscious. Garbed in the shining robes of the Lamb in the biblical *Revelation*, H.D.'s Goddess—or "Lady" as she is called in this section of *Tribute to the Angels*—embodies salvation and rebirth. She resembles the madonna of Christian tradition, even the more powerful Isis of Egyptian religion. But she appears without the Child, the male symbol of salvation. Instead, she carries a book of life whose pages are blank, waiting to be written anew by the poet. She is "not-fear, she is not-war," and "she carries over the cult / of the *Bona Dea*" (*T*, pp. 103, 104). In H.D.'s poetry of survival, the Lady is indeed the embodiment of the "woman-centered beliefs" Rich would restore to a world dangerous to all living things.

The *Trilogy* does not explicitly link war with patriarchy, with men in opposition to women. But in her profoundly antifascist epic, *Helen in Egypt*, written between 1952 and 1954, H.D. returned to the subject of war and directly connected violence with patriarchy. The narrative retells the story of Helen—the Greek Eve, "Helena, hated of all Greece"—from Helen's perspective. At the beginning, Helen has repressed all memory of her escape from a dull marriage for the springtime love of Paris. But in the course of the meditative "Pallinode" (the first of three sections in the epic), she learns to redefine her own and all women's innocence by understanding the sterility and violence at the core of the masculine ethos. The Trojan War, and by mythological extension, war itself, represents the forces of Love in confrontation with the forces of Death. Forms of the Goddess—Thetis, Aphrodite, Isis, and ultimately Helen—are regenerating Love, "a fountain of water / in that desert" where the "purely masculine iron ring" of war "died of thirst" (*HE*, pp. 48, 51, 55). The "Pallinode" presents H.D.'s view of polarized male and female worlds wherein women express the inner, spiritual powers of Eros while men command state power and weapons as bequests from the past, from father to son.

Rich did not first discover her theory of sexual polarity, war, and a countering female principle in H.D.'s epic works. Rather, Rich's own ideas provided the feminist lens through which she could see the presence of these issues in H.D.'s work. Read in this perspective, H.D. then deeply reinforced the direction of Rich's thought and the urgency of finding poetic expression for her vision. In particular, the *Trilogy* and *The Dream of a Common Language* are companion volumes whose echoing themes and forms establish reverbating intertextualities. The polarity of worlds—the forces of life and death, of love and violence—provides the underlying dualistic structure of both volumes. Where H.D. focused on cataclysmic wars, Rich broadened the "death-spiral" of patriarchy to include the institutions producing the postmodernist wasteland of hunger, atomization, and alienation. In Rich's volume, the city frequently serves as the objective correlative for the spiritual state of mind engendered by a world that devalues the "female principle."[18] Throughout "Twenty-One Love Poems," which form the structural center of *The Dream of a Common Language,* Manhattan serves as the alienating setting, representing the violent world which the lovers must inhabit, yet seek to transform with love and relationship. Just as H.D. started the *Trilogy* with her impressions of destruction on walking through her London neighborhood after a bombing raid, Rich began poem I of "Twenty-One Love Poems" with a walk through the city which produces images of violence:

> Wherever in this city, screens flicker
> with pornography, with science-fiction vampires,
> victimized hirelings bending to the lash,
> we also have to walk . . . if simply as we walk
> through the rainsoaked garbage, the tabloid cruelties
> of our own neighborhoods.
>
> (*DCL*, p. 25)

Both H.D. and Rich insist on confronting the worst representations of societal disease; neither seeks escape to a peaceful countryside that obscures the violence dominating Western culture. Both are determined to create and experience an alternative in the very heart of destruction. Their tasks take somewhat different forms, but the dynamic of transformation and the polarity out of which it emerges are similar. H.D., much more the traditional mystic, has apocalyptic visions of the forces of life amidst death, even in the terrifying firebombs of war, which incarnate the purifying "new fire . . . of regeneration" (*T*, p. 21). Rich, not particularly interested in the esoteric traditions so central to H.D.'s mythos, nonetheless searches for life in the rubble of destruction:

> We need to grasp our lives inseparable
> from those rancid dreams, that blurt of metal, those disgraces,
> . . . .
> . . . We want to live like trees,
> sycamores blazing through the sulfuric air,
> dappled with scars, still exuberantly budding,
> our animal passion rooted in the city.
>
> (*DCL*, p. 25)

Rooted in the city, rooted in the war, H.D. and Rich both find evidence of a regenerating life force associated with a desecrated "female principle." The structural center of both volumes is love, an Eros whose intangible power is the only force strong enough to confront the tangible power of society. Rich's choice of a quotation from the *Trilogy*—"I go where I love and where I am loved"—highlights the centrality of a newly defined Eros in their mythmaking. In philosophical and structural function, Rich's "Twenty-One Love Poems" parallel H.D.'s vision of the "Lady."

Both the *Trilogy* and *The Dream of a Common Language* associate the principle of life with images of matriarchal prehistory, in which, as Rich wrote, the mother's "capacity for gestation and nurture" served as an "intellectual and creative force." H.D.'s presentation of her own Atlantis myth in the final volume of the *Trilogy* has its companion in Rich's re-vision of the matriarchy myth in *The Dream of a Common Language*. Rich's epigram from the *Trilogy* comes from a section in which H.D. images her quest as the flight of the wild geese "who still (they say) hover / over the lost island, Atlantis; / seeking what we once knew." These birds abandon the "foolish circling" of the "steel sharpened on the stone; / again, the pyramid of skulls." They know:

> only love is holy and love's ecstasy
>
> that turns and turns and turns about one centre,
> reckless, regardless, blind to reality,
>
> that knows the Islands of the Blest are there,
> for *many waters can not quench love's fire.*
> (T, pp. 117, 121–22)

The remainder of the *Trilogy* tells the "tale of jars," the story of Mary Magdalene and Kaspar, to portray the recovery of Atlantis, the female principle lost to the male-dominated world at war.[19] In H.D.'s re-vision of biblical tradition, Kaspar is an Arab merchant who is suddenly interrupted by Mary's "unseemly" appearance in his shop. At the evening in "Tribute to H.D." of the Manhattan Theatre Club, Rich's reading and commentary dramatically brought to life the ensuing confrontation between Kaspar and Mary. Kaspar is offended by the indecency of her unveiled hair, by her refusal to contain this symbol of woman's power. Annoyed when she ignores his repeated rebuffs, Kaspar represents the patriarchal world that tolerates the presence of women only when their power, especially their sexual power, is controlled by men. Suddenly, however, he sees a grain of light in her hair that reveals a vision of Paradise, the Atlantis lost through man's desecration of woman. This revelation converts Kaspar to a worship of Mary, which in turn makes him worthy to bring a gift to the Child in later years. The epic ends with his journey to Bethlehem, but instead of focusing on the Child, he kneels before Mary, the primal mother who embodies the related principles of love and life. Atlantis regained is not an actual historical place, but rather a state of mind symbolized by the matriarchal woman in the iconography of the *Trilogy*.

Rich's short poem "Mother-Right" (1977) evokes the matriarchal concept as an idea which she recognizes has importance whether or not it reflects an historical reality. Echoing J. J. Bachofen's *Das Mütterrecht* (translated by Ralph Manheim as *Myth, Religion, and Mother Right*), the title of the poem identifies the intellectual subject underlying the flashing succession of condensed images as the tradition of matriarchy described in Bachofen, Frederick Engels, Jane Harrison, Robert Briffault, and Erich Neumann, the theorists of matriarchy Rich discussed extensively in her essays.[20] The man in the poem stands firmly "planted / on the horizon," regarding the earth as property to be measured out in boundaries (*DCL,* p. 59). The woman, in contrast, is a figure of motion, running with her child in a field, "making for the open." She is attuned to the earth—"the grass   the waters underneath   the air"—rather than possessive of it. The poem, however, represents a critical re-vision of the matriarchal myth. Bachofen, Briffault, and Neumann in particular have envisioned the mothers of matriarchy as soft, fecund, and inert. Progress, they believed, was achieved by the aggressive thrust of men, whose creativity is centered in the brain rather than the womb.[21] Rich's poem, in contrast, creates a matriarchal image of freedom, strength, and motion. Evoking prehistory, revised from a feminist perspective, the poem nonetheless ends with a pre-vision of the future. At the end, the woman has been trapped within man's boundaries and must recapture her freedom: "the woman   eyes sharpened in the light / heart stumbling   making for the open" (*DCL*, p. 59). Just as H.D.'s "tale of jars" bore a message for a modern world consumed in violence, Rich's poem about an imaginary prehistory ends with an omen for the present. Women must recover the power denied them by patriarchy and "mak[e] for the open." The image of the matriarchal mother stands symbolically at the center of both poets' re-vision of culture.

The emphasis on the mother in the poetry of H.D. and Rich led both women to an exploration of the mother–daughter relationship as an essential element in their reconstitution of an authentic female principle. In *Of Woman Born*, Rich outlined the causes of conflict between mothers and daughters in a phallocentric world and insisted that women must find ways to heal these divisions. Her theoretical argument serves admirably as a description of the mother–daughter dynamic in the life and poetry of H.D., as well as in her own. A number of striking biographical parallels highlight the pattern they both share: the strong desire for their mothers, born of a flawed mother–daughter bond, which in turn motivates their poetic creation of potent mother-symbols. Both women were the favorites of professor-fathers who encouraged their intellectual development. Professor Doolittle wanted his daughter to be a second Marie Curie. Like H.D.'s, Rich's mother was named Helen, and both poets associated their mothers with Helen of Troy and grew up with Poe's famous poem echoing through their feelings about their mothers.[22] Like Rich, H.D. broke away from a life built on pleasing her father and instead turned to her relationship with her mother to create the major symbols of her mythos. However, H.D.'s mother preferred her son to her daughter and was prevented by her own victimization from giving her gifted daughter the nurturance she craved. H.D.'s yearning for her mother was in part a reaction against her mother's male-identification, a response that inspired her art. As she wrote about the motivating force behind *Helen in Egypt*: "My older brother was my mother's favorite; I, my father's. But the mother is the Muse, the Creator, and in my case especially, as my mother's name was Helen."[23]

In analysis, Freud convinced H.D. that her vivid dreams and hallucinating visions were expressions of her unconscious desire to recreate the infant bond with her mother. From Freud, H.D. learned to link the mother of her desire with the mother-symbols of mythological and esoteric tradition. Divided from her real mother by Helen Doolittle's favoritism toward her brother and subservience to her father, H.D. created mother goddesses in her poetry who represent the ideal mother the patriarchy had denied her. The poet in H.D.'s epics is always implicitly the daughter of the matriarchal Goddess, whose inspiration results in both poetry and religious vision. This process, whereby the daughter births the potent mother-symbol who then nourishes her art, is paradigmatically clear in the *Trilogy*'s alchemical mythmaking. Before the lady can appear in the poet's dream, the poet must purify the goddesses desecrated by patriarchal monotheism. Through poetry, she can "swiftly re-light the flame" and return Venus, whose name now stands for "venery," back to "venerate, / venerator":

> Now polish the crucible
> and in the bowl distill
>
> a word most bitter, *marah,*
> a word bitterer still, *mar,*
>
> sea, brine, breaker, seducer,
> giver of life, giver of tears;
>
> Now polish the crucible
> and set the jet of flame
>
> under, till *marah-mar*
> are melted, fuse and join
>
> and change and alter,
> mer, mere, mère, mater, Maia, Mary,
>
> Star of the Sea,
> Mother.

(T, p. 71)

H.D.'s Goddess contains a strongly religious component based on her extensive involvement in a hermetic mysticism largely absent from *The Dream of a Common Language*. But Rich's unabashed yearning for her mother is pervasive and fundamentally similar to H.D.'s in motivation and function. In *Of Woman Born*, Rich wrote:

> There was, is, in most of us, a girl-child still longing for a woman's nurture, tenderness, and approval, a woman's power exerted in our defense, a woman's smell and touch and voice, a woman's strong arms around us in moments of fear and pain . . . The cry of that female child in us need not be shameful or regressive; it is the germ of our desire to create a world in which strong mothers and strong daughters will be a matter of course. (*OWB*, p. 225)

Rich's feminist reconstitution of a matriarchal mother-daughter bond is especially evident in "Sibling Mysteries" (1976), a poem strikingly similar to H.D.'s *Trilogy* and *Helen in Egypt*. In Rich's poem, a number of structural and linguistic parallels intensify the more significant thematic intertextuality. H.D.'s *Trilogy* is written entirely in unrhymed couplets organized into loosely connected sections. *Helen in Egypt* contains three-line stanzas similarly joined into distinct sections, each introduced by a prose inset in which the poet reflects on the verse to follow. "Sibling Mysteries" contains six sections composed of couplets and three-line stanzas; one prose inset taken from a journal entry in 1963 creates the structural commentary of two voices that is fundamental to *Helen in Egypt*. Rich's language has the instantaneous clarity, simplicity, and condensed quality which was the hallmark of imagist craft and for which H.D. was often praised.[24]

The condensed simplicity of language characteristic of H.D.'s epics and Rich's "Sibling Mysteries" clothes a structure based on memory and reflection rather than conventional narrative. Influenced by the reflective free association in classical psychoanalytic method, H.D. made her contribution to the modernist epic by constructing psychological narratives that move by association and weave past, present, future, and fantasy into a tapestry of reflection. "Sibling Mysteries" is structured on the same principle, a fact emphasized by Rich's syntactic repetitions. "Remind me how," the poet asks her sister in stanza after stanza, as she reflects on fragmented memories of the past in an effort to connect with her sister. Syntactic parallels and repetition define H.D.'s poetic craft and account for the deceptive simplicity of her line as much as her better understood imagistic technique. The presence of H.D. in some of Rich's poetry represents a literary mother–daughter bond that has nourished the change in Rich's language.[25]

Stylistic affinities exist, however, because of a fundamental thematic concurrence. "Sibling Mysteries" reverberates with H.D.'s goddesses because both women express the desire of the daughter bound in patriarchy for a potent, loving mother. Rich's poem begins with the family constellation of a mother and two daughters living both within and without "the kingdom of the sons." Divided from each other by fathers and husbands, the poet asks for her sister's help in establishing a reunion of the sisters with each other, and of both with their mother. Adapting Freud, H.D. made the personal and the mythic into palimpsestic forms of the same truths. Adapting both Freud and H.D., Rich uses the personal dynamics of her own family to represent the structure of women's oppression in patriarchy. The attempt to connect with her sister is the prototype of sisterhood, and the role of the mother in this search suggests the primacy of the maternal principle Rich has written about elsewhere. The overlapping dimensions of personal, mythical, and political are evident in the poet's memory:

> Remind me how we loved our mother's body
> our mouths drawing the first
> thin sweetness from her nipples
> . . . .
> and how she sent us weeping
> into that law
> how we remet her in our childbirth visions
>
> erect, enthroned, above
> a spiral stair
> and crawled and panted toward her

I know, I remember, but
hold me, remind me
of how her woman's flesh was made taboo to us

(*DCL*, pp. 48–49)

Rich's memory evokes the potent mother of the Eleusinian mysteries, suggested also by the title and the cultlike aura of the fragments from the past. Demeter's power—worshipped but not controlled by men—was based in her body as the symbol of a spiritual force for Eros, directed first toward her daughter Korê and then by extension to the whole universe of growing things. Ostensibly memories of shared times, Rich's recollections of hikes, streams, pregnancy, and camping trips in the first section of the poem resonate with imagery of nature as symbol and occasion of ritual. Rooted in the everyday, the poet superimposes mythic prehistory onto the common life of women:

smelling the rains before they came
feeling the fullness of the moon
before moonrise

unbalanced by the life
moving in us, then lightened
yet weighted still

by children on our backs
at our hips, as we made fire
scooped clay   lifted water

Remind me how the stream
wetted the clay between our palms
and how the flame

licked it to mineral colors
how we traced our signs by torchlight
in the deep chambers of the caves

(*DCL*, p. 47)

Fire, food, pottery, agriculture, art, childbirth, and childrearing constitute the ritual of women's everyday life and their contribution to civilization in the prehistorical period. Rich's memories move backwards in time through the "spiral stair" to the "enthroned" mother of personal and mythic prehistory. Similarly, H.D.'s Mary reveals the "message" of Atlantis "through spiral upon spiral of the shell / of memory that yet connects us / with the drowned cities of pre-history" (*T*, p. 156). In the "kingdom of the fathers," the power of the mother, of women, has been contained, defiled, or ignored. Both poets seek to unveil that power by returning to the mother as symbol of creative regeneration. Rich concludes "Sibling Mysteries":

> The daughters never were
> true brides of the father
>
> the daughters were to begin with
> brides of the mother
>
> then brides of each other
> under a different law
>
> Let me hold and tell you
>
> (*DCL*, p. 52)

Rich's conclusion for "Sibling Mysteries" emphasizes a lesbian-feminist dimension in her mythos of the mother and ultimately points to the final aspect of her bond with H.D. that I will examine. A major concern of Rich's essays and poems written after *Diving into the Wreck* is the relationships between women—not only mothers and daughters, but also friends and lovers. A poem like "Dialogue" (1972), about two women attempting to speak authentically about their lives, suggests the direction Rich's feminism was to take. So also do the central themes of isolation and the desire for human relation, connectedness, and communication in all her earlier volumes. But more than these earlier works, *The Dream of a Common Language* fuses her commitment to women and "the drive to connect," as she defines her tasks in "Origins and History of Consciousness" (1972–1974).[26] Among feminist writers—theorists and artists—Rich is especially insistent that the birth of woman's Self involves the abandonment of an individualistic ethos and the recognition of the Self's existence in relationship to others, most particularly women. Woolf's well-known call for women writers to explore women's relationships with each other (in *A Room of One's Own*) was certainly important to Rich, for she discusses the implication of Woolf's essay in her own "Conditions for Work: The Common World of Women" (*LSS*, p. 209). But H.D.'s memoir, *Tribute to Freud,* and the example of her life, have been at least as important. In the same essay, Rich uses H.D.'s account of her relationship to Bryher as her example of women's networking:

> Working together as women, . . . we can confront the problems of women's relationships, the mothers we came from, the sisters with whom we were forced to divide the world, the daughters we love and fear. We can challenge and inspirit each other . . . stand by and give courage at the birth throes of one another's insights. I think of the poet H.D.'s account of the vision she had on the island of Corfu, in the *Tribute to Freud.* (*LSS*, pp. 208–9)

Rich continues by quoting at length from H.D.'s account of the flickering lights projected onto her hotel wall in Corfu in 1920. The lights composed a set of five distinct images which H.D. believed to be fundamentally important omens about her future destiny as a poet. Her desire to translate the meaning of this "writing-on-the-wall" was a major reason she went into analysis with Freud some fourteen years later. Since H.D. herself considered these visions to be so essential to her life and art, many critics have discussed their significance. But no one has seen the Corfu visions from the woman-identified perspective Rich demonstrates. What Rich chooses to highlight reveals her own concerns and thus the particular aspect of H.D. which has influenced her. Rich notes that the woman, Bryher, who saved H.D.'s life and that of her infant daughter in 1919, sat beside H.D. during the course of the vision and in fact completed it for her. After watching the first four light-pictures take shape, H.D. concluded by saying "we were 'seeing' it together, for without her, admittedly, I could not have gone on." Rich may well be among those "who would mistrust the visionary experience," for H.D.'s deeply religious bent is not characteristic of Rich. But regarding the episode as "metaphor," Rich concludes:

> The personal relationship helps create the conditions for work (out of her vision H.D. went on to create her great, late, long poems celebrating a matriarchal world and the quests of female heroes); no less does the fact of working together deepen and sustain a personal relationship. (*LSS*, p. 209)[27]

Poems like "Phantasia for Elvira Shatayev" (1974) and "Paula Becker to Clara Westhoff" (1975–1976) explore the interconnections between women's authentic friendship and their heroic or creative work. Out of this matrix of women's relation comes "the unfinished   the unbegun / the possible" (*DCL*, p. 5). Breaking the "separateness" between women created by the patriarchy, women begin to touch their real strength and power. Love between women—love which is utterly separate from men, as the grieving, but irrelevant husband of "Phantasia for Elvira Shatayev" demonstrates—is the energizing force which makes transformation possible. For Rich, this love is ultimately lesbian—not in a reductionistic, genital sense, but in terms of women's whole being, body and soul in reaction against the patriarchy. As she wrote in "It Is the Lesbian in Us . . ." (1976),

> I believe it is the lesbian in every woman who is compelled by female energy, who gravitates toward strong women, who seeks a literature that will express that energy and strength. It is the lesbian in us who drives us to feel imaginatively, render in language, grasp, the full connection between woman and woman. It is the lesbian in us who is creative, for the dutiful daughter of the fathers in us is only a hack (*LSS*, pp. 200–201).[28]

The structure of *The Dream of a Common Language,* a volume of separate poems which nonetheless constitute a whole, embodies Rich's theory that authentic women's relationships in a patriarchy are essentially lesbian. "Twenty-One Love Poems," first published as a separate volume, occupies the center of this three-part volume. Set mainly in the city which represents the patriarchy, these poems explore how "two lovers of one gender,/ . . . two women of one generation" attempt to live, love, and work together, an accomplishment "nothing in civilization has made simple" (*DCL*, pp. 31, 35). Rich avoids the reduction of lesbianism to sexuality (as words like "sexual preference" or "sexual orientation" inevitably suggest) by portraying a range of concerns about living, working, and relating in a hostile world. But "(THE FLOATING POEM, UNNUMBERED)," a poem celebrating the woman's body and making love with a woman, makes crystal clear that the erotic component of lesbian love is essential to Rich.

"Sibling Mysteries," the poem which most echoes H.D.'s work, explores the origins and significance of that erotic component in women's love for one another and thereby helps to define what Rich means by lesbian-feminism. The overlapping of psychological and mythic dimensions makes "Sibling Mysteries" a kind of antitext to the anthropological fantasy of Freud's *Totem and Taboo,* in which he reconstructed the Oedipal origins of male rivalry as a theory of social organization. Borrowing from yet transforming Freud, Rich's poem argues implicitly that the institution of heterosexuality results from the patriarchy's success in separating women from their mothers—in making the mother's flesh "taboo to us."[29] Accomplished symbolically, reunion with the mother—indeed the sensuous mother—fuses what has been sundered and allows women to escape "the kingdom of the fathers." Women have never been "true brides" of the father, and in recovering their love of the mother, they become "brides of each other / under a different law." The concluding line—"Let me hold and tell you"—refers specifically to the poet's blood sister, and by extension to all women. For Rich, reconstitution of the world with the mother at the center is inseparable from lesbianism. In "Transcendental Etude" (1977), Rich called this longing for the mother "homesickness" and connected the desire for the mother to the "homesickness for a woman, for ourselves." Love of the mother, of the woman-lover, of the woman-self represent different forms of the same woman-identified act. "Birth stripped our birthright from us, / tore us from a woman, from women, from ourselves," she wrote (*DCL*, p. 75). She yearned to be:

lifted breathtaken on her breast, to rock within her
—even if beaten back, stranded again, to apprehend
in a sudden brine-clear thought
trembling like the tiny, orbed, endangered
egg-sac of a new world:
This is what she was to me, and this
is how I can love myself—
as only a woman can love me.

(DCL, p. 76)

Wholeness as a woman comes through a whole love of woman:
body, soul, and intellect. And it is here that poetry begins: "a
whole new poetry beginning here" (*DCL*, p. 76). Woman-iden-
tified love between women, ultimately lesbian in its defiance of
the laws of the fathers, makes the poet's work possible, *The
Dream of a Common Language* argues throughout.

At first glance, it seems as if Rich's union of mother-love with
lesbianism separates her from H.D., demonstrating dimensions
of difference rather than similarity. While the goddesses in
H.D.'s epics represent her mother and symbolize the female
principle, they coexist with the poet's search for male forms of
divinity as well. As a deeply religious poet, H.D. accepted the
fundamental premise of hermetic tradition: the existence of an
androgynous Divine One transcending all dualisms, but man-
ifested in sometimes female, sometimes male iconography.[30]
The narratives of *Helen in Egypt* and *Heremetic Definition* are
profoundly heterosexual, and the only relationships between
women that H.D. explores are the mother-daughter bond repre-
sented by the goddesses and the tie between the sisters, Helen
and Clytaemnestra. It appears as if H.D.'s love for Bryher, the
women she lived with off and on from 1919 until her death, was
never the subject of her great epics.

However, a close look at H.D.'s life, her analysis with Freud,
and her unpublished texts reveals not only her underlying com-
mon bond with Rich, but also the light which Rich's probing
perspective sheds on H.D.'s own texts. Understood in the con-
text of his theory of psychosexual development, Freud's diag-
nosis of H.D.'s "mother-fixation" connects her desire for re-
union with the mother (about which H.D. openly wrote) with

lesbianism (about which H.D. did not openly write). H.D. and Freud extensively explored the living presence of her dead parents in all the outpourings of her unconscious—mainly her dreams and hallucinations, or "occult phenomena," as she called her daytime visions. According to H.D.'s account, Freud believed that H.D. "had not made the conventional transference from mother to father." In his essays Freud had argued that conscious or unconscious lesbian desire originates in a woman's wish to recreate the early mother-daughter bond. Unlike the girl who will achieve "normal" femininity by rejecting her mother and loving her father, the lesbian remains fixated in her early love for her mother and the women who serve as mother-substitutes.[31]

H.D. ignored the prescriptive norms which pervade Freud's concepts of "normal" femininity and complex-ridden "regressions" to the pre-Oedipal stage of psychosexual development. But she fully accepted that her unconscious desire for her mother was projected onto her love for women, predominantly Bryher and Frances Josepha Gregg. H.D. met Gregg while she was engaged to marry Ezra Pound in 1910. Instead of marrying Pound, H.D. went to Europe in 1911 with Gregg and Gregg's mother. Gregg's marriage and H.D.'s own marriage to poet Richard Aldington in 1913 did not halt her continued "infatuation," as she called it, and she wrote three unpublished novels exploring that love.[32] In 1918, while Aldington was in the trenches in France, H.D. met Bryher, who took "the place of Frances." H.D. was pregnant at the time, and her seemingly ideal marriage had dissolved in betrayal and bitterness. When H.D. contracted the killing influenza of 1919 during the last month of pregnancy, Bryher's care and promise of a trip to Greece saved H.D.'s life. Two months after the birth of Perdita, the two women spent an idyllic May in the Scilly Isles, where H.D.'s occult experiences first began. During their voyage to Greece in 1920, the experiences continued and finally culminated in the "writing-on-the-wall" at Corfu. At one point in analysis, H.D. told Freud "how happy I was at Corfu . . . I told him of Bryher's care of me, our walks and drives, and said the friendship seemed to have adjusted me to normal conditions of life.

Freud qualified, 'Not normal, so much as ideal.'"[33] Freud referred, no doubt, to his belief that the relationship between H.D. and Bryher fulfilled H.D.'s unconscious wish for the ideal fusion with her mother of the pre-Oedipal period. Freud further connected the psychic visions, which occurred in Bryher's presence, indeed with Bryher's aid, to the earliest layers of infantile desire when the ego is not yet differentiated from the object of its desire. Religious experience of all types, Freud believed, reproduced the unconscious wish for fusion with the mother. H.D.'s occult experiences, her love for Bryher, and her desire for her mother were all "symptoms," Freud said, of H.D.'s "mother-fixation," the motivating impulse of lesbianism.[34]

Rich's emphasis on H.D.'s and Bryher's love for each other in her reading of the Corfu incident may seem to some a gratuitous distortion of the significance of those visions for H.D. But in actuality, Rich's approach led her to be sensitive to a series of connections that H.D. never made openly in her published work. Love for Bryher reproduced her yearning for her mother, both of which inspired her artistic and religious vision. The woman–identified family constellation encoded in H.D.'s account of her Corfu experiences parallels the sisters' desire for the mother in Rich's "Sibling Mysteries" and "Transcendental Etude." A dream H.D. discussed extensively with Freud, but described in writing only to Bryher, demonstrates the extent of the connections H.D. made between the mother-daughter bond and her love for women. H.D. wrote to Bryher about her dream:

> . . . There was a giant moon, bigger than the sun. It was rainbow coloured and like a pool of rainbow in the sky. Enormous. As I looked, there was a dim figure of a woman in the moon. She was clothed with "samite, mystic, wonderful," if you know what I mean, draped in flowing rainbow coloured robes, seated like a madonna in a curved frame. But she was not Madonna in that sense, she was Greek, she was Artemis, yet she was pregnant. "O moon of my delight that knows no wane." I shouted to you and Joan to look. A bird crossed the surface, a dark pigeon, a dove. Freud tells me it is an almost

perfect mythological state, I was in. The moon, of course, equated mother, but it was "mother in heaven." You and Joan and I were a sort of band of sisters, the Graces or Fates.

Well, I give this just in outline, but evidently it meant that I had, in the uc-n [unconscious], completely turned about to a homo layer.[35]

H.D.'s account of her dream also clarifies that her potent goddess figures originate in the interlocking connections between her love for women and her desire for her mother. The moon goddess, Artemis, madonna of her dream, suggests the Lady of *Trilogy,* the Mother of her alchemical mythmaking, and the Mary of Atlantis. In earlier texts, H.D.'s mother-figures tended to be arbiters of convention, figures of respectability against whom the daughter must rebel. The goddesses who peopled her mythologically based poems were often distancing masks for H.D.'s own ideas or emotions rather than living presences of other women. Freud's theory of myths as the dream of the tribe, however, led H.D. to fuse the personal and the mythic, the mother-figure and the mother-symbol.

H.D.'s poetic explorations of female divinity were not only religious statements, but also recreations of her mother that encoded a celebration of her love for women. While in analysis with Freud, H.D. wrote a poem, "The Master," which she refused to publish at least partially because the connection between lesbianism and a woman-centered religion necessary for the world's survival is directly the subject of the poem. The poem begins in worship of Freud, who is "near to God."[36] But while this reverence is never denied, the poet explores the dimensions of her "anger with the old man," with his "man-strength" and "mysteries." "*Woman is perfect,*" she announces, not the castrated male of psychoanalytic theory. That perfection, sufficient unto itself, is erotically based, and by extension, serves as the center of a new religion in which Rhodocleia is "that Lord become woman"—that is, the Divine taking female form. Section 5 of "The Master" parallels Rich's "FLOATING POEM" in function:

She is a woman,
yet beyond woman,
yet in woman
her feet are the delicate pulse of the narcissus bud,
pushing from earth
(ah, where is your man-strength?)
. . . .
she conjures the hills;
"rhododendrons
awake,"
her feet
pulse,
the rhododendrons
wake
there is purple flower
between her marble, her birch-tree white
thighs,
or there is a red flower,
there is a rose flower
parted wide,
as her limbs fling wide in dance
ecstatic
Aphrodite,
there is a frail lavender flower
hidden in grass;

O God, what is it,
this flower
that in itself had power over the whole earth?
for she needs no man,
herself
is that dart and pulse of the male,
hands, feet, thighs,
herself perfect.

H.D.'s epics are not explicitly lesbian in the way the poem she
suppressed defiantly is. But the goddesses in *Trilogy* and *Helen in
Egypt* are encoded versions of H.D.'s exploration of her love for

women and her belief that they embody a principle of life which the violent world of patriarchy must learn to absorb and revere. They, as well as more explicit texts which H.D. did not publish, are consistent with the vision of *The Dream of a Common Language*. Rich, familiar only with the coded epics, was nonetheless attuned to aspects of H.D.'s work which have become definitively known only after the publication of *The Dream of a Common Language*.

The perspectives which Rich and H.D. share illuminate dimensions of their seemingly different work. The aspects of H.D.'s life and writings which Rich ignores are equally revealing, particularly of the change in Rich's perspective since the publication of *Diving into the Wreck*. In "Conditions for Work: The Common World of Women," Rich concluded her discussion of H.D. and Bryher's fruitful relationship with a warning against the trap the male mentor poses for women: such a man might appear to "guide and protect his female student or colleague," even seem "willing to share his power." But his guidance offers only the "*illusion* of power," that only "allow[s] her to live, work, perhaps succeed in the common world of men. But he has no key to the powers she might share with other women" (*LSS*, pp. 209–10).

Rich did not explicitly direct her comments at H.D., but given the significance of male mentors for H.D., she certainly could have. "The Master," which substitutes H.D.'s own gynocentrism for Freud's androcentrism, nonetheless remains a poem that testifies to his genius and continuing importance to her. Other men served as her mentors and companions as well. Aside from her father, Pound was the first; but at various points in her life Aldington, D. H. Lawrence, Kenneth Macpherson, Sir Hugh Dowding, and Norman Holmes Pearson were equally important. In H.D.'s life, companionship with these men often entangled her artistic, erotic, and religious selves with an intensity which equalled her involvements with women. Rachel Blau DuPlessis has argued convincingly that H.D.'s conflicted relationships with these male lovers and companions vitalized her art, particularly the long poems of the fifties. With Pound and Aldington, H.D. enacted what DuPlessis has called "romantic thralldom," the scripts of conventional heterosexual romance.

Entrapped in a love which victimizes women, H.D. repeatedly experienced her involvements with men as a pattern that began with attraction, moved to a companionship with love and work entwined, and concluded with male rejection and betrayal. Du-Plessis has analyzed the narrative structures of H.D.'s epics as her attempt to transform those destructive heterosexual relationships into ideal centers for work and love based on mutuality and equality. The male suitor, whose love is an attack in H.D.'s actual experience, becomes in her art a twin spirit who transcends the divisions of the patriarchal world into male and female, victim and victimizer.[37] Within this context, the poet invokes the protection of the Goddess to fortify herself as she makes her forays into the dangerous territory of heterosexuality.

H.D. never gave up the hope of finding or creating the ideal male companion, converted by her influence to a humanism based in a reverence for life symbolized by the Goddess. In *Helen in Egypt,* the pervasive twin imagery expresses that desire and the transformation of Achilles from a warlord into a worshiper of Eros. Isis is the major goddess with whom Helen is identified. In Egyptian religion, Isis is the twin, lover, and savior of Osiris. After Set dismembers Osiris, Isis travels the world over in search of her lost twin-husband. Her magic revives the scattered limbs of Osiris and together they rule the underworld. This myth of the twins Isis and Osiris infuses the human drama of Helen and Achilles in H.D.'s version of the Trojan War—not the story of the mother-daughter pair, Demeter and Korê. During the war, Achilles is the prototypical "War-Lord," the Hitler who has been promised world leadership until he watches Helen walk the ramparts. The glance he shares with Helen leads to his death in his one mortal spot and his rebirth as Osiris. But in the afterworld of Egypt where Helen and Achilles meet, both realize that "it was God's plan / to melt the icy fortress of the soul, / and free the man." Achilles's love for Helen, his worship of the Goddess in her, gives him life as "the new Mortal, / shedding his glory" (*HE*, p. 10). Reflecting concepts of androgyny H.D. adapted from both esoteric tradition and psychoanalysis, this liberation of Achilles from the masculine ethos and Helen's concurrent quest for wholeness represent H.D.'s desire to transcend all dualisms, especially the polarity of male and female. The birth of their child Euphorian, whose gender is not specified, symbolizes that desire for transcendence. Taken as a whole, the complex epic begins with a separation of male and female worlds, moves to an eloquent revaluation of woman as Eros, explores the oppositions of Eros and Thanatos within all individuals, and concludes with symbolic affirmations of transcendence.

Rich has never commented directly on this aspect of H.D.'s life and work, neither to question nor to condemn. In her treatment of women writers, Rich is ever the forgiving daughter or sister, simply emphasizing what she finds important and remaining silent about what she rejects. Consequently, Rich stresses H.D.'s matriarchal ethos and relationships with women and does not address her search for an androgynous male lover-companion or her belief in the potential transformation of men. But a number of poems in *The Dream of a Common Language* carry on a silent debate with H.D. and the position she represents. "Natural Resources" (1977), in particular, presents argument and imagery which oppose while they echo *Helen in Egypt*.

The unidentified dialogue with H.D. first takes the form of Rich's self-criticism, specifically of the perspective she argued in *Diving into the Wreck* and this volume's companion essay, "When We Dead Awaken: Writing as Re-Vision." Section 13 of "Natural Resources" opens with the declaration: "There are words I cannot choose again: / *humanism   androgyny*" (*DCL*, p. 66). Written in 1972, "The Stranger" presented the gender-free poet as the "androgyne / . . . the living mind you fail to describe / in your dead language." The sex of the diver in "Diving into the Wreck" (1972) is carefully left unspecified, so that both women and men could identify with the search for the "she-he," the potentially androgynous self wrecked by a sexually polarized world.[38] In "When We Dead Awaken," Rich called eloquently for the birth of women, but she also envisioned the potential and necessity for male transformation:

> I am curious and expectant about the future of the masculine consciousness. I feel in the work of the men whose poetry I read today a deep pessimism and fatalistic grief; and I wonder if it isn't the masculine side of what women have experienced,

the price of masculine dominance. One thing I am sure of: just as woman is becoming her own midwife, creating herself anew, so man will have to learn to gestate and give birth to his own subjectivity—something he has frequently wanted woman to do for him. We can go on trying to talk to each other, we can sometimes help each other . . . but women can no longer be primarily mothers and muses for men: we have our own work cut out for us.[39]

When Rich reprinted this essay in *On Lies, Secrets and Silence*, she left out this call for man's rebirth and rewrote her concluding paragraph. The emphasis on continuing masculine sterility in the 1979 version highlights the gulf which has opened between the radical "humanism" of *Diving into the Wreck* and the separatist lesbian-feminism of *The Dream of a Common Language*. This separation is not the "simplistic dyke separatism" which Rich described as tempting for lesbians, but ultimately too narrow to accomplish the broader goals of lesbian-feminism.[40] Rather, it emerges out of Rich's belief that women must devote all their creative energies to each other. Man's all-consuming need has required "women's blood for life / a woman's breast to lay its nightmare on" and has resulted in "women stooping to half our height" (*DCL*, pp. 63, 64). "Natural Resources" argues that women must develop the "impatience" of the spider's rebuilding as they "make and make again" a new way of being. Such impatience characterizes the poet's ironic interchange with the insensitive male interviewer and contrasts with the curiosity about masculine consciousness expressed in the early version of "When We Dead Awaken." In response to the interviewer's attempt to joke about a world of "women only," she wearily explains that she must live in two worlds—one in which women are "*absent*" (the larger patriarchal world) and one in which men are "*absent*" (the lesbian-feminist subculture). She does not portray this divided world as ideal; nor does she suggest that this chasm between the sexes is biologically inevitable. The "natural resources" mined and celebrated in the poem are products of culture, not nature.

The poet's exchange with the interviewer leads her to reflect in the following four sections on the experiences which have led to her present stance. The main diversion of women's energies from themselves has been their search for "the man-who-would-understand, / the lost brother, the twin" (DCL, p. 62). This twin imagery is probably an implicit reference to Helen in Egypt, where the twin-lovers Isis and Osiris provide the mythic formula for Helen and Achilles. Rich recalls that it was never the violent man who limited her potential in the past, but instead the "comrade/twin" whose "lifeline" matched her own. Rich's imagery echoes the lightning and arrow motifs associated with H.D.'s Achilles:

> It was never the rapist:
> it was the brother, lost,
>
> the comrade/twin whose palm
> would bear a lifeline like our own:
>
> decisive, arrowy,
> forked-lightning of insatiate desire
>
> It was never the crude pestle, the blind
> ramrod we were after:
>
> merely a fellow-creature
> with natural resources equal to our own[41]
>
> (DCL, p. 62)

Looking back at the woman who wrote Diving into the Wreck, the poet now sees that "comrade/twin" as a "phantom" who has divided her from other women even more thoroughly than the rapist. "For him did we leave our mothers, / deny our sisters, over and over?" she asks. "Did we invent him, conjure him?" Rich's question hovers over H.D.'s troubled relationships with men like Pound and Aldington and the brilliant poems she constructed out of that experience.

The exchange between Rich and H.D. is a literary dialogue of resonance and dissonance which highlights essential elements of each poet. Rich found in H.D. a literary foremother whose poetry presented a vast map of woman's place and woman's transformative power in patriarchal territory. H.D.'s achievement, as

Rich has seen it, is epitomized by the paradigmatic exchange between the pompous Mage and the "sinful" Mary Magdalene in the last volume of the *Trilogy,* the witty drama that Rich brought vividly to life in her reading. To man's assumption that woman is an "unseemly" presence to be silenced or dismissed at will, H.D. countered with an insistent female presence which subjects the very foundations of culture to a process of re-vision from a woman's perspective. In H.D.'s critique of culture, Rich found confirmation of her own growing analysis of the connections between worldwide violence and the oppression of women. H.D.'s matriarchal mythos and her celebration of women in the form of mother-symbols charted for Rich a pathway which connected the female iconographies of tradition and the personal dimensions of women's love for other women. For both poets, the mother as symbol and living presence is central for women's rebirth and for the regeneration of civilization. Whether highly coded or directly affirmed, love for the mother in both poets is part of a healing self-love and a sustaining lesbian love of other women. Here, however, in the very center of similarity, the two poets part ways.

H.D.'s regeneration of woman as symbol and self took place within a context which included men as mentors, lovers, or companions. She never gave up her search for "the man-who-would-understand," for the masculine forms of divinity which she balanced with the woman-symbols she had resurrected. In contrast, the growth of Rich's lesbian-feminism coincided with her disillusionment with the radical humanism pervading her poetry of the sixties and culminating in the androgyny of *Diving into the Wreck.* As she concludes "Natural Resources," the rainbow that flies "from the walls / of cloud" holds out promise to the poet regarding centuries of patriarchal destruction only when she makes her choice:

> I have to cast my lot with those
> who age after age, perversely,
>
> with no extraordinary power,
> reconstitute the world.

> (*DCL,* p. 67)

1. H.D., *Trilogy* (New York: New Directions, 1973), p. 115; here-after identified in the text as *T*. Hilda Doolittle (1886–1961), pen name H.D., first published the *Trilogy* in three separate volumes: *The Walls Do Not Fall* (1944), *Tribute to the Angels* (1945), and *The Flowering of the Rod* (1946). The epigram opens Adrienne Rich's *The Dream of a Common Language: Poems 1974–1977* (New York: Norton, 1978); hereafter *DCL*.

2. Virginia Woolf, *A Room of One's Own* (1929; New York: Harcourt, Brace & World, 1957), p. 101.

3. "Natural resources" is the major image for women's culture in Rich's poem "Natural Resources" (*DCL*, pp. 60–67).

4. Rich, *On Lies, Secrets and Silence: Selected Prose 1966–1978* (New York: Norton, 1979), p. 35; hereafter *LSS*.

5. See Carolyn Kizer's "Pro Femina" in *No More Masks! An Anthology of Poems by Women*, ed. Florence Howe and Ellen Bass (New York: Anchor, 1973), pp. 173–74.

6. See Harold Bloom, *The Anxiety of Influence* (New York: Oxford University Press, 1973).

7. Rich, *Of Women Born: Motherhood as Experience and Institution* (New York: Norton, 1976; pb. ed. New York: Bantam, 1977), p. 257; hereafter *OWB*. Sandra Gilbert and Susan Gubar have brilliantly adapted Bloom's family paradigm for literary creativity to the anomolous position of the woman writer in *The Madwoman in the Attic: The Woman Writer and the Nineteenth-Century Literary Imagination* (New Haven: Yale University Press, 1979). They use as well a mother-daughter paradigm to describe the subculture of women writers (pp. 50–51). See also Betsy Erkkila, "Emily Dickinson and Adrienne Rich: Dreaming of a Common Language," a paper read at the Modern Language Association meeting, December 1982.

8. See Rich, "The Tensions of Anne Bradstreet," in *LSS*, pp. 21–32 and her comments about her own early development in "When We Dead Awaken: Writing as Re-Vision," in *LSS*, pp. 44–47.

9. Rich, *LSS*, p. 37; *Diving into the Wreck: Poems 1971–1972* (New York: Norton, 1973). Rich's noncombative criticism of Woolf contrasts strongly with Elaine Showalter's treatment of Woolf in *A Literature of Their Own* (Princeton: Princeton University Press, 1977). See also Rich, "Vesuvius at Home: The Power of Emily Dickinson," in *LSS*, pp. 157–83 and the theme of caged power in *DCL*.

10. Rich's discussions of H.D. are in "When We Dead Awaken," *LSS*, pp. 39, 40; "Conditions for Work: The Common World of

Women," in *LSS*, pp. 208–9; "Power and Danger: The Work of a Common Woman," in *LSS*, pp. 247, 256–57. Rich also read selections from the *Trilogy* and spoke about H.D. at "Tribute to H.D.," an evening sponsored by the Manhattan Theatre Club, May 16, 1978.

11. This essay stresses the change in Rich's thought, but for excellent discussions of important continuities in her poetry, see especially Albert Gelpi, "Adrienne Rich: The Poetics of Change" in *Adrienne Rich's Poetry*, ed. Barbara Charlesworth Gelpi and Albert Gelpi (New York: Norton, 1975), pp. 130–47 and Judith McDaniel, "Reconstituting the World. . .," reprinted in this collection, pp. 3–29.

12. Rich, *LSS*, pp. 83–84. See also pp. 195–97, 215–22, 259–74; and Wendy Martin, "From Patriarchy to the Female Principle: A Chronological Reading of Adrienne Rich's Poems" in *Adrienne Rich's Poetry*, ed. Gelpi and Gelpi, pp. 175–88.

13. Rich, *Diving into the Wreck*, pp. 3–4. For her explicitly theoretical statement connecting the violence of war with violence against women, see "Vietnam and Sexual Violence," in *LSS*, pp. 108–116.

14. See Rich, "The Antifeminist Woman," in *LSS*, p. 80.

15. Rich, *OWB*, p. 80. See also *OWB*, pp. 70–97 and *LSS*, pp. 75–77.

16. See especially H.D., *Helen in Egypt* (1961; New York: New Directions, 1974); hereafter *HE*. H.D. read widely in psychoanalysis, experienced some five months of daily analysis with Freud in 1933 and 1934, and referred specifically to his theories of Eros and the death instinct in her memoir, *Tribute to Freud* (1956; Boston: David R. Godine, 1974), p. 103. For extensive discussion of H.D.'s analysis with Freud and her exploration of these and other issues referred to in this essay, see Susan Stanford Friedman, *Psyche Reborn: The Emergence of H.D.* (Bloomington: Indiana University Press, 1981).

17. See for example H.D.'s alchemical purification of Astarte and Venus, the revelation induced by the Goddess's flowering bush, and the story of Mary Magdalene in *T.*, pp. 74–78, 82–87, 130–72. See also Susan Gubar's "The Echoing Spells in H.D.'s *Trilogy*," in *Contemporary Literature* 19 (Spring 1978): 196–218.

18. See for example "Not Somewhere Else, but Here," "Upper Broadway," and "Nights and Days" in *DCL*, pp. 39–46. See "Teaching Language in Open Admissions" for the special meaning the city has for her: "The city as object of love, a love not unmixed with horror and anger, the city as Baudelaire and Rilke had previsioned it . . . death in life, but a death emblematic of the death that is epidemic in modern society, and a life more edged, more costly, more charged with knowledge, than life elsewhere. Love as . . . energy draining but also energy

replenishing . . ." (*LSS*, p. 54). Rich's emblematic treatment of the city predates *DCL*. See for example "The Stranger," with its echoes of T. S. Eliot's "The Love Song of J. Alfred Prufrock," in *Diving into the Wreck*, p. 19.

19. In some ten pages of notes H.D. took, probably during her visit to Greece in 1932, she noted "Schleimann said Atlantis is Crete" and that "women [are] equal" in Crete; in her "Autobiographical Notes" (no page number) in the Collection of American Literature, Beinecke Rare Book and Manuscript Library, Yale University. H.D.'s "tale of jars" is mostly her own invention, but she followed a common cult of the Middle Ages in collapsing into one the three Marys of the New Testament: Mary, the virgin mother of Jesus; Mary Magdalene, the adulteress to whom Jesus revealed himself after death; Mary, sister of Martha who complained to Jesus that Mary should help her in the kitchen rather than listen to Jesus. H.D.'s symbolic fusion of Marys (the mother, the whore, the intellectual) into one woman emphasizes the prototypical nature of Mary's confrontation with Kaspar.

20. See Rich, *LSS*, pp. 73–76 and *OWB*, pp. 70–97.

21. See Rich, *OWB*, pp. 70–80 for her feminist critique of these writers.

22. H.D., *Tribute to Freud*, pp. 43–44; Rich, *OWB*, pp. 219–20.

23. H.D., *End to Torment* (New York: New Directions, 1979), p. 41.

24. In her "Ghazals," Rich had already experimented with couplets and three-line stanzas inspired by Urdu poet Mirza Ghalib (*Leaflets: Poems 1965–1968* [New York: Norton, 1969] and *The Will to Change: Poems 1968–1970* [New York: Norton, 1971]). Unlike these diffuse lines, the stanzas of "Sibling Mysteries" echo H.D.'s poetry because of their conciseness, directness and precision, qualities characteristic of imagist craft. For other formalist echoes of H.D.'s verse, see especially "Cartographies of Silence," "A Woman Dead in Her Forties," "Mother-Right," and "Natural Resources" in *DCL*.

25. For another discussion of the change in Rich's tone and language, see Joanne Feit Diehl, " 'Cartographies of Silence': Rich's *Common Language* and the Woman Poet," reprinted in this collection, pp. 91–110.

26. Rich, *Diving into the Wreck*, p. 21; "Origins and History of Consciousness," (*DCL*, pp. 7–9) reverses Erich Neumann's book of the same title by suggesting that "progress" will result from women's conscious separation from men rather than men's separation from women.

27. See H.D., *Tribute to Freud*, pp. 48–49.

28. See also Rich's insistence on a broad definition of lesbian/ femi-

nism: "It is . . . crucial that we understand lesbian/feminism in the deepest, most radical sense: as that love for ourselves and other women, that commitment to the freedom of all of us, which transcends the category of 'sexual preference' and the issue of civil rights, to become a politics of *asking women's questions* . . ." (*LSS*, p. 17).

29. Rich has subsequently developed her theoretical attack on the institution of heterosexuality in "Compulsory Heterosexuality and Lesbian Existence," *Signs* 5 (Summer 1980): 631–60.

30. Although hermetic tradition posits an androgynous Divine One, it is riddled by androcentric symbolism. As she did with psychoanalysis, H.D. had to remake this tradition from a woman's perspective.

31. See H.D., *Tribute to Freud*, p. 136; Freud, "The Psychogenesis of a Case of Homosexuality in a Woman" (1920), in *The Complete Psychological Works of Sigmund Freud* (London: Hogarth Press, 1950), vol. 2, pp. 201–31; Freud, "Femininity" (1933) in his *New Introductory Lectures*, trans. James Strachey (New York: Norton, 1965), pp. 112–35.

32. See H.D., *Tribute to Freud*, p. 152. One of these novels has just been published: *HERmione* (New York: New Directions, 1981). For extended discussion of these novels, see Susan Friedman and Rachel Blau DuPlessis, "'I Had Two Loves Separate': The Sexualities of H.D.'s *Her*," *Montemora* 8 (1981): 7–30.

33. H.D., *Tribute to Freud*, p. 168.

34. Freud, *Civilization and Its Discontents*, trans. James Strachey (New York: Norton, 1961), pp. 11–14.

35. H.D. to Bryher, 26 May 1933. H.D.'s letters to Bryher, 1918–1961, are at the Beinecke Library, Yale University.

36. H.D., "The Master" (1933–1935?), *Feminist Studies* 7 (Fall 1981): 408. See the article on the poem, "'Woman Is Perfect': H.D.'s Debate with Freud," by DuPlessis and Friedman, in the same issue, pp. 417–30.

37. Rachel Blau DuPlessis, "Romantic Thralldom in H.D.'s *Helen in Egypt*," *Contemporary Literature* 20 (Summer 1979): 178–203. DuPlessis has also developed this analysis brilliantly in her "Family, Sexes, Psyche: An Essay on H.D. and the Muse of the Woman Writer," *Montemora* 6 (1979): 137–56.

38. Rich, *Diving into the Wreck*, pp. 19, 22–24. Rich also used the term "androgyny" in her "Toward a Woman-Centered University" (1973–1974) and attacked feminist use of the term in her introductory notes to "Caryatid: Two Columns" (*LSS*, pp. 141, 108). See also her attack in *OWB*, p. 62n. Feminist theorists like Mary Daly and Janice Robinson have also renounced their early use of the term.

39. Rich, "When We Dead Awaken," in *Adrienne Rich's Poetry*, ed. Gelpi and Gelpi, p. 98.

40. Rich, "The Meaning of Our Love for Women Is What We Have Constantly to Expand," in *LSS*, pp. 223–30. "True separatism," Rich continued, "has yet to be adequately defined." See also Rich, "Compulsory Heterosexuality and Lesbian Existence," (n. 29 above) and "Notes for a Magazine: What Does Separatism Mean?" *Sinister Wisdom* 18 (Fall 1981): 83–91.

41. These lines may also be a deliberate answer to Sylvia Plath's famous lines in "Daddy" in reference to her father and husband: "Every woman adores a Fascist, / The boot in the face . . ." in *Ariel* (New York: Harper & Row, 1965), p. 50.

PART TWO   *Reviews of Rich's Poetry,*
            1951–81

W. H. AUDEN

Foreword to *A Change of World*

Reading a poem is an experience analogous to that of encounter-
ing a person. Just as one can think and speak separately of a
person's physical appearance, his mind, and his character, so one
can consider the formal aspects of a poem, its contents, and its
spirit while knowing that in the latter case no less than in the
former these different aspects are not really separate but an indis-
soluble trinity-in-unity.

We would rather that our friends were handsome than plain,
intelligent than stupid, but in the last analysis it is on account of
their character as persons that we accept or reject them. Similar-
ly, in poetry we can put up with a good deal, with poems that
are structurally defective, with poems that say nothing particu-
larly new or "amusing," with poems that are a bit crazy; but a
poem that is dishonest and pretends to be something other than
it is, a poem that is, as it were, so obsessed with itself that it
ignores or bellows at or goes on relentlessly boring the reader,
we avoid if possible. In art as in life, truthfulness is an absolute
essential, good manners of enormous importance.

Every age has its characteristic faults, its typical temptation to
overemphasize some virtue at the expense of others, and the
typical danger for poets in our age is, perhaps, the desire to be
"original." This is natural, for who in his daydreams does not
prefer to see himself as a leader rather than a follower, an ex-
plorer rather than a cultivator and a settler? Unfortunately, the
possibility of realizing such a dream is limited, not only by talent
but also by time, and even a superior gift cannot cancel historical
priority; he who today climbs the Matterhorn, though he be the

First published in the Yale Series of Younger Poets, edited by W. H. Auden
(New Haven: Yale University Press, 1951). Copyright 1967, 1979 by Adrienne
Rich. Reprinted by permission of Adrienne Rich.

greatest climber who ever lived, must tread in Whymper's footsteps.

Radical changes and significant novelty in artistic style can only occur when there has been a radical change in human sensibility to require them. The spectacular events of the present time must not blind us to the fact that we are living not at the beginning but in the middle of a historical epoch; they are not novel but repetitions on a vastly enlarged scale and at a violently accelerated tempo of events which took place long since.

Every poet under fifty-five cherishes, I suspect, a secret grudge against Providence for not getting him born a little earlier. On writing down the obvious names which would occur to everyone as those of the great figures in "modern" poetry, novels, painting, and music, the innovators, the creators of the new style, I find myself with a list of twenty persons: of these, four were born in the sixties, six in the seventies, and ten in the eighties. It was these men who were driven to find a new style which could cope with such changes in our civilization as, to mention only four, the collapse of the liberal hope of peaceful change, of revolution through oratory and literature; the dissolution of the traditional community by industrial urbanization; the exposure of the artist to the styles of every epoch and culture simultaneously; and the skepticism induced by psychology and anthropology as to the face value of any emotion or belief.

Before a similar crop of revolutionary artists can appear again, there will have to be just such another cultural revolution replacing these attitudes with others. So long as the way in which we regard the world and feel about our existence remains in all essentials the same as that of our predecessors we must follow in their tradition; it would be just as dishonest for us to pretend that their style is inadequate to our needs as it would have been for them to be content with the style of the Victorians.

Miss Rich, who is, I understand, twenty-one years old, displays a modesty not so common at that age, which disclaims any extraordinary vision, and a love for her medium, a determination to ensure that whatever she writes shall, at least, not be shoddily made. In a young poet, as T. S. Eliot has observed, the most promising sign is craftmanship for it is evidence of a capacity for detachment from the self and its emotions without which no art is possible. Craftmanship includes, of course, not only a talent for versification but also an ear and an intuitive grasp of much subtler and more difficult matters like proportion, consistency of diction and tone, and the matching of these with the subject at hand; Miss Rich's poems rarely fail on any of these counts.

They make no attempt to conceal their family tree: "A Clock in the Square," for instance, is confessedly related to the poetry of Robert Frost, "Design in Living Colors" to the poetry of Yeats; but what they say is not a parrotlike imitation without understanding but the expression of a genuine personal experience.

The emotions which motivate them—the historical apprehension expressed in "Storm Warnings," the conflict between faith and doubt expressed in "For the Conjunction of Two Planets," the feeling of isolation expressed in "By No Means Native"—are not peculiar to Miss Rich but are among the typical experiences of our time; they are none the less for that uniquely felt by her.

I suggested at the beginning of this introduction that poems are analogous to persons; the poems a reader will encounter in this book are neatly and modestly dressed, speak quietly but do not mumble, respect their elders but are not cowed by them, and do not tell fibs: that, for a first volume, is a good deal.

DONALD HALL

A Diet of Dissatisfaction

Adrienne Cecile Rich is distinguished by her uncanny ability to write. Again and again her poetry communicates the peculiar excitement of exactness. Young poets of talent generally have one of two flaws; either they are afflicted with every kind of clumsiness, and must have their poems weeded clear of dead metaphors, extra feet, clichés, and dishonest rhetoric; either that, or they are gifted with easy competence and are plagued by not always sounding quite like themselves. Adrienne Cecile Rich falls into the second category, but she does not fall far. It is easy to greet several of her poems with familiarity: "How do you do, Mr. Frost? And you, Mr. Auden?" But even if one should decide to dismiss these poems (which would be foolish), there would be many left to which one could attach no name but the author's own.

The Diamond Cutters is Miss Rich's second volume, and it is superior to *A Change of World*. The earlier book was sometimes tame, and even a little smug about its ability to keep experience away from the door. In the second book, the wolf is inside and is busy writing poems about its successful campaign. Perhaps I can suggest the qualities of *The Diamond Cutters* by quoting a few passages; the first is from "Versailles," and the others from "Apology," "Living in Sin," "The Snow Queen," and "The Insomniacs," in order.

> Merely the landscape of a vanished whim,
> An artifice that lasts beyond the wish:
> The grotto by the pond, the gulping fish
> That round and round pretended islands swim,

Donald Hall's review of *The Diamond Cutters* first appeared in *Poetry* 87 (February 1956). Reprinted by permission of the author.

The creamery abandoned to its doves,
The empty shrine the guidebooks say is love's.

*

You told us little, and are done.
So might the dead
Begin to speak of dying, then
Leave half unsaid.
Silence like thunder bears its own
Excuse for dread.

*

By evening she was back in love again,
Though not so wholly but throughout the night
She woke sometimes to feel the daylight coming
Like a relentless milkman up the stairs.

*

Yet here the Snow Queen's cold prodigious will
Commands me, and your face has lost its power,
Dissolving to its opposite like the rest.
Under my ribs a diamond splinter now
Sticks, and has taken root; I know
Only this frozen spear that drives me through.

*

I speak a dream and turn to see
The sleepless night outstaring me.
My pillow sweats; I wake in space.
This is my hand before my face.
This is the headboard of my bed . . .

Precision and frequent profundity characterize the best of her verse, a verse which can be rigorous and charming at the same time. The range within her work, the variety of tones and styles which she can assume, is the most promising of her characteristics.

By definition, perfection is not promising; we have room to hope that this young American, gifted by her elders with a set of techniques not available to most previous generations, may extend the range of her performances still further. Miss Rich's problem is to find things she cannot with all her skill do, and then try to do them. If she should become satisfied with the poems she is writing, she could repeat them until doomsday, but growth will require a diet of dissatisfaction. Two things, perhaps, she can attempt: fewer adjectives (for these come to her easily, and may block her vision of her subject), and fewer poems whose content is familiar knowledge—like the fine poem "Orient Wheat," which informs us that old people always think the world has gone to hell. Greater profundity and greater strength are within her reach. Meantime, *The Diamond Cutters* is a marvelous collection of skills and insights.

PHILIP BOOTH

"Rethinking the World"

Taking her third book's title from a movingly complex long poem, "Snapshots of a Daughter-in-Law," Adrienne Rich has self-defined the deceptively simple tones and modes of these forty new poems. Written during the past eight years, when much new poetry has (as if after Auden's directive) sung of "human unsuccess" in a confessional "rapture of distress," Miss Rich's book is demandingly quiet in its tones and persuasively selfless in its fictions. If she is often distressed with what she defines as the problems of "knowing and being known, with the undertow and backlash of love and self-love," her agony is the quiet agony of what she calls "rethinking the world," and she is never self-pitying in this, the function and perfection of her poetry. The risk this book quietly takes, and impressively fulfills, is no less than to get life said.

As the fine poem of that title tells, "Merely to Know" the world is only to know emotional emptiness. But Adrienne Rich both knows and feels, and it is a sure measure of her poetry that it realizes historical knowledge and human emotion in equal, and interrelated, depth. "Readings of History," perhaps tactically influenced by Robert Lowell's new techniques, is wholly Miss Rich's in showing us "pieces of ourselves," and it is ourselves we most see in the candid focus of her many poems about women.

A lesser poet, moving between Europe and America as a tourist to those conditions in which Miss Rich has lived, might show us only himself, as if behind the camera of these apparently casual "snapshots." But Miss Rich's individually penetrating

First published in the *Christian Science Monitor*, January 3, 1963. Reprinted by permission from the *Christian Science Monitor*. Copyright © 1963 The Christian Science Publishing Society. All rights reserved.

intellect (unmistakable as it is) focuses always on her subject: the commonplaces of human experience seen from such uncommonly candid angles that even her most domestic images are raised to the nth power of universal implication.

Newly freed from the metrical conventions of her earlier books, Adrienne Rich has lost none of her perfect pitch for the tones of language itself; and her rhythms, if flatter than before, are still modulated with the utmost subtlety. What poet of lesser skills could possibly achieve the brilliant variety of "Rural Reflections," "Antinoüs: The Diaries," "Double Monologue," "A Woman Mourned By Daughters," and, climactically, "The Roofwalker"?

Deceptively simple as the skills of these poems seem, their excellence is greatly more than mere descriptive precision or verbal technique. Just as Henry James's novels—on a larger scale—are infinitely greater than the sum of their parts, so Adrienne Rich's poems compound themselves (by the human ways of poetry-beyond-formula) to become a civilized measure of man, woman, and civilization itself.

JOHN ASHBERY

Tradition and Talent

Adrienne Rich is a traditional poet, but not a conventional one.
She has made progress since those schoolgirlish days when she
would come home from a Bach concert worried that "A too-
compassionate art is half an art." Such rhetorical questions are
now left behind. She speaks in dense, short lines that suggest the
laconic exchanges of a couple who have outlived more elaborate
forms of communication, and she emerges as a kind of Emily
Dickinson of the suburbs, bleakly eyeing the pullulation and
pollution around her, sometimes being shocked into passionate
speech:

> Whatever you are that weeps
> over the blistered riverbeds
> and the cracked skin of cities,
> you are not on our side
>
> ("Spring Thunder")

or, in this beginning:

> Ailanthus, goldenrod, scrapiron, what makes you flower?
> What burns in the dump today?
>
> ("Open-Air Museum")

In lines like these, where inner and outer reality fuse into a kind
of living fabric, Miss Rich is . . . a metaphysical poet.
  Sometimes she does succumb to the mania for overinterpreta-
tion that plagues her contemporaries. (The technical term for

John Ashbery's review of *Necessities of Life* first appeared in the *New York Herald
Tribune Book Week,* September 4, 1966. Reprinted by permission of John Ash-
bery and Georges Borchardt, Inc. Copyright © 1966.

this ailment is *objective correlativitis*. It attacks poets in their late thirties, and is especially prevalent in New England; elms are thought to be carriers.) In "Breakfast in a Bowling Alley in Utica, New York," Miss Rich, appalled by the crumminess of her surroundings, chews a defrosted sandwich steak, "thinking of wheatfields— / a gold-beige ceinture—," trying to forget about TV aerials and mobile homes until she remembers that in one of the latter there is "perhaps, a man / alone with his girl / for the first time." Everybody's hell is different, but a reader conversant with those of Burroughs, Ginsberg, and Ed Sanders, for instance, is not likely to be shaken up by Miss Rich's bowling alley, or reassured by the couple in the trailer.

But it is not often her way to present us with problems which we have to make an effort to take seriously, followed by their imaginary solutions. In this hard and sinewy new poetry she has mastered the art of tacking between alternative resolutions of the poem's tension and of leaving the reader at the right moment, just as meaning is dawning. She does this beautifully in "Mourning Picture," based on Edwin Romanzo Elmer's primitive drawing of parents on a New England lawn watching the spirit of their dead child:

> I tell you, the thread that bound us lies
> faint as a web in the dew.
> Should I make you, world, again,
> could I give back the leaf its skeleton, the air
> its early-summer cloud, the house
> its noonday presence, shadowless,
> and leave *this* out? I am Effie, you were my dream.

DENIS DONOGHUE

Review of *Leaflets: Poems 1965–1968*

Adrienne Rich's leaflets are poems written between 1965 and
1968, a bad time for those Americans who would like to be
quiet. The poems come from "the panicky life-cycle of my
tribe," messages from underground. "I wake in the old cell-
block / observing the daily executions." Mostly, the verses are
anecdotes of loss, "the clear statement / of something missing":
"the eyes reflect something / like a lost country." And the defin-
itive figure is a stretching across the void, for sanctuary, hope-
fully for relation. "If I were only colder, / nearer death, nearer
birth, I might let go / whatever's so bent on staying lost."
   The source of whatever hope remains is the feeling that
"something wants us delivered up alive," tears may still mean
mercy. Several poems keep the works going until one hand
reaches toward another, as in "Nightbreak" and "The Demon
Lover," despite the bad time, "shivering here in the half-dark
sixties. . . . / The moon, cracked every which-way, / pushes
steadily on." I relate many of these poems to the "sweetness
hardly earned" which Miss Rich celebrated in the "Autumn
Sequence" of *Necessities of Life*.
   The formal invention in *Leaflets* is mainly found in the third
section, called "Ghazals: Homage to Ghalib," a long sequence
incited by Aijaz Ahmad's literal English versions of the work of
the Urdu poet Mirza Ghalib (1797–1869). Each ghazal consists
of a group of at least five unrhymed couplets, related not by plot
but by image and association. It is useless to read the couplets as
if they were aphorisms, luminous and final. Many of them are
tedious, if taken with a presumption of concentration and force;

First published in the *New York Review of Books*, May 7, 1970. Reprinted with
permission from the *New York Review of Books*. Copyright © 1970 Nyrev, Inc.

they work best when they are received like images in a symbolist poem, one image stretching across vacancy to the next.

It is clear that Miss Rich has invested heavily in this form, the pervading note is apocalyptic—"Someone has always been desperate, now it's our turn"—and the messages, bottled and thrown into the sea, are the cries of desolation heard in a different measure in other parts of the book. The continuity throughout the different forms and measures is based upon Miss Rich's feeling for the redemptive power of language, set off against the inescapable fact that there are limits to this power. "We are our words, and black and bruised and blue. / Under our skins, we're laughing." But, two stanzas back:

> *The world, we have to make it,*
> my coexistent friend said, leaning
> back in his cell.
> Siberia vastly hulks
> behind him, which he did not make.

This is Miss Rich's special area of feeling, the shadow falling between word and desire, word and need. When the shadow obliterates her world, she longs to be released from the old burdens, the past, memory, responsibilities. In two poems, the fox is her device for this longing: the animal is self-possessed, the only tense the present, free of ancient lore, archives, and heirlooms. The poems are "5:30 A.M." and, one of the most powerful things in the book, "Abnegation."

DAVID KALSTONE

Review of *The Will to Change:*
Poems 1968–1970

The Will to Change is an extraordinary book of poems and some-
thing else as well. It has the urgency of a prisoner's journal:
patient, laconic, eloquent, as if determined thoughts were set
down in stolen moments. It takes risks—as Adrienne Rich has
been doing in her recent collections, *Leaflets* (1969) and *Neces-
sities of Life* (1966)—in the name of "living through a time / that
needs to be lived through us." There are, of course, polished
poems in this book, the kind which will eventually detach them-
selves into anthologies.

But *The Will to Change* must be read whole: for its tough
distrust of completion and for its cool declaratives which fix us
with a stare more unsettling than the most hysterical questions.
The poems are dated by year, a way of limiting their claims;
they try to be faithful to their particular moment. It is hard to
imagine one hundred new poems being dropped retrospectively
into a second edition of this book, as they were into Robert
Lowell's *Notebook*. Miss Rich's poems don't overvalue the past
in that way; they are instruments of self-scrutiny and resolve in
the present. One doesn't turn back.

Distinctions fall away—Yeats's choice between perfection of
the life and perfection of the work, for example. These poems
would like, however composed they are, to fight off the notion
of finish and form, seeing them as the enemies of a candid en-
gaged life. "A language is a map of our failures." That sentence
comes up in "The Burning of Paper Instead of Children," itself a
powerful mixture of poetry and prose. A neighbor has called to

First published in the *New York Times Book Review*, May 23, 1971. Copyright ©
1971 by The New York Times Company. Reprinted by permission.

report the punishment of his son who, along with hers, has burned a mathematics text on the last day of school. He invokes memories of Hitler as his reason.

The poem that follows fights free of that automatic imprisoning memory and is itself a tribute and a challenge to the power of books over emotions and experience. It plays through moments with a lover, the desire and impossibility of shaking away acquired feelings: "Loneliness / relieved in a book / relived in a book"; it includes moments when poverty and heroism explode grammar with their own dignified unsyntactical demands. Its prose coda resumes at white heat phrases from the disciplined poem which precedes it:

Joan, who could not read, spoke some peasant form of French. Some of the suffering are: it is hard to tell the truth; this is America; I cannot touch you now. In America we have only the present tense. I am in danger. You are in danger. The burning of a book arouses no sensation in me. I know it hurts to burn. There are flames of napalm in Catonsville, Maryland. I know it hurts to burn. The typewriter is overheated, my mouth is burning, I cannot touch you and this is the oppressor's language.

When that remark about the "oppressor's language" occurs earlier in the poem, the speaker must counter "yet I need it to talk to you." The poems bristle with the difficulties of describing experience and with the necessity of burning through to do it:

> Our whole life a translation
> the permissible fibs
>
> and now a knot of lies
> eating at itself to get undone
>
> Words bitten thru words
>
> meanings burnt-off like paint
> under the blowtorch

What strikes me most about this book is its determination. To be stern with herself is Miss Rich's first condition for personal and political commitment. There is very little joy in this version of breaking free, partly because, as she has always been in her verse, Miss Rich is too much in touch with her feelings to be simple about them and because her poetry registers those complications. The poems are about departures, about the pain of breaking away from lovers and from an old sense of self. They discover the point where loneliness and politics touch, where the exercise of radical courage takes its inevitable toll.

There is some buoyancy in the opening poem, "November 1968":

> How you broke open, what sheathed you
> until this moment
> I know nothing about it
> my ignorance of you amazes me
> now that I watch you
> starting to give yourself away
> to the wind

But even here the watchful "I" is detached, puzzled, and on guard. After the initial stirrings, expectation is seldom pleasant, as the last deliberate images of the book suggest: "To pull yourself up by your own roots; to eat the last meal in / your old neighborhood."

What remains is a watchful honesty, for which, in its two distinct sections, the book struggles to find forms—among the short poems of the first part, letters, "images," a "photograph," pieces, and finally, taking up the whole second portion of the book, a "Shooting Script." The "Valediction Forbidding Mourning," which closes the first section, is only the most explicit of the continuing farewells in the volume, willing and wishing to give up illusion, and asking to use poetry in a new way: "They gave me a drug that slowed the healing of wounds." As if written under that drug and prompted by the desire to forget an old composure, the "Shooting Script" follows.

There are fourteen poems, more concerned perhaps with the

succession of images than with ordinary syntax, and designed to find a notation true to the movement of the feelings. These are spare instructions for a photographer of the inner self. A shooting script in another sense, they are a way of gunning out, of performing the ceremony of breaking free. The sentences are plain quick cuts in which images do the work: "They come to you with their descriptions of your soul. . . . / You hang among them like the icon in a Russian play; living your / own intenser life behind the lamp they light in front of you. . . . / You are a mirror lost in a brook, an eye reflecting a torrent of / reflections. / You are a letter written, folded, burnt to ash, and mailed in an / envelope to another continent."

The analogies to film and the grammatical liberties Miss Rich takes elsewhere are hardly new to poetry, but one finds them here in disciplined service. Syntactical irregularities become a means of self-interrogation, and this is Miss Rich's discovery; for her a way to probe—as a scene in an old house:

> To float like a dead man in a sea of dreams
> and half those dreams being dreamed by someone else.
>
> Fifteen years of sleepwalking with you,
> wading against the tide, and with the tide.

What must be imagined are the consequences of those bits of sentences. The fragments raise ghosts of questions and conclusions. Because of their incompleteness, they expose fears and loyalties at the same moment and have a prodding truth of their own. Miss Rich has committed her verse to exposing the rhythm and feel of such hidden experience. It means giving up a great deal of the formative power of poetry, its ways of judging and ordering outside experience, in the name of poetry as an instrument of personal survival.

A critical friend objects that *The Will to Change* is self-enclosed. Yes, but it is also an example of rare self-discipline. What Miss Rich settles for is a method more modest, less earth-shaking than that of the early astronomers she praises in "Planetarium." If they are "levitating into the night sky / riding the polished lenses," she remains in a modern world

                    an instrument in the shape
        of a woman trying to translate pulsations
        into images   for the relief of the body
        and the reconstruction of the mind.

Her method is courageous and radical in intention. What she reveals is something more troubling and with consequences she might not at all endorse. The exposure of the pitfalls of language and of our capacity to deceive ourselves is a force deeply subversive of radical politics, to which many of these poems are committed, or indeed of any politics at all. That may, disconcertingly enough, be what makes them such good poems.

CHERYL WALKER

"Trying to Save the Skein"

There can be no doubt now that the women's movement has
had its effect on the lives of countless unknown women. Alert to
this fact, I find myself collecting odd statistics, rags of evidence I
can use or dispose of. A tracer of missing persons informs the
New York Times that in twelve years the ratio of runaway wives
to husbands has gone from one out of three hundred to one out
of two; he explains this by saying that the women's liberation
movement has given housewives who would once have suffered
in silence the courage to express their misery and frustration.
The results on the whole seem to be positive. . . .

In the literary world this process sometimes produces unusual
results. I've been watching with fascination lately one queer and
wonderful phenomenon in articles by women critics. The writer
begins in an elegant literary style, making observations full of
intelligence and insight. I am often struck by the extent of her
sophistication, the depth of her background. But suddenly the
writer (it might be Elizabeth Hardwick reviewing Doris Lessing
or Grace Schulman surveying European poetry) breaks off and
begins to speak, from the perspective of her own life, about the
problems which make literature more than an intellectual exer-
cise. So it seems that after much truck with distance and objec-
tivity, it's the proximate and subjective which govern our reac-
tions. Everywhere women are admitting this openly or in so
many words, as the women's movement encourages us to ex-
amine our lives and reconsider our premises.

Of course, criticism of this kind is somewhat disorderly. It
lacks clean lines and, like the housewife's flight and the career
women's complaint, it cannot be considered modest behavior.

Cheryl Walker's review of *Diving into the Wreck* was first published in *The Nation*,
October 3, 1973. Copyright 1973 *Nation* magazine, The Nation Associates, Inc.

But that must be why it is so compelling. For now we know we can no longer shut our eyes to those trivial personal considerations behind our acts and judgments. It has become clear that these are not trivial considerations at all, but the uneven foundations on which all our structures sit. And more than that, we have learned that we share those foundations with our neighbors. George Eliot wrote, "There is no private life which is not determined by a wider public life." And that is more true than ever right now.

Poets too are searching past and present, renouncing art as camouflage, taking risks. Adrienne Rich calls her seventh book *Diving into the Wreck*. If it were not the case that Robert Boyers in a recent article in *Salmagundi* (Spring/Summer 1973) managed to discuss Rich's work at length without ever dealing with the importance of feminism for this poet, it would hardly seem necessary to say that *Diving into the Wreck* is one more reflection of what intelligent women are feeling and thinking today because of the women's movement. Boyers severely criticizes Rich for her recent failures to respect poetic decorum. He prefers her earlier poetry which, he feels, does not "dismiss orderliness and the clean lines of a modest behavior for undifferentiated passion. The lust to be contemporary has not yet become dangerously compelling."

"The lust to be contemporary." What can that mean? I suspect that if those terms can be applied to Adrienne Rich at all, their application must not imply a merely superficial commitment to the ideals of radical feminism (for this is certainly not true of her) but a desire to identify correctly and face unflinchingly the trials of contemporary life, whatever the cost. Her anger is directed against those who would hide in tradition and decorum, refusing, like the husband in her poem "A Primary Ground," to acknowledge the evasions of their behavior:

> Sensuality desiccates in words—
> risks of the portage, risks of the glacier
> never taken
> Protection is the genius of your house
> the pressure of the steam iron
> flattens the linen cloth again

> chestnuts puréed with care are dutifully eaten
> in every room the furniture reflects you
> larger than life, or dwindling

The poetry of *Diving into the Wreck* is a poetry of risk, of search and of appetite. It has the fierce quality of certain poems by the more gifted women poets of the past but, unlike them, Adrienne Rich is on guard against her own swings of emotion. She knows too well the perils of a rage "driving / now out upon men and women / now inward upon myself." What she seeks is clarity:

> my visionary anger cleansing my sight
> and the detailed perceptions of mercy
> flowering from that anger

The risk is the risk of exploring an unknown environment, where the most trivial activities must be handled, and will become accomplishments. The search is a search for the means of survival. This poetry is deadly serious, but it is not, like so much of women's poetry in the past, death-enamored. For it is the poet's appetite, her undeniable life force, which sustains these operations. Her image is repeatedly one of a mind like a fire:

> burning itself, burning down
>
> feeding on everything
> till there is nothing in life
> that has not fed that fire

Some, I'm sure, will object to the use of the self in these poems. The poet says:

> if they ask me my identity
> what can I say but
> I am the androgyne
> I am the living mind you fail to describe
> in your dead language

What is this but self-aggrandizement and self-congratulation, some will ask, not realizing that the process women are undergoing today requires coming into a new relation to the self, requires the self-love which is not narcissism. I remember particularly two things Adrienne Rich has said: one, that she would like to write poetry which could be useful to women, and two, that the only real maturity is one in which the self is so small it disappears and so large it encompasses a great many more than one. Thus the figure, the "I," which recurs in these poems, both is and is not Adrienne Rich. In the title poem, "Diving into the Wreck," surely one of the most beautiful poems to come out of the women's movement, the explorer—simultaneously male and female—achieves something close to a mythic density. The figure is passionate but with an isolation and passion transparent to the universal. The poem is utterly personal but there is nothing in it which draws away into private life.

> I came to explore the wreck.
> The words are purposes.
> The words are maps.
> I came to see the damage that was done
> and the treasures that prevail.
> I stroke the beam of my lamp
> slowly along the flank
> of something more permanent
> than fish or weed
>
> the thing I came for:
> the wreck and not the story of the wreck
> the thing itself and not the myth
> the drowned face always staring
> toward the sun
> the evidence of damage
> worn by salt and sway into this threadbare beauty
> the ribs of the disaster
> curving their assertion
> among the tentative haunters.

Because *Diving into the Wreck* is really a log of encounters with the disasters that foster consciousness, some of its materials may strike the reader as defensive. The poem which begins, "You're wondering if I'm lonely: / OK then, yes, I'm lonely," has this quality in spite of its strength. Then too there are areas of unconverted language, poetry which falls short of tension or definition. "The Phenomenology of Anger" strikes me this way, for instance. These are literary weaknesses. But the strength of this book is not only literary but political. The love for another woman which invigorates "When We Dead Awaken" is useful in the way the poet has wished to be of use. I find myself searching my own life for that

> . . . fellow-creature, sister,
> sitting across from me, dark with love,
> working like me to pick apart
> working with me to remake
> this trailing knitted thing, this cloth of darkness,
> this woman's garment, trying to save the skein.

Few feminist poets can equal this in sheer manipulation of language, and most nonfeminist poetry seems tame or solipsistic compared to the jugular intensity of this enterprise.

In *Diving into the Wreck* we have another valuable book to add to the community of works about women's developing consciousness. All of these works share a dark, tentative atmosphere of exploration. For some this tentative quality will disqualify Adrienne Rich from serious consideration. Why is this true, I wonder, remembering a critic I admire who remarked to me after reading Ingrid Bengis's fine *Combat in the Erogenous Zone:* "I don't understand what she's writing about. These are nothing but complaints." Perhaps it is true that the complaint, the lament, is endemic to women's literature at this time. But as Rilke wrote:

> Jubilance *knows,* and Longing sits confessing,—
> only Lament is learning still; with girlish hands
> she reckons all night long the ancient evil.

Yet suddenly, oblique, unpracticed, even so
she holds a constellation of our voice
into the sky, unclouded by her breath.

So, too, does Adrienne Rich, and I, for one, must thank her.

ROSEMARY TONKS

Cutting the Marble

In order to understand [Adrienne Rich], we must go into a certain room in Manhattan where a light is on over a table. A serious woman is sitting there, writing a lesson, which is the lesson of her life. On the paper we observe free verse stanzas in a near-colloquial idiom with a somewhat scientific vocabulary; they have an anonymous appearance. An occasional cockney rhyme (sister/glamor) comes up. Reading the lines gives us the illusion, at moments, of having gained an objective picture of events, even of our own thoughts:

> In a bookstore on the East Side
> I read a veteran's testimony

introduces a fact, and related materials are used to describe thought later in the poem:

> Pieces of information, like this one
> blow onto the heap

This is well done, so that we really believe while we are reading it that it is how thoughts behave. In this instance the idiom has justified its impersonal quality by an ability to produce convincing objective effects. It is the clean diction used by all good reporters (the method of Tolstoy when he is reporting), and it is insidious because of its invisibility. The subjective factor, with all its distortions, appears to have been edited out.

Rosemary Tonks's review of *Diving into the Wreck* first appeared in the *New York Review of Books,* October 4, 1973. Reprinted with permission from the *New York Review of Books.* Copyright © 1973 Nyrev, Inc.

What we think of *as* diction is something that brings us quickly to the boil on an instinctive level by throwing colored words at us in a way for which we are unprepared, as in the writing of Rimbaud or of Gerard Manley Hopkins; or a rigid, thrilling block of modern words, with a granite frost on it, which smashes us intellectually, like a phrase of Robert Lowell's. Diction can then be identified by the autonomous life it leads; the poetry is already partly about the way it is written, and it becomes more difficult to paraphrase the content away from the page.

When a poet takes up a simpler idiom, like the one used by Adrienne Rich, subjects are of great importance. The presumption is that the poet has especially chosen a line that will allow her to cover ground of all kinds. Even so, we must be moderate in the expectations we form, for there are other difficulties in such a line—which, although fragmented, could be called a narrative line—and I shall try to show some of them. It becomes dangerous, rather than insidious, when there is insufficient fresh material within it; originally it did the work of prose and tends to be one-dimensional.

We must examine what is going on in the poems.

A cast of three or four men and women is living a life very close to the life of the newspapers; Manhattan is a living newspaper. There are refrigerators, airplanes, phone booths, hypodermics, chemicals, molecules, bombs—and subways, prisons, *rooms* where people all over the world become careworn in their efforts to face up to reality. But because these people, places, and objects are so little distinguished and personalized, we have to read minutely to assemble the essential data from which the story will begin.

There is a reason for this. The poet is careful not to impose herself on the landscape. She tries, on the contrary, to read exactly the meaning which is there, and no more, and to reproduce it without inflation. At times, a deliberately conventionalized sensibility is in fact placed so squarely before its public subject matter that we can check our emotional attitudes by it, to see whether we have them right, so to speak, as if we were checking our watches by a world clock. In the poem already quoted from, called "Burning Oneself In," we note

        the running down, for no reason
        of an old woman in South Vietnam
        by a U.S. Army truck

brings about the humane but unexceptional (and slightly ambiguous) comment at the end of the poem:

        in bookstores, in the parks
        however we may scream we are
        suffering quietly

In Miss Rich's work, the moral proportions are valid, the protagonists are sane, responsible persons, and the themes are moving on their courses. Why is it then that we are still waiting for the poetry? At once it's obvious what has happened. She has taken on too much, and the imagination is exhausted by the effort required to familiarize itself with all the burdens of the modern world. The syntax is not there to reinvent the material, is not allowed to do so, but only to expose it. Therefore everything hangs on the uniqueness of the poet's personal contribution.

But she has almost edited herself out of the picture in her initial effort to "get it right." Furthermore, as we continue to read the "narrative" line she is using, we notice that it is far more intractable than we had thought. What it can do to present facts it does very well. But once its basic character has been established in her poetry as a character of situation and event, the tone of the poetry sets hard, and it is extremely difficult to get anything else in. The line goes on quietly forcing the poet to produce more and more objective pictures in the interests of drama, tension, and news. It asks for the next action, the next scene, perhaps for the next statement—but not for the next *thought*. It would be impossible, for example, for an idea to be argued through to a conclusion. Similarly, the lines can never have finish. It is not, regretfully we admit it, the ideal classical modern line, which can do every kind of work and for which we are searching; the one with which we can talk and think—cutting the marble with what Norman Douglas called "the thought-laden chisel of Lysippus."

The only way thought and feeling can be introduced at all is on the same descriptive terms as material objects. And this, as I have shown in the first quotation, is exactly what the poet has had to do. They must match in kind and degree, or the line will not tolerate them. From now on she can only think in a certain way. The inner world that she shows us occasionally is furnished then in much the same way as the outer world; although a transfer of material objects into mental counterparts does not necessarily guarantee that we are inside, for the soul has its own landscapes.

We may perhaps conclude that the basic fault of this book lies in the nature of a subject matter already familiar being joined to impersonality of presentation: the result is abstraction, or politics.

Now the actual poetry in the book is elsewhere. It's entirely personal, and is to do with psychological survival. It appears out of nowhere, almost by accident:

> Nothing can be done
> but by inches. I write out my life
> hour by hour, word by word

and in another poem whose intention is hard to follow, but which is in general a series of pictures and comments on the poet's afflictions:

> You give up keeping track of anniversaries,
> You begin to write in your diaries
> more honestly than ever.

That is a personal admission which we find illuminating because it tells us something useful about ourselves. We know that the private face that has been turned away from us is the one that can tell us things we need to know. From this snatch, we understand that the poet is rebuilding herself; the mind is still tough and fresh, even after the intellectual toil of taking on emotions not its own, as in this good descriptive piece:

> Walking Amsterdam Avenue
> I find myself in tears

> without knowing which thought
> forced water to my eyes

It goes on, "To speak to another human / becomes a risk." The tears are said to be evoked by a sense of outrage at certain inhuman aspects of life today, according to the poem. Tears of rage can come to our eyes in the street, but usually, if we are scrupulously truthful, from less abstract causes.

At the end of the book is a section on *The Wild Boy of Aveyron*. Psychologically, it is most revealing. Some people may have read the book by J-M Itard, or seen the film by Francois Truffaut, *L'Enfant Sauvage*. Briefly, a child left for dead in the woods in eighteenth-century France manages to survive. Some years later he is discovered, caught, and brought back into society; a human wild animal. In the film (an extraordinary film leaving an indelible impression) we are shown the child reacting to rain falling on his head, to the taste of milk, and to the safety of the forests, with their hiding places, for they alone are trustworthy.

This child is the helpless animal within every lonely alienated human creature, every poet, who from early days has found himself cut off from the minds of his fellows. He does not know how to make contact with them; his only relationship is with Nature. I suspect that it's for this reason above all others that he has entered Miss Rich's imagination.

We can see that when her intellect and her ethics have got her into a corner once again in the name of poetry, and there seems to be no way out, nevertheless she manages to write in her lesson-book:

> stones on my table, carried by hand
> from scenes I trusted

This is not from the section on the wild boy; but they are certainly the stones touched, or carried, by the hand of the wild boy of Aveyron. In an attempt at wholeness the urban citizens must engross his experience within herself, for it is the part of her own story which is missing, and this is the moment in life when she needs it for her survival. In order to go back to the necessary depth, she takes the only route available from her room in the city, and makes the journey at night in her dreams:

> The most primitive part
> I go back into at night
> pushing the leathern curtain
> with naked fingers
> then
> with naked body

The regression is to an almost subhuman ancestor, frightening to consciousness, but essential to *spirit*. The day consciousness of the poet appears to stand in direct opposition to the unconscious dreamer of the night—the compensating self, who is doing all the real work, and who rights the balance by releasing buried aspects of her personality. It's no wonder that while this vital process of unification was going on, the poetry regularly escaped from stanzas about current affairs. If we carelessly forget that Orpheus was especially famous for playing to wild beasts, trees, and stones, the myth which is active within us will remind us of its own accord.

Il faut être absolument moderne; but there can also be an out-of-date modernness. Early poems by Miss Rich, such as "The Raven," "After Dark," and "In the Woods" (those essential woods) are more modern than many in her present book. That the contemporary nerve is awake in her poetry is shown in ways that pass unnoticed. For example, as we read forward we are struck by the observation that this poet never writes a love poem from which she cannot learn something useful psychologically, which forms an amusing and relevant comment on our society.

MARGARET ATWOOD

Review of *Diving into the Wreck*

This is Adrienne Rich's seventh book of poems, and it is an extraordinary one. When I first heard the author read from it, I felt as though the top of my head was being attacked, sometimes with an ice pick, sometimes with a blunter instrument: a hatchet or a hammer. The predominant emotions seemed to be anger and hatred, and these are certainly present; but when I read the poems later, they evoked a far more subtle reaction. *Diving into the Wreck* is one of those rare books that forces you to decide not just what you think about it, but what you think about yourself. It is a book that takes risks, and it forces the reader to take them also.

If Adrienne Rich were not a good poet, it would be easy to classify her as just another vocal Women's Libber, substituting polemic for poetry, simplistic messages for complex meanings. But she *is* a good poet, and her book is not a manifesto, though it subsumes manifestoes; nor is it a proclamation, though it makes proclamations. It is instead a book of explorations, of travels. The wreck she is diving into, in the very strong title poem, is the wreck of obsolete myths, particularly myths about men and women. She is journeying to something that is already in the past, in order to discover for herself the reality behind the myth, "the wreck and not the story of the wreck / the thing itself and not the myth." What she finds is part treasure and part corpse, and she also finds that she herself is part of it, a "half-destroyed instrument." As explorer she is detached; she carries a

---

knife to cut her way in, cut structures apart; a camera to record; and the book of myths itself, a book which has hitherto had no place for explorers like herself.

This quest—the quest for something beyond myths, for the truths about men and women, about the "I" and the "You," the He and the She, or more generally (in the references to wars and persecutions of various kinds) about the powerless and the powerful—is presented throughout the book through a sharp, clear style and through metaphors which become their own myths. At their most successful the poems move like dreams, simultaneously revealing and alluding, disguising and concealing. The truth, it seems, is not just what you find when you open a door: it is itself a door, which the poet is always on the verge of going through.

The landscapes are diverse. The first poem, "Trying to Talk with a Man," occurs in a desert, a desert which is not only deprivation and sterility, the place where everything except the essentials has been discarded, but the place where bombs are tested. The "I" and the "You" have given up all the frivolities of their previous lives, "suicide notes" as well as "love-letters," in order to undertake the risk of changing the desert; but it becomes clear that the "scenery" is already "condemned," that the bombs are not external threats but internal ones. The poet realizes that they are deceiving themselves, "talking of the danger / as if it were not ourselves / as if we were testing anything else."

Like the wreck, the desert is already in the past, beyond salvation though not beyond understanding, as in the landscape of "Waking in the Dark":

> The tragedy of sex
> lies around us, a woodlot
> the axes are sharpened for.
> . . . .
> Nothing will save this. I am alone,
> kicking the last rotting logs
> with their strange smell of life, not death,
> wondering what on earth it all might have become.

Given her view that the wreck, the desert, the woodlot can-
not be redeemed, the task of the woman, the She, the powerless,
is to concentrate not on fitting into the landscape but on redeem-
ing herself, creating a new landscape, getting herself born:

> your mother dead and you unborn
> your two hands grasping your head
> drawing it down against the blade of life
> your nerves the nerves of a midwife
> learning her trade
>
> ("The Mirror in Which Two Are Seen As One")

The difficulty of doing this (the poet is, after all, still surrounded
by the old condemned landscape and "the evidence of damage"
it has caused) is one of the major concerns of the book. Trying to
see clearly and to record what has been seen—the rapes, the
wars, the murders, the various kinds of violation and mutila-
tion—is half of the poet's effort; for this she requires a third eye,
an eye that can see pain with "clarity." The other half is to
respond, and the response is anger; but it is a "visionary anger,"
which hopefully will precede the ability to love.

These poems convince me most often when they are true to
themselves as structures of words and images, when they resist
the temptation to sloganize, when they don't preach at me.
"The words are purposes. / The words are maps," Rich says,
and I like them better when they are maps (though Rich would
probably say the two depend on each other and I would proba-
bly agree). I respond less fully to poems like "Rape" and refer-
ences to the Vietnam War—though their truth is undeniable—
than I do to poems such as "From a Survivor" and "August"
with its terrifying final image:

> His mind is too simple, I cannot go on
> sharing his nightmares
>
> My own are becoming clearer, they open
> into prehistory
>
> which looks like a village lit with blood
> where all the fathers are crying: *My son is mine!*

It is not enough to state the truth; it must be imaged, imagined, and when Rich does this she is irresistible. When she does this she is also most characteristically herself. You feel about her best images, her best myths, that nobody else writes quite like this.

RUTH WHITMAN

Review of *Poems: Selected and New*
1950–1974

Adrienne Rich's process of transformation over the years has been an astonishing phenomenon to watch: in one woman the history of women in our century, from careful traditional obedience (that was Auden's description of her) to cosmic awareness, defying the mode of our time, especially the sexual and political repression. She describes her own process of change in the wonderful new poem "Tear Gas."

If she began in 1951 with a control that seemed to me to be cold, she has exploded into passion and compassion, beginning in 1966 when she moved to New York from Cambridge—during the time of the Vietnam War, the student protests, the rage of the Third World, and the accelerating women's movement. "From an Old House in America" is a magnificent poem, a quieter, more comprehensive statement of her allegiance than any yet made: "Any woman's death diminishes me."

But if her poetry is now open and even occasionally violent, it carries with it the strength of those years of craft. When Rich breaks away from form, as in "The Phenomenology of Anger," it is with a strength that comes from years of control and mastery. If the tension between passion and control sometimes leans toward the side of passion, so much the better: she sees the world whole and she sees what it needs. She is poet as prophet, she is Cassandra, willing to stand in the earthquake.

> Now, again, poetry,
> violent, arcane, common,

---

hewn of the commonest living substance
into archway, portal, frame
I grasp for you, your bloodstained splinters, your
ancient and stubborn poise
—as the earth trembles—
burning out from the grain

I believe that "Diving into the Wreck" (the title poem of her previous book, which won the National Book Award) is one of the great poems of our time. It is a poem of disaster, with a willingness to look into it deeply and steadily, to learn whatever dreadful information it contains, to accept it, to be part of it, not as victim, but as survivor. When I was asked to review that earlier book, I wrote these lines of celebration for her:

Across another room,
a tremor of flame plays from her eyes,
a fire for the lost, the unmasked.

It has honed her to the wick. Sure as a rose,
she burns and burns and is not consumed.

ELEANOR WILNER

"This Accurate Dreamer"
An Appreciation of *Poems: Selected and New 1950–1974*

When I was in high school, my tough-minded English teacher expressed to me her pity and her empathy: "I'm sorry for you," she said; "you have a man's mind and a woman's emotions." I had the uneasy feeling that I had received a compliment (having, at least, a man's mind) for which I had only begun to pay. "I wonder," writes Adrienne Rich in "For L.G.: Unseen for Twenty Years" (1974), "what words of mine drift back to you? / Something like: / *But you're a man, I know it—* / *the swiftness of your mind is masculine—?*" *Poems* is a twenty-four year document that tells in the searing hieroglyphics of the imagination what it means to be a woman, to have a "man's mind," to want to keep that mind—its "swiftness" and its lucidity, and to make it your own. To keep your mind and change that one possessive, modifying masculine noun means escaping the original decree that you will be, in your desire for clarity, your own cinder. Because that mind, on which your pride is hung—in that ritual, repetitive way by which societies perpetuate their own arrangements—is your mortal enemy and your longest hope, the light by which you see, yet stand condemned and burn. Change it or be consumed—on the market, in the fire.

The measure of that change, that alchemy, is in the transformation of the central images of Adrienne Rich's poetry, a quarter of a century of transformation which this chronological collection holds up to the light; as the images shift in their rela-

---

First published in the *American Poetry Review*, March/April 1975. Reprinted with permission from the author and *American Poetry Review*.

tion to the living presence they unfold, an unflinching eye opens and gains in power as it alters, living on the double-edged risk of Blake's dictum: "they became what they beheld" and towards the final sense of what he knew: "the eye altering, alters all." *Poems* opens with "Storm Warnings" (1951), a "gray unrest," the "glass . . . falling," a fear of weather, of storms, of change; and the resigned knowledge that "Weather abroad / and weather in the heart alike come on / Regardless of prediction"; that "averting change" is not in the power of instruments the elements will shatter: "We can only close the shutters." The last verse sets the central image of the poems to follow—the isolate, self-enclosed lamp where light, set up defensively under glass, consumes the stuff that feeds it (though that last horror is still unfelt):

> I draw the curtains as the sky goes black
> And set a match to candles sheathed in glass
> Against the keyhole draught, the insistent whine
> Of weather through the unsealed aperture.
> This is our sole defense against the season;
> These are the things that we have learned to do
> Who live in troubled regions.

So much of what will become manifest in the later poems is here set neatly down in an order that will shatter with the glass, its meaning becoming clearer as the glass darkens into the "stained panes" of the later poems, as the burning grows fiercer and the imprisonment "cast-iron," the opposites of fire and ice, passion and false order, growth and restriction becoming ever more extreme until they destroy each other in a new perception. In 1973 in "The Wave," casting off even the diver's mask of *Diving into the Wreck,* she writes:

> And I think of those lives we tried to live
> in our globed helmets, self-enclosed
> bodies self-illumined gliding
> safe from the turbulence
>
> and how, miraculously, we failed

There is more to the images in the verse quoted above from "Storm Warnings"—the bright, hard maleness of that defensive mind, those "candles sheathed in glass," and the contrary female image of possibility and danger: "the keyhole draught, the insistent whine / Of weather through the unsealed aperture." The identity becomes explicit later in "When We Dead Awaken" (1971):

> The fact of being separate
> enters your livelihood like a piece of furniture
> —a chest of seventeenth-century wood
> from somewhere in the North.
> It has a huge lock shaped like a woman's head
> but the key has not been found.
> In the compartments are other keys
> to lost doors, an eye of glass.

Poems ends with the image with which it began, their consequences now fully understood: the woman, isolated in her pride, a detached leaf burning under the glass of her negative self-magnification, the eye turned against the flesh, the judgment of a woman's "masculine mind" against her own passionate kind. This time the image comes as an admonition and a last burning away of an old condition:

> Isolation, the dream
> of the frontier woman
>
> leveling her rifle along
> the homestead fence
>
> still snares our pride
> —a suicidal leaf
>
> laid under the burning-glass
> in the sun's eye

This is a kind of last judgment on judgment, against the egotism of conspiring in your own incineration. And, as this final poem is called "From an Old House in America" (1974), domesticity is turned against itself: "the snout of the vacuum cleaner / sucks the past away"; the domestic imagery of the first poems has given way to the surreal of the later ones, even as the private domain has extended itself to the public, until in this poem the subject is equally herself and America's women: the prairie wife, the witch, the "breeding-wenches," women barren or bereaved and begging the world's pardon—"*I will live for the others, asking nothing / I will ask nothing, ever, for myself.*" Now the poet speaks in a new voice; the first person has become plural:

> If it was lust that had defined us—
> their lust and fear of our deep places
>
> we have done our time
> as faceless torsos licked by fire
>
> we are in the open, on our way—
> ....
> They were the distractions, lust and fear
> but are
>
> themselves a key
> Everything that can be used, will be

"Everything that can be used, will be"—this distillation of so much living that arrives, double-tongued, to say that we can always be used if we permit it—exploited or delivered, depending on whether we use a bloody past as judge or as midwife to that other woman who has been trying so long to be born.

> your mother dead and you unborn
> your two hands grasping your head
> drawing it down against the blade of life
> your nerves the nerves of a midwife
> learning her trade
> ("The Mirror in Which Two Are Seen As One")

It is frightening and right, this image of giving birth to yourself;

your head, the old conceptions, must be cut on the hard edge of facts, the new birth drawn from the body and opening the mind.

It is fascinating to go back to the early poems at the beginning of the volume and watch the appearance of this unlived life from its entrapment in an art that was at first its only expression and watch it gain in actuality as the poetry moves away from artifice into "accurate dream." From *A Change of World* (1951) in "Aunt Jennifer's Tigers" we meet the instinctual force which her wifely role denies active expression, as she emblazons her art with the rebellious power her life refuses. Her hands heavy with "the massive weight of Uncle's wedding band," she sews her tigers with a "topaz" thread, tigers who, unlike Aunt Jennifer, "do not fear the men beneath the tree":

> When Aunt is dead, her terrified hands will lie
> Still ringed with ordeals she was mastered by.
> The tigers in the panel that she made
> Will go on prancing, proud and unafraid.

In "Mathilde in Normandy" two pages later, the "long-sleeved ladies" of a "young epoch" weave with "slow shuttles" the "swift arrows" and "outlandish attitudes of death" of their warrior lords, absent in body as the women are absent in mind: "While the bright sun on the expensive threads / Glowed in the long windless afternoons." Not yet has the war come home; not yet have these golden threads become the poet's own body, mind and nerves, as they are in "August" (1972) where the sublimated separation of art from life dissolves and image recovers its immediacy:

> If I am flesh sunning on rock
> if I am brain burning in fluorescent light
>
> if I am dream like a wire with fire
> throbbing along it
>
> if I am death to man
> I have to know it

> His mind is too simple, I cannot go on
> sharing his nightmares

No longer the unimplicated woman weaving the tapestry of man's history (betrayed only by the "knots" of her strained inattention), she picks up the thread of her own life, only to discover the outer horror of war and waste converging with the inner:

> everything outside our skins is an image
> of this affliction:
> . . . .
> even the scars of my decisions
> even the sunblaze in the mica-vein
> even you, fellow-creature, sister,
> sitting across from me, dark with love,
> working with me to remake
> this trailing knitted thing, this cloth of darkness,
> this woman's garment, trying to save the skein.
>> ("When We Dead Awaken")

The image of faithful Penelope, weaving and unweaving the self-same shroud, is here undone; the old patterns must be painfully disentangled, saving only "the skein" (with its echo of "skin") to create a wilder conception, a new kind of faithfulness:

> the faithfulness I can imagine would be a weed
> flowering in tar, a blue energy piercing
> the massed atoms of a bedrock disbelief.

The imaginative energy necessary to "imagining the existence of something uncreated" is the growing power of the recent poems, more sure in the newest poems (1973–74) than in anything written before, coming up from the "wreck" to a new vision. In *Diving into the Wreck* the signs are already there: "Outside the frame of his dream we are stumbling up the hill / hand in hand, stumbling and guiding each other / over the scarred volcanic rock" and "the composing of the thread / inside the spider's body / first atoms of the web / visible tomorrow." Images of volcanoes and weaving come together: Blake's furnaces of Los and the looms of Enitharmon, traditional male and female images of art: creative energy and connective design, requiring each other, fuse in the androgynous figure who begins to emerge. The "male" energy of the embroidered tigers of Aunt Jennifer becomes the partially humanized figure of "Orion" (1965) burning in the cold sky, his back to the celestial wall:

> you were my genius, you
> my cast-iron Viking, my helmed
> lion-heart king in prison.
> Years later now you're young
>
> my fierce half-brother, staring
> down from that simplified west
> . . . .
> But you burn, and I know it;
> as I throw back my head to take you in
> an old transfusion happens again

The transfusion here is not blood but the exchange of one "star-like eye" with another, "shooting its cold and egotistical spear / where it can do least damage." The "other," half-brother, is still the distanced projection of an unpermitted power in a world of guilt, a guilt she feels when she returns to the house and so turns back to him, aloof and "pinned aloft," safe in his distance from her life but imprisoned and pinned by that very sublimation. Three years later, the "other" appears again in "Gabriel"; closer now, more intimate, he enters her room:

> There are no angels   yet
> here comes an angel   one
> with a man's face   young
> shut-off   the dark
> side of the moon   turning to me

The unintegrated side of the feminine archetype, beast and angel, *"with fangs of fire   and a gentle heart,"* he is no Gabriel unfurling a message to a waiting Mary, but a daemon/brother afflicted like her with feelings inappropriate to the used up arts *"of love / . . . of words."* The exchange of looks is more human than the cold glance beamed between her and Orion: "We glance miserably / across the room   at each other / . . . I get your message Gabriel."

Still later, in "Diving into the Wreck," his power has been recovered as her own; she is mermaid and merman: "I am she: I am he." The self-division and self-hate, the old scar healing, a single being emerges in the last poems of the book; in "The Fourth Month of the Landscape Architect" (1973) she is no longer obsessed with her own birth, but that of something else—a strange new world:

> For now, I am myself,
> like anyone, like a man
> whose body contains simply: itself.
> I draw a too-big sweater
> over my breasts, walk into the drafting-room
> and stand there, balancing.
> The sun sprays acid points of light
> on the tools of my trade, the metal,
> the edged instruments. My work has always been
> with edges. . . .
> . . . .
> I start to imagine
> plans for a house, a park
> stretching in every direction to the horizon
> which is no horizon
> which is merely a circle of volcanoes.
> I touch stylus, T-square, pens
> of immeasurable fineness,
> the hard-edge. I am I,
> this India ink my rain
> which can irrigate gardens, terraces
> dissolve or project horizons
> flowing like lava from the volcano of the inkpot
> at the stirring of my mind.
> A city waits at the back of my skull

eating its heart out to be born:
how design the first
city of the moon? how shall I see it
for all of us who are done
with enclosed spaces, purdah, the salon, the sweatshop loft,
the ingenuity of the cloister?

Here is the integrated imagination, the meeting of sophisticated artistry and the primal volcanic energy of underground material, set in motion by fire, an art that wants the most precise delineation of the deepest immemorial powers. The androgynous figure with which the poem begins announces the Jungian figure of individuation, the unification of opposites which is the outcome of psychic maturation and the goal of religious vision—restated in the circular image of "a park / stretching in every direction to the horizon / which is no horizon / which is merely a circle of volcanoes." The volcanoes are both the periphery of the circle and its burning center: "flowing like lava from the volcano of the inkpot / at the stirring of my mind." And from this same inkpot comes the opposite of earth's fire—sky's rain, containing its own opposition: dissolution and nourishment—"India ink," shades of Kali. This is the mythic imagination, ruled by the feminine archetype of the moon and infused with the solar power of the masculine altered by its connection to the dominant "Mothers"—the solar fire is of the earth, it is volcanic: "the cratered night of female memory, where delicately and with intense care the chieftainess inscribes upon the ribs of the volcano the name of the one she has chosen." Unashamedly smeared with the memory of blood sacrifice, of the death required for rebirth, this is a kind of female apocalypse; no one can miss the ominous character of that landscape ringed in volcanoes—everything must be changed in this circle of fire, overturned, made new in the apocalyptic image of total transformation which always embodies destruction and creation in a single imaginative act.

In one of the last of the new poems, "White Night" (1974), as the poet looks across the night at her sister-neighbor awake like her in the dark, she describes the apocalyptic dawn in which inner fire and outer conflagration coalesce, suggesting simultaneous self and social renewal. The eyes of the two women meet in a flash of awareness and communion that signals the dawn:

> Her lamplight
> licks at the icy panes
> and melts into the dawn.
> They will never prevent her
> who sleep the stone sleep of the past,
> the sleep of the drugged.
> One crystal second, I flash
>
> an eye across the cold
> unwrapping of light between us
> into her darkness-lancing eye
> —that's all. Dawn is the test, the agony
> but we were meant to see it:
> After this, we may sleep, my sister,
> while the flames rise higher and higher, we can sleep.

The light of "this accurate dreamer" reverses that first image of the book—of "candles sheathed in glass" against the changing elements. In the new poem, the woman "burns like a candle" and her fire, as it "licks at the icy panes," destroys the cold separation of the detached eye, and her light melts into the flames that rise from the earth like the dawn sun, inner and outer world identified. That these two can sleep in the rising fire underlines its identity with their own power; the apocalypse terrifies only those who have not understood the alternatives and who do not believe in its restorative fires.

The enormity of this vision justifies itself imaginatively by the earlier identification Adrienne Rich has made between the carnage of her inner life and that of the outer world, a convergence made convincing by the marshalling of evidence of modern horrors that cannot be dismissed as projections, but must be seen rather, as she sees them—as social symptoms of the same inner division that makes her the victim of her own censorious "male mind," which fears her power and had taught her to hate it, and which makes of love a carnage (emphasis mine):

> There seems a spell upon
> your lovers,—all dead of wounds
> or blown to pieces . . . Nitrate!
> I'm writing, blind with tears of rage.
> In vain. Years, death, depopulation, fears,
> bondage—these shall all be borne.
> No imagination to forestall woe.
>> ("Charleston in the Eighteen-Sixties")

The earlier Adrienne Rich is "a thinking machine / that types out *useless* as *monster* / and *history* as *lampshade*" ("On Edges," 1968), who lives by cunning and hides her wildness—a red fox "gone to earth" in her own chest, who "sees from her scuffled burrow: / dull-jawed, onrushing / killer, being that / inanely single-minded / will have our skins at last" ("5:30 A.M.," 1967). To come out in the open is to risk that death that is already general; when anger finally tears her open:

> my body is a list   of wounds
> symmetrically placed
> a village
> blown open   by planes
> that did not   finish the job
>> ("Nightbreak")

"Trying to Talk with a Man" (1971) is testing bombs in the desert, but it is she (not he) who refuses sublimation, who knows what these bombs mean: "ourselves / as if we were testing anything else." And in "The Phenomenology of Anger" she makes clear that in both public and private realms there are two distinct kinds of fire: one *purely* destructive, the other transformative and healing. The first kind of fire is associated with the "masculine mind"; it is idealizing, sublimating, the elevation of a sick and helpless will-to-power into some kind of moralistic ideal that ends as bomber planes raining fire on people and on the earth with which, in its lofty, self-falsifying detachment, it has lost all human connection:

> I suddenly see the world
> as no longer viable:

you are out there burning the crops
with some new sublimate
This morning you left the bed
we still share
and went out to spread impotence
upon the world

I hate you.
I hate the mask you wear . . .

In chemistry, to sublime means to purify a solid by heating it
directly to its gaseous state and condensing the vapor back to a
solid form. When applied to life, this desire to purify clouds
everything, destroys it in the heat, and then holds up the graven
image of its new "solid," which is in fact a gravestone. The
other kind of fire is not the fire from the mind (and the sky, as it
becomes social policy), but the fire from the body (and the earth,
in her extension of it into apocalyptic fire);

white acetylene
ripples from my body
effortlessly released
perfectly trained
on the true enemy

raking his body down to the thread
of existence
burning away his lie
leaving him in a new
world; a changed
man

The first kind of fire destroys life with its lie; the second destroys
the lie and makes life possible. Here is reversed the old soul fire
where the material is burned away; what this restoring fire burns
away is the immaterial—ideas, lies, sublimations—laying bare
the actual connections between us all—"the thread of exis-
tence." To liberate life from the false conceptions and institu-
tions which enclose it requires the fire from the body's sight,
which is imagination:

we talk of destruction and creation
ice fits itself around each twig of the lilac
like a fist of law and order
your imagination burns like a bulb in the frozen soil
the fierce shoots knock
at the roof of waiting

This recent poem, "Blood-Sister," brings us to the central role of a poetry restored to, and restoring, human life. No longer a mere consolation for or complement to our everyday existence, poetry has become for Adrienne Rich—at last—enabling. The poems themselves allow us to trace the change in the way she regards poetry; it is not distinct from the way she is herself changing. In the first book, poetry is like those candles sheathed in glass: the serene composure of a contained lucidity. "At a Bach Concert" makes this explicit:

> This antique discipline, tenderly severe,
> Renews belief in love yet masters feeling,
> Asking of us a grace in what we bear.

The "proud restraining purity" she invokes to restore the "too-human heart" speaks the same language of the ideal self, the "perfect woman" burned on the male altar of her own mind, like Sylvia Plath, that "pure acetylene virgin." In "The Diamond Cutters" (1955) the poet (reminding us a little of Emily Dickinson with her amethyst, the "Purple—from Peru") has her diamond from Africa, "this coldest one," ice which the artist "with tools refined" must incise to "set / The final spoke of flame / In that prismatic wheel." The diamond is "intelligence," hard enough to resist the pressures of Africa, "dredged up from dark," "the adversary" of the poet whose material it is—the poet who must be equally hard to work this cold and precious substance which is that light contained in glass, mind lit by its passionate antagonist.

In 1963, with *Snapshots of a Daughter-in-Law,* the poetry loses its finely chiselled lines and perfect composure; the forces of rebellion gather against playing "Time's precious chronic invalid" and the careful builder of the earliest poems finds herself on the half-finished roof of the house she tried to build, the roof tilting (and burning) crazily like "a listing deck, the wave / of darkness about to break / on their heads. . . ." The lines, like the wave, have begun to break where they will; she can no longer be contained under the roof she labored so hard to raise:

> I'm naked, ignorant,
> a naked man fleeing
> across the roofs
> who could with a shade of difference
> be sitting in the lamplight
> against the cream wallpaper
> reading—not with indifference—
> about a naked man
> fleeing across the roofs.

The cozy distance between art and life has vanished for her; from now on, poetry can no longer contain and express the unlived; it must take the risks she is taking with her life; it must become, increasingly, a rite of passage. The 1963 book of her departure ends, not surprisingly, with a door: "If you go through / there is always the risk / of remembering your name." And "The door itself / makes no promises. / It is only a door."

In the next book, *Necessities of Life* (1966): "Listen. The glass is breaking" and the amazing trees, "like newly discharged patients," are stumbling out into the night; "The moon is broken like a mirror, / its pieces flash now in the crown / of the tallest oak." Life has broken the image, and in the books that follow things are often in pieces, at war; words fail before the atrocities they name: "no imagination to forestall woe." But the writing goes on; two years later poems are seen as something more than paper "because the imagination crouches in them. / . . . I am thinking how we can use what we have / to invent what we need." Imagination, not to forestall woe, but to invent out of it, to pick up the signals for a new shape out of the deep clouds of the old, false perceptions:

> I have been standing all my life in the
> direct path of a battery of signals

> the most accurately transmitted most
> untranslatable language in the universe
> I am a galactic cloud so deep   so invo-
> luted that a light wave could take 15
> years to travel through me   And has
> taken   I am an instrument in the shape
> of a woman trying to translate pulsations
> into images   for the relief of the body
> and the reconstruction of the mind.
>
> ("Planetarium")

And in *The Will to Change* (1971), she writes:

> free in the dusty beam of the projector
> the mind of the poet is changing
>
> the moment of change is the only poem
>
> ("Images for Godard")

The final image of poetry in *Poems,* "The Fact of a Door-frame" (1974), brings all the earlier images together but in the fresh conjunction that marks transformation. I want to quote it all:

The Fact of a Doorframe

> means there is something to hold
> onto with both hands
> while slowly thrusting my forehead against the wood
> and taking it away
> one of the oldest motions of suffering
> as Makeba sings
> a courage-song for warriors
> music is suffering made powerful
>
> I think of the story
> of the goose-girl who passed through the high gate
> where the head of her favorite mare
> was nailed to the arch

and in a human voice
If she could see thee now, thy mother's heart would break
said the head
of Falada

Now, again, poetry,
violent, arcane, common,
hewn of the commonest living substance
into archway, portal, frame
I grasp for you, your bloodstained splinters, your
ancient and stubborn poise
—as the earth trembles—
burning out from the grain

The Africa that once created only a diamond-hard resistance has found its living female warrior voice, Makeba; the severed head of "my dead poet" Orpheus has gone "backward against the wind" (1968) to become the oracular mare: female, animal, human; the "antique discipline" of the first poems has become "an ancient and stubborn poise." The poem, "hewn of the commonest living substance," becomes a portal for passage and a support for suffering that bears the marks of its damage: "your bloodstained splinters." The imaginative moment of the poem is apocalyptic: "the earth trembles—burning out from the grain." The more obvious sense of "burning out" is balanced by the sense of the fire emanating from the earth's fertility (and the grain of the poetic wood of the portal); the original power is reinstated and the oldest judges reconvened:

Who is here. The Erinyes.
One to sit in judgment.

One to speak tenderness.
One to inscribe the verdict on the canyon wall.
                    ("From an Old House in America")

In this poem that closes the book, this poem about the past that opens the future, she invokes finally "the Mother of reparations," that last word with its double sense of repair and making amends. Two images, connected to and torturing the thread image with which connections are made, appear and reappear throughout the poems: the knot and the scar. The knot first appears in "Mathilde in Normandy," quoted earlier, where the female tapestry weavers reveal the anxiety which "played havoc with the skein, and the knots came / when fingers' occupation and mind's attention / Grew too divergent. . . ." The knots and the scars of false joining and real division are related as in barbed wire whose "every knot is a knife / where two strands tangle to rust"; "a knot of lies / eating at itself to get undone." These are the false entanglements brought about by unreal conceptions, knots which always become knives:

> In the heart of the queen anne's lace, a knot of blood.
> . . . .
> and there, all along, the tiny dark-red spider
> sitting in the whiteness of the bridal web,
>
> waiting to plunge his crimson knifepoint
> into the white apparencies.
>
> Little wonder the eye, healing, sees
> for a long time through a mist of blood.
>
> ("The Knot")

The awful divisions and necessary separations which these knots carry as knives leave terrible scars: "Yet always the tissue / grows over, white as silk / hardly a blemish / maybe a hieroglyph for scream." In this same poem, "Meditations for a Savage Child" (1972), the scar records a primal act of violent separation—the cutting of the child's throat by those (his parents?) who left him out to die. The oldest writing of the world, "a cave of scars," birth and wound confounded, the old white lines and the recent "red–black scrawl / a red mouth slowly closing / . . . these scars bear witness / but whether to repair / or to destruction / I no longer know." But in the last poem these opposites seem reconciled in the confession of the damage and the recognition of the Mother of reparations: the female poetic imagination as healer of the ancient fault.

In "A Primary Ground" (1972), Adrienne Rich returns to the house she left so long ago, the house and wife both designed to soothe and sanctify a fearful male ego, where "Protection is the genius of your house":

> But there is something else:
> your wife's twin sister, speechless
> is dying in the house
> You and your wife take turns
> carrying up the trays,
> understanding her case, trying to make her understand.

The horror of that imprisoned, speechless twin has not been eroded with time; suddenly you remember Jane Eyre, the perfect governess, patiently in service and in love downstairs; upstairs, the violent and mad Mrs. Rochester, her "speechless" twin. And you know again the dreadful image of a woman burning her better part—Mrs. Rochester flaming in the burning rafters, horribly laughing. And the rotten, romantic aftermath: Jane getting her heart's desire, the secret desire of all women who have incinerated their natural twin, thinking her unnatural—Mr. Rochester blind, helpless, completely dependent on her loving ministrations, in her power at last. These are the real man-haters, *not* Adrienne Rich—make no mistake about it. Jane and Mrs. Rochester, the latter who has her modern apotheosis in Jane Rhys, the self-aware and sullen victim, certain of her fate, hating herself and men with equal vehemence. And Mr. Rochester who has fulfilled the fear that ruled him: "their terror of blinding / by the look of her who bore them."

The moment when the attrition begins to end, when the circles of guilt begin to open, is documented—seen clearly now—by Adrienne Rich in the new poem, "The Alleged Murderess Walking in her Cell" (1973), a poem that seemingly owes much to her own life and something to that of Natalya Gorbanevskaya (see Rich's "Caryatid: A Column" in *The American Poetry Review*, September/October, 1973), a political prisoner in a Soviet mental hospital and pregnant, accused of insanity, guilty in fact of opposing tyranny. In a retrospective poem, a twenty-one-year-old Adrienne Rich seen with the eyes of 1973 is imprisoned and pregnant, with a real child perhaps—more importantly with a budding self it would take twenty years to bring to full being. She is accused: "they said I'd helped beat a man to death, / even my lover said so." That moralizing lover (depicted in the early poems) that the young and the guilty choose so carefully, who fills the double need to live and to be punished for it. But the accused woman carries within her "a bead of life / lit from with-in. / . . .Then began that whispered conversation / telling each other we were alive, / twins in the prison womb." But she is then unsure "what / it means, that we have each other," and she worries that this new life will be used against her—she has a right to worry. But, at last, the two words—not words, a life: "the blue pulse of your life / with its blind stroke: *Not-Guilty*." It is heart evidence, this *Not-Guilty;* the unconscious "blind stroke" that mocks the accuser's sight and ends his power. The "bead of life" has become the woman who has forgiven herself and won her own mind, who has left behind that simpler world of false oppositions, who knows that "the line divid-ing / lucidity from darkness / is yet to be marked out" ("From an Old House in America").

It is not the first time that the Mothers have entered history at a bloody moment to claim their own. There have been many such times, but I am thinking particularly of Medea, who made her entrance on the Greek stage when Athens had grown cold, imperial, opportunist and corrupt. Medea, intimate of Hecate and protected by Helios, the sun-god older than Apollo. And I remember again, though I have not thought of it for years, the words of a student, a young black woman, that ended an exam essay on the *Medea:* "I know," she wrote, "that Medea is sup-posed to be a monster. But I shall always adore her."

RIMA SHORE

"To Move Openly Together /
in the Pull of Gravity"
A Review of *Twenty-One Love Poems*

To begin speaking of *Twenty-One Love Poems* by discussing its
title might seem hopelessly academic. Like the poems them-
selves, the title is wonderfully simple—but deceptively so. This
would be a different book were its poems unnumbered, were it
called simply *Love Poems;* for this poetry spills over its form,
breaking the limit set by its title. There are twenty-*two* poems
(the lines which seem most like a conventional love poem are
called "THE FLOATING POEM, UNNUMBERED"). In this
way the title reflects what, in an important sense, this love poet-
ry is about—and perhaps suggests something of what love is
about and what poetry is about: recognizing limits (conventions,
laws, boundaries) and breaking through them.

Here the idea of overstepping boundaries—the old American
theme of the road less travelled—takes on special weight, for this
is love poetry written by a woman to a woman, "a woman's
voice singing old songs / with new words . . .":

XIII

The rules break like a thermometer,
quicksilver spills across the charted systems,
we're out in a country that has no language
no laws, we're chasing the raven and the wren
through gorges unexplored since dawn
whatever we do together is pure invention

Rima Shore's review is reprinted from *Conditions: One,* April 1977. It is a review
of the first edition of *Twenty-One Love Poems,* published in 1976 by Effie's Press,
Emeryville, California.

the maps they gave us were out of date
by years . . . we're driving through the desert
wondering if the water will hold out
the hallucinations turn to simple villages
the music on the radio comes clear—
neither *Rosenkavalier* nor *Götterdämmerung*
but a woman's voice singing old songs
with new words, with a quiet bass, a flute
plucked and fingered by women outside the law.

The desert is a metaphor, not a setting, for this love. Rich
locates herself not in an unbounded expanse, but in the city, on
the island of Manhattan. The opening poem is a kind of pro-
logue, insisting on this setting—not a postcard view, not a pic-
turesque skyline, but a real city of tenements and garbage. There
is passion here, but it is "passion rooted in the city." The insis-
tence on ordinary life prepares us for the poems that follow.
Their long lines, their sometimes prosaic feel, their range of
experience, give a sense that Rich is breaking out of the confines
of narrowly "poetic" poetry. This kind of poetry—we might
call it establishment poetry—seems to be personified in poem IV
by the man who lets a door almost close on the poet, then
berates her when she makes it through:

. . . I'm lugging my sack
of groceries, I dash for the elevator
where a man, taut, elderly, carefully composed
lets the door almost close on me.—*For god's sake hold it!*
I croak at him.—*Hysterical,*—he breathes my way.

In her poems Rich communicates the great difficulty of her de-
fiance, but also her conviction that to a woman's hands may be
entrusted the most difficult of tasks:

. . . in these hands
I could trust the world, or in many hands like these,
handling power-tools or steering-wheel
or touching a human face. . . .

(VI)

Poetry has its place in the setting of daily life as the poet's work. In *Twenty-One Love Poems,* Rich handles words like the power-tools they are, using them to build another world, to touch another human being. These lines struck me as another expression of her determination to break out of the confines of taut, elderly, carefully composed poetry.

The second poem introduces the poet, her lover, their smaller setting. It introduces poetry itself, almost as a character in the narrative, and it introduces the notion of gravity which becomes so central.

> I wake up in your bed. I know I have been dreaming.
> Much earlier, the alarm broke us from each other,
> you've been at your desk for hours. I know what I dreamed:
> our friend the poet comes into my room
> where I've been writing for days,
> drafts, carbons, poems are scattered everywhere,
> and I want to show her one poem
> which is the poem of my life. But I hesitate,
> and wake. You've kissed my hair
> to wake me. *I dreamed you were a poem,*
> I say, *a poem I wanted to show someone . . .*
> and I laugh and fall dreaming again
> of the desire to show you to everyone I love,
> to move openly together
> in the pull of gravity, which is not simple,
> which carries the feathered grass a long way down the
> > upbreathing air.

Twenty-One Love Poems seems to grow out of this "desire to show you to everyone I love," and yet the lover remains for the most part unseen and unheard. Our glimpse of this love affair is mostly of the moments in between—not the waking, not the parting, but the moment after waking, the moment after parting. We see not the lover, but her reflection in the poet's ordinary life, as in poem IV we see

> . . . the early light of spring
> flashing off ordinary walls, the Pez Dorado,
> the Discount Wares, the shoe-store. . . .

We see not her lover, but the impact she makes, as in poem VIII, looking at the dark ocean we don't see the wave itself; we are rather . . .

> looking down the red rocks to where a soundless curl
> of white told me a wave had struck,
> imagining the pull of that water from that height.

This image returns us to the notion of gravity's pull. If these poems are down-to-earth, it is in a very literal sense. The physical world is always visibly present, even if our view is filtered through the poet's sensibility (a filtering process which becomes an image in poem XVI, when the poet is "watching red sunset through the screendoor of the cabin"). There is always:

> that detail outside ourselves that brings us to ourselves,
> was here before us, knew we would come, and sees beyond us.
>
> (XI)

But while the poems and their passion are "rooted in the city," the poet uses dream and metaphor to break out of the limits she has set. In the center of the book, she crosses over into another unbounded expanse; in sleep, the poet and her lover become planets, separate worlds, turning in the same universe.

XII

> Sleeping, turning in turn like planets
> rotating in their midnight meadow:
> a touch is enough to let us know
> we're not alone in the universe, even in sleep:
> the dream-ghosts of two worlds
> walking their ghost-towns, almost address each other.
> I've wakened to your muttered words
> spoken light- or dark-years away
> as if my own voice had spoken.
> But we have different voices, even in sleep,
> and our bodies, so alike, are yet so different
> and the past echoing through our bloodstreams

is freighted with different language, different meanings—
though in any chronicle of the world we share
it could be written with new meaning
we were two lovers of one gender,
we were two women of one generation.

Reading this poem, I remembered a grade school trip to the
Hayden Planetarium, where a series of scales told what our
weight would be on each heavenly body. Each world, we
learned, has its own unique gravitational force. We imagined
how we would float effortlessly on the moon, how our heavi-
ness on Jupiter would take some getting used to.

The gravitational pull of this poetry, of the world it creates,
takes some getting used to. Familiar ideas and sensations take on
new weight; familiar words take on new meanings. Light seems
denser, water heavier; time moves in a different way. I think one
reason why this is so striking in the context of love poems is that
it comes so close to the feeling of being in love—the difficulty of
reorienting oneself, the sensation of "my body still both light
and heavy with you" (IV), the fresh awareness of possibilities
and limitations:

> At twenty, yes; we thought we'd live forever.
> At forty-five, I want to know even our limits.
> I touch you knowing we weren't born tomorrow,
> and somehow, each of us will help the other live,
> and somewhere, each of us must help the other die.
>
> (III)

One can think of gravity in another sense as well, for the
poetic process has its own downward pull, from idea to image,
from passion to paper:

> What kind of beast would turn its life into words?
> What atonement is this all about?
> —and yet, writing words like these, I'm also living.
> Is all this close to the wolverines' howled signals,
> that modulated cantata of the wild?
>
> (VII)

Rich recognizes the power of poetry, "imagining the pull," the modulating force. And yet, the poetry seems to take on a life of its own which breaks through the surface of the words, just as when the lover tells the story of her life in poem XVIII, "a tremor breaks the surface of your words." When this happens, the poet becomes again a woman outside the law; she defies the law of gravity, and the twenty-second love poem becomes a *floating* poem:

(THE FLOATING POEM, UNNUMBERED)

Whatever happens with us, your body
will haunt mine—tender, delicate
your lovemaking, like the half-curled frond
of the fiddlehead fern in forests
just washed by sun. Your traveled, generous thighs
between which my whole face has come and come—
the innocence and wisdom of the place my tongue has found there—
the live, insatiate dance of your nipples in my mouth—
your touch on me, firm, protective, searching
me out, your strong tongue and slender fingers
reaching where I had been waiting years for you
in my rose-wet cave—whatever happens, this is.

This breathtaking poem insists on the physicality of passion, but it leaves us with a sense of floating, and gives new meaning to the lines

> to move openly together
> in the pull of gravity, which is not simple,
> which carries the feathered grass a long way down the
> upbreathing air.

(II)

The floating poem comes near the book's center, in the midst of a journey (we have left the island of Manhattan for a time, we are on the sea, we travel to another island). It comes between two poems/episodes which place the lovers in postcard settings gone awry. In the first, they cruise between islands, but there is a storm. The poet recalls that they vomited into plastic bags, their insides literally spilling out, and that "I never felt closer to you" (XIV). In the second, they are on a beautiful beach too wind-swept to lie on. They retreat to another place, where the beds are too narrow for two. Rich places the floating poem between these two moments full of the closeness which comes from resisting the elements together.

> If I cling to circumstances I could feel
> not responsible. Only she who says
> she did not choose, is the loser in the end.
>
> (XV)

The theme of choice is crucial in *Twenty-One Love Poems,* the first book of poetry explicitly about a lesbian relationship that Adrienne Rich has published. It is full of a sense of determina-tion. It reads sometimes like a dedication to that poem "which is the poem of my life" (II).

> If I could let you know—
> two women together is a work
> nothing in civilization has made simple,
> two people together is a work
> heroic in its ordinariness . . .
>
> (XIX)

Reading this book, you get the sense that it is special, that Rich has thought of it as special, that she wants it to be thought of as special. The very beautiful edition hand set by Bonnie Carpenter of Effie's Press, a small women's press, reflects great care.

Rich ends *Twenty-One Love Poems* with the conviction that she has chosen: "I choose to walk here. And to draw this circle." Closing her circle of poems, she returns to the image of the poet alone; for in this love poetry, she does not address only her silent lover:

> and I discern a woman
> I loved, drowning in secrets, fear wound round her throat
> and choking her like hair. . . .
> and soon I shall know I was talking to my own soul.
>
> (XX)

Sometimes when she addresses her lover, it seems she could as well be addressing her poetry—her poetry come to life. This comes as no surprise, for from the very beginning ("*I dreamed you were a poem . . .*" [II]), the poet has spoken of her lover and her poetry in a single breath.

> I can hear your breath tonight, I know how your face
> lies upturned, the halflight tracing
> your generous, delicate mouth
> where grief and laughter sleep together.
>
> (XVI)

And finally, she speaks to another silent woman—to her reader. For moving through these poems, "where grief and laughter sleep together," the poet and her reader move openly together, in the pull of the poetry's gravity. To reorient oneself to the force of Adrienne Rich's world is, as we have been warned, not simple. But it is an effort which is rewarded. For whatever happens with us, her world will haunt ours.

HAYDEN CARRUTH

Excellence in Poetry

I have known Rich's work for years, have liked it immensely, have watched it mature with a steady, personal directedness that is rare. Consequently I am not surprised that her new book is her best. Beyond that, it is important, both poetically and thematically, to our general human evolution, especially because in the work itself these two elements, poetry and theme, cannot be separated. Here is a new awareness totally assimilated to timeless aesthetic procedures. This would be rare at any time; now it is unique.

The new poems spring from the same locus of thought and feeling that has generated Rich's recent polemical writing, particularly her book *Of Woman Born,* which has stimulated so much discussion since it appeared a couple of years ago. But whereas I found in the polemic minor points of irrationality, even hysteria, that rather spoiled the whole effect, the poems are firm, assured, calm. They are *reasonable*—to draw the distinction between rationality and reason that Camus made years ago—and that is what counts in poetry. They are true to the poet's vision. I don't know if Rich's radical feminist ideology contains mechanisms that might be made to account for this difference between her prose and poetry, and in the present discussion I don't care. What is important is that Rich is a poet, a genuine poet, and has been all her life. Whatever the state of the world, she would be writing fine poems. If the actual state of the world has driven her to devote part of her energy to polemic, she remains a poet primarily. And I do not imply by this that the ideology is unim-

Hayden Carruth's review of *The Dream of a Common Language* was published in *Harper's* Magazine, November 1978. Copyright © 1978 by Harper's Magazine. All rights reserved. Reprinted from the November 1978 issue by special permission.

portant to the poetry. On the contrary, the ideology is what has permitted her to combine traditional poetic resources with continual personal experiment, exactly the combination that has always produced the strongest literature.

The heart of this book is a sequence of sonnetlike love poems—no, call them true sonnets. For if they do not conform to the prescribed rules, they certainly come from the same lyrical conception that made the sonnet in the first place, and it is long past time to liberate the old term from its trammeling codes of technique. Here is one from the sequence:

Every peak is a crater. This is the law of volcanoes,
making them eternally and visibly female.
No height without depth, without a burning core,
though our straw soles shred on the hardened lava.
I want to travel with you to every sacred mountain
smoking within like the sibyl stooped over her tripod,
I want to reach for your hand as we scale the path,
to feel your arteries glowing in my clasp,
never failing to note the small, jewel-like flower
unfamiliar to us, nameless till we rename her,
that clings to the slowly altering rock—
that detail outside ourselves that brings us to ourselves,
was here before us, knew we would come, and sees beyond us.

(XI)

It is an outstanding poem but typical as well of Rich's way of writing: the genuinely literate sentences woven into genuinely poetic measures, cadences, and patterns of sound; the easy, perfectly assimilated classical allusion; the sense of immediate, unique experience; the details—here the female mountain and flower—turned into generalized insights of humane value. These are the resonances we find in all the poems. A mind is here, a loving mind, in and of this world, including all this world's cultural inheritance, yet still asserting, firmly and calmly, its own independence and newness.

At one point Rich writes:

There are words I cannot choose again:
humanism   androgyny

meaning that in the present condition of society the poet finds herself so embattled that she can only fight back with equally militant means; that is, by adopting an antimale, frankly sexist posture. She implies that this is the case with all women. But she also implies, I believe, that the hope has not been entirely lost of a time when these old words and the vision embodied in them, "the dream of a common language," may still come true, at least for significant numbers of people. I cannot think of any book more likely to help induce such a change than this one by Adrienne Rich.

OLGA BROUMAS

Review of *The Dream of a Common Language*

> *But this is the saying of a dream*
> *on waking*
> *I wish there were somewhere*
> *actual we could stand*
> *handing the power-glasses back and forth*
> *looking at the earth, the wildwood*
> *where the split began*
> —"Waking in the Dark," *Diving into the Wreck*

The Dream of a Common Language is a document, both historical and emotional, of one woman's fierce desire and dedication to actualizing that wish among women and, failing that, to accurately describe the somewhere she finds herself, speechless, standing.

For a poet who has held speech to be synonymous with existence,

> Only where there is language is there world
> ("The Demon Lover," 1966)

and whose identity as a woman, articulate, serious, imperative, has defined and extended the parameters of our collective understanding of identity, the struggle to bring back the dream into the actual is a struggle with, a struggle against death.

This is the most difficult, complex, demanding of Rich's work. Not only is it heroic, as any pitting of the living will against the dark must be; it is, in the midst of the battle, a radical redefinition *of* the heroic

---

Olga Broumas's review first appeared in *Chrysalis,* no. 6 (1978). Reprinted by permission from the author.

                    in its ordinariness
      the slow-picked, halting traverse of a pitch
      where the fiercest attention becomes routine
      —look at the faces of those who have chosen it.
                          ("Twenty-One Love Poems," XIX)

Revision, willfulness, change: these are familiar themes in the
long work of a poet whose first book, in 1951, was called *A
Change of World*. What is unfamiliar about this book is the full
focus of those energies being riveted unflinchingly on the nature
of interrelationships among women. In previous volumes,
largely, though not exclusively, she was addressing men in the
name of women; here, the *you* is almost always female, and
where it is not, as in "Phantasia for Elvira Shatayev" ("leader of
a women's climbing team, all of whom died in a storm on Lenin
Peak, August 1974"), in which Rich speaks through Shatayev to
her husband, it is an abstract *you,* a *you* no longer personal, a
being she no longer engages with, only speaks to from afar,
from another life, and with no belief or desire in
communication.

Everything in Rich's work, both poetry and prose, has pre-
pared the way for this book, in theory, in the mind. The actual
book is a shock I've found difficult to recover from. I have felt
moved, angry, challenged, betrayed, confronted, comforted.
I've had, as a friend reviewing it for another publication said to
me the other day, "to come to terms with it, for my own life."
I've had to rediscover the original meaning of criticism, *krisis,*
the decisive encounter that transforms.

The Dream of a Common Language. The emphasis, grammati-
cal and actual, is not on *common,* which is where I first placed it
in my own fierce desire for that reality, but on *dream*. The com-
mon language requires another one to hear it, to speak it, to
reply. Alone, one dreams of/in it. The commonality of a lan-
guage, dialogue, implies a tremendous risk for anyone, but cer-
tainly for a poet whose voice has matured in

                  Isolation, the dream
                  of the frontier woman

leveling her rifle along
the homestead fence

still snares our pride
—a suicidal leaf
("From an Old House in America," 1974)

The risk is so great because one cannot enter dialogue at will;
one can only express one's desire, willingness, hunger to do so.
It is the giving up of power on faith of another, greater perhaps,
certainly different power. It is, for the poet, an ultimate act of
faith, not only to understand and speak about the nature of
dialogue, but to undertake it, risking, possibly, to fail.

Rich's challenge to men in her last poem before this book:

I try to understand
he said

what will you undertake
she said

will you punish me for history
he said

what will you undertake
she said
("From an Old House in America," 1974)

becomes the challenge she herself has faced—and answered:

I have to cast my lot with those
who age after age, perversely,

with no extraordinary power,
reconstitute the world.
("Natural Resources," 1977)

The problem, and the complexity, is that Rich has extraordi-
nary powers—of perception, eloquence, rhythm, courage, the
rare fusion of vision and action, the ability to suggest not only to

others but to herself a course of action in the mind and follow it in the next breath in the world. A few months ago I came across a poem by Wendell Berry, "Healing," and copied these lines from it, inserting them in my copy of *Women and Honor:* "The possible is infinite in the mind, finite in the world. But to fulfill the possible is to enlarge it."

The Dream of a Common Language is, with the exception of one poem ("Nights and Days"), about what has been or is possible among women in the world as we know it. Its limitations constitute the gap between the infinite of the imaginary and the contradictions of the extant; between the force of the single, well-exercised will and voice and the long, hard way toward commonality, of love, of language, of trust.

The core of the book is "Twenty-One Love Poems," which one thousand of us have jealously owned, and a great many more have read, in its beautiful, small edition from Effie's Press. Eight poems precede it in a section called "Power," and ten follow it in a section called "Not Somewhere Else, but Here."

"Power" begins with "Power," a poem about Marie Curie, suffering from radiation sickness:

> She died   a famous woman   denying
> her wounds
> denying
> her wounds   came   from the same source as her power

"Not Somewhere Else, but Here" ends with a long poem, "Transcendental Etude," a meditation on the poet's own source of power, language, that comes to a multiple conclusion: the wound

> No one who survives to speak
> new language, has avoided this:
> the cutting-away of an old force that held her
> rooted to an old ground
> the pitch of utter loneliness
> where she herself and all creation
> seem equally dispersed, weightless, her being a cry
> to which no echo comes or can ever come.

and the healing:

> *I am the lover and the loved,*
> *home and wanderer, she who splits*
> *firewood and she who knocks, a stranger*
> *in the storm,* two women, eye to eye
> measuring each other's spirit, each other's
> limitless desire,
>> a whole new poetry beginning here.

The thirty-one lines that follow and conclude are so different in tone, in diction, pacing, rhythm and intent, so deliberate and quiet, so self-contained, that they stand apart almost as a separate poem.

> Vision begins to happen in such a life
> as if a woman quietly walked away
> from the argument and jargon in a room
> and sitting down in the kitchen, began turning in her lap
> bits of yarn, calico and velvet scraps,
> . . . .
> . . . the musing of a mind
> one with her body, experienced fingers quietly pushing
> dark against bright, silk against roughness,
> pulling the tenets of a life together
> with no mere will to mastery,
> only care for the many-lived, unending
> forms in which she finds herself.

This woman, at home in her surroundings, having chosen them, and in herself tender, thoughtful, meticulous, becomes emblematic in her silence. Vision, not language, begins here— "care for the many-lived, unending / forms in which she finds herself." The path from "Power" to this quietude, this centered sense of self, is threefold. Primarily, there are the poems to the loved one: "Origins and History of Consciousness"; "Splittings"; "Cartographies of Silence"; "Twenty-One Love Poems"; "Not Somewhere Else, but Here"; and "Upper Broadway." There are ten poems in the voices of historical women, like the "Phantasia for Elvira Shatayev," or to a specific person. And there are three poems in an interior voice, meditations: "Nights and Days," "Toward the Solstice," "Transcendental Etude."

The distinction according to voice is an important one because voice is inseparable from the ear for which it is intended in any case, but certainly in this book, whose emphasis is on the nature and qualities of space between voice and ear. Here, even smaller distinctions of address acquire a significance beyond the moral, the political. In the twenty-seven poems to the loved one there are two ("Splittings" and "Not Somewhere Else, but Here") where she is not addressed directly—both are poems of painful separation, the first one geographical, the second one complete. The use of *her/she* instead of *you* acknowledges the distance grammatically and also acknowledges an emotion too overwhelming to allow clear vision of the other person.

Scrupulous attention to the small and large details of language, a constant reexamination of their function and scope, is as essential to Adrienne Rich's poetry as the uses to which she puts that language. Every volume has been a further exploration of the responsibilities and limits of words as tools. I want to follow this exploration primarily through the poems to the loved one, because they constitute the major part of this volume and because, rooted as they are in the most immediately personal, tangible details of the poet's life, they embody a politics and poetics I most deeply feel.

The sequence I am calling "poems to the loved one" begins with "Origins and History of Consciousness." It is the title-cut: "The dream of a common language" surfaces here.

> No one lives in this room
> without living through some kind of crisis.
>
> No one lives in this room
> . . . .
> Without contemplating last and late
> the true nature of poetry. The drive
> to connect. The dream of a common language.

Two women meet, recognize each other, love.

> . . . We did this. Conceived
> of each other, conceived each other in a darkness
> which I remember as drenched in light.
>
> > I want to call this, life.

> But I can't call it life until we start to move
> beyond this secret circle of fire
> where our bodies are giant shadows flung on a wall

The secret circle is not enough. Sexuality alone, by which women have been defined whether we chose to love men or women, whether we chose at all, is not enough. The gesture of these poems is one of desire for a totality of living, openness, communication and trust, in the now, the immediate, the real:

> Wherever in this city, screens flicker
> with pornography, with science-fiction vampires,
> victimized hirelings bending to the lash,
> we also have to walk . . . if simply as we walk
> through the rainsoaked garbage, the tabloid cruelties
> of our own neighborhoods.
> We need to grasp our lives inseparable
> from those rancid dreams, that blurt of metal, those disgraces,
> and the red begonia perilously flashing
> from a tenement sill six stories high
>
> > ("Twenty-One Love Poems," I)

and later, in XIX,

> > (I told you from the first I wanted daily life,
> > this island of Manhattan was island enough for me.)

I began "Twenty-One Love Poems" expecting to read twenty-one poems about love, whatever that has come to mean in my life, but certainly something of the praiseful, the sexual, the lyric. Instead I found one long poem, in twenty-two sections, about a deep and anguished proximity of two lives, indeed of love, two lives that only once (in "THE FLOATING POEM, UNNUMBERED," meaning everywhere, meaning despite) shed their specific realities: of residence, age, politics, beliefs, limitations. "THE FLOATING POEM" tells not only of a physical intimacy, but of the place of physical intimacy in an "honorable human relationship—that is, one in which two peo-people have the right to use the word 'love' " (*Women and Honor*). It is not the physical which defines this love as lesbian, but the absolute and primary attention directed at the other. Sister-hood—that is, primary and bonding love from women—is, like motherhood, a capacity, not a destiny. It must be chosen, exercised by acts of will; "Twenty-One Love Poems" de-scribes as many instances, acts of the will. The sexual, requiring the least will, floats, unnumbered, informing the sequence the way a canvas is painted in a certain light, but is not about the light.

> Whatever happens with us, your body
> will haunt mine—tender, delicate
> . . . .
>
> your touch on me, firm, protective, searching
> me out, your strong tongue and slender fingers
> reaching where I had been waiting years for you
> in my rose-wet cave—whatever happens, this is.

What comes to happen is silence; the loved one does not, cannot, will not fully enter the dialogue and thereby transform the dream.

Your silence today is a pond where drowned things live
I want to see raised dripping and brought into the sun.
. . . .
. . . . I fear this silence,
this inarticulate life. I'm waiting
for a wind that will gently open this sheeted water
for once, and show me what I can do
for you, who have often made the unnameable
nameable for others, even for me.

(IX)

And

> If it [the poem] could simply look you in the face
> with naked eyeballs, not letting you turn
>
> till you, and I who long to make this thing,
> were finally clarified together in its stare
>
> > ("Cartographies of Silence")

"Now every refusal of language is a death," the linguist Roland Barthes has said. And Rich's final line in *Poems: Selected and New* was

> Any woman's death diminishes me

"Twenty-One Love Poems" records painfully, painstakingly, the slow process of a death by silence, by lack of speech.

> . . . a woman
> I loved, drowning in secrets, fear wound round her throat
> and choking her like hair. And this is she
> with whom I tried to speak, whose hurt, expressive head
> turning aside from pain, is dragged down deeper
> where it cannot hear me,
> and soon I shall know I was talking to my own soul.
>
> > (XX)

The tenderness and restraint of these poems, long after the poet has understood the silence, having tried and tried to break it, are what haunt and teach me most. The animal wild cry of pain, of loss—one of the most evocative and searing articulations of that primal cry—is in the third person, does not involve the loved one in its private grief ("Not Somewhere Else, but Here"). There is no accusation:

> . . . No poison cup,
> no penance. Merely a notion that the tape-recorder
> should have caught some ghost of us: that tape-recorder
> not merely played but should have listened to us,

and could instruct those after us:
this we were, this is how we tried to love,
and these are the forces they had ranged against us,
and these are the forces we had ranged within us,
within us and against us, against us and within us.

(XVII)

When a woman speaks from her heart, when she grounds her words in the experience she has lived, when she reads with the full faith that she will be heard, understood, she is a wave coming to shore. (Ellen Bass)

In the absence of that faith, a woman's voice falters. It is significant that the poems not to or about the loved one are poems in a persona, or to a specific person. They continue the theme of love, as variously defined and possible as there are women, and the theme of power and visionary anger, anger that transforms, wasting no time in complaints. They are acts of vision, demystification, of courage and intelligence ("Sibling Mysteries" encapsulates in six pages the anthropological states of woman), but their poetic voice falters.

> If in this sleep I speak
> it's with a voice no longer personal

says Elvira Shatayev, who, being dead, speaks in fact in the disembodied or many-bodied voice. The impersonal in other poems diminishes their power, their ability to be both symbolic and inextricable from an individual, graspable reality. Often it is a matter of tone, of pacing, difficult to pin down in a few lines. Sometimes the metaphor is far-removed or stereotyped:

> this fraying blanket with its ancient stains
> we pull across the sick child's shoulder
>
> or wrap around the senseless legs
> of the hero trained to kill

("Natural Resources")

Sometimes the line is prosy, overwritten:

> in a weekend's destructive power,
> triggers fingered by drunken gunmen, sometimes
> so inept as to leave the shattered animal
> stunned in her blood. . . .
>
> ("Transcendental Etude")

These are symptoms of a deeper phenomenon, a voice diminished in its drive to connect, faltering in its faith that it will be heard, understood, a voice that risked extending its certitude beyond the halfway point and was not met. The fragmentation of line is not a stylistic device but a representation of an actual fragmentation:

> Spilt love   seeking its level   flooding other
> lives   that must be lived   not somewhere else
> but here   seeing through blood   nothing is lost
>
> ("Not Somewhere Else, but Here")

> I have written so many words
> wanting to live inside you
> to be of use to you
>
> Now I must write for myself . . .
>
> ("Upper Broadway")

The first poem to herself is "Nights and Days," a poem in the imaginary voice, in the infinity of the possible, a poem in the pure language of a dream. The first and last stanzas, identical, are in the rhythm and tense of the future, powerfully lyrical and visionary.

> The stars will come out over and over
> the hyacinths rise like flames
> from the windswept turf down the middle of upper Broadway
> where the desolate take the sun
> the days will run together and stream into years
> as the rivers freeze and burn

and I ask myself and you, which of our visions will claim us
which will we claim
how will we go on living
how will we touch, what will we know
what will we say to each other.

Pictures form and dissolve in my head

The middle three stanzas begin this way, in the present tense,
pictures in a dream defining in specific ways what/how is possi-
ble, how/what she desires. It may seem paradoxical that the way
back toward a common language begins with a fantasy, a speech
to one's self; and yet, commonality is an ethics, and as such
concerned with value—from the Latin root *val*, indicating cour-
age, discernment, and praise—which, though it does not exist
until it is manifest and tested in the world, must be envisioned
and revisioned in the mind, the heart, the most private quarters.
"Nights and Days," "Toward the Solstice," and "Transcen-
dental Etude" are the three poems where Rich does not inhabit

> . . . any place but the mind
> casting back to where her solitude,
> shared, could be chosen without loneliness,
> not easily nor without pains to stake out
> the circle, the heavy shadows, the great light.
>
> (XXI)

The pages of these poems are the most intimate in the book. I
feel not only allowed, but invited into that circle, drawn by the
mind of a woman whose work and life have been an act of
becoming conscious against the established order:

> Every act of becoming conscious
> (it says here in this book)
> is an unnatural act
> ("The Phenomenology of Anger," 1972)

Consciousness, truth, love are becoming synonymous.
Truth, Rich says in *Women and Honor*, is not one thing, or even a

system. It is an increasing complexity. Truth, like poetry, often surprises by an unpredictability that on second look seems obvious, self-evident. The common language can begin in soliloquy; love is a total and intelligent caring in which the sexual is a kind of light. The common language may indeed be *silent,* emblematic, composed of acts of great care, beginning with the encircled self of each woman

> becoming now the sherd of broken glass
> slicing light in a corner, dangerous
> to flesh, now the plentiful, soft leaf
> that wrapped round the throbbing finger, soothes the wound;
> and now the stone foundation, rockshelf further
> forming underneath everything that grows.

("Transcendental Etude," 1977)

SARA MANDELBAUM

Adrienne Rich's *Wild Patience*

For nearly a decade, Adrienne Rich's poetry has been rooted in a passionate belief in "the will to change" and in a need to imagine "what *can* be." In *A Wild Patience Has Taken Me This Far,* she has not abandoned this aesthetic, but she does seem to have taken pause and given herself over to that "severer listening" she once described. Although her work has always been imbued with a keen sense and appreciation of history (if also a certain mistrust of it), these new poems are united in a fierce, exacting determination to pursue memory in order to "ease the hold of the past / upon the rest of my life / and ease my hold on the past."

Disdainful of the nostalgia that she feels has gripped the peculiarly ahistorical moment in which we live ("Nostalgia," she writes, "is only amnesia turned around"), Rich beckons past ghosts as well as still-living family members to prod her memory and haunt her imagination. Susan B. Anthony, Jane Addams, Willa Cather, Emily Dickinson, Ethel Rosenberg, her grandmothers, her father, her mother-in-law, and sister are among those she summons—both to allow them to speak as they themselves would be heard, and to address them herself. In one of the strongest poems, "The Spirit of Place" (dedicated to her lover/companion Michelle Cliff), there is a section in which the poet attempts in a final address to rescue the memory of Emily Dickinson, whose life has been so oversimplified and trivialized by the "experts." Rich writes with affection:

Sara Mandelbaum's review is reprinted from *Ms.,* December 1981. Reprinted with permission from *Ms.* and from the author.

with the hands of a daughter I would cover you
from all intrusion   even my own
saying   rest to your ghost

with the hands of a sister I would leave your hands
open or closed as they prefer to lie
and ask no more of who or why or wherefore

with the hands of a mother I would close the door
on the rooms you've left behind
and silently pick up my fallen work

To the mother-in-law who, after years of silence, longs to be
told "something true," Rich plainly replies: "Your son is
dead / ten years, I am a lesbian, / my children are themselves."
In the striking poem, "For Ethel Rosenberg," Rich makes vital
and revelatory connections between her own life and the fate of
this woman (Ethel Rosenberg's execution coinciding with the
week of Rich's wedding), raising complex and painful questions
about loyalty and disloyalty, punishment and crime. In a climac-
tic moment of reckoning, Rich addresses herself to this ghost she
has conjured up:

Ether Greenglass Rosenberg   would you
have marched to take back the night
collected signatures

for battered women who kill
What would you have to tell us
would you have burst the net

While Rich dares to ask these questions, which at first might
seem uncomfortably inappropriate, she is too scrupulous ever to
use the memory of the women she evokes for her own political
ends. Finally, she writes:

I must allow her to be at last

political in her ways   not in mine
her urgencies perhaps   impervious to mine

The familiar themes persist in this new volume: the omni-present threat of "male dominion"; colonization and rape of the land, which she understands anew through the lens of Native American history and the southwestern landscape; the intellectual/activist mission that a woman has to embrace the complexity of experience, "knowing better than the poem she reads / knowing through the poem . . ."; the conviction that the truth of women's lives not be obliterated yet again, as when she writes of "the matrices we weave / web upon web, delicate raf-ters / flung in audacity to the prairie skies / nets of telepathy con-trived / to outlast the iron road . . ."; and, of course, the daily, ordinary heroism of women everywhere.

Her journey into the past does not leave Rich's poetry un-altered. She has become, I think, less sanguine about the mind's freedom to choose unfettered from "the hawk-wind / poised to kill" (in the poem, "What Is Possible"), and less likely to advo-cate change purely for its own sake. The radicalism of her vision remains strong and invigorating; the writing as lyrical, polemi-cal, and moving as ever—and even more honest. In addition, Rich leaves us with what few other living poets are able to offer their readers: the images with which to build a strategy for survival.

PART THREE

Reviews and Studies of Rich's Prose

JANE LAZARRE

Adrienne Rich Comes to Terms
with "The Woman in the Mirror"

What if, in response to centuries of pontification on a subject as central to life as the relationship between children and their mothers, we suddenly hear the sound of a woman's wild, mocking laughter? What if we next hear her cackling whisper that our illusions can no longer be tolerated? What if the true complexities of her life and history are then thrust into the self-satisfied privacy of our individual lives?

The first responses will be fear, anger, and resistance. And I believe these are the reasons, in part, for the very mixed reception being given Adrienne Rich's compelling and compassionate new book, *Of Woman Born: Motherhood as Experience and Institution*. I believe this resistance (I am thinking particularly of Helen Vendler's and Francine Gray's reviews in the *New York Review of Books* and the *New York Times*) to be a response to two separate aspects of the book.

One aspect is the structure of the book, Rich's radical departure from the usual methodological distancing devices to blend her personal experience as a mother and daughter with her iconoclastic scholarship into the history of women as mothers, and a cross-cultural and historical analysis of birth-giving customs. Like many other feminist artists and scholars, Adrienne Rich is committed to joining "subjective experience" with "objective research." This joining is the beginning of a feminist contribution to a theory of knowledge, and we are only groping, still at the beginning. But in contrast to other reviewers who wish Rich had written "one book or the other," I have found the joining in

Jane Lazarre's review of *Of Woman Born* first appeared in the *Village Voice,* November 8, 1976. Reprinted with permission from the *Village Voice*.

293

Of Woman Born to be achieved with grace and meaning. Adrienne Rich is a great poet, a woman trained in the art of transforming the one into the other and then finding her way back again.

Categories are like tunnels we have dug to the truth. And since the usefulness of these tunnels has resided in their neat separateness, it is threatening when someone not only insists on joining two we had thought to be eternally distinct but then suggests that without this joining our precious truth is at best distorted, at worst illusory. Thus, many critical readers may be more comfortable with Juliet Mitchell's analysis of patriarchy than Adrienne Rich's—because Rich insists on the usefulness and absolute relevance of her personal experience, thereby suggesting its universality. They will wish that Rich had not muddied our well-dug tunnels, creating landslides, confusing us. Yet Mitchell and Rich share the same premise: that patriarchy—that system that systematically excludes women and "female" qualities from creative, publicly affirmed power—is first manifested in the family in the persons of our own fathers (however adored), our own husbands (however beloved), and our own sons (however cherished).

There is the second, more challenging cause for resistance to Rich. For against this power of the fathers, she posits unashamedly and without apology the possibility of female power, not to dominate but to reclaim that biologically based power of the mother. This power, she shows us through personal example and historical analysis, has been cruelly misdirected, violently repressed, domesticated, and rendered impotent; in some cases turned murderous. The sometimes tragic result is best described in a chilling chapter on "Violence: The Heart of Maternal Darkness," which should forever vanquish the self-serving illusion that the child-abusing mother is *the other*—a being totally without relation to ourselves.

When the idea of female power is not clothed in continuous subtle apology, when the author does not reiterate every few paragraphs that one's focus on women does not imply a lack of concern for the other half of the human race, she is inevitably accused of being antimale. This fact is reflected in our own personal lives for, as every strong woman knows, if we do not continually censor our strengths, obediently trimming their cutting edges, if we do not unceasingly direct our attention to the subtle messages and needs of men, if we do not pretend to allow them to dominate us, most men and many women will find us unattractive, unlikeable, and castrating.

Of Woman Born is not antimale, nor antifather, but antipatriarchy. In the chapter entitled "Mothers and Sons" Rich speaks tenderly about her life with her three sons. Her affirmation of the mother-rage I know so well, her courageous and brutal exposure of that painful myth of maternal serenity, healed my inner wounds as I read, and fed the process of restoration of my self-respect as a mother. I never doubted her love for her boys (to say that a child's conception was an accident is not to say that the child was unwanted, as one reviewer suggested; even to say that the child was unwanted at first is not to say that he was not later desperately wanted). I was inspired by the example of her lifelong devotion to them and theirs to her as they begin their joint search for a new kind of manhood predicated on their shared confrontation with the true meaning of motherhood—rather than the more usual repression and thus blinding fear of the potentially evil aspect of the mother's face. Rich's story of a vacation in the country when the boys were small is one of the most moving depictions I have read of mother-child intimacy, a model of a long moment of love freely given, of life defined out of human need. And, surely, we should be able to investigate and describe this unique bond—mother and child have, after all, been of one body for nine months—without, on every page, having to assure everyone that, yes, the father is important, too.

The relationship between women and men is not the focus of the book; Rich is more concerned with exploring the relationship between women and their children, between women and their own failed or lost or potential power. And here I feel I must identify a personal attitude, because women who share this attitude with me have used it as a setting from which a negative criticism of the book must spring. I am married to a man who is as involved with the daily responsibilities of childrearing as any man I know. He was often the primary nurturer of our second baby. Also, I am sexually drawn to men much more than I am to women. Furthermore, I had in many ways a strongly positive relation to my father and I am utterly committed to my children, both boys. At no point did I find *Of Woman Born* to be exclusive of a profound love or respect for the individual males in one's life. After all, in some sense my father's tenderness, or my childrens' father's, is irrelevant—because culturally they are exceptions and personally they must still function in a broader conception of "masculinity," destructive as it is to the male self. I found, however, my belief in the redefinition of fatherhood as an absolute social priority asserted several times in Rich's analysis.

But the heart of the book is, as it should be, the chapter on "Motherhood and Daughterhood." It is, first of all, women who must, in the words of one of Adrienne Rich's poems, "come to terms with the woman in the mirror." It is this reconciliation with the hitherto either despised or romanticized female self: with our menstrual blood, with our birth-giving powers, with our creativity, that feminism explores. This chapter is the next to the last. By the time we reach it, we have read self-critical and yet redemptive descriptions of maternal anger and anguish. We have explored with Rich the recurring theme of female power as evidenced in history and mythology—not in any simplistic assertion of a past gynocracy, a golden age of matriarchal power, but rather in a search through the labyrinths of patriarchal power for whatever signs of mother primacy are to be found—in art, in religion, in social organization. (And unquestionably there were instances of this power, a tribute to the irrepressibility of the psyche's wholeness, if not recorded history's.) We have read also of the domestication of motherhood, that special network of women's oppression that rests on trivialization as well as on violence, the encouraging, generation after generation, of a terrible psychic dependency in women ratified by a tutoring of daughter by mother to become utterly centered upon the needs of a man and to bury faith in the power of a woman.

The cruelly ironic paradigm of this intertwining of historical and psychological forces is, of course, woman's relinquishing of her power over the experience of childbirth itself, a process which Rich analyzes with careful respect for the complex gains and losses we derived from the medical establishment's progress in the development of the technology of childbirth and the social degeneration of the female midwife. Rich does not suggest that we banish medical knowledge from the birth chamber. But she does suggest that women ought to recapture the field of obstetrics from the men who now dominate it and who so often force us, the birth givers, to play supporting actress to their starring role; who, more dangerously to both infant and mother, precisely because they cannot give birth, are less apt to understand the felt realities and individual requirements of that profound psychological and physiological test of the human spirit.

As women, we run the risk of playing the supporting role to any man who enters our lives. We have been well taught. Among several other pieces of women's literature, Rich analyzes Virginia Woolf's portrait of Mrs. Ramsay in *To the Lighthouse,* the quintessentially maternal, male-directed woman whom Woolf contrasts to Lily Briscoe, the young painter who must struggle with all her being to protect her dream of autonomy from the male whose power lies not only in his confidence, but in his *attractiveness.* Rich refers to the missed intimacy between these two women as "the most complex and passionate vision of the mother-daughter schism in modern literature."

Over and over, our lives are illuminated by the source of Rich's vision in the "Motherhood and Daughterhood" chapter. Here the poet and the scholar join to tell of the Eleusinian Mysteries, the ancient ritual of reconciliation and affirmation between daughter and mother—moving not only because of its religious and historical interest, but because as daughters so many of us have felt "wildly unmothered." Here we glimpse a symbolic and sacred expression of what we have lost—the loving protection of a powerful mother—and what we might possibly create anew in our own mothering. Unlike some others, I do not find Rich's discussion of the biological uniqueness of the mother-daughter bond, or the erotic lesbian poetry (which is included in this chapter), to be in the least foreign to my experience. Rather, the first redefined for me in a regenerative way my lifelong search to recapture my love for my dead mother, which existed (as in Rich's own life) long before I began to nurture my identification with my father. The poetry affirmed the fulfilling physical dimension my love for women friends has come to include since the women's movement has made permissible the erotic feelings many of us—lesbian and heterosexual—expressed privately in childhood in the dark of night and under the covers on our endless "sleep-over dates."

And, certainly, I found myself revealed by the words of the poet Sue Silvermarie when she says to her son:

> i tremble to see your temptations.
> how clear for me what losing you would mean.
> how confusing for you
> little man, already
> you're lured by what passes for power,
> and is, by half.
> what do i do with your guns?

"She fears," Rich reminds us, "the *price* of his penis." I know of no feminist mother of sons who has not, in a thousand daily ways, been confronted by this anguished fear: What spiritual price will he pay, this child of my body, closest person to my heart, for being a boy? I do not wish my sons were girls, but I recognize that there is a vacuum in our lives where an authoritative "manhood" used to stand, and that it is up to me and my sons' father to fill that vacuum daily, risking continually that we shall damage some thread that should have been left in place or leave a pattern that should have been torn away. This struggle is chronicled by Adrienne Rich in twin chapters on daughters and sons and, despite the incessant theories and proofs that I will thereby damage my son's somehow always precarious "masculinity," I yearn to say to him with Robin Morgan, "you shall be a child of the mother / as of old, and your face will not be turned from me. . . ."

The notion of female power, when honestly explored, releases our deepest fears, at once unconscious and institutionalized, of women. To discuss raising children, giving birth or investigating history, within this sort of consciousness, should never be considered a betrayal of our sons or our male lovers. Rich warns of the more dangerous betrayal when she asks us to imagine a continuum: a poverty-stricken, oppressed teenage mother on the one end, giving birth to her third child, her first menstrual period having been her last; and on the other, a factory for the artificial creation of babies. Socialism will eliminate the first human outrage, Rich tells us, but who can be sure that it will prevent the second? It is the poet's vision which reveals that socialist values—as critical as those values are—will be insidiously betrayed without the primacy of a strong feminism.

Simultaneously, she counters other feminist writings supporting the mechanization of childbirth with a self-expressive humanism clearly derived from the joining of her own motherhood with feminism. She does not negate the usefulness of a class analysis, as she has been accused of doing. In fact, she is careful to record the distinctions in the oppression of mothers of different social classes. Rather, her concern is to eliminate both ends of the spectrum, her direction the exploration of the biological and psychological unities that connect all women across racial and class lines.

Like many others, I have waited for *Of Woman Born*. It is the best analysis I have seen of what we mean when we speak of *patriarchy*. And it is, through the experience of an exquisitely sensitive and brilliant poet, an opening up of my soul.

KATHLEEN BARRY

Reviewing Reviews
Of Woman Born

Prior to the publication of *Of Woman Born,* the *New York Review of Books* published a scathing review of Adrienne Rich's book, condemning it as "partisan writing" filled with the "rhetoric of violence."[1] Almost immediately the *New York Times Book Review* and every other major reviewer followed the lead set by the *New York Review.* The reading public was left with the question "What is this book about?"

The reviews had their impact. Many bookstores that would have ordered the book did not do so. And the airwaves were silent—several major TV talk show interviews which had been arranged by the publisher were cancelled.

Most censorship is explicit and as such provides an inducement to sales. But the understood censorship of *Of Woman Born* does not involve a patronizing attempt by authorities to protect public or private morals. It is true censorship of knowledge and of ideas—censorship in its most fundamental sense.

Most Americans are socialized in an educational system which presents knowledge as immediately and once-and-for-all knowable. A fact is a fact is a fact. . . . And yet, historically we are aware that "facts" change when contradictory evidence is presented. Whether it is the Copernican system disproving the notion of the earth as the center of the universe or the feminist movement and the research of Masters and Johnson challenging the belief that the vagina is the primary source of eroticism for women, what has been presumed as fact will inevitably be altered when faced with evidence to the contrary.

Kathleen Barry's review-essay was first published in *Chrysalis,* no. 2 (1977). Reprinted with permission from the author.

But it is not the mere presentation of new facts which causes the reconstitution of previously defined "knowledge." Knowledge, new or old, arises—is developed and nourished—within an ideology. There is no such thing as value-free knowledge. Further, the ideological base of knowledge is rooted in political attitudes.[2] From its base of political power, the dominant group in society assumes the responsibility and authority for the promulgation and dissemination of knowledge and values. When, during the Middle Ages, the Church virtually controlled society, any knowledge that threatened its view of the world was suppressed. Likewise, in all five thousand years of patriarchal culture, knowledge about the role, status, or function of women has been disseminated—distorted or carefully selected—according to patriarchal values. As a result, one of the greatest abuses of women by male-dominated society has been the theft of our potential through the perpetuation of gigantic myths about who we really are.

In *Of Woman Born,* Adrienne Rich returns motherhood to women. And she returns it with feminist vision. By breaking through patriarchal mythology she exposes the essence of the domination of women through the institution of motherhood. She neither idealizes nor mandates motherhood. She does show us the ways in which it has been used to limit female potential, at the same time bringing us a vision of what motherhood can mean to all women once it is free of men's domination and control.

Of Woman Born was created out of a history of feminist thought and writing. It is not a one-woman statement on motherhood. Rather, it brings together and expands present thinking on the subject and will serve as a source for other writing and research for years to come. The book asks the most basic questions about motherhood and thus challenges the most fundamental precepts of patriarchy.

It is for this reason that censorship of *Of Woman Born* has come about. What is being censored is intricately bound to the methods of censorship. One of the most successful strategies for silencing the written work of women is through damaging reviews *by* women. Most review publications have come to recognize the effectiveness of "catfighting" they themselves create.

First, when male domination is being condemned in a work, a denunciation of that work by a male lacks credibility. Second, there is always an audience for women attacking women; it fits the notion that women are women's own worst enemy. And, finally, women can often more articulately defend men than men themselves.[3] It has long been the function of women to uphold the values that oppress them and these values are so ingrained as to be unseen. It will require a lengthy, arduous learning process to get beyond them. Unfortunately, many women are still willing and available to defend the old order.

Speaking in defense of men and their definition of motherhood, Helen Vendler in the *New York Review of Books* manages to obfuscate her intent and the purpose of the review by stating, "The selectivity of quotation throughout is a fault common to all ideological writing. It will be said that all writing is ideologically motivated. To that remark there is no response."[4] Of course there *is* a response! It is the point of this essay to demonstrate that all writing is ideologically motivated—including attacks on feminist writing, attacks which derive from and support patriarchal ideology.

I am not suggesting that there should be no critical review of this book or of any feminist writing. Indeed, our thinking can only grow and expand through honest and thoughtful criticism. But what I do find appalling is the extent to which women will go to take part in CENSORSHIP of a feminist view to protect bruised male egos and patriarchal power.

Writing for the *New York Times Book Review*, Francine Du Plessix Gray joins the infighting. Being careful not to allow the reader the benefit of quotes from Rich's book, Gray bemoans the fact that Rich does not keep motherhood "private" and its societal phenomena unquestioned. While she is pleased with Rich's personal revelations, she does not want them connected with an institutional analysis of motherhood. Gray rages when Rich steps over this boundary. "When she writes about 'motherhood as an institution' one feels that her considerable intelligence has been momentarily suspended by the intensity of her rage against men."[5] Disliking the historical context in which Rich analyzes motherhood, Gray writes it off as a mythologizing of history. That, of course, presumes that patriarchal history gives us the truth and nothing but the truth.

Ultimately neither motherhood nor feminism can be silenced. Despite censorship tactics, *Of Woman Born* continues to sell at a high rate of demand. Yet the attempts at censorship must be exposed and understood. The attack on Rich's book is a political attack against feminism and must be dealt with as a political issue. The attack is, first, a signal to us that through feminist analysis we are challenging patriarchy at its core. But it also reminds us that we are not yet powerful and that those who *are* in power can still try to silence us.

Of Woman Born should spur us on to even greater challenges of patriarchy's control over us—and so should its attempted suppression.

NOTES

1. Helen Vendler, "Myths for Mothers," *New York Review of Books,* September 30, 1976, pp. 16–17.

2. Karl Mannheim, in *Ideology and Utopia* (1936; New York: Harcourt, Brace & World, 1968), discusses the political dimensions of the social context of knowledge: "Political discussion . . . penetrates more profoundly into the existential foundation of thinking than the kind of discussion which thinks only in terms of a few selected 'points of view'. . . . Political discussion is, from the very first, more than theoretical argumentation; it is the tearing off of disguises—the unmasking of those unconscious motives which bind the group existence to its cultural aspirations and its theoretical arguments" (pp. 34–35).

3. One notable example of what happens to men's writing when they try to defend themselves against the articulate prose of women can be found in the slightly hysterical review of *Of Woman Born* by Alexander Theroux in *Boston Magazine* See pp. 304–8 in this collection.

4. Vendler, p. 17.

5. Francine Du Plessix Gray, "Amazonian Prescriptions and Proscriptions," *New York Times Book Review,* October 10, 1976, p. 3.

ALEXANDER THEROUX

Reading the Poverty of Rich

The propagandistic title—exaggeration, you assume, for emphasis—doesn't quite prepare one for the sad, monomaniacal lunacies attempting to prop it up in this book, which is less a feminist manifesto than the "Confessions of St. Adrienne." A hodgepodge of ten aggrieved essays, its stridency makes me seriously wonder why the author is living in New York rather than in one of the famous matriarchates, with the Nairs of India or the Ghats of the Indian Ocean. This book is an absolute, radical witchery; the bookend to its male chauvinist counterpart, Otto Weininger's insane *Sex and Character* (1906) in which, among other delights, can be found this little *tranche:*

> Coitus is the price man has to pay to women, under the Asiatic system, for their oppression. . . . Man must free himself of sex, for in that way, and that way alone, can he free women. In his purity, not, as she believes, in his impurity, lies her salvation. She must certainly be destroyed, as woman. . . . Every form of fecundity is loathsome, and no one who is honest with himself feels bound to provide for the continuity of the human race.

Extremism, pushed, must necessarily meet its opposite. Who but a pedant will distinguish between the factual brutality of Hitler and Stalin, converse ideologues?

Of Woman Born attempts an articulation of two sets of problems: first, Ms. Rich's personal ones, and then those same problems, in defiance of the laws of formal logic, raised to the universal ones of women in general. Adrienne Rich, born in 1929 of

Alexander Theroux's review of *Of Woman Born* is reprinted from *Boston Magazine,* November 1976. Reprinted with permission.

upper-middle-class Jewish parents, has been since the early fifties a self-proclaimed poet, feminist, woman, and mother, and this latest effort concentrates on the latter persona, addressing itself to the subject of "motherhood as experience and institution." Of her experience, anon. Of the institution—well, for her it's as if to probe into the workings of the mind of Gilles de Rais, Rhodesian domestic policy, or the proscriptions of Andersonville. The aim of institutionalized motherhood, as she'd have it, is simply that *all* women "shall remain under male control." With that panoptic judgment made—proved—she proceeds to less obvious matters.

For Adrienne Rich, history—the biased efforts of "patrivincialists," i.e., male scholars with intellectual defects (a redundancy to her)—has got it all wrong, for, since "the majority of theorists on child-raising, pediatricians, psychiatrists are male," the unavoidable conclusion follows that patriarchal history has rigorously deceived the world on the subjects of family and childhood and that, in the process, women have been relegated to nothing more than a subgroup, Q.E.D. But so objective, well-researched, and scholarly is Adrienne Rich's reassessment (". . . I have invaded various professional domains, broken various taboos. I have used the scholarship available to me where I found it suggestive . . .") that in the foreword of her book she is able to assert categorically, "Most women in history have become mothers without choice." She later remarks: "The ancient continuing envy, awe, and dread of the male for the female capacity to create life [!] has repeatedly taken the form of hatred for every other female aspect of creativity." Don't trouble yourself with the logic. Miraculous revisionism is always the upshot of a scholarship used when it is found suggestive. Weininger, using the same method, proves by algebra that women have no souls.

"Woman," Kant once wrote, "does not betray her secret." Rich belies him. She quotes us chapter and verse from the miseries of her own private life, detailing from diaries and notes, along with some perfunctory and inevitable joys, all the anxiety, physical weariness, boredom, and terror of motherhood. We are apprised, along the way, of what institutionalized motherhood has caused, with what she sees as typical and life-bright pictures of it: how women have had to give birth in piggeries; how one "scapegoat" decapitated and chopped up two of her children; how another, crusading feminist Shulamith Firestone, went to the heart of the matter: "Pregnancy is barbaric." We are treated to a vivid review of the difficulties of menstruation, labor, childbirth, breast-feeding, the mercilessness of child care. A conspiracy is discerned in it all: "We come to understand how *both* childbearing and childlessness have been manipulated to make women into negative quantities or bearers of evil." And who is at fault? Men. Fathers, husbands, uncles, grandpas, sons, the lot. There is not one generous remark about men in the entire book.

Patriarchy, Adrienne Rich writes, is

> the power of the fathers: a familial–social, ideological, political system in which men—by force, direct pressure, or through ritual, tradition, law, and language, customs, etiquette, education, and the division of labor—determine what part women shall or shall not play, and in which the female is everywhere subsumed under the male.

With that established, Rich—in hysteria, in hate, and in hyperbole—spins into one of the most misanthropic tarantellas imaginable. She blames men for monopolizing medical technology. She blames men for being in the *position* to strengthen and support women. She blames men for overpopulation, for eliminating midwives, for countenancing the pain of childbirth and for eliminating it. She blames men for the word "widow," which means *without*. She even blames "the majority of 'concerned' or profeminist men'" for they "secretly hope that 'liberation' will give them the right to shed tears while still exercising their old prerogatives." She blames Tolstoy for frightening her in a scene of parturition in *War and Peace*. She blames the Roman Catholic Church for defining the Virgin Mother "entirely by her relationship to God the Son," and while she's about it, I mean what the hell, she blames God, for "it is out of the struggle for paternal control of the family that God the Father is created." I may be wrong, I'm not certain, but I don't believe she included masculine rhymes, male holly bushes, or mascular plugs.

"This book," writes Rich, "is rooted in my own past." I

don't think one has to reach further to ascertain the *essential* motive of the book, allowing all the while, of course, that many of her complaints in terms of women's rights are at once argument-proof, sound, and well-made. St. Augustine's early Carthaginian mistakes are not unrelated to his theology. *Of Woman Born* strikes me, frankly, as a kind of nervous breakdown, an exorcism, an examination of conscience. Motherhood-as-experience: this aspect of the book seems to me scrupulously honest and, at times, heartbreaking. Her life is seamed with regret:

> I became a mother in the family-centered, consumer-oriented, Freudian-American world of the 1950s. My husband spoke eagerly of the children we would have; my parents-in-law awaited the birth of their grandchild. I had no idea of what *I* wanted. . . .

But, to me, it's clear she did—she wanted to be a poet, she wanted to be happy, she wanted, in Hopkins's terms, to "selve." Nevertheless, she quickly had three children and lived what she adjudges now a stereotypical life, a wifehood, a motherhood, for twenty years, with the domestic duties hers and her husband's professional life considered the real work of the family. Clearly, she wasn't meant for such sacrifices or, better, she preferred to devise sacrifices of her *own* making. Unfulfilled, guilt-ridden, depressed, she decided to be sterilized a mere twenty-four hours after the birth of her third child. The marriage was terminated. Her husband committed suicide. And since then, she says, she has been trying to give birth to herself—a phrase by which, perhaps, we can charitably interpret the inscrutable title of this book.

The autobiographical business, then, is hardly incidental to the book, nor is it given out to be; it shuttles along, weaving through, as it informs and shapes, the rubric of one thesis and then another. It *explicates*—perhaps absolves—her rage. And it slowly becomes the undisguised and primal fact of the book that Ms. Rich, a Radcliffe graduate, a poet, an intellectual of sorts, simply resented—while feeling guilty for it—the artistically creative chances stolen from her as she tried to conform to the "patriarchal" conception of motherhood her parents, her mimetic youth, her contemporary experience tried to instill. "In 1945," she confesses, "I was writing poetry seriously and had a fantasy of going to postwar Europe as a journalist, sleeping among the ruins in bombed cities, recording the rebirth of civilization after the fall of the Nazis. . . . I have a very clear, keen memory of myself the day after I was married: I was sweeping a floor."

There is a tension described here, one passionately evinced, for which one can have nothing but sympathy and to which a shared regret is quickly brought. There is a reason, and it's a simple one, for no one alive, male or female, couldn't in some form or other publish—or at least wish to—similar laments about his or her own life, asking only that the reader somehow share it, understand it, and reach out to touch that sorrow with an extended hand of compassion and gentle grace. We understand *this* Adrienne Rich. She locates the pain in all of us: a black South African, a starving Glaswegian, a humpbacked child in Boston. How many books! How much grief!

This is the virtue of this book, one, alas, in pieces, chilled by polemic, blunted by a hacking didacticism. The autobiography here was not researched; it didn't have to be; it was experienced firsthand, born of suffering, of struggle, of pain—and with the vulnerability of the author we can, as we should, only commiserate. But for the pages of exclusivist and misandrous rubbish in *Of Woman Born,* for the cruel exaggerations that can only further widen the already wide rift between the sexes, for the agitprop, for the sloganeering, for the absurd and crapulous poetry thrown in to support the unilateral myths in the history to which she'd have us subscribe, I can only say I find most of it mercyproof, reasonless, blackhearted, and unfair. There is a narcissism in this part of the book that makes argument a joke. It smells of a dissertation, glossed only with sources that fit the scope of its narrowness. And saddest of all, in its soliloquy, somniloquy, and self-conscious attitudinizing, it commits the very sins it accuses in others, which is why, though touching upon the genre of the "confession," it but parodies the growing mercy and learned wisdom of Augustine's.

ELLEN MOERS

A Poet's Feminist Prose

That Adrienne Rich is one of America's most important and gifted poets is of course a known fact here; it is also known abroad, as a year of travel from Tokyo to Sydney to Paris informed this reviewer in 1978. Less well known is her quality as a writer of prose. This fact alone justifies the publication of this collection of twenty-two essays that might otherwise be lost, for they originally appeared in such places as *Chrysalis: A Magazine of Women's Culture; Chronicle of Higher Education; Parnassus: Poetry in Review; Heresies: A Feminist Magazine of Art and Politics; College English; Ms.; Sinister Wisdom*—as well as the "Op-Ed" page of the *New York Times*. Some were introductions to other people's books, some were talks never printed.

Adrienne Rich's prose moves with force, clarity, energy; and soothes with a poet's grace and elegance. The only bad prose in the volume is its title, which conveys a wholly inaccurate idea of whining and whimpering within. Feminism, pedagogy and literature, not lies, secrets and silence, are the subjects covered by her essays. The literary studies are brilliant: on Anne Bradstreet, on *Jane Eyre* and on Emily Dickinson, about whom Adrienne Rich may have written the single best critical essay we have.

On pedagogy she is always interesting, especially when writing about the SEEK program (Search for Education, Elevation and Knowledge) in which she taught at the City College of New York in the late 1960s. "Claiming an Education," the convocation address she delivered at Douglass, the distinguished women's college of Rutgers University where she now teaches, could be repeated yearly with pleasure and profit to entering college students of both sexes, and must be one of the liveliest models of the genre. She comments: "If university education means anything beyond the processing of human beings into expected roles, through credit hours, tests and grades, it implies an ethical and intellectual contract between teacher and student. . . . Too often, all of us fail to teach the most important thing, which is that clear thinking, active discussion, and excellent writing are all necessary for intellectual freedom, and that these require *hard work*."

On feminist issues, which loom largest here and affect all her subjects, Adrienne Rich says much that we have heard before from others; but she usually says it better. Feminist readers, who may feel they need not read another word on women's issues, will find themselves mining this collection for quotable epigrams on such matters as consciousness-raising ("it is no longer such a lonely thing to open one's eyes"); token women; day-care centers; male psychiatrists (blaming "the waste of [society's] young on the 'bad' mothers who have somehow failed to be superhuman"); women's studies; abortion; the problems and challenges of black feminism ("beleaguered . . . between the twin grindstones of gynephobia and racism"); sexist advertising and the ever-present threat of rape.

She writes: "If it is dangerous for me to walk home late of an evening from the library, *because I am a woman and can be raped,* how self-possessed, how exuberant can I feel as I sit working in that library? How much of my working energy is drained by the subliminal knowledge that, as a woman, I test my physical right to exist each time I go out alone?" Extreme? Recently, when I left the library of a California university late one afternoon, a woman student came up to warn me not to take the direct route to the parking lot through a small wood, as it was the principal scene of campus rape.

For the purpose of scholars, Adrienne Rich's most important feminist subject is lesbianism, because lesbianism (of capital importance to modernism in the arts) has a slim bibliography, to which she unfortunately contributes only a few scattered pages here. Perhaps another book is in view.

Antifeminist readers, who do not understand what "patriarchal society" means, can learn a lot from the critical use of the concept Adrienne Rich makes in her studies of Brontë and Dickinson. (The wide-ranging and hostile overtones given by women to the word patriarchal are hardly of recent coinage. Harriet Beecher Stowe, in her historic letter announcing that she was writing *Uncle Tom's Cabin,* referred to slavery as "the 'patriarchal institution.'") In "Vesuvius at Home: The Power of Emily Dickinson," it is with the authority of a woman poet that Adrienne Rich discerns will, power and freedom in Dickinson's poems, many of which "seem to me a poet's poems—that is, they are about the poet's relationship to her own power, which is exteriorized in masculine form, much as masculine poets have invoked the female Muse." She reads "He fumbles at your Soul" (#315) and "He put the Belt around my Life" (#273) not as love poems to some never-to-be-discovered adored male, but as poetry in an ancient mystic tradition in which metaphors "of seduction and rape [are] merged with the intense force of a religious experience." In "I'm ceded—I've stopped being Theirs—" (#508) Rich finds the theme not only of confirmation but of "self-confirmation" as a woman: "It is a poem of movement from childhood to womanhood, of transcending the patriarchal condition of bearing her father's name and 'crowing—on my Father's breast—.' She is now a conscious Queen 'Adequate—Erect / With Will to choose, or to reject.'"

From time to time in this volume Adrienne Rich returns to motherhood, the subject treated in *Of Woman Born* (1976). Here I find myself in frequent disagreement, and hope, if I ever meet her, to have a debate based on our mutual experience of mothering during the fearful 1960s. Her interests in the subject run to politics and sexuality; mine to economics and aesthetics. But that mothers alone must determine the optimum conditions under which they do the work of motherhood is her central point, on which I can imagine no possible disagreement. As she puts it, the goal "is to release the creation and sustenance of life into the same realm of decision, struggle, surprise, imagination, and conscious intelligence, as any other difficult, but freely chosen, work."

This collection is not a personal memoir about a poet who has also been a daughter, wife, mother, divorcée* and lesbian, but it provides one shattering revelation about her education. She went to a highly selective, competitive all-girls high school and then to Radcliffe, of which she writes: "I never saw a single woman on a lecture platform, or in front of a class . . . and never again was I to experience, from a teacher, the kind of prodding, the insistence that my best could be even better, that I had known in high school. Women students were simply not taken very seriously."

Those women of the same generation who went to Vassar found women professors dominating the faculty: women of such scholarly distinction, of such variety of temperament and personal life, that there was no question of looking for a "role model" needle in a haystack; no need to compare female with male professors; and no women students, only students. There is an important book to be written on the varying imprint of the "Seven Sisters" colleges on distinguished American women of the last half-century. For literary starters, Mary McCarthy of Vassar, Adrienne Rich of Radcliffe, and Sylvia Plath of Smith.

The generosity with which Adrienne Rich has given herself to feminist causes in the last decade has made this collection out-of-date in one odd way, even though most of its essays were written in the late 1970s. She seems not to have had time to acknowledge and enjoy the accomplishments of the feminist movement. She seems not to know many young women of 1979, off to their careers in banking or government, intelligently handling their personal lives. But they know Adrienne Rich and what she has written. Thanks are due her from all who raise, teach, work with, marry or are young women.

---

*Moers is in error here; Rich left her marriage, but I do not think that she and Alfred Conrad were divorced. For Rich's mention of the separation, see *Of Woman Born* (New York: Norton, 1976; pb. ed. Bantam, 1977), p. 13.

ANN BARR SNITOW

Review of *On Lies, Secrets and Silence: Selected Prose 1966–1978*

> *It could be said that a women's university-without-walls exists*
> *already in America. . . .*
>
> —P. 126

Of particular interest to educators in this excellent collection of
essays by the feminist poet Adrienne Rich are the many pieces
that raise by implication such questions as the following: Are
women's studies programs a fad? What are the shortcomings of
a male-centered university? How would a woman-centered uni-
versity be different? Are there two cultures, one male, one
female? The varied essays here are parts of one struggle against
"the erasure of women's political and historic past which makes
each new generation of feminists appear as an abnormal excres-
cence on the face of time" (pp. 9–10). They are also reminders in
a period of backlash that an insurgent, communal female culture
continues to develop in America beyond the range of media
report.

In an essay already a classic of the women's movement,
"When We Dead Awaken: Writing as Re-Vision," Rich gives a
history of her own education that is a devastating indictment of
what this culture teaches its young girls. She describes the slow
death of the spirit of a girl who, in search of her self, reads the
books her teachers put uncritically into her hands:

> She meets the image of Woman in books written by men. She
> finds a terror and a dream, she finds a beautiful pale face . . .
> she finds Juliet or Tess or Salomé, but precisely what she does

Reprinted from *Harvard Educational Review* 49 (November 1979). Copyright ©
1979 by President and Fellows of Harvard College. Reprinted by permission.

not find is that absorbed, drudging, puzzled, sometimes inspired creature, herself, who sits at a desk trying to put words together. (P. 39)

The irony that concludes this essay is that this male culture, so alienating a subject matter to teach a female apprentice, is itself crumbling inward, obsessively calling up its sacred cows, without new insight, or any fresh, redemptive hopes.

But it is when Rich comes to analyze the situation of women in the university that she becomes most original and most suggestive. She describes how men, however sympathetic, however aware of male cultural bankruptcy, of "depersonalization, fragmentation, waste, artificial scarcity" (p. 130), are nevertheless hard put to imagine women students as central in the process of change, as potential cultural leaders, as powerful. Men fear feminism, she argues, and do not know why. "Much male fear of feminism is infantilism—the longing to remain the mother's son, to possess a woman who exists purely for him" (p. 221). Rich sees university life as traditionally based on plays for power among men, in which women are felt to be out of place.

How might this antifemale bias be dispelled in the university? Not, Rich makes plain, by tokenism, Letting a few, or even a sizable number of "special" women in cannot change the texture of the university experience as a whole. "For us, to be 'extraordinary' or 'uncommon' is to fail. History has been embellished with 'extraordinary,' 'exemplary,' 'uncommon,' and of course 'token' women whose lives have left the rest unchanged" (p. 255). In "Toward a Woman-Centered University" she speaks more about free day care than about the female classics, more about making common cause among women professors, students, and staff than about improving feminist scholarship—this in spite of the fact that the volume affords superb examples of the new feminist literary criticism, necessary reading for anyone teaching Anne Bradstreet, Charlotte Brontë, Emily Dickinson, or Anne Sexton.

And what of women's studies, that unloved daughter, that interdisciplinary hybrid growth clinging for dear life to the unfriendly rock of so many universities?

Women in colleges where a women's studies program already exists . . . still are often made to feel that the "real" curriculum is the male-centered one; that women's studies are (like Third World studies) a "fad"; that feminist teachers are "unscholarly," "unprofessional," or "dykes." (P. 136)

Rich posits a feminist scholarship and politics that could make a virtue of this marginality. She redefines the situation into two curricula, one male: exhausted, pessimistic, threadbare; the other, female: fresh and dangerous, only just emerging from lies, secrets, silence.

As Rich knows, the reality is that although women's studies programs are still proliferating, very few have taken firm root. Each must face the question of how to link itself structurally with the university, how to survive, and how to influence the whole community, without finally being watered down or subsumed by those with no particular stake in feminist issues. Even in the rare universities where women's studies programs have the clout to command funds, they are isolated. At best they represent an alternative; at worst they are for most students something that need never touch their lives.

However, at this stage, integration into the general curriculum of what Rich calls "women's questions" (p. 17) is impossible. Schools have shown themselves strangely immune to influence. Even the idea of an enlarged canon of readings, often proposed by blacks and women, does not take. And in courses where female writers or female experiences are discussed, the feminist criticism which crucially modifies traditional approaches is rarely a part of the intellectual equipment of even the most well-meaning male teacher who assigns the new texts.

Right now women's studies programs have a better chance of educating women in an enclave. A program serves as a local habitation where what Rich calls "unspeakable" material can be discussed. The intellectual fruits of this fertile environment have already proved extraordinary. Feminist historians like Joan Kelly Godal are reperiodizing history, finding, for example, that the Renaissance was no Renaissance for women, while the Middle Ages was a period of flourishing female culture. Psychologists like Dorothy Dinnerstein are revising earlier explanations for the nearly universal asymmetry between the public and private roles of the two sexes. Feminist critics are unearthing and developing an appreciation for a female tradition in art. Rich gives different examples, and her footnotes are a fine bibliographic source for the new scholarship in all areas, though, regrettably, there is no cumulative list provided of these materials.

Perhaps the pressure behind these new ideas will build up, as it tends to do behind that which is suppressed, until there is an explosion which the rest of the university cannot choose but hear. Certainly, women's studies will continue to be a major source of intellectual breakthrough in the next decade. One of the great gifts that feminism has to offer the university is an idea of integration, an attack on dichotomous thinking: mind and body; love and death; children and career; gay and straight; right brain and left; autonomy and relation; sex oppression and race oppression[1]—all the treacherous splits that are the hallmarks, perhaps also the death warrant, of Western culture.

It remains to be seen whether women's studies will survive to make its gift to the university. If feminism cannot make itself felt there, it will continue to emerge elsewhere in that "university-without-walls [that] exists already in America." The various movements towards feminist change are powerful, and the larger question is whether or not they will be overtaken by the sort of material crises that can close a chapter of one particular civilizing effort. Rich writes:

> I know that the rest of my life will be spent working for transformations I shall not live to see realized. I feel daily, hourly impatience, and am pledged to the active and tenacious patience that a lifetime commitment requires: there can be no resignation in the face of backlash, setback, or temporary defeat; there can be no limits on what we allow ourselves to imagine. Because the past ten years of feminist thinking and action have been so full, so charged with revelations, challenges, as well as with anger and pain, we sometimes think of that decade as if it had been fifty years, not ten. *Why haven't we come further?* But in the great evolution of women that this century's radical feminism envisions, we have only

begun. And yet this longer historical view seems unbearable to me when I consider the urgency of each woman's life that may be lost, poured away like dishwater, because history does not move fast enough for her. (P. 271)

If Adrienne Rich cannot tell how to enact the new ideas on parallel lines with the old, yet finally make these lines cross—the women's studies paradox, which must in the end be resolved— she can well dramatize what it means to see a woman's life lost.

> Look at a classroom: look at the many kinds of women's faces, postures, expressions. Listen to the women's voices. Listen to the silences, the unasked questions, the blanks. Listen to the small, soft voices, often courageously trying to speak up, voices of women taught early that tones of confidence, challenge, anger, or assertiveness, are strident and unfeminine. Listen to the voices of the women and the voices of the men; observe the space men allow themselves, physically and verbally, the male assumption that people will listen, even when the majority of the group is female. Look at the faces of the silent, and of those who speak. (P. 243)

As every teacher knows, passive women students are legion. But there is a new group visible alongside them who have worked or studied in groups of women, learned about their "much-politicized biology" (p. 240), learned about their history. These, says Adrienne Rich, are less "vulnerable to the projections of male fantasy"; "ignorance of ourselves has been the key to our powerlessness" (p. 240). Insofar as this is true, the university has potential as an honorable and important locale for feminist political work.

Adrienne Rich's writings are a reminder of the vital link that can exist between the academy and the radical imagination. A serious student, a careful carver of distinctions, she is also the poet working toward cultural transformation within her own medium. When she published her first book of poems in 1951, W. H. Auden praised her for knowing her place in the tradition, for writing poems "neatly and modestly dressed . . . [which] respect their elders but are not cowed by them."[2] But that volume was called *A Change of World,* and it is a change of world she has increasingly wanted. She is now a powerful critic of the tradition into which she was once so warmly accepted as a well-behaved token.

Rich's most recent book of poems is called *The Dream of a Common Language.* Her essays provide a gloss to that title: "dream" because women are still committed to lies and secrets that keep them from speech; "common" because women's culture will pay "passionate attention to *all* female experience" (p. 213), will be shared, a maximizing of private and collective intelligence; "language" because communication is power, not the power of dominance but the power to speak and be believed, to enact fully what one is.

Appropriately enough, the best thing in the volume is the essay in which Rich comes closest to fusing the poet and the duteous, much-valued political worker: "Women and Honor: Some Notes on Lying." The piece is laid out in impressionistic fragments, a technique which may one day be recognized as a potential form for scholars. She understands why women lie; she wants to warn them how much there is to lose through this lying. In telling self-protective lies to others, women have sometimes forgotten they are lying, have closed the door to the subconscious, and have given up on the unrewarded project of finding out who they are. This loss of authenticity is one of oppression's most subtle and vicious by-products.

The university has always rhapsodized about its unbiased quest for truth. Can it expand into an intellectual home for women who make this search? This volume reminds us what will remain if it cannot: a place where traditions cannot fuse, where unequal and discontinuous cultures coexist, always with "the unspeakable," with lies, between them.

NOTES

1. Rich has a brilliant, ground-breaking essay, "Disloyal to Civilization," about "the special history of polarization" (p. 280) between black and white women.

2. Foreword to *A Change of World.* Reprinted in this collection, pp. 209–11.

GLORIA BOWLES

Adrienne Rich as Feminist Theorist

In the introduction to the first issue of *Sinister Wisdom* which she edited with Michelle Cliff, Adrienne Rich wrote:

> We believe that many more women should be writing theory. The word "theory" has bad associations for some: abstract writing, rhetoric, something detached from practice, from action, from daily needs. Yet theory can take many forms. . . . Theory essentially means thinking, reflecting on, what has happened to us and drawing some kind of general principles from that. . . . Unfortunately, when we explore our concrete experiences without theory-making, we are left with isolated instances, feelings of victimization, therapy insights, perhaps, but no sense of how these experiences belong to a larger whole, or how we can move out from them not just as individuals but *with* large numbers of other women. . . .[1]

Adrienne Rich is one of our most important feminist theorists. She wants her writing to inspire dialogue and spirited critique. Her authoritative prose style betrays her a bit; because it is so forceful, it does not seem to admit disagreement. Yet she writes not to inspire overweening admiration but to move feminist theory in directions that will help us to live more honestly.[2] Few of Rich's works have engendered as much debate as her essay on "Compulsory Heterosexuality and Lesbian Existence," which appeared in *Signs* in Summer 1980, and two articles on black women writers, "Wholeness Is No Trifling Matter," published in the *New Women's Times Feminist Review* in December 1980 and January 1981.[3] As we might expect, these articles are

Previously unpublished, 1981.

linked thematically, reflecting Rich's thought at the beginning of the decade of the eighties. In this brief essay, I will attempt to sound some of the themes which these articles raise and to respond to them. No doubt some of my propositions will be as controversial as Rich's but they are intended to be part of the dialogue which contributes to feminist theory. This article is inspired by my discussions with feminist friends and colleagues, that oral tradition of feminist theory-making which has been repeated all over the United States and Europe, wherever women have had access to Rich's work.[4]

"Compulsory Heterosexuality and Lesbian Existence" is both a contribution to feminist theory and a challenge to feminist scholarship. Rich has several purposes here. First, she wants to show how women have had little choice about their relationships with men, that heterosexuality is compulsory and that it is enforced by all means possible, from brute force to mass advertising. Although it does obscure enormous differences in women's love relationships with men, I think this argument, compellingly made, has some merit and gives us much to ponder and use in the years to come. It is very difficult to know how many women really choose heterosexuality. It is clear that everything in this society conspires to prevent us from entertaining any idea that we might have a choice.

One of the ways heterosexuality is enforced is by suppressing permission for feelings among women. This leads Rich to lesbianism, a term she wants to rescue from the realms of the clinical and the perverse. First, she wants "lesbianism" to be purged of its sex-only ring. That she has to do this is partly because our culture is sex-mad. Lillian Faderman had the same problem with a different wrinkle as she was working on her history of lesbian relationships from the Renaissance to the present day. She had a hard time convincing some contemporary feminists that women who did not sleep together were in fact lesbians. For Faderman, the working definition of "lesbian" is

a relationship in which two women's strongest emotions and affections are directed toward each other. Sexual contact may be a part of the relationship to a greater or lesser degree, or it may be entirely absent. By preference the two women spend most of their time together and share most aspects of their lives with each other. "Romantic friendship" described a similar relationship.[5]

I do not think that sophisticated women's studies scholars, some of whom are lesbians, think of lesbianism only in terms of sexual activity, although we are aware we must confront this prejudice in our introductory courses. Rich cites several works of feminist scholarship as examples of heterosexual bias. While I do not excuse this bias, I think it is important to remember that these books were written several years ago. Feminist scholarship is developing rapidly; not one of us would write the same thing today that we wrote three years ago, any more than spokeswomen for the movement would make the same statements they made earlier.

Besides ridding lesbianism of its sex-only connotation, Rich has a subsidiary point and, I think, an interesting one: she also wants to remove lesbianism from the realm of the exotic, that decadence we associate with turn-of-the-century Paris, say, when because of class privilege and wealth, some women were permitted public lesbianism. I think we need to explore further the meanings behind the displays of lesbianism, homosexuality, and transvestism on the continent and in England in this period, the manifestation of the permitted "perverse," which is so far from the day-to-day existence of real lesbians and homosexuals. What Rich asks us to do, then, is essentially to reconceptualize "lesbianism." That means disassociating our imaginations from the nineteenth-century aristocrats who rode around in carriages—and for me, by extension, from the cult of masculine dress which is part of the contemporary lesbian scene. It is to think in free, unstereotyped ways, to conceive of lesbian existence as one possible way to be more ourselves.

Instead of "lesbianism," Rich proposes the terms "lesbian existence" and "lesbian continuum":

> *Lesbian existence* suggests both the fact of the historical presence of lesbians and our continuing creation of the meaning of that existence. I mean the term *lesbian continuum* to include a range—through each woman's life and throughout

history—of woman-identified experience; not simply the fact that a woman has had or consciously desired genital sexual experience with another woman. If we expand it to embrace many more forms of primary intensity between and among women, including the sharing of a rich inner life, the bonding against male tyranny, the giving and receiving of practical and political support; if we can also hear in it such associations as *marriage resistance* and the "haggard" behavior identified by Mary Daly . . . we begin to grasp breadths of female history and psychology which have lain out of reach as a consequence of limited, mostly clinical, definitions of "lesbianism."[6]

Some women I have talked with, now sitting on the fence, poised between heterosexuality and they know not what, like this definition because it ends their feelings of being "left out," places them instead on a continuum *with other women*. There are also objections. My first one was: if we make all female love part of the "lesbian continuum," then what do we call the experience of women who have come out and suffered enormously for doing so? To give the appellation "lesbian" such a broad definition is to reduce the significance of those few who are courageously trying to force the society to broaden its ideas of what is possible and fruitful in this world. Of course, what Rich wants to do is to put the lives of declared lesbians and undeclared lesbians in context, to *join* us. She is thinking of all history; I wish to focus on particular periods, our own, for example, when women pay great costs for coming out. Early in women's studies, we brought forth generalizations because we did not have enough scholarship to be specific, to explore women's differences. Now I think we should be trying to get away from generalizations in order to better understand both our commonalities and our differences.

In the *Signs* article, black women are one illustration of the lesbian continuum. There, Rich makes few distinctions between black and white women writers since her main purpose is to advocate the idea of a continuum. In the *New Women's Times Feminist Review* articles on black women writers, Rich is more explicit about the origin of the lesbian continuum: "Do we identify first as white or first as female, we who claim that the 'bonds of womanhood' are the original and primary connection?"[7] This "original and primary connection," then, is the basis for the lesbian continuum. Although she has not put it so neatly, I read Rich's process of knowing this way: we realize that heterosexuality is compulsory; we unearth the importance of female bonding, which has taken place throughout our lives; we discover the *primary* connection between ourselves and other women. All of the individual primary connections make up a lesbian continuum across history, lesbian in the sense both of emotional and erotic attachments, and erotic understood in its broadest sense.

The assertion of a primary connection among women is no surprise to those who have read Rich's prose and poetry over the last few years. Of course, there are many feminists who would disagree that "'the bonds of womanhood' are the . . . primary connections." I find it difficult to imagine connections with either women or men as primary—it is all too primal, too Laurentian sounding to me. Relationships among questioning people are in such disarray today, obscured by roles and power, that I think definitive pronouncements on our kinds of connections are premature. Moreover, I think I would always oppose any hypothesis that declares one kind of relationship "primary." This kind of an argument, albeit in a shadowy kind of way, seems to invoke Nature, in the sense of some fixed and determinate origins of humankind. Such theories have been used against women and I think it is dangerous for us to be arguing along similar lines.[8]

Rich finds vivid examples of these "original and primary connections" among twentieth-century black women writers: "It is impossible to miss the fact that the predominant values and vision of Black women's fiction are female. . . ." White women can learn from this; in fact, "white women, white feminists, white lesbians . . . cannot fully comprehend female struggle and woman-to-woman bonding without the work of these writers."[9] Later she writes that the fiction of black women is an expression of the lesbian continuum:

> I have written elsewhere of the institution of compulsory heterosexuality as blocking women's capacity to bond with women, and as obscuring the *lesbian continuum* in and out of

which all women's lives move, individually and histori-
cally. . . .

Black women's fiction provides endless instances of this
lesbian continuum, even when it does not directly reflect the
experience of Black lesbians. . . .[10]

The contemporary novels of black women are compelling, in
connection still with politics and survival; white women's nov-
els seem to drift into disquisition on life style. I keep waiting for
the eloquent fiction that reflects the kind of life-in-struggle led
by contemporary white feminists. Yet to invoke black women
as exemplary because they illustrate the primary connections
(and thus the lesbian continuum) is highly problematic. As
women of privilege, educated, white middle-class critics, I think
we need to be particularly careful about appropriating the work
and the lives of women of color to validate our theories. Too
many of our formulations are "culture-bound," as the an-
thropologists say. Middle-class white women in contemporary
America have been alienated from each other but we are a tiny
portion of the world's female population. In the *Signs* article,
Rich quotes black lesbian feminist critic Lorraine Bethel, who
wrote that "Black women have a long tradition of bonding
together."[11] Yes, there has always been bonding among black
women; but some black feminists would not agree that this has
been their primary connection. Barbara Christian, author of
*Black Women Novelists: The Development of a Tradition,
1892–1976,* says:

> . . . a characteristic of the culture that black women come
> from is that intense friendship amongst women has always
> been an important element. That does not mean that this is
> the *only* element that is important. . . . The relationship be-
> tween the self and the community, for example. And the
> community consists of children as well as men as well as
> elders.[12]

When we are told that the bonding of black women is exem-
plary, we are led to ask: What kinds of bonding? Under what
circumstances does bonding take place? Are there differences in

bonding among black and white women and other women of color? Among working-class and aristocratic women? What about interracial bonding?

Ultimately, it is a little greedy—and much too general—to claim all kinds of female bonding and all of black women's writing for the lesbian continuum. Perhaps our fears of being different are surfacing again in the eighties, a time so uncongenial to feminism. But if theory is for praxis, if we want to advance our ideas so that we can transform idea into action *in order to improve the lives of women,* then we must be as specific as possible. In her newest book of poems, *A Wild Patience Has Taken Me This Far,* Rich is immersed in women's history; through the poems she is

> trying to clarify   connect
>
> past and present   near and far
> the Alabama quilt
> the Botswana basket
> history
>
>   ("The Spirit of Place")[13]

The "wild patience" brings on an urge to simplify in order to clarify and connect, and an even stronger urge to recognize how very difficult it is to know the past. Women's history is one of the most compelling of the new studies of women as it invites us to identify imaginatively with the lives of women in the past. In so doing, we must be aware of differences and of the dangers of seeing the past through the lens of the present. We must always stifle the urge to simplify, that urge born of anger, impatience or a lack of knowledge.

Thus, we can question whether we should even be trying to develop ideas of a "continuum" ("a thing whose parts cannot be separated or discerned").[14] And we need to ask ourselves: for whom are we making theory? If it is only for ourselves, for our discussions, then we have become just another study, another academic discipline. If I were to talk with a peasant woman in Greece about "female bonding," she would understand immediately what I mean—the ties between women, the unspoken putting up with men. But if I spoke of a "lesbian continuum," she would be utterly confused and immediately alienated. For feminist scholars to assume heterosexuality and to put lesbianism on the margin is unacceptable. To abandon distinctions between lesbianism and female bonding is also unacceptable.

In essence, theory formulation means to put forth ideas, to apply and then revise these ideas in order to make a closer fit between theory and reality as we women perceive it. We do not expect that any of our formulations will be definitive or "right" for all time. In fact, we are dedicated to the process of discussion and reformulation. Now, feminist scholars are facing the limitations of any theory which does not include women of color and lesbians. Adrienne Rich has always helped us to see the blank spaces in feminist thought. Her work constantly challenges our own, asking us to rethink, to see anew—to change. Her articles on lesbianism and black women have raised questions that will be with us for some time.[15]

NOTES

1. Adrienne Rich, "Notes for a Magazine," *Sinister Wisdom* 17 (1981): 6.

2. The relationship of the "personal" to current feminist theory-making needs much more discussion. As feminists, we seem to assume that our theories begin with personal experience. But to what extent does our personal get expressed in articles on theory? Are we "copping to our biases," as the old movement phrase would have it, or are we now legitimizing only "pure theory"? Through her poetry and prose, Adrienne Rich is generous about making public the relevant "personal." Is academic feminism, on the other hand, promoting objective "distance"? For a fascinating discussion of the use of the personal in feminist social science, see Liz Stanley and Sue Wise's advocacy of "vulnerability" in research: "Back into 'The Personal,' or Our Attempt to Construct Feminist Research," in *Theories of Women's Studies II,* ed. Gloria Bowles and Renate Duelli-Klein (Berkeley: Women's Studies Program, 1981).

3. "Compulsory Heterosexuality and Lesbian Existence," *Signs* (Summer 1980): 631–60; "'Wholeness Is No Trifling Matter': Some Fiction by Black Women," *New Women's Times Feminist Review,* December 1980/January 1981, pp. 10–13 and February/March 1981, pp. 12–13, 20–24.

4. In Britain, for example, feminist bookstores sell single copies of the "Compulsory Heterosexuality . . ." essay. Many discussions of Rich's latest work took place at meetings of the National Women's Studies Association in Storrs, Connecticut, June, 1981.

5. Lillian Faderman, *Surpassing the Love of Men* (New York: William Morrow, 1981), pp. 17–18. Faderman's subtitle gets at the distinctions: *Romantic Friendship and Love Between Women from the Renaissance to the Present.*

6. "Compulsory Heterosexuality . . . ," pp. 648–49. *Signs* is publishing responses to Rich's essay. The first response, from Martha E. Thompson, takes issue with the idea that "compulsory heterosexuality is the central factor in women's oppression." *Signs* (Summer 1981): 790–94. See vol. 7 (Autumn 1981) for responses from Ann Ferguson, Jacquelyn N. Zita, and Kathryn Pyne Addelson.

7. "Wholeness . . . ," *New Women's Times Feminist Review*, February/March 1981, p. 20. Rich's first article on racism in the women's movement, "Disloyal to Civilization: Feminism, Racism, Gynephobia," was published in *Chrysalis* in 1978 and republished in *On Lies, Secrets and Silence.* I am not dealing with that essay here because of lack of space and because the more recent essays are related in specific themes. But I do want to acknowledge the starting point for her writing about racism.

8. See, for example, Monique Wittig, "One Is Not Born a Woman," *Feminist Issues* 1 (Winter 1981): 47–54.

9. "Wholeness . . . ," *New Women's Times Feminist Review*, December 1980/January 1981, p. 10.

10. "Wholeness . . . ," *New Women's Times Feminist Review*, February/March, 1981, p. 22.

11. Lorraine Bethel, quoted by Adrienne Rich, "Compulsory Heterosexuality . . . ," p. 658. The entire quotation reads: "Black women have a long tradition of bonding together . . . in a Black/women's community that has been a source of vital survival information, psychic and emotional support for us. We have a distinct Black woman-identified folk culture based on our experiences as Black women in this society; symbols, language and modes of expression that are specific to the realities of our lives. . . . Because Black women were rarely among those Blacks and females who gained access to literary and other acknowledged forms of artistic expression, this Black female bonding and Black woman-identification has often been hidden and unrecorded except in the individual lives of Black women through our own memories of our particular Black female tradition."

12. Gloria Bowles, Diane Le Bow and Barbara Christian, "Toward a Multi-Ethnic Feminist Literary Criticism: The Process of One Session at NWSA 1981," forthcoming in *Proceedings of the National Women's*

Studies Association Third Annual Conference, Storrs, Connecticut, June 1981. Barbara Christian's book was published by Greenwood Press in 1980.

13. *A Wild Patience Has Taken Me This Far: Poems 1978–1981* (New York: Norton, 1981), p. 41.

14. *Webster's New World Dictionary,* 2d College ed., s.v. "continuum."

15. Clearly, as these citations show, the emergence of feminist periodicals and newspapers in the last ten years has been crucial to the process of theory-making.

Bibliography

I. Primary Materials

POETRY

A Change of World. New Haven: Yale University Press, 1951.

The Diamond Cutters and Other Poems. New York: Harper & Brothers, 1955.

Snapshots of a Daughter-in-Law. Poems 1954–1962. New York: Harper & Row, 1963; New York: W. W. Norton, 1967; London: Chatto & Windus, 1970.

Necessities of Life: Poems 1962–1965. New York: W. W. Norton, 1966.

Selected Poems. London: Chatto & Windus, 1967.

Leaflets: Poems 1965–1968. New York: W. W. Norton, 1969; London: Chatto & Windus, 1972.

The Will to Change: Poems 1968–1970. New York: W. W. Norton, 1971; London: Chatto & Windus, 1973.

Diving into the Wreck: Poems 1971–1972. New York: W. W. Norton, 1973.

Poems: Selected and New 1950–1974. New York: W. W. Norton, 1975.

Twenty-One Love Poems. Emeryville, California: Effie's Press, 1976.

The Dream of a Common Language: Poems 1974–1977. New York: W. W. Norton, 1978.

A Wild Patience Has Taken Me This Far: Poems 1978–1981. New York: W. W. Norton, 1981.

PROSE

Included here are citations for Rich's articles, reviews, columns, books of prose, transcripts of speeches and panel presentations, forewords and afterwords to books by other writers, responses to questionnaires, letters to editors (and letters written by others in response to Rich's), and

---

Note: An asterisk indicates that the work is included in this volume.

excerpts from Rich's communications which are quoted by other writers. Entries are alphabetized and listed by year of publication (or presentation, if Rich read the material publicly prior to publication). I have also cited some secondary materials in this section to guide readers to responses to Rich's letters to editors, and to reviews of books which include commentary on a foreword or afterword by Rich. These pieces are cross-referenced and cited in both sections of the bibliography.

1963

Review of *The Lordly Hudson: Collected Poems of Paul Goodman. New York Review of Books,* first issue, undated, 1963, p. 27.

1964

"Beyond the Heirlooms of Tradition." Review of *Found Objects* by Louis Zukofsky. *Poetry* 105 (November 1964):128–29.
"Mr. Bones, He Lives." Review of *77 Dream Songs* by John Berryman. *The Nation,* May 25, 1964, pp. 538, 540.
"On Karl Shapiro's *The Bourgeois Poet.*" In *The Contemporary Poet as Artist and Critic: 8 Symposia,* edited by Anthony Ostroff. Boston: Little, Brown and Company, 1964, pp. 192–94.
"Poetry and Experience: Statement at a Poetry Reading, 1964." Quoted in "Adrienne Rich: The Poetics of Change," by Albert Gelpi. In *American Poetry Since 1960,* edited by Robert Shaw. Cheadle, Cheshire: Carcanet Press, 1973, pp. 132–33. Reprinted in *Adrienne Rich's Poetry: Texts of the Poems, The Poet On Her Work, Reviews and Criticism,* edited by Barbara Charlesworth Gelpi and Albert Gelpi. New York: Norton, 1975, p. 89.

1965

"Reflections on Lawrence." Review of *The Complete Poems of D. H. Lawrence,* edited by Vivian De Sola Pinto and F. Warren Roberts. *Poetry* 106 (June 1965):218–25.

1966

"Six Anthologies." Review. *Poetry* 108 (August 1966):343–45.

1967

"For Randall Jarrell." In *Randall Jarrell 1914–1965,* edited by Robert

Lowell, Peter Taylor, and Robert Penn Warren. New York: Farrar, Straus & Giroux, 1967, pp. 182–83.

"The Tensions of Anne Bradstreet." In *The Works of Anne Bradstreet,* edited by Jeanine Hensley. Cambridge: Harvard University Press, 1967. Reprinted in Adrienne Rich, *On Lies, Secrets and Silence: Selected Prose 1966–1978.* New York: W. W. Norton, 1979, pp. 21–32.

1968–69

"Ghalib: 'The Dew Drop on the Red Poppy. . . .' " *Mahfil* 5 (1968–69):59–69.
    Rich's translations of the Urdu poet Ghalib.

1969

"Living with Henry." Review of *His Toy, His Dream, His Rest* by John Berryman. *Harvard Advocate* (John Berryman issue), 103 (Spring 1969):10–11.

1970

"Jean Valentine: *Pilgrims.*" Review. *Chicago Review* 22 (Autumn 1970):128–30.

1971

Adrienne Rich to Aijaz Ahmad. Quoted in *Ghazals of Ghalib: Versions from the Urdu by Aijaz Ahmad, W. S. Merwin, Adrienne Rich, William Stafford, David Ray, Thomas Fitzsimmons, Mark Strand, and William Hunt,* edited by Aijaz Ahmad. New York: Columbia University Press, 1971, pp. xxv–xxvi.
    Rich comments on her fascination with the ghazal form.
Introduction to "(Reflections) of a Convict, Poems From Prison," by Luis Talamantez. *Liberation* 16 (November 1971):10.
"A Tool or a Weapon." Review of *For You* and *The Clay Hill Anthology* by Hayden Carruth. *The Nation* October 25, 1971, pp. 408–10.
"When We Dead Awaken: Writing as Re-Vision." Paper presented at the Modern Language Association Commission on the Status of Women in the Profession forum on "The Woman Writer in the Twentieth Century," 1971. Published in *College English* 34 (October 1972):18–30. Reprinted in *The Norton Reader,* edited by Arthur M. Eastman, et al. 3d ed. New York: W. W. Norton, 1973, p. 104. Revised [updated] and reprinted in *American Poets in 1976,* edited by

William Heyen. New York: Bobbs-Merrill, 1976, pp. 276–92. Reprinted in *On Lies, Secrets and Silence*, pp. 33–49.

1972

"The Anti-Feminist Woman." Review of *The New Chastity, and Other Arguments Against Women's Liberation* by Midge Decter. *New York Review of Books*, November 30, 1972, pp. 34–40. Reprinted in *On Lies, Secrets and Silence*, pp. 69–84.

"The Case for a Drop-Out School." *New York Review of Books*, June 15, 1972, pp. 33–35. Reprinted in *Starting Your Own High School*. The Elizabeth Cleaners Street School People. New York: Random House, Vintage Books, 1972.

"Poetry, Personality, and Wholeness: A Response to Galway Kinnell." *FIELD: Contemporary Poetry and Poetics*, no. 7 (Fall 1972):11–18.
Kinnell's "Poetry, Personality, and Death" appeared in *FIELD*, no. 4 (Spring 1971):56–75. Both his essay and Rich's are reprinted in *A Field Guide to Contemporary Poetry and Poetics*, edited by Stuart Friebert and David Young. New York: Longman, 1980, pp. 203–32.

Review of *Welcome, Eumenides* by Eleanor Ross Taylor. *New York Times Book Review*, July 2, 1972, p. 3. Reprinted in *On Lies, Secrets and Silence*, pp. 85–88.

Review of *Women and Madness* by Phyllis Chesler. *New York Times Book Review*, December 31, 1972, p. 1.

"Teaching Language in Open Admissions." In *The Uses of Literature*, edited by Monroe Engel. Cambridge: Harvard University Press, 1973, pp. 257–73. Reprinted in *On Lies, Secrets and Silence*, pp. 51–68.

"Voices in the Wilderness." Review of *Monster* by Robin Morgan. *Washington Post Book World*, December 31, 1972, p. 3.

1973

"Caryatid: A Column." *American Poetry Review* 2 (January/February 1973); (May/June 1973); (September/October 1973). The first two essays, "Vietnam and Sexual Violence" and "Natalya Gorbanevskaya," are reprinted in *On Lies, Secrets and Silence*, pp. 107–19.

"Jane Eyre: The Teachings of a Motherless Woman." *Ms.* 2 (October 1973):68. Reprinted in *On Lies, Secrets and Silence*, pp. 89–106. An earlier version of the essay was presented as a lecture at Brandeis University in 1972.

Review of *The Women Poets in English: An Anthology*, edited by Ann
Stanford. *New York Times Book Review*, April 15, 1973, p. 6.
"The Sisterhood of Man." Review of *Beyond God the Father: Toward a
Philosophy of Women's Liberation* by Mary Daly. *Washington Post Book
World*, November 11, 1973, pp. 2–3.

1974

"Anne Sexton: 1928–1974." Memorial presentation at City College of
New York, 1974. In *On Lies, Secrets and Silence*, pp. 121–23.
"Dedication to Self-Determination." *Off our backs* 4 (June 1974):20.
"New Women's Poetry." Letter to the Editor. *New York Times Maga-
zine*, December 24, 1974, p. 38.
> Written in response to M. L. Rosenthal's "Like the Shark, It
> Contains a Shoe: The Aroused Language of Modern Poetry."
> *New York Times Magazine*, November 24, 1974, p. 13. See also
> Rosenthal's response to Rich's letter in December 24 issue.
"The Origins of Feminist Myth-Making." Review of *The First Sex* and
Tribute to Elizabeth Gould Davis. *Boston Phoenix*, September 10,
1974, p. 15.
"Women's Studies—Renaissance or Revolution?" Paper read at the
University of Pennsylvania Women's Studies Conference, Novem-
ber 14, 1974. Published in *Women's Studies* 3 (1976):121–26.

1975

"Feminism and Fascism: An Exchange [with Susan Sontag]." *New York
Review of Books*, March 20, 1975, pp. 31–32.
> Response to Sontag's "Fascinating Fascism," a piece on Leni
> Reifenstahl, in the *New York Review of Books*, February 6, 1975.
Introduction to *Voices: A Play for Women* by Susan Griffin. Brooklyn,
New York: The Feminist Press, 1975.
Prefatory Note to *Amazon Poetry: An Anthology*, edited by Elly Bulkin
and Joan Larkin. New York: Out & Out Books, 1975.
"The Theft of Childbirth." Reviews of *Immaculate Deception: A New
Look at Childbirth in America* by Suzanne Arms and *Birth Without
Violence* by Frederick Leboyer. *New York Review of Books*, October
2, 1975, pp. 25–30.
"Toward a Woman-Centered University." In *Women and the Power to
Change*, edited by Florence Howe. New York: McGraw-Hill, 1975,
pp. 15–46. Excerpts reprinted in the *Chronicle of Higher Education* 10
(July 26, 1975):32. Complete essay reprinted in *On Lies, Secrets and
Silence*, pp. 125–55.

"Vesuvius at Home: The Power of Emily Dickinson." Earliest version presented at Brandeis University; revised version presented as Lucy Donelley Martin lecture at Bryn Mawr College; published in *Parnassus: Poetry in Review* 15 (Fall/Winter 1976):49–74. Reprinted in *On Lies, Secrets and Silence*, pp. 157–83.

"Women and Honor: Some Notes on Lying." Presented at the Hartwick College Women Writers' Workshop in Oneonta, New York in June, 1975; first published in Pittsburgh by Motheroot Publications as a pamphlet in 1977. Reprinted in *Heresies: A Feminist Journal of Art and Politics* 1 (1977); in French translation by Les Editions du Remue-Menage, 1979; and in *On Lies, Secrets and Silence*, pp. 185–94.

"Writers' Choice." Reviews of *Maps and Windows* by Jane Cooper, *Ordinary Things* by Jean Valentine, and *Through the Flower: My Struggle As A Woman Artist* by Judy Chicago. *Partisan Review* 42 (1975):155–56.

1976

"A Challenge to All Your Ideas About Motherhood and Daughterhood: From Adrienne Rich's Extraordinary Book." *Ms.* 5 (October 1976):60.

> Excerpts from "Motherhood and Daughterhood," chapter 9 of *Of Woman Born*. See responses by Carol Fulkerson and Mary Helen Washington and Rich's reply to Washington in Letters to the Editor, *Ms.* 5 (February 1977):4, 6–7. For annotation see pp. 349 and 351 herein.

"Anger and Tenderness." *The Second Wave: A Magazine of the New Feminism* 4 (Spring 1976):3–11.

> With some revisions, this essay appears as the first chapter of *Of Woman Born*.

"Conditions for Work: The Common World of Women." Foreword to *Working It Out: 23 Women Writers, Artists, Scientists, and Scholars Talk About Their Lives and Work*, edited by Sara Ruddick and Pamela Daniels. New York: Pantheon Books, 1977. Reprinted in *Heresies: A Feminist Publication on Art and Politics* (Lesbian Art and Artists issue) 1 (Fall 1977), and in *On Lies, Secrets and Silence*, pp. 203–14.

Foreword to *The Other Voice: 20th Century Women's Poetry in Translation*, edited by Joanna Bankier, et al. New York: W. W. Norton, 1976.

"It Is the Lesbian in Us. . . ." Presented at a Modern Language Association panel sponsored by the Women's Commission and the Gay Caucus, December 28, 1976. Reprinted in *On Lies, Secrets and Silence*, pp. 191–202.

"The Kingdom of the Fathers." *Partisan Review* 43 (1976):17–37.
> With some revisions, this essay appears as the third chapter of *Of Woman Born*.

"Mother and Son, Woman and Man." *American Poetry Review* 5 (September/October 1976):6–13.
> This essay is the eighth chapter of *Of Woman Born*.

"Motherhood in Bondage." *New York Times* "Op-Ed" page, November 20, 1976. Reprinted in *On Lies, Secrets and Silence*, pp. 195–97.

Of Woman Born: Motherhood as Experience and Institution. New York: W. W. Norton, 1976; pb. ed. New York: Bantam, 1977.

Response to Jan Clausen's questionnaire, "Publishing as a Political Act." In Clausen, "The Politics of Publishing and the Lesbian Community." *Sinister Wisdom* 1 (Fall 1976):95–115.

1977

"Claiming an Education." Presented at Douglass College Convocation, September 6, 1977. Published in *The Common Woman* (New Brunswick, New Jersey), n.d. Reprinted in *On Lies, Secrets and Silence*, pp. 231–35.

Foreword to *The Lesbian: A Celebration of Difference* by Bernice Goodman. Brooklyn, New York: Out & Out Books, 1977.

Introduction to *Ordinary Women/Mujeres Comunes: An Anthology by New York City Women*, edited by Sara Miles, Patricia Jones, Sandra Maria Esteves, and Fay Chiang. New York: Ordinary Women Books, 1978.

"Husband-Right and Father-Right." Introduction to *Legal Kidnapping* by Anna Demeter. Boston: Beacon Press, 1977. Reprinted in *Chrysalis: A Magazine of Women's Culture*, no. 5 (1978):105–8, and in *On Lies, Secrets and Silence*, pp. 215–22.

Letter to the Editor. *Ms.* 5 (February 1977):7.
> Reply to Mary Helen Washington's letter about the excerpt from *Of Woman Born* published in *Ms.* in October 1976, "A Challenge to All Your Ideas about Motherhood and Daughterhood." Cited on p. 351.

"The Meaning of Our Love for Women Is What We Have Constantly to Expand." Presented at the women's rally during Gay Pride demonstration in Central Park, 1977; published as a pamphlet in Brooklyn, New York by Out & Out Books in 1977. Reprinted in *On Lies, Secrets and Silence*, pp. 223–30.

"Power and Danger: Works of a Common Woman." Introduction to *The Work of a Common Woman: The Collected Poetry of Judy Grahn*. Oakland, California: Diana Press, 1978; New York: St. Martin's

Press, 1978. Reprinted in *On Lies, Secrets and Silence*, pp. 247–58.

Review of *The Female Experience: An American Documentary* by Gerda Lerner. *New York Times Book Review*, March 20, 1977, p. 5.

"There Is a Fly in This House." Review of *Housework* by Joan Larkin. *Ms.* 5 (February 1977):46.

"The Transformation of Silence into Language and Action." Presented at the Lesbians and Literature panel of the Modern Language Association convention, Chicago, in December, 1977, and for the Turning Point Project at the University of Massachusetts, Boston, in 1978. Published in *Sinister Wisdom*, no. 6 (Summer 1978):17–25.

1978

"Disloyal to Civilization: Feminism, Racism, Gynephobia." Partially presented at the MLA panel "The Transformation of Silence . . ." and partially presented for the Turning Point Project (see entry above). Complete version in *On Lies, Secrets and Silence*, pp. 275–310.

"Motherhood: The Contemporary Emergency and the Quantum Leap." Presented at the Women's Resource and Policy Development Center Conference on The Future of Mothering, Columbus, Ohio, in June, 1978. Published in *On Lies, Secrets and Silence*, pp. 259–73.

Personal communication with Mary Daly, January 1978. Quoted by Mary Daly, in *Gyn/Ecology: The Metaethics of Radical Feminism*. Boston: Beacon Press, 1978, pp. 322–23n.

> Statement on conflict between desire to learn more about the condition of women and horror at the discovery of materials on pornography, female child abuse, and female sexual enslavement.

Review of *Woman and Nature* by Susan Griffin. *New Women's Times Feminist Review*, November 1978, p. 5.

"Taking Women Students Seriously." Presented to the New Jersey College and University Coalition on Women's Education, May 9, 1978; published in *Radical Teacher: a newsjournal of socialist theory and practice*, no. 11 (March 1979):40–43. Reprinted in *On Lies, Secrets and Silence*, pp. 237–45.

1979

"Commencement Address to Smith College Class of 1979." *Smith Alumnae Quarterly* 70 (August 1979):8–10. Excerpts published in "Adrienne Rich on Privilege, Power, and Tokenism." *Ms.* 8 (September 1979):42–44.

"In Support of Mary Daly." Letter to the Editor. *New Women's Times,* April 27–May 10, 1979, p. 8.

On Lies, Secrets and Silence: Selected Prose 1966–1978. New York: W. W. Norton, 1979.

"The Problem with Lorraine Hansberry." *Freedomways: A Quarterly Review of the Freedom Movement* 19 (1979):247–55.

Review of *Gyn/Ecology: The Metaethics of Radical Feminism* by Mary Daly. *New York Times Book Review,* February 14, 1979, p. 10.

1980

Afterword to *Take Back the Night: Women on Pornography,* edited by Laura Lederer. New York: William Morrow and Company, 1980, pp. 313–20.

"Compulsory Heterosexuality and Lesbian Existence." *Signs: Journal of Women in Culture and Society* 5 (Summer 1980):631–60.

> For three women's responses to this essay, see "Viewpoint: On 'Compulsory Heterosexuality and Lesbian Existence': Defining the Issues." *Signs* 7 (Autumn 1981). Articles by Kathryn Pyne Addelson, Ann Ferguson, and Jacquelyn N. Zita are cited in Articles in Serials section. See pp. 346, 348, and 351–52. See also the response by Martha E. Thompson cited on p. 351.

Commencement Speech for Smith College Graduate School of Social Work, August 13, 1980. *Smith School for Social Work Journal,* Fall 1980.

Foreword to *The Coming Out Stories,* edited by Julia Penelope Stanley and Susan J. Wolfe. Watertown, Massachusetts: Persephone Press, 1980.

> For commentary on Rich's Foreword, see Marguerite Fenton, Review of *The Coming Out Stories. The Second Wave: A Magazine of the New Feminism* 5 (Summer 1980):47–48; Jane Gurko, "Coming out, coming in, coming home." *New Women's Times Feminist Review,* no. 13 (December 1980/January 1981):18–20.

"Response." Letter to the Editors. *Sinister Wisdom,* no. 14 (Summer 1980):104–5.

> Rich comments on Elly Bulkin's article in *Sinister Wisdom,* no. 13, about white feminism and racism in Mary Daly's *Gyn/Ecology* and in the lesbian/feminist press.

" 'Wholeness Is No Trifling Matter': Some Fiction by Black Women." *New Women's Times Feminist Review,* no. 13 (December 1980/January 1981):10–13; no. 14 (February/March 1981):12.

> See response by Holly Brough, "Naming Names." Letter to the

Editors. *New Women's Times Feminist Review*, no. 15 (April/May 1981):2. For annotation see p. 347.

1981

"An Interview with Audre Lorde." *Signs: Journal of Women in Culture and Society* 6 (Summer 1981):716–36.

"Interview with Audre Lorde." In *Woman Poet—The East,* edited by Elaine Dallman. Reno, Nevada: Women-in-Literature, 1981, pp. 18–21.

"Notes for a Magazine." *Sinister Wisdom,* no. 17 (Summer 1981):4–5.
Rich discusses her expectations and desires for the journal, which she and Michelle Cliff began to edit with this issue.

"Notes for a Magazine: What Does Separatism Mean?" *Sinister Wisdom,* no. 18 (Fall 1981):83–91.
See citations for "Responses" from Barbara Smith and Sydney Spinster in Articles in Serials section, p. 350.

" 'Wholeness Is No Trifling Matter': Some Fiction by Black Women."
See 1980 entry.

1982

Adrienne Rich to Barbara Mor. "Responses." *Sinister Wisom,* no. 21 (Fall 1982):119–21.
Critical response to Mor's letter to the Editors about anti-Semitism and brief remarks about *Sinister Wisdom's* editorial practices. For Mor citation and annotation, see p. 349.

"An Open Letter to the Women's Movement." In "Community Voices: Anti-Zionism and Anti-Semitism." *Gay Community News* 9 (May 29, 1982):5, and in "Anti-Zionism Is Anti-Semitism." *New Women's Times* 8 (June 1982):3.
Letter signed by Evelyn T. Beck, Nancy K. Bereano, Gloria Z. Greenfield, Melanie Kaye, Irena Klepfisz, Bernice Mennis, and Adrienne Rich.

"Split at the Root." In *Nice Jewish Girls: A Lesbian Anthology,* edited by Evelyn Torton Beck. Watertown, Massachusetts: Persephone Press, 1982, pp. 67–84.

1983

"The Eye of the Outsider: The Poetry of Elizabeth Bishop." Review of *The Complete Poems, 1927–1979. Boston Review* 8 (April 1983):15–17.

"A Footnote on 'Being There': Being Here." *Off our backs: a women's news journal* 13 (October 1983):10–11.

Rich's impressions of Nicaraguan women's needs and the contradictions within both North American feminist thought and the Sandanista Revolution. Presented at the New York Feminist Forum, "Women in Struggle—Medgar Evers, Nicaragua, Seneca," October 28, 1983. For a review of Rich's presentation, see Sarah Schulman, "Feminist Forum: Provocative, Contradictory," *Gay Community News* 11 (November 12, 1983):3.

"Notes for a Magazine." *Sinister Wisdom*, no. 24 (Fall 1983):3–5.

Reflections on the 2½ years that Rich and Cliff edited *Sinister Wisdom*.

II. Secondary Materials

BOOKS

Adrienne Rich's Poetry, A Norton Critical Edition: Texts of the Poems, The Poet on Her Work, Reviews and Criticism. Edited by Barbara Charlesworth Gelpi and Albert Gelpi. New York: W. W. Norton, 1975.

The only full-length book about Adrienne Rich's poetry, the *Norton Critical Edition (NCE)* contains an excellent selection of poems from 1951–75; two essays and one brief statement by the poet; transcripts of "Three Conversations" between Rich and the editors; eight critical essays; biographical information; and a bibliography of Rich's poetry and prose through 1975. Especially useful in the classroom. Editors' notes provide definitions and historical references. Materials from the *NCE* section, "The Poet on Her Work" are cited with the other primary materials in this bibliography by the year of publication or initial presentation. Critical selections are cited under Chapters and Articles in Books, Reviews, and Articles in Serials. *NCE* is reviewed with Rich's *Poems: Selected and New*. See entries for Morris and Dahlen in Reviews section.

CHAPTERS AND ARTICLES IN BOOKS, PAMPHLETS

Most materials cited below are primarily about Rich's work, although some are about Rich and one or two other poets. The articles which have appeared in journals as well as books are cited both here and in the Serials section.

Boyers, Robert. "On Adrienne Rich: Intelligence and Will." In *Adrienne Rich's Poetry,* edited by Barbara Charlesworth Gelpi and Albert Gelpi, pp. 148–60; first published in *Salmagundi* 22–23 (Spring–Summer 1973):132–48.

> Favorable critique of poems through *The Will to Change.* Praises Rich's authenticity and constraint, her focus on "the tension . . . between . . . what we know and how we feel," particularly in *Necessities of Life.* Unfavorable commentary on the changes beginning in *Leaflets:* "how charged she has become with the nauseous propaganda of the advance-guard cultural radicals."

Chenoy, Polly N. " 'Writing These Words in the Woods': A Study of the Poetry of Adrienne Rich." In *Studies in American Literature: Essays in Honour of William Mulder,* edited by Jagdish Chander and Narinder S. Pradhan. Delhi: Oxford University Press, 1976, pp. 194–211.

> Praises Rich's affirmation and political commitment in the face of war and the destruction of the environment: "to use what one has, to help heal the wounds of the world in some small measure, to join sundered relationships, and somehow manage to hold out, these are the themes of many of Ms. Rich's poems." Sees *Diving into the Wreck* as "an apparent abandonment of hope."

Christ, Carol P. "Homesick for a Woman, Homesick for Ourselves: Adrienne Rich." In *Diving Deep and Surfacing: Women Writers and Spiritual Quest.* Boston: Beacon Press, 1980, pp. 75–96.

> Analysis of Rich's "spiritual journey" and "new naming of self and world" in *Diving into the Wreck* and *The Dream of a Common Language.* Emphasis on her search through the "wreck," her recognition of "the nothingness at the heart of patriarchal marriage and politics," and her desire to "weave a new culture—not from scratch, but from the threads our foremothers have left us."

DuPlessis, Rachel Blau. "The Critique of Consciousness and Myth in Levertov, Rich, and Rukeyser." In *Shakespeare's Sisters: Feminist Essays on Women Poets,* edited by Sandra M. Gilbert and Susan Gubar. Bloomington: Indiana University Press, 1979, pp. 280–300. First published in *Feminist Studies* 3 (1975):199–221; revised version, "Lyric Documents: The Critique of Personal Consciousness in Levertov, Rich, and Rukeyser," in *Myth and Ideology in American Culture,* edited by Regís Durand. Villeneuve d' Ascq: Univ. de Lille, 1976, pp. 65–80.

> Comparative study of "the invention of reevaluative quest myths" which enable women poets to address the "conflict between the claims of the self and the claims of others." Historical

interpretation of the split between women's psyches and social norms, and the poets' desires to "extend the model of personal changes of consciousness to produce social change."

Gelpi, Albert. "Adrienne Rich: The Poetics of Change." In *American Poetry Since 1960: Some Critical Perspectives,* edited by Robert Shaw. Cheadle, Cheshire: Carcanet Press, 1973, pp. 123–43; reprinted in *Adrienne Rich's Poetry,* edited by Barbara Charlesworth Gelpi and Albert Gelpi, pp. 130–48.

Critical overview through *The Will to Change* with analysis of changes in American poetry during Rich's career. Explications of numerous poems, reflections on thematic continuities and changes, discussion of the usefulness of Jungian interpretation, and particular attention to the development of Rich's feminism: "Adrienne Rich's new poems show an absorption of animus-powers into a growing sense of identity as woman and identification with women, and consciousness is the key."

Harrison, Barbara Grizzuti. "Imagination and Ideology." In *Off Center.* New York: The Dial Press, 1980, pp. 79–85; first published in the *New Republic,* June 2, 1979, pp. 35–37.

Extremely hostile review of *On Lies, Secrets and Silence:* "It's an unhappy fact of life and of prose that ideology tends to coarsen, and sometimes to fossilize, the moral imagination. . . . [F]eminists of Ms. Rich's ilk now contend that only *women's* concerns are of universal importance . . . assigning to themselves the right, of course, to define 'women's concerns.' This implied reactionary separatism inevitably leads to the conclusion that there are no truly universal concerns. . . ."

Howard, Richard. "Adrienne Rich: 'What Lends Us Anchor But the Mutable?'" In *Alone with America: Essays on the Art of Poetry in the United States Since 1950.* New York: Atheneum, 1969, pp. 423–41; enlarged ed. 1980, pp. 493–516.

"Underground Streams," Howard's review of *Diving into the Wreck,* is reprinted from *Harper's Magazine,* December 1973; review of *The Will to Change* is excerpted from *Partisan Review,* Winter 1971–72; and general commentary on volumes through *Leaflets* appears only in *Alone with America.* "What is striking, what is even stricken about Adrienne Rich's poetry is her probity and resource in the face of fracture. . . . For she is, like her radical affiliates, determined to overcome. She is Sylvia Plath in reverse, not eager or even willing to be still . . . but rather letting the stillness be broken within and around her."

Jong, Erica. "Visionary Anger." In *Adrienne Rich's Poetry*, edited by Barbara Charlesworth Gelpi and Albert Gelpi, pp. 171–74; first published in *Ms.* 2 (July 1973):31–33.

> Positive critique of Rich's ideas about feminism, androgyny, redemption and survival in a "death-dealing culture." Consideration of *Diving into the Wreck* as continuation of Rich's themes in earlier volumes. "Rich is one of very few poets who can deal with political issues in her poems without letting them degenerate into socialist realism . . . . Her feminism is a natural extension of her poetry because, for her, feminism *means* empathy. And empathy is the essential tool of the poet."

Juhasz, Suzanne. "The Feminist Poet: Alta and Adrienne Rich." In *Naked and Fiery Forms: Modern American Poetry by Women, A New Tradition*. New York: Harper-Colophon, 1976, pp. 177–204.

> General commentary on the political implications of feminist poetry, the new forms and themes women are exploring, and the feminist refusal "to treat poetry as a metalanguage that needs to be decoded to reveal meaning." Critique of early oblique poems about interpersonal conflict, using Rich's prose to address changes in her work during the late sixties and early seventies.

Kalstone, David. "Adrienne Rich: Face to Face." In *Five Temperaments: Elizabeth Bishop, Robert Lowell, James Merrill, Adrienne Rich, and John Ashbery*. New York: Oxford University Press, 1977, pp. 129–69.

> Critical overview through *Poems: Selected and New*. Comparison of Rich with (male) poets of her generation, especially Merrill. Focus on poetry of dialogue and relationship, the changes beginning in *Necessities of Life* and increasing with Rich's political growth. Brief remarks about the loss of "the coiled sexual tension," the "deliberate narrowing of focus," as Rich writes more directly to, for, and about women.

Martin, Wendy. "From Patriarchy to the Female Principle: A Chronological Reading of Adrienne Rich's Poems." In *Adrienne Rich's Poetry*, edited by Barbara Charlesworth Gelpi and Albert Gelpi, pp. 175–89.

> Study of the cultural and historical changes that have nurtured Rich's growth as a feminist poet. Discussion of the developing connections between inner and outer, self and nature, which are severed in patriarchal society. Emphasis on the power and reverence for life that Rich derives from her use of women's history. "Rich returns to the ancient origins of the community of women in order to more fully comprehend her own experience as a mod-

ern woman; this poetic exploration of matriarchal community—
the female principle—has important political consequences."

Middlebrook, Diane Wood. "Three Mirrors Reflecting Women: Poetry
of Sylvia Plath, Anne Sexton, and Adrienne Rich." In *Worlds into
Words: Understanding Modern Poets*. New York: Norton, 1978, pp.
65–95.

> Traces the evolution of Rich's feminism through discussion of
> *Snapshots of a Daughter-in-Law* and her prose writings about the
> fifties. "The significance of sexual identity dawns in poems from
> this period of Rich's life like the inescapable recognition of symp-
> toms of a mortal illness." Brief comment on differences between
> Rich and the women poets with whom she is often compared.

Milford, Nancy. "This Woman's Movement." In *Adrienne Rich's Poet-
ry*, edited by Barbara Charlesworth Gelpi and Albert Gelpi, pp.
189–202.

> Overview through *Diving into the Wreck*, including discussion of
> her own early identification with Rich, conflicts of women writ-
> ers, and Rich's changing ideas about the power of language and
> history. "Adrienne Rich is working out the destiny of her para-
> doxical identities: American woman and American poet. . . . An
> American woman living through that time of radical change in
> human sensibility that Auden said had not come. But that was a
> quarter of a century ago and Auden is dead."

McDaniel, Judith. *Reconstituting the World: The Poetry and Vision of
Adrienne Rich*. Argyle, New York: Spinsters, Ink, 1978. 24 pages.*

> Overview through *The Dream of a Common Language*, tracing
> Rich's changing forms and focusing on her growth toward les-
> bian/feminism. Commentary on her movement "beyond that
> range explored by the confessional poets" and interpretation of
> recurrent myths and images which have new meaning as Rich
> reconceptualizes power from a feminist perspective. "As a poet
> and a feminist, Adrienne Rich knows that she must live a life that
> allows her to make connections with other women, connections
> which will unite her inner reality and her outer environment."

Radycki, Diane. "Diane Radycki on Adrienne Rich on Paula Moder-
sohn-Becker." In *Voices of Women: 3 Critics on 3 Poets on 3 Heroines*,
edited by Cynthia Navaretta. New York: Middlemarch Associates,
1980, pp. 23–35.

> Short essay praising Rich's poem, "Paula Becker to Clara West-
> hoff" (from *The Dream of a Common Language*) and providing
> information about the painter's life. "In empathy, in absolute

identification with a woman who lived more than seventy years ago, Rich risks Becker's innermost feelings. . . . She challenges us to the impossible dialogue with the voices of women unheard in their lifetimes."

Whelchel, Marianne. " 'Phantasia for Elvira Shatayev' as Revolutionary Feminist Poem." In *Toward a Feminist Transformation of the Academy: II, Proceedings of the Sixth Annual Great Lakes College Association Women's Studies Conference,* edited by Beth Reed, et al. Great Lakes College Association, 1982.

> Close reading of Rich's poem about the Russian women's climbing team (from *The Dream of a Common Language*) intended to "show how the women's experience becomes a model for the audience and how Rich creates community with the audience and challenges [readers] to change." Commentary on differences between "consciously political" and "revolutionary" poetry. Parts of this essay are extended in Whelchel's "Mining the 'Earth-Deposits': Women's History in Adrienne Rich's Poetry."*

Vendler, Helen. "Adrienne Rich." In *Part of Nature, Part of Us: Modern American Poets.* Cambridge: Harvard University Press, 1980, pp. 237–62. Review of *Diving into the Wreck* was first published as "Ghostlier Demarcations, Keener Sounds." *Parnassus: Poetry in Review* 2 (Fall/Winter 1973). It was reprinted in *Adrienne Rich's Poetry,* edited by Barbara Charlesworth Gelpi and Albert Gelpi, pp. 160–71. Review of *Of Woman Born* was published in the *New York Review of Books,* September 30, 1976, pp. 16–18.

> Review of *Diving* and retrospective study of earlier volumes. Discussion of other poets and changes in American poetry during Rich's career. Negative commentary about Rich's feminism, anger, and prose "propaganda": "I hope that the curve into more complex expression visible in her earlier books will recur . . . , and that these dispatches from the battlefield [in *Diving*] will be assimilated into a more complete poetry." Hostile review of *Of Woman Born,* charging Rich with "sentimentality," "the rhetoric of violence," "ideologically motivated writing," and "refus[ing] full existential reality to men."

REFERENCE GUIDES

American Literary Scholarship: An Annual (1979). Edited by James Woodress. Durham, North Carolina: Duke University Press, 1981, pp. 337–70.

> In "Poetry: The 1940s to the Present," Sandra M. Gilbert com-

ments on several articles about Rich and refers readers to an essay by Joyce Greenberg and a review by Carol Muske. See pp. 349 and 362 herein.

American Women Writers: A Critical Reference Guide from Colonial Times to the Present. Edited by Lina Mainiero. Vol. 3. New York: Frederick Ungar Publishing, 1981, pp. 462–64.

Brief bibliography of Rich's works and essay by Sheema Hamdani Karp. "Above all her voice is directed towards other women, sharing her perceptions and partaking of a common experience."

Book Review Index. Detroit: Gale Research Company, 1965–76.

Contemporary Poets. 2d. ed. Edited by James Vinson. New York: St. Martin's Press, 1975, pp. 1270–71.

Biographical paragraph and bibliography of Rich's poetry through *Diving into the Wreck,* critical overview by Hayden Carruth on Rich's importance for American poetry. "Many poets, perhaps most poets, in America today are writing *about* revolution. The poetry of Adrienne Rich *is* revolution. . . ."

Contemporary Poets. 3d. ed. Edited by James Vinson. New York: St. Martin's Press, 1980, pp. 1257–60.

Biographical information and brief essay by Lois Gordon.

Contemporary Poets in American Anthologies, 1960–1977. Edited by Kirby Congdon. Metuchen, New Jersey: Scarecrow Press, 1978.

Cites anthologies in which Rich's poems appear.

Crowell's Handbook of Contemporary American Poetry. Edited by Karl Malkoff. New York: Thomas Y. Crowell Co., 1973, pp. 253–60.

Critical overview of Rich's poetry through *The Will to Change* with commentary on anti-war and "confessional" poems and Rich's ambivalence about the power of language. "In the end, Adrienne Rich . . . has revised the formula governing poetry between the two world wars; for Rich, poetry is not the ally of order but of anarchy."

Current Book Review Citations. Edited by Paula de Vaux. New York: H. W. Wilson, 1976–81.

Granger's Index to Poetry, 1970–1977. Edited by William James Smith. New York: Columbia University Press, 1978.

An Index to Book Reviews in the Humanities. Williamston, Michigan: Phillip Thomson. 21 vols. to date. 1960–.

International Who's Who in Poetry. 4th ed. (1974–75). Edited by Ernest Kay. Cambridge and London: Melrose Press, 1976, pp. 377–78.

Brief bibliography and biographical paragraph.

Literary History of the United States. 4th ed. Edited by Robert E. Spiller, et al. New York: Macmillan, 1974, p. 1426.

> Brief critical overview of Rich's poetry.

Modern American Literature: A Library of Literary Criticism. 4th ed. Edited by Dorothy Nyren Curley, Maurice Kramer, and Elaine Fialka Kramer. New York: Frederick Ungar Publishing, 1969, pp. 66–68.

> Excerpts from reviews of Rich's poetry: Alfred Kreymborg on *A Change of World;* Donald Hall on *The Diamond Cutters;* Randall Jarrell and Richard Howard on *Snapshots of a Daughter-in-Law;* Jerome Judson, Robert Lowell and Hayden Carruth on *Necessities of Life.*

The Oxford Companion to American Literature. 4th ed. Edited by James D. Hart. New York: Oxford University Press, 1965, p. 709.

> Very brief bibliography of Rich's volumes of poetry through *Snapshots of a Daughter-in-Law.*

The Penguin Companion to American Literature. Edited by Malcolm Bradbury, Eric Mottram, and Jean Franko. Harmondsworth, England: Penguin Books, 1971, p. 217.

> Bibliography of Rich's volumes of poetry through *Necessities of Life;* paragraph overview.

Who's Who of American Women. 12th ed. (1981–1982). Chicago: Marquis Who's Who, 1981, p. 621.

> Very brief biographical paragraph and list of Rich's books.

World Authors, 1950–1970. Edited by John Wakeman. New York: H. W. Wilson, 1975, pp. 1207–09.

> Excerpts from reviews: Alfred Kreymborg and W. H. Auden on *A Change of World,* Randall Jarrell on *The Diamond Cutters,* Robert Lowell on *Snapshots of a Daughter-in-Law* and *Necessities of Life,* and David Kalstone on *The Will to Change;* critical overview through *The Will to Change.*

ARTICLES IN SERIALS

Most materials cited below are primarily about Rich's work, although some are about Rich and one or two other poets. Pieces which have been published in books as well as in serials are cited both here and in the Articles in Books section. Letters to the Editor about Rich's work are included here.

Addelson, Kathryn Pyne. "Words and Lives: On 'Compulsory Heterosexuality and Lesbian Existence'—Defining the Issues." *Signs: Journal of Women in Culture and Society* 7 (Autumn 1981):187–99.

See also Ferguson and Zita entries in this section; Addelson responds to their critiques of Rich's essay. Suggests that a useful definition of *lesbian* "must cut across normal-deviant lines," and shows how Rich's "lesbian continuum" enables us to "examine the past (and present) not in terms of hierarchical institutions but in terms of women's own understandings within the historical contexts of life patterns they were creating."

Allen, Carolyn. "Failures of Word, Uses of Silence: Djuna Barnes, Adrienne Rich, and Margaret Atwood." *Regionalism and the Female Imagination* (University Park, Pennsylvania), 4 (1978):1–7.

Overview of Rich's changing attitudes toward language, imagery, and silence as her political awareness has grown and she has sought alternatives to the discourse of male-dominated culture.

Atsumi, Ikuko. "Adrienne Rich: America Josei Shi Renaissance No Gunzo" (Some Figures in the American Renaissance of Women's Poetry). *Eigo Sienen* (The Rising Generation) (Tokyo), 122 (March 1, 1977):30–31.

Barry, Kathleen. "Reviewing Reviews: Motherhood Censored—*Of Woman Born.*" *Chrysalis: A Magazine of Women's Culture,* no. 2 (1977):7–9.*

Analysis of the mainstream critical responses to Rich's prose study. "The vital theoretical breakthroughs of Rich's book were greeted with the same hysteria that results whenever the dominant culture feels seriously threatened by new ideas."

Bere, Carol. "A Reading of Adrienne Rich's 'A Valediction Forbidding Mourning.'" *Concerning Poetry* (Bellingham, Washington) 11 (1978):33–38.

Detailed interpretation of "a pivotal poem in Rich's poetic landscape." Her "leavetaking . . . is saying farewell to a whole way of being in this world."

Boyers, Robert. "On Adrienne Rich: Intelligence and Will." *Salmagundi* 22–23 (Spring–Summer 1973):132–48.

For reprint information and annotation, see p. 340.

Brough, Holly. "Naming Names." Letter to the Editor. *New Women's Times Feminist Review,* no. 15 (April/May 1981):2.

Objection to "Rich's insensitive and racist use of the term 'light-skinned Black' to describe Whites who are part Black and Mulattoes [sic]" in "'Wholeness Is No Trifling Matter,'" cited on pp. 337–38.

DuPlessis, Rachel Blau. "The Critique of Consciousness and Myth in Levertov, Rich, and Rukeyser," *Feminist Studies* 3 (1975):199–221.

For reprint information and annotation, see p. 340.

Farwell, Marilyn R. "Adrienne Rich and an Organic Feminist Criticism." *College English* 39 (October 1977):191–203.

> Thought-provoking analysis of a relatively unexplored subject. Focuses on the moral functions of language, the poet/poem relationship, and the emphases that distinguish Rich from other feminist critics. "Rich has provided the only sustained attempt at what I would call an organic feminist criticism, a literary theory based directly on a feminist philosophy."

Feit Diehl, Joanne. "'Cartographies of Silence': Rich's *Common Language* and the Woman Poet." *Feminist Studies* 6 (Fall 1980):530–46.*

> Exploration of Rich's concept of "re-vision" and her poetic effort to overcome "otherness," to discover women's "First Idea." "As outsider, Rich seeks a way to reappropriate language, to . . . free [it] from its patriarchal origins. . . . The relation of a lesbian ontology to the poetic praxis, however, is not so direct as Rich would have us believe."

Ferguson, Ann. "Patriarchy, Sexual Identity, and the Sexual Revolution: On 'Compulsory Heterosexuality and Lesbian Existence'—Defining the Issues." *Signs: Journal of Women in Culture and Society* 7 (Autumn 1981):158–72.

> Response to Rich's assertion of what constitutes a useful definition of *lesbian;* discussion of labeling theory and what it means for women to choose the lesbian label; extensive information about the historical development of lesbian identity; criticism of Rich's "lesbian continuum" formulation, which "does not clearly distinguish between three different goals of definitional strategy: first, valorizing the concept *lesbian;* second, giving a sociopolitical definition of the contemporary lesbian community; and finally, reconceptualizing history from a lesbian and feminist perspective." See Zita and Addelson entries in this section; these women respond to Ferguson's essay. See also Thompson entry in this section for response to Rich's essay.

Flynn, Gale. "The Radicalization of Adrienne Rich." *Hollins Critic* 11 (October 1974):1–15.

> Generally favorable overview of poems through *Diving into the Wreck,* tracing the development of Rich's attitudes toward history and the changing structures of her poems. Self-contradictory commentary on Rich's feminism: "To label Adrienne Rich a 'Women's Liberation Poet' is like billing *Crime and Punishment* a murder mystery." Four pages later, Rich "seems ready to burn not only her bra, but her breasts."

Friedman, Susan. "Adrienne Rich and H.D.: An Intertextual Study." *Signs: Journal of Women in Culture and Society* 9 (Winter 1983).*

Fulkerson, Carol. Letter to the Editor. *Ms.* 5 (February 1977):4.

Thoughts about motherhood and relationships with women triggered by reading *Of Woman Born* excerpt in *Ms.*

Gilbert, Sandra M. "'My Name Is Darkness': The Poetry of Self-Definition." *Contemporary Literature* 18 (Fall 1976):442–57.

Perceptive study of the differences in the meaning of "confessional" poetry when written by women and men. Emphases on women's socialization away from power, object relations in women's poetry, and "otherness" in men's poetry about women. "The male confessional poet . . . writes in the certainty that he is the inheritor of major traditions, the grandson of history. . . . The female poet, however, even when she is not self-consciously confessional like Plath or Sexton, writes in the hope of discovering or defining a self, a certainty, a tradition."

Greenberg, Joyce. "By Woman Taught." *Parnassus: Poetry in Review* 7 (Fall/Winter 1979):99–103.

Journal written after Greenberg's completion of two courses taught by Rich at Douglass College in 1976. Focuses on the author's changes and Rich's teaching style. Moving piece, possibly the only publication about a student's experience in a course with Rich. "Overall, she seems more interested in my development as a woman than in my development as a poet. I wonder if this is her way of showing me the two are synonymous."

Janows, Jill. "Mind-Body Exertions: Imagery in the Poems of Adrienne Rich." *Madog* (Wales) 3 (Winter 1979):4–18.

Detailed interpretations of "The Tourist in the Town" (from *The Diamond Cutters*), "Necessities of Life," "Images for Godard" (from *The Will to Change*), "Diving into the Wreck," and "The Lioness" (from *The Dream of a Common Language*). Exploration of Rich's movement from tourist/observer to participant/agent. Discussion of her changing beliefs about the power of language, integration of mind and body, and imaginative identification with women like and unlike herself in *The Dream of a Common Language*.

Mor, Barbara. Letter to the Editors. *Sinister Wisdom,* no. 21 (Fall 1982):103–7.

Clarification of Mor's views of Jewish feminism and anti-Semitism. Criticism of Selma Miriam's "unauthorized use of personal correspondence" in "Anti-Semitism in the Lesbian Community," *Sinister Wisdom,* no. 19.

Morris, Susan. "The Moment of Change." Special Section on Adrienne Rich. *Anonymous: A Journal for the Woman Writer* (Fresno, California), 2 (1975):5–9.

Detailed interpretation of three poems from *The Will to Change,* about the poet's power and her temporary inability to use it: "I Dream I'm the Death of Orpheus," "The Burning of Paper Instead of Children," and "Images for Godard." Favorable commentary on Rich's transformation of suffering into words that "applaud the living."

Muske, Carol. "Backward into the Future."

See Reviews section, p. 362.

Ostriker, Alicia. "Her Cargo: Adrienne Rich and the *Common Language.*"

See Reviews section, p. 362.

Pinkert, Rosalie. "To Question Language." Special Section on Adrienne Rich. *Anonymous: A Journal for the Woman Writer* (Fresno, California), 2 (1975):10–15.

Favorable commentary on Rich's poems about the politics of sexuality, particularly in *Diving into the Wreck.* Discussion of Rich's repudiation of masculine culture and the fear, anger, and isolation it creates for women. "Her poetry is an almost brutal portrayal of reality, yet . . . she maintains an optimism for humanity and the future."

Smith, Barbara. "Response." Letter to the Editor. *Sinister Wisdom,* no. 20 (Spring 1982):100–104.

Criticism of "Notes for a Magazine: What Does Separatism Mean?" Discussion of Rich's failure to explain why she conceptualizes separatism in racial terms. Commentary about her lack of attention to the differences between the theory and the practice of separatism. For Rich citation see p. 338.

Spinster, Sydney. Letter to the Editor. *Sinister Wisdom,* no. 20 (Spring 1982):104–5.

Discussion of the point of view represented by Rich's "Notes for a Magazine: What Does Separatism Mean?" "The article feels to me like a challenge to a debate between non-Separatist Lesbian-Feminists and Lesbian Separatists. But there is a great power imbalance in this debate. The moderator, and the forum itself, is non-Separatist." For Rich citation see p. 338.

Tanenhaus, Beverly. "The Politics of Suicide and Survival: The Poetry of Anne Sexton and Adrienne Rich." *Bucknell Review* 24 (1978): 106–18.

Incisive analysis of the ways Sexton and Rich use the parts of themselves that have traditionally been considered "masculine." In Rich's poetry, "Jungian imagery is appropriated into feminist terms," and "access to friendships between women" frees the poet to survive into a better future.

Thompson, Martha E. "Comment on Rich's 'Compulsory Heterosexuality and Lesbian Existence.' " *Signs: Journal of Women in Culture and Society* 6 (Summer 1981):790–94.

Critique of the contradictions of institutionalized heterosexuality. Response to Rich's assessment of the relationships between lesbianism and feminism, individual and collective resistance to compulsory heterosexuality. Questions about the type of strategy she believes is implicit in Rich's theory and doubts about the purpose of conceptualizing "compulsory heterosexuality [as] the central factor in women's oppression."

Van Dyne, Susan R. "The Mirrored Vision of Adrienne Rich." *Modern Poetry Studies* 8 (1978):140–73.

Chronicles and analyzes changes in Rich's use of distance and identity, personae and negative capability. Criticizes the feminist who "is willing . . . to renounce the role of poet for spokesperson," but appreciates the structures Rich has developed to heal the powerful/powerless dichotomy.

Washington, Mary Helen. Letter to the Editor. *Ms.* 5 (February 1977):4.

Response to "Motherhood and Daughterhood" excerpt from *Of Woman Born*. Comment on her appreciation of the book; criticism of "the total absence of any references to black women and their treatment of mother-daughter relationships." Rich's response follows. For Rich citation, see p. 334 herein.

Zita, Jacquelyn N. "Historical Amnesia and the Lesbian Continuum: On 'Compulsory Heterosexuality and Lesbian Existence'—Defining the Issues." *Signs: Journal of Women in Culture and Society* 7 (Fall 1981): 172–87.

Detailed response to Ann Ferguson's "Patriarchy, Sexual Identity, and the Sexual Revolution" (commentary on Rich's essay, cited in this section), and direct discussion of "Compulsory Heterosexuality." Criticism of Ferguson's "automatically exclusive" definition of *lesbian*, "reliance on" male theorists of sexuality, and "socialist-feminist approach [which] undermines the full consideration that should be given to the matrix of institutional coercions that enforce women's erotic loyalty to men." Favorable discussion of Rich's "lesbian continuum," which "includes lesbian existence as a source of power and knowledge available to women, as a phenomenon that would continue to exist outside of its present historically necessary mode of resistance to patriarchy."

REVIEWS, ANNOUNCEMENTS OF PUBLICATIONS AND AWARDS

The annotations in this section are intended to distinguish between reviews and brief notices in publications which ordinarily publish reviews. Letters to the Editor in response to reviews of Rich's work are also included here. For general information about most of the reviews listed below, see the excellent annotated bibliography in Margaret Morrison's dissertation, "Adrienne Rich: Poetry of Re-Vision" (George Washington University, 1977).

A Change of World (1951)

Bogan, Louise. "Verse." *New Yorker,* November 3, 1951, pp. 150–51.
Humphries, Rolfe. "Verse Chronicle." *The Nation,* July 28, 1951, pp. 76–77.
Kreymborg, Alfred. "Voices That Speak in Verse." *New York Times,* May 13, 1951, p. 27.
Miller, Vassar. Review of *A Change of World. Hopkins Review* 6 (Spring-Summer 1953):197–200.
"Yale Younger Poets Award." *Publishers Weekly* 158 (December 16, 1950):2502.

The Diamond Cutters and Other Poems (1955)

Golffing, Francis. "A Corroboration of Life." *Western Review* 22 (Autumn 1957):72.
Hall, Donald. "A Diet of Dissatisfaction." *Poetry* 87 (February 1956): 299–302.*
Holmes, John. "Three Voices." *New York Times Book Review,* April 8, 1956, p. 22.
Jarrell, Randall. "New Books in Review." *Yale Review* 46 (September 1956):100–103. Reprinted in *Adrienne Rich's Poetry,* edited by Barbara Charlesworth Gelpi and Albert Gelpi. New York: W. W. Norton, 1975, pp. 127–29.
Review of *The Diamond Cutters. Booklist* 52 (December 1, 1955), p. 142.
Review of *The Diamond Cutters. Kirkus Reviews* 23 (July 1, 1955):460.
Review of *The Diamond Cutters. U.S. Quarterly Book Review* 11 (December 1955):476.

Whittemore, Reed. "One's Own True Tone." *New Orleans Poetry Journal* 2 (April 1956):21–25.

Snapshots of a Daughter-in-Law (1963)

Booth, Philip. "'Rethinking the World.'" *Christian Science Monitor,* January 3, 1963, p. 15.*

Flint, R. W. "Poetry." *New York Review of Books,* first issue, undated, 1963, p. 26.

Gunn, Thom. "New Books in Review." *Yale Review* 53 (October 1963):135–44.

Harrison, Tony. Review of *Snapshots of a Daughter-in-Law. London Magazine,* April/May 1971, p. 163.

Howard, Richard. "Poetry Chronicle." *Poetry* 102 (July 1963):250–60.

Jerome, Judson. "For Summer, A Wave of New Verse." *Saturday Review,* July 6, 1963, pp. 30–32.

"Loitering Between Dream and Experience." *Times Literary Supplement,* January 22, 1971, p. 92.

Nicholl, Louise Townsend. "Compulsive Balancing." *Spirit: A Magazine of Poetry* 29 (January 1963):181–82.

Nyren, Dorothy. Review of *Snapshots of a Daughter-in-Law. Library Journal* 88 (January 1, 1963):108.

Patten, Brian. "Vulnerable Poets." *Books and Bookmen* 16 (February 1971):26.

Pendleton, Conrad. "Ichor from Apple and Nettle." *Voices* (Portland, Maine), no. 181 (May–August 1963):29–33.

Porter, Peter. "Dazzling Landscapes." *The Observer,* January 3, 1971, p. 30.

Review of *Snapshots of a Daughter-in-Law. New Statesman,* December 4, 1970, p. 772.

Robinson, Edgar: "Four Lady Poets." *Chicago Review* 21 (December 1969):110–116.

Necessities of Life (1966)

Ashbery, John. "Tradition and Talent." *New York Herald Tribune Book Week,* September 4, 1966, p. 2.*

Burke, Herbert C. Review of *Necessities of Life. Library Journal* 91 (June 15, 1966):3218.

Carruth, Hayden. "In Spite of Artifice." *Hudson Review* 19 (Winter 1966/1967):689.

———. "To Solve Experience." *Poetry* 109 (January 1967):267–68.

Gelpi, Albert J. "Disclosing the 'Secret in the Core.'" *Christian Science Monitor,* August 18, 1966, p. 5.

Lowell, Robert. "Modesty Without Mumbling." *New York Times Book Review,* July 17, 1966, p. 5.

Morse, Samuel French. "Poetry 1966." *Contemporary Literature* 9 (Winter 1968):112–29.

Review of *Necessities of Life. Booklist* 63 (September 15, 1966):92.

Review of *Necessities of Life. Kirkus Reviews* 34 (May 1, 1966):501.

Stephens, Alan. "Twelve New Books of Poetry, 1966." *Denver Quarterly* 1 (Winter 1967):101–12.

Sullivan, D. H. "Good, Clear, Shark-Infested Water and High Grade Motor Oil". *Northwest Review,* no. 1 (Summer 1967):113–16.

Tillinghast, Richard. "Worlds of Their Own." *Southern Review,* n.s. 5 (April 1969):582–96.

Vendler, Helen. "Recent American Poetry." *Massachusetts Review* 8 (Summer 1967):541–60.

Wilson, Robley, Jr. "Not Awfully Plain." *Carleton Miscellany* 8 (Winter 1967):103–7.

Selected Poems (1967)

Dodsworth, Martin. "The Human Note." *The Listener,* November 30, 1967, p. 720.

Grant, Damian. "Short Measure." *Tablet* (London), May 4, 1968, p. 446.

Hamilton, Ian. "New Poetry." *The Observer,* December 31, 1967, p. 20.

Holmes, Richard. "Poets: Ferlinghetti, Amis, Coward, and Love, love, love." *The Times,* December 16, 1967, p. 18.

Kavanagh, P. J. Review of *Selected Poems. Manchester Guardian,* November 2, 1967, p. 11.

Sargeant, Howard. "Light Coming or Darkness Going." *Poetry Review* (London), 59 (Summer 1968):113.

Symons, Julian. "Parlour Games." *New Statesman,* November 3, 1967, p. 595.

"Unamerican Editions." *Times Literary Supplement,* November 23, 1967, p. 1106.

Leaflets (1969)

Booth, Philip. "Truthfulness Is the Essence." *Christian Science Monitor,* July 24, 1969, p. 7.

Donoghue, Denis. "Oasis Poetry." Review of *Leaflets*. *New York Review of Books*, May 7, 1970, pp. 35–38.*

James, Clive. "The Influence of Auden." *The Observer*, April 16, 1972, p. 32.

Kalstone, David. "Poetry Has Made Friends with Everyone." *New York Times Book Review*, February 13, 1972, p. 3.

Leibowitz, Herbert. "The Muse and the News." *Hudson Review*, 22 (Autumn 1969):497–507.

"Moving Around." *Times Literary Supplement*, June 9, 1972, p. 651.

Review of *Leaflets*. *Booklist* 65 (July 15, 1969):1252.

Smith, Ray. Review of *Leaflets*. *Library Journal* 94 (May 15, 1969):1975.

Stanford, Derek. Review of *Leaflets*. *Books and Bookmen* 17 (June 1972):86.

Van Duyn, Mona. "Seven Women." *Poetry* 115 (March 1970):430–39.

The Will to Change (1971)

Brownjohn, Alan. "Forebodings." *New Statesman*, March 16, 1973, p. 384.

Cotter, James Finn. "Women Poets: Malign Neglect?" *America*, February 17, 1973, pp. 140–42.

"Fundamentals and Beyond." *Times Literary Supplement*, April 20, 1973, p. 442.

Howard, Richard. Review of *The Will to Change*. *Partisan Review* 38 (Winter 1971–72):484. Reprinted in *Alone with America*.

    See full citation for reprint in Articles in Books section, p. 341.

Kalstone, David. Review of *The Will to Change*. *New York Times Book Review*, May 23, 1971, pp. 31–32.*

Knox, Sandra. "Cane Wins Poetry Society Medal." *New York Times*, April 24, 1971, p. 27.

    Announcement of Rich's receipt of the Shelley Memorial Award of the Poetry Society of America.

Knudson, Rozanne. Review of *The Will to Change*. *Library Journal* 96 (August 1971):2515.

Lattimore, Richard. "Poetry Chronicle." *Hudson Review* 24 (Autumn 1971):499–510.

Murray, Michelle. "The Poetic Order Changeth." *National Observer*, May 31, 1971, p. 19.

Oates, Joyce Carol. "Evolution." *Modern Poetry Studies* 2 (1971):190.

Review of *The Will to Change*. *Booklist* 68 (October 1, 1971):129.

Review of *The Will to Change*. *Choice* 8 (December 1971):1330.

Review of *The Will to Change*. *Kirkus Reviews* 39 (March 1, 1971):277.

"Selection of Recent Titles." *New York Times Book Review,* June 6, 1971, p. 37.

> Four line announcement of *The Will to Change.*

Whitehead, James. Review of *The Will to Change. Saturday Review,* December 18, 1971, p. 37.

Diving into the Wreck (1973)

Alderson, Sue. Review of *Diving into the Wreck. West Coast Review* 10 (October 1975):45–47.

Atwood, Margaret. Review of *Diving into the Wreck. New York Times Book Review,* December 30, 1973, pp. 1–2.*

Bowering, Marilyn. Review of *Diving into the Wreck. Malahat Review* (Victoria, British Columbia), 33 (January 1975):129–30.

Cotter, James Finn. Review of *Diving into the Wreck. America,* February 2, 1974, p. 78.

"Eclectic Reading." *New York Times,* April 20, 1974, p. 30.

> Rich's receipt of National Book Award for *Diving into the Wreck* is mentioned in editorial.

Fraser, Kathleen. "Songs of Experience." *Washington Post Book World,* December 23, 1973, p. 2.

Flynn, Gale. "The Radicalization of Adrienne Rich."

> See Articles in Serials section, p. 348.

Howard, Richard. "Underground Streams." *Harper's,* December 1973, pp. 120–21.

> For reprint information and annotation, see Articles in Books section, p. 341.

Jong, Erica. "Visionary Anger." *Ms.* 2 (July 1973):30–34. Reprinted in *Adrienne Rich's Poetry,* edited by Barbara Charlesworth Gelpi and Albert Gelpi. New York: W. W. Norton, 1975, pp. 171–74.

Pastan, Linda. Review of *Diving into the Wreck. Library Journal* 98 (May 15, 1973):1588.

Perloff, Marjorie G. "The Corn-Porn Lyric: Poetry 1972–1973." *Contemporary Literature* 16 (Winter 1975):84–125.

Prescott, Peter S. "Looking for Life." *Newsweek,* December 24, 1973, p. 84.

Pritchard, William H. "Poetry Matters." *Hudson Review* 26 (Fall 1973):585–88.

"Pynchon, Singer Share Fiction Prize." *New York Times,* April 17, 1974, p. 37.

> Brief announcement of Rich's receipt of National Book Award.

Review of *Diving into the Wreck. Choice* 10 (October 1973):1198.

Review of *Diving into the Wreck*. *Publishers Weekly* 203 (April 16, 1973):51.

Review of *Diving into the Wreck*. *Virginia Quarterly Book Review* 49 (Fall 1973):140.

Review of *Diving into the Wreck*. *Washington Post Book World,* May 20, 1973, p. 15.

    Brief announcement of *Diving into the Wreck*.

Robinson, James K. "Sailing Close—Hauled and *Diving into the Wreck:* From Nemerov to Rich." *Southern Review* 11 (Summer 1975):668–80.

Savery, Pancho. "Confrontations with the Self." *Epoch* (Ithaca, New York), 23 (Autumn 1973):120–21.

Schulman, Grace. Review of *Diving into the Wreck*. *American Poetry Review* 2 (September/October 1973):11.

Shapiro, Harvey. "Two Sisters in Poetry." *New York Times,* August 25, 1973, p. 21.

Smith, Raymond. "With a Gift for Burning." *Modern Poetry Studies* 5 (Spring 1974):84.

Stimpson, Catharine R. Review of *Diving into the Wreck*. *Southern Humanities Review* 10 (Winter 1976):81–84.

Sukenick, Lynn. Review of *Diving into the Wreck*. *Village Voice,* April 25, 1974, p. 23.

Tonks, Rosemary. "Cutting the Marble." *New York Review of Books,* October 4, 1973, pp. 8–10.*

Vendler, Helen. "'Ghostlier Demarcations, Keener Sounds.'" *Parnassus: Poetry in Review* 2 (Fall–Winter 1973):5. Reprinted in *Adrienne Rich's Poetry,* edited by Barbara Charlesworth Gelpi and Albert Gelpi. New York: W. W. Norton, 1975, pp. 160–79; also in Helen Vendler, *Part of Nature, Part of Us: Modern American Poets.* Cambridge: Harvard University Press, 1980, pp. 237–62.

Walker, Cheryl. "'Trying to Save the Skein.'" *The Nation,* October 8, 1973, pp. 346–49.*

Weisman, Steven R. "World of Books Presents Its Oscars." *New York Times,* April 19, 1974, p. 24.

    Short announcement of Rich's National Book Award for *Diving into the Wreck*.

Poems: Selected and New (1975)

Bell, Pearl K. "Poets of Our Times." *New Leader,* May 26, 1975, pp. 3–5.

Brown, Rosellen. "'The Notes for the Poem Are the Only Poem.'" *Parnassus: Poetry in Review* 4 (Fall/Winter 1975):50–67.

Clemons, Walter. "Adrienne Rich: A Retrospective." *New York Times Book Review,* April 27, 1975, p. 5.

Cotter, James Finn. Review of *Poems: Selected and New. America,* January 31, 1976, pp. 80–81.

Dahlen, Beverly. "The Poetry of Adrienne Rich." Review of *Poems: Selected and New; Adrienne Rich's Poetry: A Norton Critical Edition;* and *Twenty-One Love Poems. San Francisco Review of Books* 2 (September 1976):19–21.

Fraser, G. S. "Free and Uneasy." *Partisan Review* 45 (1978):151–53.

Goldstein, Laurence. "The Evolution of Adrienne Rich." *Michigan Quarterly Review* 15 (Summer 1976):360–66.

Hartsell, Elinor Emmons. "No Quiet Place." *Southern Review* 12 (April 1976):422–25.

Henninger, Mary Nugent. "A Female Trio: Gender Means Little." *National Observer,* June 21, 1975, p. 21.

McLellan, Joseph. "Briefly Noted: *Poems: Selected and New.*" *Washington Post Book World,* May 18, 1975, p. 4.

Morris, John N. "'The Songs Protect Us, in a Way.'" Review of *Poems: Selected and New* and *Adrienne Rich's Poetry: A Norton Critical Edition. Hudson Review* 28 (Autumn 1975):446–50.

"1975: A Selection of Noteworthy Titles." *New York Times Book Review,* December 7, 1975, pp. 70–72.

    Four-line announcement of *Poems: Selected and New.*

Pastan, Linda. Review of *Poems: Selected and New. Library Journal* 100 (February 15, 1975):397.

Poss, Stanley. "'Such Women Are Dangerous / to the Order of Things.'" *Western Humanities Review* 29 (Autumn 1975):388–91.

Pritchard, William H. "Despairing at Styles." *Poetry* 127 (February 1976):292–302.

Review of *Poems: Selected and New. Booklist* 75 (July 15, 1975):1159.

Review of *Poems: Selected and New. Choice* 12 (July 1975):684.

Review of *Poems: Selected and New. Kirkus Reviews* 43 (February 1, 1975):168.

Review of *Poems: Selected and New. Publishers Weekly* 207 (February 3, 1975):74.

"Selected Vacation Reading List." *New York Times Book Review,* June 1, 1975, p. 29.

    Four line announcement of *Poems: Selected and New.*

Spiegelman, Willard. "Voice of the Survivor: The Poetry of Adrienne Rich." *Southwest Review* 60 (Autumn 1975):370–88.

Wells, Denzil. "A Fine Nine." *Village Voice,* December 15, 1975, p. 73.

Whitman, Ruth. "Three Women Poets." *Harvard Magazine,* July/August 1975, pp. 66–67.*

Wilner, Eleanor. " 'This Accurate Dreamer': An Appreciation of *Poems: Selected and New.*" *American Poetry Review* 4 (March/April 1975): 4–7.*

Of Woman Born (1976)

Barry, Kathleen. "Reviewing Reviews—*Of Woman Born.*"*
    See Articles in Serials section, p. 347.

Baruch, Elaine Hoffman. "Of Mothers and Fathers." *Dissent* 25 (Winter 1978):98–102.

Casari, L. E. Review of *Of Woman Born. Prairie Schooner* 52 (Summer 1978):206–7.

Christ, Carol P. "Motherhood: Spirit and Flesh." *Cross Currents* 28 (Summer 1978):244–47.

Cook, Catherine. "The Back of the Hand That Rocks the Cradle." *National Observer,* November 13, 1976, p. 23.

Crutcher, Anne. "Motherhood—An Unmixed Blessing." *Washington Star,* October 17, 1976, p. F4.
    See Shanahan entry, p. 360, for citation of Letter to the Editor in response to Crutcher's review.

Daly, Mary. "Our Mothers, Our Daughters." *The Real Paper,* December 4, 1976, p. 6.

Gardiner, Judith Kegan. "The New Motherhood." *North American Review* 263 (Fall 1978):72–76.

Gargan, C. Review of *Of Woman Born. Best Sellers* 36 (February 1977):354.

Glazer, Nona. Review of *Of Woman Born. Contemporary Sociology* 6 (July 1977):480–82.

Gottlieb, Annie. "On Reading: Feminists Look at Motherhood." *Mother Jones,* November 1976, pp. 51–53.

Gray, Francine Du Plessix. "Amazonian Prescriptions and Proscriptions." *New York Times Book Review,* October 10, 1976, p. 3.

Hall, Joan Joffe. Review of *Of Woman Born. New Republic,* November 6, 1976, pp. 28–30.

Hirsch, Marianne. "Review Essay: Mothers and Daughters." *Signs: Journal of Women in Culture and Society* 7 (Autumn 1981):200–222.

Jacob, John. Review of *Of Woman Born. Booklist* 73 (November 15, 1976):436–37.

Janeway, Elizabeth. Review of *Of Woman Born. Chrysalis: A Magazine of Women's Culture,* no. 2 (1977):132–35.
    See also Dorothy Bryant, "A Reader's Response to the Review of *Of Woman Born.*" Letter to the Editor. *Chrysalis,* no. 3 (Spring 1978):6; Janeway, "Author's Reply" in same issue, p. 6; Elly

Bulkin, "Homophobia in *Chrysalis?!*" Letter to the Editor. *Chrysalis*, no. 4 (Summer 1978):6; and Janeway, "To Each Her Own," in same issue, p. 6.

Larkin, Joan. "Theory." *Sinister Wisdom* 1 (Fall 1976):89–91.

Lazarre, Jane. "Adrienne Rich Comes to Terms with 'the Woman in the Mirror.'" *Village Voice*, November 8, 1976, pp. 81–82.*

Lerner, Gerda. "Motherhood in Historical Perspective." *Journal of Family History* 3 (Fall 1978):297–301.

Maraini, Dacia. "Viewpoint." Translated by Mary Jane Ciccarello. *Signs: Journal of Women in Culture and Society* 4 (Summer 1979): 687–94.

McPherson, Elizabeth. "On Becoming Pregnant." *America*, February 26, 1977, pp. 172–73.

Mednick, Martha S. Review of *Of Woman Born*. *Contemporary Psychology* 22 (July 1977):535–36.

Mitchell, Sally. Review of *Of Woman Born*. *Library Journal* 101 (October 15, 1976):2189.

Newton, Niles. Review of *Of Woman Born*. *Psychology Today*, January 1977, pp. 88–90.

O'Connell, Mary. "Rich's Bleak Portrait of Motherhood." *Panorama—Chicago Daily News*, October 16–17, 1976.

Prescott, Peter S. "A Woman's Lot." *Newsweek*, October 18, 1976, p. 106.

Review of *Of Woman Born*. *Choice* 13 (January 1977):1504.

Review of *Of Woman Born*. *Kirkus Reviews* 44 (August 15, 1976):954–55.

Review of *Of Woman Born*. *Publishers Weekly* 210 (August 23, 1976):64.

Review of *Of Woman Born*. *Washington Post Book World*, December 5, 1976, p. H9.

    Short announcement of publication.

Rothman, Barbara Katz. Review of *Of Woman Born*. *Journal of Marriage and the Family* 40 (May 1978):438–41.

Rudikoff, Sonya. "Motherhood and the Many Myths of Men." *Washington Post Book World*, November 14, 1976, pp. L1–2.

Shanahan, Thomazine. "Error of Omission: Response to Anne Crutcher." Letter to the Editor. *Washington Star*, November 7, 1976, p. G3.

    See Crutcher entry, p. 359.

Stone, Elizabeth. "Those Love-Hate Relationships Between Mothers and Daughters." *Weight Watchers*, August 1979, p. 40.

Theroux, Alexander. "Reading the Poverty of Rich." *Boston Magazine*, November 1976, pp. 46–47.*

Tweedie, Jill. "Alone Together." *Saturday Review,* November 13, 1976, pp. 28–31.

Vendler, Helen. "Myths for Mothers." *New York Review of Books,* September 30, 1976, pp. 16–18.

  For reprint information and annotation, see Articles in Books section, p. 344.

Waelti-Walters, Jennifer. Review of *Of Woman Born. Malahat Review* (Victoria, British Columbia), no. 42 (April 1977):136–37.

Wrightsman, Lawrence S. Review of *Of Woman Born. Contemporary Psychology* 23 (September 1978):663.

Twenty-One Love Poems (1976)

Dahlen, Beverly. "The Poetry of Adrienne Rich." Review of *Poems: Selected and New; Adrienne Rich's Poetry: A Norton Critical Edition;* and *Twenty-One Love Poems. San Francisco Review of Books* 2 (September 1976):19–21.

Shore, Rima. " 'To Move Openly Together / In the Pull of Gravity.' " *Conditions: One,* no. 1 (April 1977):113–18.*

The Meaning of Our Love for Women Is What We Have Constantly To Expand (1977)

Zimmerman, Bonnie. Review of *The Meaning of Our Love for Women is What We Have Constantly To Expand. Conditions: Six* 2 (Summer 1980):232–37.

The Dream of a Common Language (1978)

Atwood, Margaret. "Unfinished Women." *New York Times Book Review,* June 11, 1978, p. 7.

Broumas, Olga. Review of *The Dream of a Common Language. Chrysalis: A Magazine of Women's Culture,* no. 6 (1978):109–13.*

Carruth, Hayden. "Excellence in Poetry." *Harper's,* November 1978, pp. 81–88.*

———. "A Year's Poetry." *The Nation,* December 23, 1978, p. 712.

Estrin, Barbara L. "Rich Woman, Poor Man: *The Dream of a Common Language." Salmagundi,* no. 44–45 (Spring–Summer 1979):224–34.

Hall, Donald. "Everything That Grows." *The Nation,* July 1, 1978, pp. 21–22.

Hughes, Mary Gray. "Summer Becomes a Poet." *VISION* (Dallas), April 1979.

Jacob, John. Review of *The Dream of a Common Language*. *Booklist* 74 (July 1, 1978):1659.

Johnson, Alia. "Communications." *Co-Evolution Quarterly*, no. 25 (Spring 1980):122.

McDaniel, Judith. "To Be of Use: Politics and Vision in Adrienne Rich's Poetry." *Sinister Wisdom*, no. 7 (Fall 1978):92–99.

Muske, Carol. "Backward into the Future." *Parnassus: Poetry in Review* 7 (Fall/Winter 1979):77–90.

Oates, Joyce Carol. "Joyce Carol Oates on Poetry." *New Republic*, December 9, 1978, pp. 25–30.

Ostriker, Alicia. "Her Cargo: Adrienne Rich and the *Common Language*." *American Poetry Review* 8 (July/August 1979):6–10.

Pastan, Linda. Review of *The Dream of a Common Language*. *Library Journal* 103 (March 1, 1978):569.

Review of *The Dream of a Common Language*. *Choice* 15 (November 1978):1219–20.

Review of *The Dream of a Common Language*. *Kirkus Reviews* 46 (February 1, 1978):169.

Review of *The Dream of a Common Language*. *Publishers Weekly* 213 (February 20, 1978):112.

Ward, Andrew. "Short Review." *Atlantic*, June 1978, p. 100.

Webster, Harvey Curtis. "Six Poets." *Poetry* 133 (January 1979): 227–34.

Whitehill, Karen. "A Whole New Poetry." *Virginia Quarterly Review* 55 (Summer 1979):563–67.

Wood-Thompson, Susan. Review of *The Dream of a Common Language*. *Feminary* 10 (Autumn 1979):68–79.

Yenser, Stephen. "New Books in Review." *Yale Review* 68 (Fall 1978):83–102.

Young, Vernon. "Poetry Chronicle: First, Second, and Third Person— Singular." *Hudson Review* 31 (Winter 1978–79):677–92.

On Lies, Secrets and Silence (1979)

Butscher, Edward. Review of *On Lies, Secrets and Silence: Selected Prose, 1966–1978*. *Booklist* 75 (June 1, 1979):1474–75.

Eaglen, Audrey B. Review of *On Lies, Secrets and Silence: Selected Prose, 1966–1978*. *Library Journal* 104 (June 1, 1979):1258–59.

Gargan, C. Review of *On Lies, Secrets and Silence: Selected Prose, 1966–1978*. *Best Sellers* 39 (August 1979):191.

Harrison, Barbara Grizzuti. Review of *On Lies, Secrets and Silence: Selected Prose, 1966–1978*. *New Republic*, June 2, 1979, pp. 37–39.

For reprint information and annotation, see Articles in Books section, p. 341.

Moers, Ellen. "A Poet's Feminist Prose." *New York Times Book Review*, April 22, 1979, p. 12.*

O'Connell, Mary. "Richly Oppressive." *Chicago Sun-Times*, April 15, 1979.

Rainone, Francine. Review of *On Lies, Secrets and Silence: Selected Prose, 1966–1978*. *Frontiers: A Journal of Women's Studies* 5 (Spring 1980): 75–76.

Review of *On Lies, Secrets and Silence: Selected Prose, 1966–1978*. *Choice* 16 (September 1979):836.

Review of *On Lies, Secrets and Silence: Selected Prose, 1966–1978*. *Kirkus Reviews* 47 (March 15, 1979):376.

Review of *On Lies, Secrets and Silence: Selected Prose, 1966–1978*. *New York Times Book Review*, December 30, 1979, p. 23.

Review of *On Lies, Secrets and Silence: Selected Prose, 1966–1978*. *Publishers Weekly* 215 (February 19, 1979):98.

Russ, Joanna. "Forsaking the Opposite Sex." *Washington Post Book World*, May 6, 1979, p. F6.

Snitow, Ann Barr. Review of *On Lies, Secrets and Silence: Selected Prose, 1966–1978*. *Harvard Educational Review* 49 (November 1979): 546–49.*

A Wild Patience Has Taken Me This Far (1981)

Grosholz, Emily. "Poetry Chronicle." *Hudson Review* 35 (Summer 1982):324–25.

Juhasz, Suzanne. Review of *A Wild Patience Has Taken Me This Far*. *Library Journal* 106 (October 15, 1981):2033.

Kilgore, Kathryn. "Rituals of Self-Hatred, Arts of Survival." *Village Voice Literary Supplement*, December 1981, p. 20.

Mandelbaum, Sara. "New Poetry: Adrienne Rich's *Wild Patience*." *Ms.* 10 (December 1981):21–22.*

Milford, Nancy. "Messages From No Man's Land." *New York Times Book Review*, December 20, 1981, p. 7.

"Notes on Current Books." *Virginia Quarterly Review* 58 (Spring 1982):58–59.

Parini, Jay. "Selves and Others." *Times Literary Supplement*, November 12, 1982, p. 1251.

Review of *A Wild Patience Has Taken Me This Far*. *Booklist* 78 (November 15, 1982):423.

Review of *A Wild Patience Has Taken Me This Far*. *Publishers Weekly* 220 (October 2, 1981):110.

Vendler, Helen. "All Too Real." *New York Review of Books,* December 17, 1981, pp. 32–35.

Wood-Thompson, Susan. Review of *A Wild Patience Has Taken Me This Far*. *Little Lamos Review* 2 (February 1982):2–4.

INTERVIEWS

Shaw, Robert and Plotz, John. "An Interview with Adrienne Rich." *The Island* 1 (May 1966):2–8.

Plumly, Stanley; Dodd, Wayne; and Tevis, Walter. "Talking with Adrienne Rich." *Ohio Review* 13 (1971):29–46.

Kalstone, David. "Talking with Adrienne Rich." *Saturday Review: The Arts,* April 22, 1972, pp. 56–59.

Abramson, Neal and Wainer, Nora Roberts. "Interview: Talking with Adrienne Rich." *CITY Magazine* (City College of New York), no. 3 (Winter 1974–75):52–56.

Gelpi, Barbara Charlesworth; Gelpi, Albert; and Rich, Adrienne. "Three Conversations." In *Adrienne Rich's Poetry,* edited by Gelpi and Gelpi, pp. 105–22. New York: Norton, 1975.

Grimstad, Kirsten and Rennie, Susan. "Adrienne Rich and Robin Morgan Talk About Poetry and Women's Culture." In *The New Women's Survival Sourcebook,* edited by Grimstad and Rennie, pp. 106–111. New York: Alfred A. Knopf, 1975.

Boyd, Blanche M. "Interview: Adrienne Rich." *Christopher Street,* January 1977, pp. 9–16.

Bulkin, Elly. "An Interview with Adrienne Rich." *Conditions: One* 1 (April 1977):58–60; *Conditions: Two* 1 (October 1977):53–66.

Miner, Valerie. "An Interview with Adrienne Rich and Mary Daly." *San Francisco Review of Books* 3 (October 1977):8–14.

Lorde, Audre and Rich, Adrienne. "An Interview with Audre Lorde." *Signs: Journal of Women in Culture and Society* 6 (Summer 1981): 713–36.

Lorde, Audre and Rich, Adrienne. "Interview with Audre Lorde." In *Woman Poet—The East,* edited by Elaine Dallman, pp. 18–21. Reno, Nevada: Women-in-Literature, 1981.

THESES AND DISSERTATIONS

Chenoy, Polly Nadshir. "Dives and Descents: Thematic Strategies in the Poetry of Adrienne Rich and Ann Stanford." Diss., University of Utah, 1975.

Bowles, Gloria Lee. "Suppression and Expression in Poetry by American Women: Louise Bogan, Denise Levertov, and Adrienne Rich." Diss., University of California—Berkeley, 1976.

McMillen, Barbara Fialkowski. "A Study of the Formal and Thematic Uses of Film in the Poetry of Parker Tyler, John O'Hara, and Adrienne Rich." Diss., Ohio University, 1976.

Morrison, Margaret. "Adrienne Rich: Poetry of Re-Vision." Diss., George Washington University, 1977.

Whelchel, Marianne. "'Re-forming the Crystal': The Evolution of Adrienne Rich as Feminist Poet." Diss., University of Connecticut, 1977.

Scarborough, Margaret Noel. "Songs of Eleusis: The Quest for Self in the Poetry of Sylvia Plath, Anne Sexton, and Adrienne Rich." Diss., University of Washington, 1978.

Titus, Mary. "Adrienne Rich's Poetic Process." Senior thesis, Skidmore College, 1978.

Hudson-Martin, Carol Ann. "Moments of Change: The Poems of Adrienne Rich." Diss., University of Notre Dame, 1979.

Pope, Deborah. "The Pattern of Isolation in Contemporary American Women's Poetry: Louise Bogan, Maxine Kumin, Denise Levertov, Adrienne Rich." Diss., University of Wisconsin—Madison, 1979.

Bracewell, Marilyn. "From Androgyny to Community in the Poetry of Adrienne Rich." Diss., University of Texas—Austin, 1980.

Keyes, Claire J. "The Aesthetics of Power: A Stylistic Approach to the Poetry of Adrienne Rich." Diss., University of Massachusetts, 1980.

Vanderbosch, Jane. "The Education of Adrienne Rich: From Re-Vision to Revelation." Diss., University of Iowa, 1980.

About the Contributors

Biographical notes are provided only about the essay contributors, the writers who sent their work in response to solicitations specifically for this collection.

Gloria Bowles grew up in Michigan and received her B.A. in Ann Arbor, where she was a senior editor of the *Michigan Daily*. She received her Ph.D. in comparative literature from the University of California at Berkeley. One of the founders of the Women's Studies Program at Berkeley, she has been the coordinator of the program since its inception seven years ago. She is currently writing a book on Louise Bogan, and she is co-editor of *Theories of Women's Studies*.

Joanne Feit Diehl is an associate professor of English at the University of California at Davis. She is the author of *Dickinson and the Romantic Imagination*, "'Come Slowly—Eden': An Exploration of Women Poets and Their Muse," and other essays about feminist literary theory and nineteenth-century American literature.

Susan Stanford Friedman is an associate professor of English and women's studies at the University of Wisconsin at Madison. Author of *Psyche Reborn: The Emergence of H.D.* and co-author of *A Woman's Guide to Therapy*, she is currently at work on a book about H.D.'s prose and a study of childbirth and women's creativity in literature.

Gertrude Hughes is an associate professor of English at Wesleyan University. She received her Ph.D. from Yale, where she wrote a dissertation on the durability of Emerson's affirmations of life. She is currently working on *Genius and Gender*, a book about how the literary imaginations of female American poets reflect female experiences of daily work.

Claire Keyes is an associate professor of English at Salem State College, where she helps edit the literary magazine *Soundings East*. She has published critical reviews and poetry in a variety of small magazines, including *Primavera, Sojourner,* and *Tendril*.

Wendy Martin is a professor of American literature at Queens College of the City University of New York, where she has taught since 1968. She is the founding editor of *Women's Studies: An Interdisciplinary Journal,* and the author of several articles on the early American novel and American women writers. She has published two books: *An American Sisterhood: Feminist Writings from Colonial Times to the Present* and *An American Triptych: Anne Bradstreet, Emily Dickinson, Adrienne Rich.*

Judith McDaniel is a feminist poet, critic, and teacher. Her articles and reviews of modern and contemporary poets have appeared in *Contemporary Literature, Conditions, Women in Literature, Sinister Wisdom,* and other journals. She is one of the founders of Spinsters, Ink, a feminist publishing company.

Adrian Oktenberg makes her living as an attorney in New Jersey. She has taught Women's Studies at the University of Puget Sound and Evergreen State College in Washington State, and at Portland State University in Oregon. Her poetry and criticism have appeared in *New Letters, Ploughshares,* and other journals. She is currently at work on a book of feminist theory about fat women.

Jane Vanderbosch received her Ph.D. in Administration/English from the University of Iowa. She is now an honorary postdoctoral "fellow" in Women's Studies and a research associate in the Office of Women at the University of Wisconsin at Madison. Her research interests include a study of academic novels by women and the radical educational theories of Virginia Woolf, Adrienne Rich, and Susan Griffin.

Marianne Whelchel grew up in Chicamauga, Georgia, and attended LaGrange College, Purdue University, and the University of Connecticut. She has taught at an Atlanta high school, a community college, Trinity College (Connecticut), Miami University (Ohio), and in programs for adult and minority students. She is currently teaching United States literature and Women's Studies at Antioch; revising her dissertation on Adrienne Rich for book publication; researching nontraditional literature by women (oral testimony, letters, diaries); and documenting the lives and work of Ohio quilters through interviews and photographs.

POETS ON POETRY

David Lehman, General Editor
Donald Hall, Founding Editor

New titles

Thom Gunn, *The Occasions of Poetry*
Edward Hirsch, *Responsive Reading*
Philip Larkin, *Required Writing*
James Tate, *The Route as Briefed*

Recently published

John Hollander, *The Poetry of Everyday Life*
William Logan, *All the Rage*
Geoffrey O'Brien, *Bardic Deadlines*
Anne Stevenson, *Between the Iceberg and the Ship*
C. K. Williams, *Poetry and Consciousness*

Also available are collections by

A. R. Ammons, Robert Bly, Philip Booth, Marianne Boruch,
Hayden Carruth, Fred Chappell, Amy Clampitt, Tom Clark,
Douglas Crase, Robert Creeley, Donald Davie, Peter Davison,
Tess Gallagher, Suzanne Gardinier, Allen Grossman, Thom Gunn,
John Haines, Donald Hall, Joy Harjo, Robert Hayden,
Daniel Hoffman, Jonathan Holden, Andrew Hudgins,
Josephine Jacobsen, Weldon Kees, Galway Kinnell, Mary Kinzie,
Kenneth Koch, Richard Kostelanetz, Maxine Kumin,
Martin Lammon (editor), David Lehman, Philip Levine,
John Logan, William Matthews, William Meredith, Jane Miller,
Carol Muske, John Frederick Nims, Gregory Orr, Alicia Ostriker,
Marge Piercy, Anne Sexton, Charles Simic, Louis Simpson,
William Stafford, May Swenson, Richard Tillinghast,
Diane Wakoski, Alan Williamson, Charles Wright,
and James Wright